The Makers of the Modern Middle East

The Makers of the Modern Middle East
T G Fraser
with Andrew Mango and Robert McNamara

HAUS BOOKS
London

First published in Great Britain in 2011 by
Haus Publishing Ltd
70 Cadogan Place
London SW1X 9AH
www.hauspublishing.com

A CIP catalogue record for this book is available from the British Library

ISBN 978-1-906598-95-2

Typeset in Sabon by MacGuru Ltd
info@macguru.org.uk
Printed in Great Britain by CPI Antony Rowe, Chippenham and Eastbourne
Maps by Martin Lubikowski, ML Design, London

Contents

Preface and Acknowledgements

Historians have long known that the settlements negotiated at the end of the First World War had ramifications well beyond Europe. Much of Volume VI of H W V Temperley's monumental study *A History of the Peace Conference of Paris*, published in 1924, was devoted to the affairs of the Middle East and the attempts to set in place a peace settlement with the Ottoman Empire and its successors. As such, the contributors ranged across Turkey, Syria, Iraq, Egypt, Palestine and Persia, as well as the Zionist movement.[1] Since then, there have been many investigations of how the region was transformed during the critical years between 1914 and 1923, some of them becoming classic studies.[2]

This book approaches the problem of post-war reconstruction from three very different perspectives; namely, the emerging but increasingly insistent claims of Arab nationalism, Turkish nationalism and Zionism. Whilst these movements, which recast the political shape of the region in spite of the imperial ambitions of the triumphant European powers, transcend any individual, three leaders emerged, who by any reckoning became the makers of the modern Middle East. The Hashemite Prince

---

1 H W V Temperley (ed), *A History of the Peace Conference of Paris*, Vol VI, (Oxford University Press, London, New York, Toronto: 1924) Chapter 1, 'The Near and Middle East'.

2 See, for example, George Antonius, *The Arab Awakening* (Hamish Hamilton, London: 1988) and Leonard Stein, *The Balfour Declaration* (Vallentine, Mitchell & Co Ltd, London: 1961). For a discussion of Antonius's book, see Chapter 1.

Feisal, with British encouragement, raised the standard of Arab nationalism against centuries of Turkish rule, only to see his hopes of an Arab kingdom destroyed, albeit with compensation for him in Iraq and for his brother in Transjordan. From an obscure university position in the north of England, the Russian-born scientist Dr Chaim Weizmann enlisted the support of key British politicians for a Jewish national home in Palestine in the shape of the Balfour Declaration, and then translated that document into a British League of Nations Mandate for Palestine charged with bringing it into effect. The Turkish soldier Mustafa Kemal came to prominence in the successful defence of the Gallipoli peninsula in 1915, and then went on to lead and inspire his country's defiance of the victorious Allied powers to establish a modern, secular Turkish republic, becoming Atatürk, the 'Father of the Turks'. What their movements achieved, and failed to achieve, are part of their legacies nearly a century later.

This volume was suggested to me by Dr Barbara Schwepcke of Haus Publishing, who realised that the deliberations of the post-First World War Peace Conference relating to the Middle East could be approached from three very different perspectives. This was apparent from three volumes she had published in *The Makers of the Modern World* series under the editorship of Professor Alan Sharp: namely, Andrew Mango, *From the Sultan to Atatürk: Turkey*; Robert McNamara, *The Hashemites: The Dream of Arabia*; and my own, *Chaim Weizmann: The Zionist Dream*. This book, thus, attempts to bring these studies together into an account of a seminal period of Middle Eastern history.

The Middle East is an area both of fascination and controversy. As an historian who has taught and researched its history at universities in Northern Ireland and the United States for over four decades, I have been lucky enough to have visited its countries many times, in the belief, taught me years ago by the late Professor L F Rushbrook Williams, that it is essential for a scholar to get the 'feel' for the societies under review. His kindly interest in my work as an apprentice historian of the Middle East and South Asia is a memory I will always cherish. I have never encountered anything other than the hospitality for which the Middle East is justly renowned, and I retain the fondest memories of the people I have met and who have educated me in its affairs. If I have become convinced of anything, it is that those brought up in the West should have a proper appreciation of, and acknowledge, just how much world civilisation has owed to the contributions of the peoples of the Middle East.

Unfortunately, it is also a part of the world which has endured more than its fair share of turmoil and tragedy, and this, too, must be acknowledged and understood. Tragic events in the Middle East have become standard fare in the headlines for decades, and it is, alas, all too tempting to develop an indifference towards them, or worse. Such a path is neither realistic nor justifiable. This book proceeds from the belief that a sympathetic, but not uncritical, understanding of Middle Eastern affairs is a *sine qua non* for the informed citizen. *The Makers of the Modern Middle East*, then, analyses a critical series of events before, during, and after the Paris Peace Conference when the future shape of the Middle East as we have come to know it came into focus.

I am particularly grateful to my fellow authors Andrew Mango and Robert McNamara for their tolerance as I worked with their texts, and for their general advice. Barbara Schwepcke of Haus and Jaqueline Mitchell patiently encouraged me through the unfamiliar experience of making a coherent text from three volumes. Janet Farren deployed her customary skills in assisting with the preparation of the work for the publisher. The Series Editor of *The Makers of the Modern World*, Alan Sharp, read and commented on the text, as, amidst all the other priorities of academic life, did Dr Leonie Murray of the University of Ulster, saving me from many errors of expression and emphasis. Finally, my wife, Grace, was, as ever, an unfailing source of critical understanding and support.

T G Fraser, MBE
Emeritus Professor of History and Honorary Professor of Conflict Research,
University of Ulster

1

The Birth of Nationalisms

The Middle East on the eve of war

In 1900 the Middle East was barely, if we may borrow Prince Metternich's dismissal of Italy, a 'geographical expression'. In the early 21st century its affairs could not be ignored. At the end of the First World War, the term 'Middle East' was being used by the British, who had come to dominate the region as the result of military conquest, and it has since passed into common usage, which may serve as some defence against accusations of Eurocentrism. Definitions of the region have varied over time, but the limits of this book are marked by the boundaries of what was then the Ottoman Empire. The Turks emerged in the 8th century CE when the Seljuks, guided, according to national legend, by a grey wolf, conquered territories in central Asia. Their name is commemorated in the modern city of Seljuk in Anatolia. Converting to Islam, the Turks, led by the House of Osman, commonly known as the Ottomans, came into conflict with the Christian Byzantine empire, heir to ancient Rome. In 1453, the armies of Mehmed II, 'the Conqueror', took Constantinople, a pivotal event in world history.

At its height, the Ottoman Empire extended from the Turkish heartland in Anatolia across Egypt and North Africa, conquering much of the Arab territories as far as the Shatt al-Arab waterway, and in Europe pressing through the Balkans to the gates of Vienna.[1] The Sublime State, as it was officially known, was both an Asian and a European empire, its capital uniquely spanning two continents across the narrow Straits of the Bosphorus, one of the most strategic waterways in the world. Constantinople, or Istanbul as it was known to the Turks, with its incomparable skyline etched by the mosques of Aya Sophia, Sultanahmet and Süleymaniye, the first of these also a reminder of the region's Roman and Byzantine inheritance, was one of the great cities of the world. It was then both imperial and cosmopolitan.[2] From his accession in 1876 until his forced abdication in 1909, the empire was ruled by Abdülhamid II, who, like the Habsburgs and the Romanovs, presided over a fascinating range of peoples and religions.

The Ottoman Empire in the new century

At the heart of Abdülhamid's empire were the Turks, numbering, perhaps, some 10 million. The empire was ruled by the House of Osman, the Sultan uniting with his temporal rule the office of Caliph, or protector of the Islamic faith.[3] By the early 20th century, the empire was the last remaining major Islamic polity in a world dominated by the imperialisms of the major Christian powers and Japan, a fact which bound the Turks to their Arab subjects, of whom there were around 7 million. This fact also attracted Muslims across the Islamic world, not least those of British India. Amongst the cities of the empire were Mecca and Medina, the holy cities of Islam, and Jerusalem, sacred to Jews, Christians and Muslims, the world's three great monotheistic faiths. Whilst the bulk of the empire's Muslims, belonged to the Sunni, or 'Orthodox', branch of Islam, in the historic lands of the Tigris and Euphrates were Najaf and Karbala, the holy cities of the Shias, whose people did not instinctively identify with Ottoman rule.[4] Shias, the minority branch of the Islamic

---

1 Lord Kinross, *The Ottoman Centuries: The Rise and Fall of the Turkish Empire* (Perennial edition, New York: 2002) Parts 1 and 2.
2 While European diplomats were accredited to Constantinople, the Turks themselves used Istanbul. For reasons of consistency, I have used the latter, which the Turks insisted upon after 1923.
3 See entry for 'Turkey' in *Encyclopaedia Britannica*, 11th edition, Vol XXVII (Cambridge University Press, Cambridge: 1911) pp 426–7.
4 Charles Tripp, *A History of Iraq* (Cambridge University Press, Cambridge: 2007) p 12.

faith, believed that the true successors of the Prophet Muhammad were his son-in-law 'Ali and his descendants. The two cities held particular sanctity for the Shias since 'Ali was buried in Najaf and his son, Husayn, who had been killed in battle, was buried in Karbala. They found an affinity with those across the border in Persia, or Iran as it became in 1935, which was the main centre of Shia power. The Shias of the Tigris and Euphrates did not sit entirely comfortably in an empire in which the dominant Turks, as well as most Arabs, were Sunnis, and this was to pose problems in later years once independence came to the region.

Nor was it an homogeneously Muslim empire, since there were also significant Jewish and Christian minorities. Jews were to be found in the holy cities of Judaism, Jerusalem, Safed, Tiberias and Hebron, as well as in considerable numbers in Baghdad, where they had lived since the Babylonian captivity of the 6th century BCE. Jerusalem, especially its Old City, held a unique place because of its significance for Jews, Christians and Muslims. This deep religious feeling found its focus for Jews in the Western Wall, the only remaining fragment of their Temple which the Roman conquerors of Jerusalem had left intact, while for Muslims the adjacent Dome of the Rock and Al-Agsa Mosque comprised the Haram al-Sharif (the 'Noble Sanctuary'), their most sacred shrine after Mecca and Medina. For Jews the site was the Temple Mount. Also in the Old City was the Church of the Holy Sepulchre, sacred to Christians. In more recent years, as we will see, Zionist Jews from eastern Europe had also begun to settle. Around Mount Lebanon were the Maronites, a Christian denomination enjoying close links with France and Rome. The region's Byzantine heritage survived, too, since the Patriarch of Constantinople was the acknowledged head of the eastern Christian Church, as well as of the empire's thriving Greek community. İzmir, or Smyrna, on the Aegean coast, the second city of the empire in terms of population, was half-Greek, while it was estimated that there were some 150,000 Greeks residing in Constantinople. It was inevitable that they would be suspected of partiality towards their kinsmen across the border, who had won their independence in the 1820s.

The position of two other substantial non-Turkish minorities, the Kurds and Armenians, was even more problematic, not least because large numbers of them were also to be found in other countries. Outside the Ottoman Empire, the Muslim Kurds were a minority population in the north-west of neighbouring Persia, whilst the Christian Armenians were stretched across Turkey, Persia and Russia, whose officials were not above encouraging their national aspirations. Armenians were also aware of the success of the Christian Slavs in prising the Turks out of the Balkans. The Turks, in turn, used the Kurds as a counter to the Armenians. Massacres of Armenians in 1895–6 set an uneasy precedent. When we also include smaller communities such as the Alawites, Chaldaeans, Circassians and Druzes, then the rich diversity of the empire becomes clear, although, as its former Habsburg rival was discovering, this was not always an advantage in an age of burgeoning nationalisms.

Although it was emphatically a Muslim polity, believers in other monotheistic religions were accorded recognition through the *millet* system, under which they ran their own affairs. *Millet* status was accorded to the Latin Catholic, Greek Orthodox, Armenian Catholic, Armenian Gregorian, Syrian and United Chaldaean, Maronite, Protestant and Jewish communities. Nor did the Jews forget that it was the Turks who had given refuge to many of them after their expulsion from Andalucia in the late 15th century. The *millet* system both acknowledged and respected the empire's rich variety.[5]

It was, of course, in the Balkans that the most immediate threat to the empire lay. From the time when the unfortunate Grand Vizier Kara Mustafa had failed in his bid to take Vienna in 1683, the Habsburg armies, led by their great commander Prince Eugene, had steadily pushed the Turks back through the Balkans. Austrian expansion came to rest with the *de facto* acquisition of the Ottoman provinces of Bosnia and Herzegovina in 1878, a poisoned chalice for the dynasty if ever there was one, but by then the Turks were being further challenged in the Balkans. If the Austrians had led the charge to expel the Turks from central and south-eastern Europe, their task was taken up by the Russians, who encouraged the Serbs and Bulgarians to move for independence, just as they had earlier done with the Greeks.[6] By the time of the Congress of Berlin in 1878, Romania, Serbia and Montenegro were also independent, and Bulgaria was soon to follow. The empire's long-standing dominance in the Balkans finally came to end in the Balkan Wars of 1912–13, which left it with a rump of territory in eastern Thrace, although crucially still in possession of Istanbul

---

5 'Turkey', *Encyclopaedia Britannica*.
6 Justin McCarthy, *The Ottoman Peoples and the End of Empire* (Arnold, London: 2004) p 51.

and the Bosphorus and the Dardanelles, which linked the Black Sea to the Aegean, the Mediterranean and the seas beyond.

By then, it may truly be said that it had become a Middle Eastern empire. The Ottoman Empire still held suzerainty over Egypt, with its fertile Nile valley and the historic cities of Cairo and Alexandria, but this had become a fiction. Since 1882, the country had been ruled by the British, whose interest was generated by the opening in 1869 of the Suez Canal, which provided a key route to their possessions in the east, notably the Indian Empire. Their proconsuls, men like Lords Cromer and Kitchener, paid no heed to the Sultan. Then, in 1911–12, Italy seized Tripolitania and Cyrenaica in a war notable for the first use of bombs dropped from aircraft, a dismal precedent for the century to come.[7] Italy's colonial adventure also marked the emergence of a young Ottoman major, Mustafa Kemal. In effect, the Turks had been shut out of their historic lands in North Africa as well as in Europe.

The 'Young Turks'

If it were an empire in geographical retreat, the seeds of renewal were there, nevertheless. The Ottoman state entered the First World War on the side of the Central Powers in 1914 in a reckless gamble by a group of adventurers, led by a triumvirate consisting of two young career officers, Enver and Cemal, and one civilian, Talât. Enver, the leading spirit, was 33 years old in 1914, Cemal was 42 and Talât 40. Enver became Commander-in-Chief (formally Deputy Commander-in-Chief, since the Sultan was nominal C-in-C), Cemal Navy Minister, commander of the Southern Front and Governor of Syria (which included Lebanon and Palestine), and Talât Minister of the Interior and then Grand Vizier (Prime Minister). These leaders of the Committee of Union and Progress, or Young Turks, as they were known in the West, had risen to power and fame in Ottoman Macedonia in the first decade of the 20th century. Their character had been moulded by their experience in fighting the irregular bands of Balkan nationalists – Slav Macedonians, Bulgarians, Greeks, Serbs and, finally, Albanians. Nationalist irregulars were known in Turkish as *komitacı* (committee-men), a designation which became a byword for ruthlessness, violence and treachery, but also reckless courage. Such men were needed

---

7 Alan Palmer, *The Decline and Fall of the Ottoman Empire* (John Murray, London: 1992) p 214.

to carve nationally homogeneous states out of a multinational empire – a process which involved massacres, deportations and the flight of millions of refugees. Enver, Cemal and Talât were Turkish *komitacıs* in a literal sense, too, as leaders of the Committee of Union and Progress (CUP), whose members were known as Unionists (*İttihatçı*). They were initiated in quasi-Masonic ceremonies in which oaths were sworn on guns and holy books. They conspired against the absolutist regime of Sultan Abdül-hamid II, forced him to reintroduce constitutional rule in 1908, deposed him in 1909 and seized power in a coup in 1913. They believed initially that constitutional rule would reconcile all the ethnic communities of the Ottoman Empire and turn them all into loyal Ottoman citizens under the banner of freedom, fraternity and justice. It was their version of the ideals of the French Revolution, which they admired as the 'Great Revolution'. But they admired Napoleon even more and also the German and Japanese militarists whose example confirmed their belief that might was right.

Like many other young officers, Mustafa Kemal was attracted to revo-lutionary politics in the hope that they might transform the fortunes of the empire. When the Young Turks acted against the Sultan in 1908, he was a member of their movement, although not a prominent one. Mustafa, to give him his original name, was born some time in the winter of 1880–1 in the cosmopolitan city of Salonica, now Thessaloniki in Greece. His father, Ali Riza, worked in the timber trade and as a customs officer, providing a decent middle-class income for his young wife Zübeyde. Mustafa was only a child when his father died, but he remained close to his mother, even after her remarriage. In 1899, he entered the imperial war college, doing well there and proceeding to Staff College. That he was an able and assiduous student is amply born out by his subsequent career. No less significantly, he was also attracted to politics, leading to a brief arrest and effective banishment to a military unit in Damascus. Here, too, according to his own account he helped spread revolutionary ideas in Beirut, Jerusalem and Jaffa.

Various staff and regimental appointments followed the Young Turk revolution, but it was Italy's invasion of Tripolitania and Cyrenaica which gave him the opportunity to make his mark. Travelling in disguise through British-ruled Egypt, he was soon in action against the Italians. With a small force of Turkish regulars and thousands of Arabs, he helped pin down the Italian forces on the coast. It was to no avail, however. Faced with the ability of the Italian fleet to bombard Beirut and the Dardanelles, as well as more immediate threats in the Balkans, the empire was forced to cede its two provinces in October 1912. His return to Turkey saw him posted as military attache to Sofia the following year, which brought promotion to lieutenant-colonel. If in 1914, he was not amongst the most prominent officers in the Ottoman army, he was certainly a well-trained and serious-minded professional, who had experienced active service against a modern European enemy. He also had an acute political brain.[8]

Despite its defeats, the Ottoman state punched well above its weight. This was partly due to the hardihood and courage of Turkish conscripts. 'The Turkish peasant will hide under his mother's skirts to avoid conscription, but once in uniform he will fight like a lion', a Russian expert on Turkey wrote during the war.[9] But there was another reason, to which most Western observers were blind and which historians have come to notice only recently. While the rural masses were illiterate and ignorant of the modern world, there was an elite of experienced and well-trained Turkish civil servants and army officers. Although the reforms of the 19th century (known as the *Tanzimat*, meaning 'the (re)ordering') were routinely decried in the West as inadequate and a sham, by the beginning of the 20th century Ottoman administration compared well with that of other contemporary empires – so much so that many of its former subjects came to regret its eventual dissolution. A recent study suggests that in the Arab lands placed under British and French Mandates at the end of the First World War, there was little improvement for indigenous Muslims in such basic areas as average life expectancy, education, communications and public order.[10] Ottoman civil administration was organised on French lines, while in the army French and British advisers were largely replaced by Germans from the reign of Abdülhamid II onwards. The efficiency of Ottoman governors and commanders was often overlooked by Western critics, however, who decried their rule as backward and corrupt. Foreign observers also overlooked the fact that many of the Greeks, particularly along the Aegean coast, were immigrants from the newly independent Greek kingdom who found life under Ottoman rule more rewarding than in their own country. The Young Turks scored their

---

8 Andrew Mango, *Atatürk* (John Murray, London: 1999) Chapters 1–7.
9 The expert was V A Gordelevski, a Russian Turcologist, in a rare Tsarist wartime publication.
10 McCarthy, *The Ottoman Peoples and the End of Empire*, pp 171–92.

only diplomatic success in 1913 when the Balkan allies fell out among themselves, allowing Enver to reclaim Edirne (Adrianople) and with it eastern Thrace up to the river Meriç (Maritza/Evros) as the last Ottoman foothold in Europe. If the empire was no longer a European power, it had not ceased to be of interest to the powers of Europe.

The Ottoman Empire and its Arab population

By the eve of war, the Ottoman Empire was predominantly a Middle Eastern empire, whose future was likely to turn on relations between the Turks and their most numerous subjects, the Arabs. At the outbreak of the First World War, the Turks had ruled the heartlands of the Arab World encompassing the modern-day states of Syria, Iraq, Jordan, Israel, Saudi Arabia and Arab North Africa for four centuries. Syria, Iraq, Jordan and Palestine were known as the Fertile Crescent due to the important rivers, notably the Tigris and Euphrates, that provided the water resources that made the areas conducive to human settlement. The Ottomans, the last of the great Islamic Turkish tribes to forge a major empire, had conquered the Arab lands in 1517, ruling them, without serious opposition, until the beginning of the 20th century. Only in the last decades of Ottoman rule did proto-nationalist challenges begin to become evident in the Arab territories.

When it emerged in the 7th century CE, Islam was initially synonymous with being Arab. However, within a century of the Arab conquests, religion rather than ethnicity or nationality became 'the Supreme bond',[11] which partly accounts for the willingness of the Arabs to accept Muslim Turkish overlords. Another reason was the nature of Ottoman rule. While ostensibly one of the most centralised empires in the world with all power held by the Sultan, this was, as one observer noted, 'make-believe'.[12] Outside the main urban centres, such as Damascus, Aleppo, Mosul and Baghdad, government control was weak and the Arabic-speaking societies of the Fertile Crescent were split into groupings based on family, tribal, ethnic and religious ties.[13] While Turkish-speaking

---

11 C Ernest Dawn, 'From Ottomanism to Arabism: The Origin of an Ideology', *The Review of Politics*, Vol 23, No 3 (Jul 1961) p 378.

12 English Arabist, traveller and diplomat Gertrude Bell, cited in David Fromkin, *A Peace to End All Peace* (Andre Deutsch, London: 1989) p 35.

13 Ira Lapidus, *A History of Islamic Societies* (Cambridge University Press,

governors, in theory, held supreme power in the Arabic-speaking regions, in practice linguistic barriers and a lack of military power meant they were dependent on local tribal leaders, the urban rich and religious leaders to maintain even a modicum of influence. These leading groups were known as the *a'yan* or 'notables'. The politics of these notables was the dominant fact of political life in the Ottoman Middle East in the 19th and early 20th century.[14]

One area of the Arab world held particular significance, Palestine. Although the word 'Palestine' was widely understood to refer to the area, it was not even a single provincial entity under the empire, with the northern part lying under the *vilayet*, or administrative district, of Beirut and the southern region constituting the *sanjak* of Jerusalem, while across the river Jordan spread the *vilayet* of Syria. The Palestinians reflected the broader Arab society of the empire in that there were identifiable Christian communities, especially in cities like Bethlehem and Nazareth, which had associations with the life of Christ, but the overwhelming majority were Sunni Muslims. Palestinian Arab society was predominantly agricultural. While there was some industry, for example the soap trade of Nablus, most urban economic activity, such as handicrafts, weaving and construction, was related in some way to the agricultural sector. The main inhibiting factor for Palestinian agriculture was, as it has remained, the availability of water for irrigation, or rather the comparative lack of it. The country's principal river, the Jordan, was unsuitable for irrigation purposes, and hence the peasant cultivators of Palestine had to be careful that their farming methods and crops were adapted to this and did not cause the erosion of what fertile soil they had. The winter crops were wheat and barley, while in the summer sesame and durra were harvested. Palestinian figs and olives were well known, and sheep and goats provided the livestock, well adapted to the hilly terrain of the country's interior.[15]

Cambridge: 2002) p 535.

14 Characterised in Albert Hourani, 'Ottoman Reform and the Politics of Notables', in William R Polk and Richard L Chambers (eds), *Beginnings of Modernisation in the Middle East: The Nineteenth Century* (University of Chicago Press, Chicago: 1968) pp 41–68.

15 Frank Adams, 'Palestine Agriculture', in *Palestine: A Decade of Development, The Annals of the American Academy of Political and Social Science* (November 1932) pp 72–83.

The cultivators were the *fellahin*, who constituted the backbone of the Palestinian population. Passionately attached to the land they farmed, their title to it was often insecure, at least by European standards. The land of Palestine was held under various systems, decided according to the Turkish land law of 1858. Much of it was designated as state, or *miri*, land, which was then allotted to peasant cultivators, subject to continuous cultivation. Under the *Musha'a* system, land was rotated, which at least ensured that everyone would have a share of the better land, but did not encourage soil improvement or fertilisation.[16] A further significant element of the Palestinian population were the Bedouin, who led a nomadic way of life, chiefly in the Negev Desert in the south but also in Galilee. While village leaders were important in their locality, power and status in Palestinian society rested primarily with the urban elites, who were also extensive landowners. The leading Palestinian *a'yan* families, the Husaynis, Nashashibis, Khalidis, Jarallas and Nusseibehs, were to provide the leadership of Arab Palestine for the period under review. The Husaynis enjoyed particular prestige since they had provided the city's mayor and for a long period the religious office of Mufti of Jerusalem had generally been held by a member of the family. In time, the Husaynis were to emerge as the driving force behind Palestinian Arab nationalism.[17]

The emergence of Arab nationalism

For many years, it was widely accepted that Arab nationalism, in its early stages, arose from contact with the West. Unsurprisingly, the first signs of a distinctively Arab nationalism begin to emerge in the urban areas of Ottoman Syria, where European and American cultural and educational influence was beginning to grow in the late 19th century in tandem with increased Western political and economic penetration of the region. European and American missionary work was linked to the Holy Places in Palestine but also grew from a desire, especially among Protestant congregations, to convert Muslims. Direct proselytisation was illegal but there seems to have been a vague, and ultimately forlorn, hope that Arab

---

16 Adams, 'Palestine Agriculture', pp 72–83.
17 Philip Mattar, *The Mufti of Jerusalem: Al Hajj Amin Al-Husayni and the Palestinian National Movement* (Columbia University Press, New York: 1988) pp 6–7.

Christians might transmit their faith to Muslims.[18] A handful of Syrian Christians, educated in the American and French missionary schools in the Lebanon that were established in the 19th century, began to develop a quasi-secular Arab nationalism, however. This included the revival of many classical Arabic literary texts and the translating of Western texts into Arabic. In the 1860s a Syrian Christian, Ibrahim al-Yaziji, articulated an early vision of Arab nationalism. He viewed the Ottoman conquest as a disaster for the Arabs who had regressed from being a technically advanced and learned civilisation to one that remained mired in backwardness and more interested in religion than science. Throwing off the Ottoman yoke, in his view, would allow the Arabs to resume their previous trajectory of learning and advancement. However, this secular vision of Arab nationalism was anathema to the vast bulk of Muslim Arabs, who remained committed to, or at least dispassionate about, the Ottoman Empire.[19]

George Antonius, in his 1938 book *The Arab Awakening*, perhaps the key text of modern Arab nationalism, saw the genesis of Arab nationalism within these very small cultural movements in late 19th-century Ottoman Syria. Since the Second World War, there has been increasing scepticism regarding some of Antonius's claims regarding the origins of Arab nationalism and his account of the Arab Revolt during the First World War, however.[20] Even a sympathetic observer notes that it is not only 'a work of historical narrative, but also of political advocacy'.[21] Relying essentially on oral evidence, Antonius almost certainly overplayed the role of a small Lebanese grouping, the Secret Society, which

---

18 M E Yapp, *The Making of the Modern Near East, 1792–1923* (Longman, Harlow: 1987) pp 132–3.

19 Dawn, 'From Ottomanism to Arabism', pp 10–11.

20 Among critical looks at Antonius are Sylvia G Haim, '"The Arab Awakening", A Source for the Historian?', *Die Welt des Islams*, Vol 2, No 4 (1953), pp 237–50; Elie Kedourie, *England and the Middle East: The Destruction of the Ottoman Empire, 1914–1921* (London, Boulder: 1987) pp 29–66, 107–41; Elie Kedourie, *In the Anglo-Arab Labyrinth: The McMahon-Husayn Correspondence and Its Interpretations 1914–1939* (Cambridge University Press, Cambridge: 1976) pp 64–136, 266–9; Albert Hourani, '"The Arab Awakening", Forty Years Later', in Derek Hopwood (ed), *Studies in Arab History: The Antonius Lectures, 1978–87* (Macmillan, Basingstoke: 1990) pp 21–40.

21 Hourani, '"The Arab Awakening", Forty Years Later', p 26.

distributed placards agitating against the Ottomans in the late 1870s. This agitation, it is likely, was more to do with particular local factors involving Maronite Christians than the genesis of an Arab nationalism aimed against the Turks.[22]

Some 30 years later there were more concrete signs of a nascent Arab nationalism. The spur was the 1908 Young Turk revolution. Arab reaction was initially enthusiastic. The initial phase of liberalism delivered by the CUP saw political activity permitted in the empire, including the formation of specifically Arab parties. Yet it soon became clear that the Young Turks' flirtation with liberalism and pluralism was merely a veneer behind which lurked a Turkish nationalist agenda, which reinforced tendencies towards centralisation and Turkification already evident in the Ottoman Empire. Indeed, there is little evidence that the Young Turks drove forward these policies to any greater extent than the old regime had.[23] However, by briefly opening up Ottoman politics, they made it harder to go back to the old authoritarian system.

After 1912, in a reaction to the end of the period of reform, parties with an agenda of Arab autonomy began to emerge in Syria. The most important of these, according to Antonius, was the Decentralisation Party. Other bodies of importance, again in Syria, were secret societies with similar manifestos including al-Fatat (the Young Arab Society) and al-Qahtanyia. Antonius would seek later to link these groupings into the Hashemite revolt against the Ottomans from 1916, thereby creating a bond between the more urban-based nationalism of the streets of Damascus and that of the arid deserts from which the Hashemites sprung.

According to its critics, however, Antonius's vision of the origins and development of Arab nationalism was exaggerated and fallacious. The pro-independence or autonomy-minded Arabs of Syria were a tiny minority, numbering around 350 members according to a recent authoritative

22 Antonius, The Arab Awakening, pp 37, 80, 81; Zeine N Zeine, Arab-Turkish Relations and the Emergence of Arab Nationalism (Khayat's, Beirut: 1958) pp 56, 57, 68.
23 See C Ernest Dawn, 'The Origins of Arab Nationalism', in Rashid Khalidi et al, The Origins of Arab Nationalism (Columbia University Press, New York: 1991) pp 18–19.

survey,[24] and Hashemite ambitions were nearly all to do with their own aggrandisement rather than a high-minded commitment to Arab nationalism.[25] Today, the dominant scholarly interpretation of the origins of Arab nationalism is C Ernest Dawn's hypothesis that the stirrings of Arab nationalism in the early part of the 20th century emerged not from Western-influenced Christian Arabs but from reform-minded Muslims in the religious elite. It also arose from the conflict among the Arab notables and the elite, particularly in the major cities such as Damascus. Those who held favour, land and office due to Ottoman patronage tended to support the *status quo* while those excluded from this spoils system began to agitate against it.[26] Even among the recalcitrant, there was little desire for complete independence. Most Arabs would have been content to 'remain within the frame of the Ottoman unity, as long as their proper place was recognised by the Turkish rulers'.[27] There were also enormous differences between city and countryside. Writing nearly 90 years ago, the influential English Arabist Gertrude Bell was perhaps closer than Antonius to the true state of Arab nationalism around the early years of the 20th century when she wrote, 'There is no nation of Arabs; the Syrian merchant is separated by a wider gulf from the bedouin than he is from the Osmanli [Ottoman] …'.[28] At the beginning of the 20th century national politics in Syria remained 'an urban game largely isolated from village needs and wishes'.[29]

---

24 Eliezer Tauber, *The Emergence of the Arab Movements* (Frank Cass, London: 1993) p 406; C Ernest Dawn, *From Ottomanism to Arabism: Essays on the Origins of Arab Nationalism* (University of Illinois Press, Urbana: 1973) pp 152–3, puts the figure at only 144.

25 Most notably, Efraim Karsh and Inari Karsh, *Empires of the Sand: The Struggle for Mastery in the Middle East, 1789–1923* (Harvard University Press, Cambridge MA: 1999) are very hostile to what they consider the imperialist ambitions of Sherif Hussein and the Hasehemites.

26 A useful summation of Dawn's more than three decades of musing on the subject is in Dawn, 'The Origins of Arab Nationalism', pp 3–31.

27 Majid Khadduri, *Political Trends in the Arab World: The Role of Ideas and Ideals in Politics* (Johns Hopkins Press, Baltimore: 1970) p 19.

28 Cited in Martin Kramer, *Arab Awakening and Islamic Revival: The Politics of Ideas in the Middle East* (Transaction Publishers, New Brunswick: 1996) p 24.

29 Raymond A Hinnebusch, *Authoritarian Power and State Formation in Ba'thist Syria: Army, Party and Peasant* (Westview Press, Boulder, CO: 1990) p 45.

The Hashemites

When the standard of Arab independence from the Turks was raised, this came not from the urban elite, but from a somewhat unexpected source, the Hashemites, the leading family in one of the empire's most remote districts, the Hejaz. The Hejaz was a narrow strip of land that extended from just south of what is now the Jordanian port of Akaba to nearly as far as the northern border of the Yemen. It now lies within the Kingdom of Saudi Arabia, although it was then a *vilayet* of the Ottoman Empire. Indeed it was practically the only part of the Arabian Peninsula where the writ of the Ottomans ran at all. Situated on a barren and inhospitable stretch of coastline, its importance lay in the fact that two of the holiest sites of Islam lay within it: Mecca, the holiest city, and Medina, the first city to accept the word of Prophet Muhammad. It was remote from the capital, poor and thinly populated. Indeed, it is estimated that towards the end of the 19th century, the combined population of the three main towns of the Hejaz – Mecca, Medina and Jeddah – was little more than 100,000, with perhaps another 400,000 nomadic tribesmen in the hinterland around them.[30] The territory lacked natural resources and much of the urban population was devoted to the study and practice of religion.

Its main source of income was the influx of pilgrims from all corners of the Muslim world, who as part of their religious duty were compelled, at least once in their life, to make the annual *haj* to the Holy Places at Mecca. The presence of the holiest cities of Islam within the Hejaz conferred considerable benefits upon the area. It was not subject to conscription or normal levels of Ottoman taxation. Indeed, it tended to be a net recipient of aid, as well as receiving subventions from relatively wealthy Muslim states such as Egypt. It has been argued that 'religion determined the social, economic, and, to a lesser degree, the political history of western Arabia [i.e., the Hejaz] in the nineteenth century'.[31] It remained a pre-modern, highly traditional society. There were little outward signs of nationalism or other modern political ideas permeating the area during the 19th century, and nor is there much evidence that

---

30 W Ochsenwald, *Religion, Society and the State in Arabia: The Hijaz under Ottoman Control 1840–1908* (Ohio State University Press, Columbus, OH: 1984) p 17.
31 Ochsenwald, *Religion, Society and the State in Arabia*, p 220.

before the beginning of the 20th century the Hashemites showed any great political ambitions.[32]

Nearly 13 centuries after the death of the Prophet, those who were descended from him were entitled to use the title 'Sherif' (usually translated as eminent, distinguished or noble).[33] Among the most important of these Sherifian families was the House of Beni Hashem (hence 'Hashemites'), from the Prophet's Quraysh tribe. Sherif Hussein ibn Ali of the Hashemites filled the most important position in the Hejaz, as Grand Sherif and Emir of Mecca, from 1908. Hussein's branch of the Hashemites had been raised out of relative obscurity when, during the 19th century Muhammad Ali, the ruler of Egypt, who had ruled over the Hejaz, installed Hussein's grandfather as Grand Sherif and Emir of Mecca.[34]

The power that came with this position tended to be more religious than political and the Hashemites, though Arab, were also part of the Ottoman establishment. The independence of the Grand Sherifs was circumscribed by the presence of a Turkish governor or *Vali* in Medina and the presence of some 7,000 troops. However, communications with Istanbul before the completion of the Hejaz railway in 1908 were slow and difficult, and distance from the imperial capital generally allowed the Emir of Mecca a reasonable degree of autonomy. Yet, as one writer in the 19th century stated, the Emir of Mecca was still a 'mere creature of the Porte, removable at the pleasure of the Sultan. Besides, he has no influence whatever, political or spiritual, beyond his own assigned district'.[35] Indeed the ultimate control of the Ottomans over the Hashemites and Hejaz was demonstrated by the practice of bringing important members of leading families of the Hejaz, such as the Hashemites, to the capital as enforced guests of the Sultan.

However, it should also be borne in mind that Ottoman rule and the Turkish garrison also afforded a degree of security for the Hejaz. The

---

32 W Ochsenwald, 'Ironic origins: Arab nationalism in the Hijaz', in Khalidi et al, *The Origins of Arab Nationalism*, p 190.

33 James Morris, *The Hashemite Kings* (Faber and Faber, London: 1959) p 18.

34 Kedourie, *In the Anglo-Arab Labyrinth*, p 11.

35 Cited in Tufan Buzpinar, 'Opposition to the Ottoman Caliphate in the Early Years of Abdülhamid II: 1877–1882', *Die Welt des Islams*, New Series Vol 36, Issue I (Mar 1996) p 67.

Arabian Peninsula was a dangerous place with plenty of tribes and religious rivals (the Imam of Yemen, the Wahhabis and by the early 20th
century the rising power of Ibn Saud) seeking to extend their influence.
Since 1800 the British had been busy securing key positions and acquiring allies amongst the various Emirs on the coastal peripheries of the
peninsula.[36]

The Caliphate

When, after his accession, Abdülhamid II emphasised that as ruler of the
Ottoman Empire he held the title of Caliph, there were voices of opposition. Some were proto-Arab nationalists who demanded the restoration
of an Arab Caliphate. Some prophetic traditions, of admittedly dubious
origin, claimed that the Caliphate could only be held by members of
the Prophet's own tribe, the Quraysh. Dissent also came from British
government officials – many in the India Office and Indian Civil Service
– who did not like the Ottoman Sultan having such potential influence
over the near 100 million Muslims in British India. One retired British
civil servant suggested the Hashemite Emir of Mecca, a member of the
Quraysh, would be a more pliable Caliph of Islam 'for he lives by the
side of our road to India and would be as completely in our power as the
Suez Canal'.[37] It was a prescient comment, for the idea of a relationship
between the Hashemites and the British would come to the surface again
at a critical point in Middle Eastern affairs, albeit in the context of Arab
nationalism rather than the Caliphate.

The Rise of Sherif Hussein[38]

Hussein ibn Ali was born in 1853 in Istanbul. Half-Circassian, half-Arab,
his family connections to the Aoun clan, a branch of the Hashemites,

---

36 See Elizabeth Monroe, *Britain's Moment in the Middle East 1914–1956*
(Methuen, London: 1963) pp 11–23.
37 Cited in Buzpinar, 'Opposition to the Ottoman Caliphate in the Early Years of
Abdülhamid II', p 80.
38 What follows is substantially based on R Baker, *King Husain and the Kingdom
of Hejaz* (Oleander Press, Cambridge: 1979); Kedourie, *In the Anglo-Arab
Labyrinth*; A Susser and A Shmuelevitz (eds), *The Hashemites in the Modern Arab
World: Essays in Honour of the Late Professor Uriel Dann* (Frank Cass, London:
1995); Morris, *The Hashemite Kings*; Joshua Teitelbaum, *The Rise and Fall of
the Hashemite Kingdom of Arabia* (Hurst, London: 2001); and Haifa Alangaria

were what made him important, as he was 37th in the line of descent from the Prophet.[39] There were approximately 800 members of the rival Aoun and Zaid clans who could claim this sacred lineage. At various times, one branch or the other would be ascendant and would hold the title of Emir or Grand Sherif of Mecca. In the 1880s and 1890s, the Zaid branch was dominant.

At the time of the outbreak of the First World War, Hussein was over 60. Nonetheless, he was a striking looking, black-robed, turban-clad figure with an almost snow-white beard. T E Lawrence, the British army officer who would have a key role in the Arab Revolt, described him as 'outwardly so clean and gentle-mannered as to seem weak; but this appearance hid a crafty policy, deep ambition, and an un-Arabian foresight, strength of character and obstinacy'.[40] Hussein was in many respects a charismatic figure, learned in Arabic literature and familiar with the intrigues of international diplomacy. His Ottoman upbringing had also bred some rather unattractive qualities in the Sherif. According to Lawrence, 'Hussein when young had been honest, outspoken … [but] he learned not merely to suppress his speech, but to use speech to conceal his honest purpose. The art, over-indulged, became a vice from which he could not free himself.'[41]

His early years are shrouded in mystery. We do know that as a leading scion of the Hashemite family he was an enforced guest of the Sultan for more than 15 years from 1892 or 1893 to 1908. His confinement, if it could be even called that, was extremely benign. The Sultan, not wishing to be accused of treating a Sherifian badly, had Hussein, his wife and four sons, Ali (1879–1935), Abdullah (1880–1951), Feisal (1883–1933) and Zeid (1898–1970), established in a comfortable villa on the Bosphorus. Three of the four sons (Ali, Abdullah and Feisal) were to become kings of three of the successor states of the Ottoman Empire.

Hussein became a prominent citizen in the capital, and was, in many respects, assimilated into the Ottoman way of life. Turkish appears to have come as easily to him as Arabic. He was, though, extremely

The Struggle for Power in Arabia: Ibn Saud, Hussein and Great Britain, 1914–1924 (Ithaca Press, Reading: 1998).

39 Morris, The Hashemite Kings, p 23.

40 T E Lawrence, Seven Pillars of Wisdom (Wordsworth, London: 1997) p 84.

41 Lawrence, Seven Pillars of Wisdom, p 86.

strong-willed and independent-minded, and was probably too dangerous a figure to have ever been left to return to the Hejaz by the despotic
Sultan Abdülhamid II.[42] However, events intervened. When the Young
Turks assumed power in 1908, Abdülhamid's powers were truncated, and
he was deposed after a year. The position of Grand Sherif of Mecca fell
vacant around the same time as the revolution, thanks to the deposition of the holder Sherif Ali Abdullah ibn Muhammad and the sudden
death of his successor. Hussein was a leading candidate for the position,
although his succession was by no means a formality. He was helped by
his political views and an ability to ingratiate himself with key players.
A deeply reactionary figure in many respects, he was not an admirer of
the Young Turks, and his hostility to the new government may well have
attracted Abdülhamid to Hussein's candidature. There is also some evidence that the British government viewed him as a suitable candidate,
thanks to Hussein's timely overtures to the British Ambassador to Constantinople, in which he claimed to have written to Arab chiefs in the
Hejaz to influence them to favour British interests in the Arabian Peninsula.[43] Abdülhamid also viewed the Caliphate and the loyalty this engen-
dered amongst his Islamic subjects as a key element in his survival. It was
in his interests therefore to have a figure opposed to the Young Turks in
the important position of Grand Sherif of Mecca. Hussein, according
to his son Abdullah, pledged that if the CUP made life too difficult for
Abdülhamid, he could have asylum in the Hejaz.[44]

Hussein as Sherif and the Ottomans

In 1908 Hussein was made Sherif and returned to the Hejaz. However,
there is some evidence that once he had done so, Hussein raised his sights
and began to contemplate that he, not the Ottoman Sultan, should be
Caliph. His son Abdullah testifies in his memoirs that Hussein was loyal
to the Ottomans at this time and that his main argument with Istanbul
was the secularising reforms of the CUP. In his view, the Young Turks,
'were ill advised when they converted the Imperial Caliphate administration into a racial "Constitutional" government and replaced the Islamic
and therefore ultimately Arab supervision of the State by a Western

---

42 Morris, *The Hashemite Kings*, pp 24–5.
43 Teitelbaum, *The Rise and Fall of the Hashemite Kingdom of Arabia*, p 41.
44 Teitelbaum, *The Rise and Fall of the Hashemite Kingdom of Arabia*, p 41.

juridical control'.[45] In contrast to this, right from the beginning of his reign, Hussein made clear that traditional Islamic law, the *Sharia*, was what guided him.[46] Hussein's priority upon arrival in the Hejaz was to consolidate his power base and increase his influence at the expense of the Turkish *Vali*. Indeed, by 1911 the British were reporting that Hussein had completely outmanoeuvered the various *Vali* sent there and the government of Mecca was essentially in his hands. A British dispatch from 1914 reported that on his arrival in 1908, Hussein had 'created a good impression, and it was hoped that he would not prove extortionate and would restore security in the country about Mecca'. After initial clamping down on brigandage, Hussein appears to have tolerated it. The British consul in Mecca reported that the murderers of three Indian pilgrims had links to the Grand Sherif.[47]

However, Hussein needed to be circumspect in his challenges to the various *Vali* and Ottoman authorities, for going too far could lead to his deposition. Indeed his earliest achievement was to bring the increasingly fractious Bedouin tribes adjacent to the Hejaz under control. The Ottomans, who after 1910 had much greater military priorities in the Balkans and in Libya, encouraged Hussein to extend his power into eastern Arabia and to assert Ottoman control against the two independent tribal leaders Ibn Saud and the Idrisi of Asir. According to the British consul in Jeddah, Hussein viewed these campaigns as a means by which he could consolidate his own power and autonomy.[48] But the tentacles of Ottoman and Turkish control over the Hejaz were beginning to grow, not wither. Telegraph wires linked the capital to the Hejaz from the end of the 19th century and by 1908, communications were revolutionised by the completion of the Hejaz railway that linked Damascus to the city of Medina and the other Holy Places. The railway was greeted with considerable hostility by the Bedouin tribes of the Hejaz, who viewed the 'Iron Donkey' as a serious threat to their main sources of

45 Abdullah, *Memoirs of King Abdullah of Transjordan* (Cape, London: 1950) p 70.
46 J Nevo, 'Abdullah's memoirs as historical source material', in Susser and Shmuelevitz, *The Hashemites in the Modern Arab World*, p 166.
47 Sir Louis Mallet to Sir Edward Grey, 18 March 1914, in G P Gooch and Harold Temperley, *British Documents on the Origins of the War, 1898–1914*, Vol X, Part II (HMSO, London: 1938) p 827, hereafter *British Docs*.
48 Alangaria, *The Struggle for Power in Arabia*, p 63.

income: the guiding, transportation and occasional robbing of pilgrims. Significantly, the Young Turks appear to have viewed the railway and its eventual extension to Mecca as the cornerstone of the consolidation of more direct Ottoman rule in western Arabia. Indeed Medina, the town at the end of the railway line, began to come under much greater Ottoman influence in the years up to 1914.

Hussein, upon his installation as Sherif, encouraged attacks on the trains and he assiduously resisted entreaties from the Young Turks to extend the line down to his power base at Mecca.[49] It is clear, however, that Hussein's autonomy in the years leading up to the outbreak of the First World War was becoming increasingly circumscribed. His son Abdullah complained about the tyranny of the Turks to the French Ambassador in 1912 and around this time the first tentative contacts between Abdullah and the British may have taken place.[50] The key event in the deterioration of the Hashemite position was the installation of Vehib Bey as the *Vali* in April 1914. Made of much more formidable stuff than his predecessors, he soon began clipping Hussein's wings. Vehib was determined that the dual control over the Hejaz would end and more direct Ottoman rule be established. Hashemite supporters in the administration were summarily dismissed and replaced by Ottoman placemen. Abdullah's contacts with the British, seeking their support for autonomy for the Hejaz, in February and April 1914, appear to have been directly motivated by the growing pressure being placed on his father by Vehib.[51] It is clear that Ibn Saud, Hussein's great rival for supremacy in Arabia, who was also subject to Ottoman sovereignty, had far more autonomy in the isolated Nejd territories of central Arabia.

Hussein's clashes with the Ottomans were very much related to his own desires for self-aggrandisement and protection from the increasing encroachments on his powers by Ottoman officials. His Arab nationalist credentials were 'questionable'.[52] Indeed, there is little evidence of any significant Arab nationalist pressures in the Hejaz. Within the

---

49 See James Nicholson, 'The Hejaz Railway', *Asian Affairs*, Vol 37, No 3 (2006) pp 320–36 for the story of the railway.
50 Teitelbaum, *The Rise and Fall of the Hashemite Kingdom of Arabia*, p 69.
51 Teitelbaum, *The Rise and Fall of the Hashemite Kingdom of Arabia*, pp 69–70.
52 A I Dawisha, *Arab Nationalism in the Twentieth Century: From Triumph to Despair* (Princeton University Press, Princeton: 2003) p 35.

socio-economic makeup of the region there were none of the key group-ings (journalists, army officers and intellectuals) that were present at the creation of other nationalisms.[53] To speak of 'nationalism' in the Hejaz, therefore, is a misnomer. The Arab Revolt, there at least, sprang almost entirely from a clash over power between the Hashemites, who considered themselves an elite whose privileges and autonomy were being threat-ened, and the Ottomans, who wanted to forge a modern centralised state. If the Ottomans had shown more skill in handling Hussein, the Sherif would have been most unlikely to lead a revolt against the Ottomans. The revolution in international politics brought about by the First World War, especially the willingness of all powers to support persons or groupings with grievances within their enemies' territories for subversive purposes, would provide Hussein with the means to take advantage of a unique opportunity to expand his power.

The Zionist movement

It was into this complex and evolving world of the Ottoman Empire and Arab politics that from the early 1880s the movement of Jews from eastern Europe began. Its immediate cause was the persecution and dis-crimination felt by the world's largest Jewish community, that of the Russian Empire's Pale of Settlement. At the time of Chaim Weizmann's birth in 1874, the Tsarist empire, which had acquired much of Poland in the late 18th century, held the largest Jewish population in the world. From 1772 onwards, the Jews were compelled to live in the western parts of the empire in an area designated the Jewish Pale. While many of them lived in cities like Vilnius, Odessa and Warsaw, or in large towns like Pinsk, many others grouped together in small towns known in Yiddish, the lingua franca of Eastern Europe's Jews, as *shtetls*. Weizmann's birth-place, Motol, was just such a *shtetl*.

The movement Hibbat Zion ('Love of Zion'), which pioneered the migration of Jews to Palestine, was founded in 1882. It was essentially a response to renewed persecution of the Jews in the Tsarist empire, and, despairing of assimilation, its members looked instead to Palestine. In November 1884, their first conference was held at Katowice, just across the border in Prussian Silesia. Anti-Semitism had been on the increase in the empire, stoked by its political and economic problems and the growth

---

53 See Ochsenwald, 'Ironic Origins: Arab Nationalism in the Hijaz', pp 189–203.

of Slavophile sentiments, but what gave it new impetus was the assassination in St Petersburg in March 1881 of Alexander II the 'Tsar Liberator', so called on account of his emancipation of the serfs, albeit in a manner which did not much benefit them. Of the six revolutionaries convicted of the murder, one was a young Jewish woman, Khasia Helfman. This event served to unleash a series of pogroms, as anti-Jewish riots were known, which began soon after the coronation of Alexander III and swept across areas as far apart as Warsaw and Odessa. Then, on 3 May 1882, the 'May Laws' were enacted which placed the Jews of the empire under even more severe restrictions than they had so far endured. Increasingly marginalised within the empire, hundreds of thousands of Jews emigrated, some across the border to the more tolerant Habsburg lands, others further afield to Britain and, especially, to the United States. Between 1882 and the outbreak of war in 1914, some 2.6 million Russian Jews emigrated to America, most of them to New York.

In 1882, a small group of Hibbat Zion members made their way to Palestine, where their first settlements were Rishon le-Zion, Rosh Pinnah and Petah Tikvah, followed by others such as Rehovoth, Hadera and Metulla. The settlements were not an immediate success, for the simple reasons that they were inadequately funded and that the settlers were inexperienced farmers. It was an inauspicious beginning for modern Jewish settlement in Palestine, which might have fallen at the first hurdle had it not been for the intervention of Baron Edmond de Rothschild, philanthropist and scion of the great French banking and winemaking dynasty. As the little settlements started to founder, Rothschild was persuaded to help, providing considerable financial backing, albeit at the cost of close supervision by his agents. With their assistance, a wine industry was created, followed by citrus production, which succeeded in stimulating an economic base for the settlement. These were the precursors of political Zionism.

Zionism had no single point of origin. The Jews were too widely dispersed, and their situations too different, for that. Although ideas of political action began to surface amongst Jewish intellectuals in the 19th century, the term itself appears to have been used first by the Austrian Nathan Birnbaum in April 1890 in his journal *Selbstemanzipation*. 'Zion' referred, of course, to Jerusalem. Although he created the term 'Zionism', Birnbaum was to part company from it later. Neverthless, his ideas anticipated those of another Viennese who is regarded as the real father of modern Zionism, Theodore Herzl, or in Hebrew, Benyamin Ze-ev Herzl.[54]

Theodore Herzl

Herzl's origins were in the German-speaking Jewish middle class of the Habsburg Empire, a world away from the *shtetls* to the east. He was born on 2 May 1860 in the city of Pest, which in 1872 united with its twin across the Danube to become Budapest, the capital of the Hungarian part of the empire. In 1878, he became a law student at the University of Vienna, then one of the most culturally vibrant cities in Europe, albeit one in which anti-Semitism was beginning to stir. Although he gained employment as a state lawyer, his real ambitions lay in literature, and while he struggled to have his plays accepted he found his niche, that of a writer of feuilletons for the press. These were short, finely crafted pieces much prized by educated Viennese, and in 1888 he was engaged to write them for the *Wiener Neue Freie Presse*, the capital's leading newspaper.

Two things conspired to change Herzl's essentially assimilationist position. The first was the growing success in Viennese municipal politics of the Christian Social Party led by Dr Karl Lueger. Lueger, who was prepared to espouse anti-Semitism to advance his party's fortunes, was elected Lord Mayor of Vienna in 1895, and although Emperor Franz Josef refused three times to confirm him in the position, such was his popularity in the city that he assumed the office in 1897, holding it until his death in 1910. Adolf Hitler was later to extol his virtues in *Mein Kampf*. If confirmation were needed of the rising tide of anti-Semitism in Europe, then Herzl received it as Paris correspondent for his newspaper at the time of the Dreyfus affair in 1894–5. Captain Alfred Dreyfus, an assimilated Jew, was convicted, wrongly as it was later shown, of selling military secrets to Germany. On 5 January 1895, Herzl witnessed the formal degradation of Dreyfus in the courtyard of the École Militaire in Paris. What particularly appalled Herzl about this miserable spectacle was the crowd outside chanting 'Death to the Jews'.[55] The success of

---

54 For the history of Zionism, see Walter Laqueur, *A History of Zionism* (Schocken Books, New York: 1972) and Nahum Sokolow, *History of Zionism 1600–1918*, 2 Vols (Longmans, Green and Co, London: 1919).
55 Alex Bein, *Theodore Herzl* (The Jewish Publication Society of America, Philadelphia: 1941) pp 112–16.

Lueger's party in March that year further exposed the degree of anti-Semitism in two of Europe's most sophisticated cities, Paris and Vienna, and set the scene for the book Herzl was to publish the following year.

His book, or rather pamphlet, was published in Vienna and Leipzig on 14 February 1896. It had the somewhat ponderous title of *Der Judenstaat: Versuch einer modernen Lösung der Judenfrage*, normally rendered in English as *The Jewish State: An Attempt at a Modern Solution of the Jewish Question*, though a more accurate translation would be *The Jews' State*. Based on his recent dismal experiences in Vienna and Paris, his premise was essentially the pessimistic one that the pursuit of assimilationism was a false trail. The fact that Jews had given their loyalty to and had tried to enrich their countries through their contributions to the economy, art and science was in vain. The history of anti-Semitism, he went on to argue, had made the Jews into a people who could make a state. He foresaw the need for an organisation to work towards this, proposing a Society of Jews which would prepare the way and a Jewish Company which would carry the project forward. There were two possible locations for such a state. The first was Argentina, which he argued had plenty of good land and a small population. The other was their historic homeland of Palestine. If that were to be granted by the Ottoman Sultan, it could become an outpost of Western civilisation. Such was the essence of his book, which went on to describe the future state in romantic, not to say visionary, terms. The idea of a Jewish state, and an organisation to bring it into being, had entered the public domain.[56]

For many, perhaps most, assimilationist Jews of western and central Europe, Herzl's book opened up issues about anti-Semitism that they had hoped were becoming a thing of the past. The 19th century had seen Jews advance into prominent positions in various European countries. Some of them were converts to Christianity, for example, the German composer Felix Mendelssohn and the British statesman Benjamin Disraeli, both favourites of Queen Victoria. Others held to their Jewish faith, asserting that they were a religious community like the Catholics, Anglicans or Lutherans. It was from the assimilationist Jews that some of the most determined opposition to Zionism came. In the winter of 1896/7, Herzl

---

56 See Theodore Herzl, *The Jewish State: An Attempt at a Modern Solution of the Jewish Question* (H Pordes, London: 1972, 6th edition, revised, with foreword by Israel Cohen; original edition 1896).

nevertheless worked single-mindedly to put his ideas into effect. His efforts culminated in the First Zionist Congress at Basle in Switzerland in August 1897. A seemingly modest affair of 197 delegates, it was historic, and the programme it approved was brief and to the point. The purpose of Zionism was to secure a home for the Jews in Palestine. In order to achieve this, Jews were to be encouraged to settle there, an organisation was to be created, Jewish national sentiment was to be fostered, and government consent secured.[57] The achievement of the Zionist programme might have seemed a distant dream, but the essential first step had been taken. While Herzl was well aware that Zionism had to negotiate with the Ottoman rulers in Istanbul, whose writ ran in Palestine, notably absent from his analysis, then and later, were the Arabs of Palestine.

The men and women of the Second *Aliya*, or 'Immigration', which began in 1904, were impelled by the failed Russian revolution of 1904–5 and the renewed spate of pogroms which broke out in its wake. What marked them out from their immediate predecessors were their socialist convictions allied to a belief that the Jews needed to work for themselves as part of their national development. An historic initiative of the Second *Aliya* was the adoption and fostering of the Hebrew language. Most arrivals at that time would have spoken Yiddish, and would almost certainly also have known Russian or possibly Polish. German, of course, was the language of choice for the cultivated Central European Jewish middle class. Hebrew was the sacred language of the scriptures and worship in the synagogue, revered as such. But revival of language was an integral part of the story of national reawakening in Europe, and Zionism proved to be no different. The driving force behind this development was Eliezer Ben Yehuda, originally Perlman, who settled in Palestine in 1882, and who preached, and practised, the exclusive use of Hebrew. Ben Yehuda clearly recognised the need to bring this ancient language into the modern age if it were to have any future, and this was embodied in the ten-volume Hebrew dictionary, *Thesaurus Totius Hebraitatis*, he published from 1910.[58] His lead was enthusiastically taken up by the new immigrants, although regarded with suspicion and disfavour by many orthodox Jews for whom Hebrew was a sacred language not to be used for mundane matters.

---

57 'The Basle Declaration', in Walter Laqueur (ed), *The Israel-Arab Reader* (Pelican Books, London: 1970) pp 28–9; Laqueur, *A History of Zionism*, pp 103–8.
58 Sokolow, *History of Zionism*, Vol I, p 287; Vol II, pp 81, 284.

Foundations were also being laid in other ways. In 1908, Dr Arthur Ruppin set up the Palestine Office in Jaffa, the purpose of which was to bring some impetus and organisation to land purchase. The following year, in the apparently unpromising sand dunes to the north of the ancient Arab port of Jaffa, a start was made on a new suburb which in time was to grow into a thriving Jewish metropolis. This was called Tel Aviv, 'the hill of the spring'. By 1914 it had attracted around 2,000 inhabitants. The driving force behind it came from the Russian Jewish immigrant Meir Dizengoff, who became chairman of the Town Council in 1910, and whose name was to become synonymous with the city's development for almost three decades. Although it was to suffer a serious setback during the war, under Dizengoff's direction Tel Aviv was to expand dramatically in the 1920s and 1930s, in time overshadowing Jaffa.[59] Elsewhere, in the years preceding the First World War, Jews were settling in Haifa and new suburbs were springing up in Jerusalem. In short, however modestly, Zionism was establishing the basis for subsequent urbanisation. It was all very different to established Turkish and Arab societies.

Chaim Weizmann: origins of a Zionist leader

The man who was to assume such a pivotal part in the future of the Middle East, Dr Chaim Weizmann, was far from the centre of these events, even although he had been involved in Zionist affairs almost from the start. The small community of Motol shaped the first 11 years of Weizmann's life. Apart from its two synagogues, it had little of what later generations would term amenities. But by the standards of the Pale at that time, Weizmann's family enjoyed a decent, if modest, lower middle-class way of life. Ozer Weizmann, Chaim's father, was engaged in the timber trade, the mainstay of the local economy, employing men to cut logs which were then tied into rafts and floated down the rivers Pina, Bug and Vistula to Danzig, as modern Gdansk was then called, on the Baltic. Rachel Leah, Ozer's wife, had 15 children, of whom 12 survived into maturity. Chaim was her third.[60]

---

59 Dr Yehuda Slutsky, 'Under Ottoman Rule (1880–1917)', in Israel Pocket Library, History from 1880 (Keter Publishing House, Jerusalem: 1973) p 17.
60 Chaim Weizmann, Trial and Error: The Autobiography of Chaim Weizmann (Hamish Hamilton, London: 1949) pp 11–27; Jehuda Reinharz, Chaim Weizmann: The Making of a Zionist Leader (Oxford University Press, New York and Oxford:

If the Weizmann household was comfortable by the standards of the time, it was only won at the price of hard work on the part of Ozer and Rachel Leah, and in the knowledge that for the Jews life in the Pale could always be precarious. From the age of four until he was 11, Chaim Weizmann attended *cheder*, the little schools which provided instruction in Hebrew and the Jewish law and scripture. While he seemingly had no high opinion or kindly memory of some of his teachers, they embedded in him a profound sense of his own Jewish identity, reinforcing the atmosphere he absorbed at home.[61] Although he was to outgrow his origins, the values of Russian Jewry were to be the essential element in his later devotion to Zionism, setting him apart from, and often at odds with, some of the most prominent Jewish figures in Western Europe and the United States. This sense of where he was grounded comes across vividly in his first surviving letter, written in 1885 to Shlomo Sokolovsky, his tutor in the Russian language, which he needed to acquire in order to advance his education. Weizmann was concerned to reassure him that he would not abandon Judaism, and expressed his ardent support for the new Hibbat Zion movement. Interestingly, in view of the central role it was to assume in his life, he mentioned England, a country which he could only have imagined, as the one European state that would look favourably on the Jews.[62]

It was, then, armed with a growing knowledge of Russian to add to his Yiddish and Hebrew, that Weizmann left Motol to begin his secondary education at the Real-Gymnasium in Pinsk, some 25 miles (40 kilometres) away. Two things stand out from his time there, each of which was to mould his subsequent career. Few things can be as inspirational in a young life as a schoolmaster or schoolmistress with talents beyond the ordinary and so it proved with Weizmann, since his interest in science, and chemistry in particular, was captured and fostered by a teacher called Kornienko.[63]

1985) p 7; Norman Rose, *Chaim Weizmann: A Biography* (Weidenfeld and Nicolson, London: 1986) pp 16–18.

61 Weizmann, *Trial and Error*, pp 13–14.

62 Weizmann to Shlomo Tsvi Sokolovsky, Motol, Summer 1885, in Leonard Stein (ed), *The Letters and Papers of Chaim Weizmann*, Series A, Vol I, Summer 1885–29 October 1902 (Oxford University Press, London: 1968) pp 35–7; hereafter *LPCW*, Vol I.

63 Weizmann, *Trial and Error*, pp 34–5.

Of even greater significance for the future were Weizmann's contacts with Pinsk's large and varied Jewish community, since Jews formed the majority of the town's population, with a wider social and educational mix than any he had so far encountered. The town's professional and business classes were strongly assimilationist, but amongst Jews of Weizmann's social background the new Hibbat Zion movement had taken hold. Its local leader was Rabbi David Friedman, who had been a leading figure at the Katowice conference. As Kornienko had done with chemistry, Friedman clearly fired the adolescent Weizmann, who worshipped in the synagogue attached to his house, and in the evenings plodded the streets of Pinsk raising money for the cause. Such was his introduction to the nascent Zionist movement with which his name was to become indelibly linked.[64] Although he was later to become somewhat dismissive of Pinsk, this was with the experience of a great city like Berlin behind him.[65] Unprepossessing and drearily provincial Pinsk might have been, but it shaped him just the same.

Weizmann: scientist and Zionist

At the age of 19, Weizmann decided to pursue his higher education in Germany. His opportunity came when he was offered a part-time position as teacher of Hebrew and Russian at a leading Jewish boarding school at Pfungstadt. This was evidently a miserable time for him. He was homesick, poorly fed and repelled by the prevailing assimilationism of the German Jews he encountered. After two terms, he returned home in poor health. Though Pfungstadt had been an acute disappointment, an upturn in his father's business affairs now enabled him to enrol at the prestigious Charlottenburg Polytechnikum in Berlin in 1893.[66] Apart from a break back in Pinsk in 1895–6, Weizmann studied there until 1897 when he followed his mentor, Professor Bystrzycki, to the University of Fribourg in Switzerland, from which he graduated with his doctorate *magna cum laude* in 1899. He now had the credentials needed to follow an academic career in chemistry, which he began as a *Privat Dozent*, which carried no formal salary but was the vital first step, at the University of Geneva.[67]

---

64 Weizmann, *Trial and Error*, pp 38–40.
65 Reinharz, *Chaim Weizmann: The Making of a Zionist Leader*, pp 35–6.
66 Weizmann, *Trial and Error*, pp 44–50.
67 Weizmann, *Trial and Error*, pp 69, 76; Reinharz, *Chaim Weizmann: The*

To his later chagrin, Weizmann was not present at the historic Basle Congress, but that did not mean that during his time in Berlin he was not fully caught up in the beginnings of Zionism nor watching these events with keen interest. There is a symmetry between his progress in Pinsk and that in Berlin. In the former, he had been inspired by Kornienko and Friedman, whereas in Berlin if Bystrzycki fostered his scientific development, his evolution as a Zionist was in no small measure the result of his association with the writer and philosopher Asher Zvi Ginsberg, who had adopted the name Ahad Ha'am, 'One of the People'. Weizmann wrote in his autobiography that he was to Zionist students like himself what Mazzini had been to Young Italy.[68] While Weizmann was to develop a marked talent for quarrelling with his fellow Zionists, Ahad Ha'am, who died in Tel Aviv in 1927, was not one of them. However, unlike Herzl, actually having visited Palestine in 1891, Ahad Ha'am knew that the Arabs would not readily surrender to the Zionists, and sounded a warning to that effect.[69]

Weizmann's view of *Der Judenstaat* was that it contained nothing that was original, and that it ignored the work of others, like Birnbaum. There was certainly truth in this, but he also conceded that what gave the book its force was the personality of its author. Herzl's unique gift to Zionism was the fact that he moved from writing the book, which could have become no more than a historical curiosity, to organising and inspiring the First Zionist Congress. Weizmann should have attended this as a delegate from Pinsk, but that year his father's business fortunes declined, and he decided to travel to Moscow in an attempt, unsuccessful as it turned out, to sell a dyestuff formula he had developed. Moscow, of course, was technically barred to him as lying outside the Pale, and the difficulties he encountered made him late for the Congress.[70]

He was able to make up for this absence at the Second Zionist Congress at Basle in 1898, and from then on was a regular attender and participant. During this time he made the acquaintance of the leading Russian Zionist, Menahem Mendel Ussishkin, an early member of the Hibbat Zion movement in Odessa. Over the years this gifted, if sometimes

---

Making of a Zionist Leader, p 51; Rose, *Chaim Weizmann,* p 44.

68 Weizmann, *Trial and Error,* pp 51–2.
69 Stein, *The Balfour Declaration,* pp 90–1.
70 Weizmann, *Trial and Error,* pp 61–8.

turbulent, man was to become a key collaborator of Weizmann, joining him in the presentation to the Paris Peace Conference, although the two parted company over the issue of partition in the late 1930s, shortly before Ussishkin's death in 1941.[71]

Weizmann began to make his mark at the Fifth Zionist Congress in 1901 on a subject which was to capture his imagination, education, and in particular the concept of a Jewish university. In December 1901, a youth conference, largely inspired by Weizmann, led to the establishment of a group within Zionism known as the Democratic Faction. At the Fifth Zionist Congress which took place immediately afterwards, his Democratic Faction introduced a motion asking for a preparatory study for a Jewish university. Despite something of a spat with Herzl, the idea was taken forward.[72] That there was no permanent rift between the two men was demonstrated the following year when Herzl asked Weizmann to draw up a plan for a Jewish university.[73] Although the idea proved premature, Weizmann continued to nurse it, and it led to an important meeting. After visiting his family in Pinsk for Passover in 1903, he made his way to Warsaw to meet Nahum Sokolow, who chaired a local committee on behalf of the proposed university.[74] It was the beginning of a remarkable partnership. Born in Russian Poland in 1861, Sokolow was an author of distinction in both Hebrew and Polish. Moving to London in 1914, he was to become an indispensable aide to Weizmann in the critical negotiations of the First World War, joining him in presenting the Zionist case in Paris in 1919, as well as writing a classic history of the Zionist movement.

Even more important during this period was Weizmann's growing attachment to an attractive young Russian medical student, Vera Chatzmann, whom he met at the Jewish Club in Geneva in November 1900. Although he was eight years her senior, Weizmann and Vera shared a

71 Weizmann, *Trial and Error*, pp 80–1.

72 Professor Hugo Bergmann, 'Dr Weizmann's conception of the Hebrew University', in Paul Goodman (ed), *Chaim Weizmann: A Tribute on his Seventieth Birthday* (Victor Gollancz Ltd, London: 1945) p 94; Reinharz, *Chaim Weizmann: The Making of a Zionist Leader,* pp 86–91.

73 Weizmann to Theodore Herlz, Vienna, 21 May 1902; Weizmann to Theodore Herzl, Vienna, 4 June 1902; Weizmann to Theodore Herzl, Vienna, 25 June 1902: *LPCW*, Vol I, 204, 207, 209, pp 263–9.

74 Weizmann, *Trial and Error*, pp 103–5.

love of music, and they began to meet for tea in the Café Landolt in Geneva. But Weizmann was still making his way in the academic world and increasingly involved in the world of Zionism, while Vera had her medical degree to complete.[75]

The 'Uganda Offer'

Herzl was driven by the concept of the *Judennot*, the need of the Jews to find relief, and confirmation that the dawn of a new century had not altered this need came with a new outbreak of pogroms in the Tsarist empire, normally associated with the activities of the monarchist societies commonly known as the Black Hundreds. Weizmann soon found himself caught up in this, Zionism's first major crisis. In the week of Passover and Easter 1903, crowds rampaged through the city of Kishinev, now Chisinau in Moldova, killing some 50 Jews, injuring over 1,000 and destroying 1,500 houses. The Kishinev pogrom, which was but the first in a series, confirmed Herzl in his pessimistic forecast of the Jews' future. At this point, on 20 May 1903, his colleague Leopold Greenberg, editor of the *Jewish Chronicle*, had a fateful meeting with Joseph Chamberlain, the British Colonial Secretary. Chamberlain told him that Kishinev had convinced him that Herzl was right to argue that the Jews needed to get out of Eastern Europe, but questioned where they could go. The Zionists had been talking of possibilities in El Arish in the Sinai Desert and of Cyprus, but Chamberlain dismissed these, suggesting instead land in East Africa, where he believed that a million people could be settled. In subsequent communications with Chamberlain, this offer was confirmed as fertile land in what would later become Kenya, though it has always been known as the 'Uganda Offer'.[76]

Herzl was well aware that East Africa was not Palestine, but was all too conscious of what was happening in the Russian empire, which he had just visited, and that the world's greatest empire was holding out the possibility of a rescue plan. It was on that basis that he presented the offer to the Sixth Zionist Congress in Basle in August 1903. The Congress voted on the somewhat tortured resolution that it appoint an advisory

---

75 Weizmann, *Trial and Error*, p 145; Vera Weizmann, *The Impossible Takes Longer: Memoirs by the Wife of Israel's First President as Told to David Tutaev* (Hamish Hamilton, London: 1967) pp 1–3, 12–13.
76 Bein, *Theodore Herzl*, pp 439–41.

committee to assist a smaller committee which was to go to East Africa to investigate the possibility, but everyone knew that what was really at stake was the principle. The vote went in Herzl's favour by 295 to 178, but with 132 abstentions. What mattered was the nature and scale of the opposition, with which Weizmann was fully engaged. What was interesting about the opposition was that it was rooted in the large Russian delegation, including those from Kishinev, the very people whose fate Herzl sought to ease.

Weizmann, still a delegate from Pinsk, denounced the Uganda scheme at a meeting of the Russian delegation, concluding with the peroration that the British would make them a better offer.[77] It was a sulphurous affair, in which Weizmann's father and brother supported Herzl, and it was to get still worse. Ussishkin, who had been absent in Palestine at the time of the Congress, launched a bitter attack on the Uganda project when he returned to Russia. Then the Russian leaders, the *Neinsager* or 'Nay-sayers' as they were known, met at Kharkov to pass a resolution denouncing Herzl for violating the original Basle Programme of 1897, which had committed the movement to Palestine. With his movement in disarray, Herzl laboured throughout the winter of 1903/4 to effect some kind of reconciliation, but for some time he had been suffering from heart problems and on 3 July 1904 he died, aged only 44.[78] The 'Uganda Offer' did not long survive him, being rejected at the Seventh Zionist Congress in 1905. Leadership of the movement passed to David Wolfssohn, a German Jew of Lithuanian birth, whom Weizmann caustically dismissed as possessing neither personality nor vision.[79] That Zionism was now led from Berlin was to become a matter of some consequence a decade later, although that could not have been foreseen at the time.

Weizmann, Manchester and British politics

In 1904 Weizmann moved to the University of Manchester in the north of England. The circumstances are not altogether clear, but he saw no future in Geneva, and he had a good doctorate, backed up by a number of patents and research papers. Despite his opposition to it, the 'Uganda Offer' had shown that British politicians were responsive to Zionism,

77 Weizmann, *Trial and Error*, pp 110–17.
78 Bein, *Theodore Herzl*, pp 453–503.
79 Weizmann, *Trial and Error*, p 146.

and he had a letter of introduction to Professor William Henry Perkin of the University of Manchester, whose chemistry department he knew had a good reputation. Perkin was willing to rent him a laboratory, and with this somewhat unpromising beginning Weizmann set about learning English and gaining a foothold in the university. It says something for his determination that by January 1905 he was ready to give his first chemistry lecture in English, and in July he was appointed assistant in the chemistry department.[80] When Vera completed her medical degree in Switzerland the following year, the way was open for them to marry. With Weizmann often absent on Zionist business, and money sometimes scarce, it was a hard enough start to the marriage, but it survived, and Vera subsequently went on to her own distinguished medical career.[81] Their first son, Benjamin, was born in 1907, followed by Michael in 1916.

Manchester was a far cry from the hurly-burly of continental Zionist politics, but neither was it a backwater. A highly political city, the Conservative Member of Parliament for its Eastern Division since 1885 had been Arthur James Balfour. A lifelong bachelor, communicant in both the Presbyterian Church of Scotland and the Anglican Church of England, he had an interest in philosophy beyond what was normally expected of politicians, publishing respected books on the subject. His languid manner concealed a man of steel. From 1887 to 1891, he had held the demanding post of Chief Secretary for Ireland, and his handling of that country's affairs at a particularly turbulent time had earned him the title 'Bloody Balfour' and forced him to carry a pistol for several years. Becoming Prime Minister in 1902, he presided over an administration which tore itself apart on the issue of tariff reform. At the end of 1905, he resigned in favour of the Liberals, provoking a general election. It was, of course, his Colonial Secretary who had raised the prospect of the 'Uganda Offer', and Balfour was sufficiently interested in the matter to find out why the Zionists had turned against it. The essential link was his Conservative Party chairman in Manchester, Charles Dreyfus, who was also chairman of the Manchester Zionist Society. It was Dreyfus, a keen supporter of the Uganda scheme as it happened, who recommended to

---

80 Weizmann, *Trial and Error*, pp 123–34.
81 Vera Weizmann, *The Impossible Takes Longer*, pp 30–5; Rose, *Chaim Weizmann*, p 113.

Balfour that he should meet Weizmann as one of its leading opponents. It was to prove the most fateful encounter of Weizmann's life.[82]

Their meeting took place on 9 January 1906 in the Queen's Hotel in Manchester's Piccadilly, in the midst of the general election which resulted in Balfour losing his seat. Balfour was clearly concerned to find out why the 'Uganda Offer', which he had supported, had aroused such opposition, especially since he felt that it offered a practical way forward. Weizmann responded by emphasising the spiritual side of Zionism, which he maintained could only be fulfilled by Palestine, and asked if he were to offer Paris instead of London would Balfour accept it. To Balfour's reply that they already had London, Weizmann countered that the Jews had had Jerusalem when London was still a marsh. It is difficult to gauge the real impact of this meeting, particularly since Balfour made no effort to maintain the contact, but his niece and biographer Blanche Dugdale recorded how he often referred to the conversation and the impression Weizmann had made on him. For his part, Balfour wrote in his introduction to Sokolow's *History of Zionism* that their conversation had converted him to the view that if a home were to be found for the Jews it would have to be in Palestine. Weizmann, too, was convinced of the importance of this.[83]

Balfour was a sophisticated political veteran, but Weizmann was also in contact with the young Winston Churchill, who, having defected from the Conservatives, was contesting North-west Manchester in the Liberal interest. The two men met on two occasions in the course of the election.[84] As Colonial Secretary in 1921–2 Churchill was to become a major influence on the affairs of Palestine, while his later career belongs to history. In short, far from being an isolated outpost, Manchester was offering Weizmann openings in British politics which he could scarcely have imagined when he moved there, and which were to prove of incalculable value in the years ahead.

---

82 Blanche E C Dugdale, *Arthur James Balfour, First Earl of Balfour* (Hutchinson, London: 1936) Vol I, pp 325–6; Weizmann, *Trial and Error*, p 142.

83 Weizmann, *Trial and Error*, pp 142–5; Dugdale, *Arthur James Balfour*, Vol I, pp 326–7; 'Introduction by the Rt Hon A J Balfour, MP' 20 September 1918, in Sokolow, *History of Zionism*, Vol I, pp xxix–xxxiv; Reinharz, *Chaim Weizmann: The Making of a Zionist Leader*, pp 270–5.

84 Reinharz, *Chaim Weizmann: The Making of a Zionist Leader*, pp 275–7.

Manchester also provided him with his Zionist base. His opposition to Herzl and the 'Uganda Offer' had made him *persona non grata* with Leopold Greenberg of the *Jewish Chronicle*, and he was not invited to address Zionist meetings in the capital. Instead, he used Manchester as a base to tour the scattered Jewish communities in the cities of the north of England, as well as in Glasgow and Edinburgh. These poor Jewish groups responded to him in a way in which the British Jewish elite did not. In 1909, many of the most prominent Anglo-Jewish figures, including Leopold de Rothschild, Claude Montefiore, Sir Philip Magnus, Robert Waley Cohen and Osmond d'Avigdor Goldsmid, denounced what they saw as opinions which alienated them from other Englishmen. They were supported in this by the Chief Rabbi, who issued a statement to the effect that the Jews were a religious community and not a nation. This was a portent of the opposition Weizmann was to face in 1917.[85]

In 1907, Weizmann undertook his first visit to Palestine, a climactic moment in his life. It was his introduction to the land which had long been the focus of his dreams. If his autobiography is to be believed, the experience was not altogether positive. He particularly disliked Jerusalem, whose Jewish life he castigated as lacking in dignity and existing on charity. His attitude did not greatly change over time, it seems, although he did note the potential of Mount Scopus for erecting a building which could reflect the city's Jewish legacy. What, of course, he was encountering in the city was the community of pious, often elderly, and generally poor Jews who were supported through the *Hallukah*, charitable collections taken in the synagogues of Europe. Although this system had existed for generations, Weizmann, the modern man of science, could not believe that its dependants had anything to offer a future Jewish homeland. Neither was he greatly impressed by many of the more recent Jewish colonies, since they, too, he felt, were dependent on charity, albeit of a different kind. Nor did he like the fact that they were employing Arab labourers. However, he did note with approval a number of settlements where recently arrived Russian Jews, who had come into the country from 1904, were offering better hope for the future through the enterprise they were showing, not least through their ability to compete with Arab labour.[86]

---

85 Stein, *The Balfour Declaration*, pp 80–1.
86 Weizmann, *Trial and Error*, pp 161–9; Reinharz, *Chaim Weizmann: The Making of a Zionist Leader*, pp 316–17.

Although he never forgot his origins in the Pale, and regularly sent money home to help his younger siblings with their education, Weizmann was becoming increasingly settled in England, and his ties with Pinsk were becoming more tenuous, especially with the death of his father in 1911. His scientific reputation was also growing. By 1913, he could claim an enviable list of patents and scientific papers. When Perkin moved to the chair of chemistry at Oxford in 1913, Weizmann felt that the quality of his research and commitment to teaching made him an obvious candidate to succeed him, but the Manchester chair went to a rival candidate, while Weizmann had to console himself with the new title of Reader in Biochemistry. While professorships at British universities were less common than they have since become, and there was certainly no shame to his failure to get the chair, equally there is no doubt that Weizmann regarded what had happened as a major setback. An alternative did present itself in the form of an invitation to head a department in the Zionist Organisation in Berlin, but while in his disappointment he was tempted to accept, Vera absolutely refused to go. Weizmann swallowed his pride and remained in Manchester, with what fateful consequences for Zionism we now know.

That he would soon rise to the summit of the movement was far from obvious. Wolfssohn still directed affairs from Berlin, while others, Ussishkin, Sokolow and Ha'am amongst them, were established figures, as were the distinguished authors Israel Zangwill and Max Nordau, whose writings had put them at the forefront of intellectual life, while the American Louis D Brandeis was about to come to the fore in that vibrant Jewish community.[87] Although we know a great deal about the Zionist movement before 1914, much more than is known about the state of Arab aspirations, the fact remains that its prospects were problematic. The Turks were in no mood to surrender anything of their position in Palestine to the Jews, any more than they were to the Arabs, who were a considerable majority of the population.

---

87 Weizmann, *Trial and Error*, pp 173–4; Vera Weizmann, *The Impossible Takes Longer*, p 39; Reinharz, *Chaim Weizmann: The Making of a Zionist Leader*, pp 359–67; David Vital, *Zionism: The Crucial Phase* (Clarendon Press, Oxford: 1987) pp 120–1.

Ottoman diplomacy and the European crisis: Germany and Britain

Historically, the European powers which had been most concerned in the affairs of the Ottoman Empire had been Austria, Britain and Russia, although the French and Italians had also managed to rob it of North African possessions. Unlike them, Germany had not attempted to plunder the empire, but in the late 19th century Berlin took an increasing interest in its affairs. This was powerfully symbolised by Kaiser Wilhelm II's state visits in 1889 and 1898. On the latter occasion he visited Damascus and Jerusalem, where a breach had to be made in the city's historic wall at Jaffa Gate to allow his somewhat theatrical entry on a charger. It was Germans who constructed the Hejaz railway and, more significantly, from 1899 the ambitious railway which was projected to run from Istanbul through Anatolia to Baghdad and Basra. Under the auspices of the Baghdad Railway Company, construction began in 1903, but such was the difficult nature of the terrain that it was never to be completed. German and Austrian banks also financed the Oriental Railway linking the capital with Central Europe and German finance was behind the city's electricity and telegraph services.

This economic penetration of the empire was not unique to Germany, however.[88] Anxious to bring their armed forces more into line with those of their European rivals, the Turks looked for help to the two obvious candidates, the British to overhaul their navy, the Germans to reform the army. A British naval mission led by Admiral Arthur Limpus arrived in 1912. The money to transform the navy was raised through enthusiastic public subscription, patriotic women even selling their hair, with the result that in 1911 work began on Tyneside on the dreadnought battleship the *Reshadieh*, while in 1914 another dreadnought then being built in Britain for the Brazilian navy was purchased as the *Sultan Osman I*. With these two powerful vessels due for completion in the summer of 1914, the Turkish navy would have become a force to be reckoned with, especially in the Black Sea where the Russians had no warships able to match them, and against the Greeks in the Aegean.[89]

---

88 For the history of the railway, see Sean McMeekin, *The Berlin–Baghdad Express: The Ottoman Empire and Germany's Bid for World Power 1898–1918* (Allen Lane, London: 2010); A J P Taylor, *The Struggle for Mastery in Europe 1848–1918* (Oxford University Press, London: 1954) pp 383–5.
89 Winston S Churchill, *The World Crisis 1911–1918* (Odhams Press Ltd, London: 1938 edition), Vol I, pp 436–7.

German influence in the army went back to 1883 when Colmar von der Goltz had headed a military mission, beginning his years of exemplary service to the empire, which were only brought to end with his death from typhus while commanding in Mesopotamia in 1916. A new German mission came in 1913 under Liman von Sanders.[90] Yet, while Germany's economic and military influence in the empire was marked, this did not mean that the Sublime State would automatically enter any future conflict on its side. Anglo-French influence remained well entrenched in the economy. Armstrong Vickers owned the docks on the Golden Horn, while British interests predominated in such diverse economic areas as the Euphrates and Tigris Steam Navigation Company, Istanbul's telephone system and the Ottoman Bank, as well as in the navy. The French, too, had a significant economic presence.[91] On 28 June 1914, however, when Archduke Frank Ferdinand, heir to the Austro-Hungarian Empire, and his wife Sophie were assassinated in the former Ottoman city of Sarajevo, events were set in train which four years later saw the Middle East transformed in ways which few could have envisaged.

---

90 Palmer, *The Decline and Fall of the Ottoman Empire*, pp 170–1, 220–2.
91 W W Gottlieb, *Studies in Secret Diplomacy during the First World War* (George Allen & Unwin Ltd, London: 1957) pp 19–22.

2

Wartime Promises and Expectations

What the future of the Middle East might have been if the world had not gone to war in 1914 no one can now tell, but what is indisputable is that the First World War had a dramatic impact on the region, leaving a legacy that remains to this day. Once war began, it soon became clear that this was a struggle on an epic scale, forcing the powers to speculate on what a peace settlement might look like. It was not inevitable that the Ottoman Empire would enter the war on the side of the Central Powers, but in November 1914 the rulers of Turkey joined their fate to that of Berlin and Vienna. Despite the fact that Turkish military forces were less technologically advanced than those of the other powers, Germany and Austria-Hungary had gained a major asset.

The Turks threatened Britain at two key points in the Middle East. The first was the Suez Canal through which Britain was drawing troops and supplies from India, Australia and New Zealand. The other was the Persian Gulf, the source of oil for the five fast battleships of the *Queen Elizabeth* class, the cutting edge of the Royal Navy. Turkish troops were ominously close to the recently developed British oil facilities at Abadan, across the Persian border. Just as dangerous to the Entente powers was Turkey's appeal in the Islamic world, through the office of Caliph, since France recruited widely in her North African territories, while the Indian Army, the British Empire's sole professional reserve, drew heavily on the Muslim community in the north-west of the subcontinent. Moreover, the fertile plains of the Punjab were dangerously close to the turbulent

The Ottoman Empire 1914

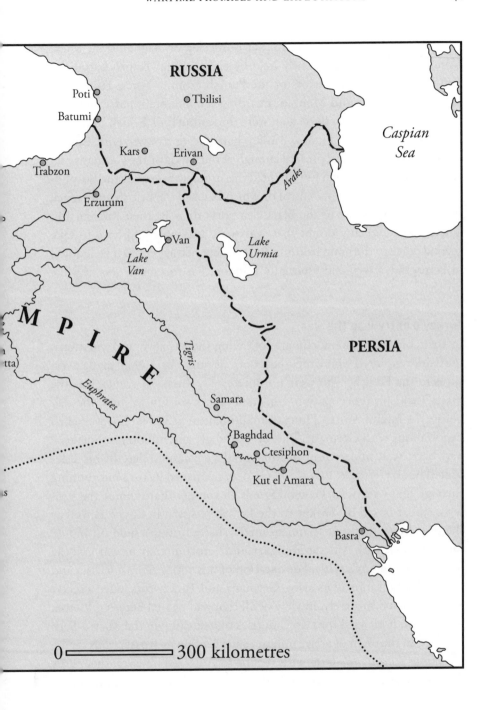

Muslim tribal regions of the frontier bordering on Afghanistan, where Britain's writ was precariously held by eight regular British battalions and their Indian compatriots of the Punjab Frontier Force. From their stations at Quetta and Mardan, guarding the mountain passes and the crossings of the Indus, these men were the sentinels of British India, but many were Muslims. Finally, Turkey had a long frontier with Russia, whose armies were hard pressed enough at the hands of the Germans and Austrians. The Ottoman Empire held the strategic Straits of the Bosphorus and the Dardanelles, control of which blocked the British and French from using that route to the Black Sea ports to assist their Russian ally. There was never any doubt that war with Turkey would have to take second place to the main fronts in Europe, but neither could it be ignored in Petrograd, Paris, and especially London. Far too much was at stake for that.

Turkey's entry into the war

In the febrile diplomatic climate following the Sarajevo assassinations, the Turks explored where their best options might lie. Cemal made overtures to the French, who were not interested. Russia, it seems, was the main Turkish preoccupation, understandably so. On 22 July, the day before the fateful Austro-Hungarian ultimatum to Serbia, Enver opened negotiations with Germany. Turkey's strategic and military importance had been well understood in influential German circles. In his celebrated book *Germany and the Next War*, published in 1912 but running through many editions, General Friedrich von Bernhardi noted the strategic threat posed by Turkey to the British position in Egypt as well as the possibility that pan-Islamism might shake Britain's hold on India.[1] On 2 August, with Austria-Hungary and Serbia already at war and the day after Germany's critical declaration of hostilities against Russia and general mobilisation of its army, Germany and Turkey concluded a secret alliance treaty. Bizarrely, in view of all that had passed between Vienna and Berlin, it pledged the two countries to neutrality in the Austro-Serb conflict. In the event of active military intervention by Russia, thus giving Germany a *casus foederis* with regard to Austria-Hungary, this *casus foederis* would also apply to Turkey. With Germany's declaration of

---

1 General Friedrich von Bernhardi, *Germany and the Next War* (Edward Arnold, London: 1914; original edition (Stuttgart: 1912) pp 95–6.

war on Russia this had already been overtaken by events. Germany also pledged itself to placing its military mission at Turkey's disposal, while the Turks agreed that the mission should have an effective influence on their army. Finally, Germany promised to defend Turkish territory. What is plain is that fear of Russia was the key to the operation of the alliance. Whether the agreement firmly bound Turkey to enter the war on Germany's side is less clear, since two months were to elapse before hostilities began against the Russians. The ambiguities and apparent inconsistencies in the treaty almost certainly reflect the fact that it was being drafted as the hectic diplomatic events in Europe unfolded. Even so, it is instructive of the way Turkish thinking had gone, as well as the direction a future military relationship would take.[2]

Unaware of the treaty, but conscious of the strength of German influence, the British played for time. One reason for this was the view of Lord Kitchener, now Secretary of State for War, but with a wealth of Indian and Egyptian knowledge behind him, that Britain had to avoid war with Turkey until the troops of the Indian Army, then being rushed to the European front, had passed through the Suez Canal.[3] It is too easily forgotten that the only professional reserves at the British Empire's disposal on the outbreak of the First World War were the men of the 3rd Lahore and 7th Meerut Divisions and the Secundrabad Cavalry Brigade of the Indian Army, which arrived safely in France from the end of September. What the British war effort would have been without them, Sikhs, Dogras, Baluchis, Jats, Punjabi Muslims, Garwhalis, Pathans and Nepali Gurkhas, trained for the mountain warfare of the North-West Frontier of India but now deployed on the very different and unfamilar plains of France and Flanders, is hard to imagine.[4] Critically for the British war effort, they did come through the Suez Canal without hindrance.

It is a paradox that what helped persuade Turkey's rulers towards war against the Entente powers was not so much the army's link with

---

2 'The Turco-German Treaty of Alliance, 2 August 1914', in M S Anderson, *The Great Powers and the Near East 1774–1923* (Edward Arnold, London: 1970) p 157; Mango, *Atatürk*, pp 132–4.

3 Viscount Grey of Fallodon, KG, *Twenty-Five Years 1892–1916* (Hodder and Stoughton, London: 1925) Vol II, p 165.

4 Lt-Col J W B Merewether, CIE and Lt-Col Sir Frederick Smith, Bart, *The Indian Corps in France* (John Murray, London: 1918).

Germany but a series of events affecting the navy, where British influence under Admiral Limpus was strong. This chain of events began on 28 July 1914 with the decision of the First Lord of the Admiralty, Winston Churchill, to acquire the two battleships under completion, and on 3 August the British embassy was told to inform the Turks that the *Sultan Osman I*, which was about to embark on sea trials, was being requisitioned. In doing this, Churchill was undoubtedly motivated by the considerable additional strength these two powerful ships would bring the Royal Navy's battle line, but his action provoked predictable fury in Turkey.[5] Compensation was, however, at hand from an unexpected quarter. On the outbreak of war, Germany had a small squadron in the Mediterranean, the modern battlecruiser *Goeben* accompanied by the light cruiser *Breslau*, commanded by Admiral Wilhelm Souchon. After a brief action in the western Mediterranean, the squadron was ordered to head for Istanbul, instead of the Austrian naval base at Pola in the Adriatic, as the British commanders seem to have assumed. Evading the Royal Navy's hapless pursuit, on 10 August the two ships entered the Dardanelles and the following day were purchased by the Turkish government, in response, so the British were informed, to their detention of the *Sultan Osman I*. While not equal to the gunpower of the two ships seized by the British, they were modern vessels well able to dominate the Black Sea, and their presence in Istanbul under the Turkish flag immeasurably strengthened the German link.[6]

On 29 October, Admiral Souchon forced the issue. Now commanding the Turkish ships *Sultan Selim* and *Midilli*, as his command had been renamed, he bombarded the Russian Black Sea ports of Odessa, Sevastopol and Novorossisk. War with Russia, France and Britain followed immediately. On 14 November, the Sultan issued a call for jihad, or holy war, against the three enemy powers, but, contrary to the hopes and expectations of men like Bernhardi, throughout most of the Islamic world this fell with a dull thud. In India, the influential Nizam of

---

5 Winston S Churchill, *The World Crisis, 1911–1918*, Vol I, p 437; see also *Correspondence Leading to the Rupture of Relations with Turkey*, Cmd. 7628: 1914, *The Times Documentary History of the War*, Diplomatic, Part 3 (Printing House Square, London: 1919) Vol IX.
6 Mr Beaumont to Sir Edward Grey, Constantinople, 11 August 1914, *The Times Documentary History of the War*, Vol IX, p 94.

Hyderabad issued a *firman* rallying Muslims to the Allied cause, and, even more significantly, the call drew no support from Sherif Hussein, the Guardian of Islam's Holy Places.

Weizmann and Britain's war aims

The fate of Turkey now became an Allied war aim. This was evident almost from the start. On 9 November 1914, the British Prime Minister Herbert Asquith made a speech in London's Guildhall in which he raised the future of the Ottoman Empire. In an early move, Egypt was proclaimed a British protectorate, erasing the fiction of Ottoman suzerainty. The possible fate of Palestine also excited the interest of the distinguished Liberal Herbert Samuel (1870–1963), Member of Parliament for Cleveland. A first-class graduate of Oxford University, Samuel had already made his mark in British history by becoming the first Jew to sit in the Cabinet, if we discount the Anglican Benjamin Disraeli. A representative of the assimilated Jewish elite that Weizmann instinctively distrusted, Samuel, by his own admission, had taken no real part in Zionism until the war with Turkey gave him cause to think about it.[7] On the same day that Asquith delivered his Guildhall speech, Samuel visited his Cabinet colleague the Foreign Secretary Sir Edward Grey, arguing that in the event of a Turkish defeat they should think about the possibility of a Jewish state in Palestine.[8]

Meanwhile, Weizmann, who had made a difficult journey back from an attempted family holiday in Switzerland, was also alive to the new possibilities, and here again the Manchester connection proved to be invaluable to him. A useful conduit proved to be a bright young journalist on the *Manchester Guardian* and Zionist colleague in the city, Harry Sacher.[9] Shortly after his return to Manchester, Weizmann met over dinner C P Scott, editor of the newspaper for over four decades and a man with ready access to the highest reaches of the Liberal Party. Evidently intrigued by his new acquaintance, Scott invited Weizmann to his house to discuss Jewish affairs. After Weizmann had confided in him his

7 The Rt Hon Viscount Samuel, *Memoirs* (The Cresset Press, London: 1945) p 139.
8 Samuel, *Memoirs*, pp 140–1; Vital, *Zionism: The Crucial Phase*, pp 92–3.
9 Jonathan Schneer, *The Balfour Declaration: The Origins of the Arab-Israeli Conflict* (Bloomsbury, London: 2010) p 116.

hatred of the Russian Empire, which was candid of him given that the two countries were fighting on the same side, and spoken of the Jewish hopes for Palestine, Scott pointed out that there was now a Jew in the Cabinet, adding that he would like to put him in touch with the Chancellor of the Exchequer, David Lloyd George.

Seizing the opportunity, Weizmann followed up the meeting with a letter to Scott on 12 November, in which he argued that if Britain could encourage Jewish emigration to Palestine as a British dependency, then the Jews could develop it and help safeguard the Suez Canal. This was precisely the line of argument which he was to refine over the next few years, and which would form the basis of the case he eventually placed before the Peace Conference. Equally, there is no doubt that Weizmann instantly grasped the implications of Asquith's Guildhall speech, since on the same day of his letter to Scott he also wrote to Ahad Ha'am in quite excited terms, saying that the speech should prompt them into action, and that in the event of victory Britain would be in control of Palestine.[10]

Scott proved to be as good as his word. At a breakfast meeting with Lloyd George on 27 November, he raised the future of Palestine. Lloyd George seemed interested in the idea of some kind of partly Jewish state, and revealed that Samuel had already discussed this with him. He responded positively to Scott's idea of a meeting with Weizmann, suggesting that this should also include Samuel.[11] This could not take place for a couple of months, but Scott had opened up a crucial contact, since Lloyd George was destined to be in a position to shape the course of events. While that lay in the future, Lloyd George was already one of the leading, not to say most contentious, figures in British political life. Born in Manchester in 1863 of Welsh origin, he had been Chancellor since 1908, had played a significant part in the search for an Irish settlement between 1912 and 1914, and was to go on to hold the key offices of Minister of Munitions in 1915–16 and Minister of War in

10 Weizmann, *Trial and Error*, pp 190–1; Weizmann to Ahad Ha'am, London, 12 November 1914; Weizmann to Charles P Scott, Manchester, 12 November 1914, in Leonard Stein (ed), *LPCW*, Series A, Vol VII, August 1914–November 1917 (Oxford University Press, London and New York: 1975) 32, 33, pp 37–9; hereafter *LPCW*, Vol VII.

11 Trevor Wilson (ed), *The Political Diaries of C.P. Scott 1911–1928* (Collins, London: 1970) p 113.

1916. Then, in December that year, he replaced Asquith to lead Britain to victory in the war, and came to play a central role in the subsequent Peace Conference.

Weizmann had his first meeting with Samuel on 10 December 1914. Samuel revealed that he had been quietly watching Zionism for some time, and that with Turkey in the war, the realisation of its aims was possible. He wanted Weizmann to keep in contact.[12] The promised meeting with Lloyd George took place over breakfast on 15 January 1915. The account Weizmann gave in his autobiography, which places the meeting in early December 1914, says that Samuel, Scott and the Labour MP Josiah Wedgwood were also present. In general, Lloyd George seemed well disposed to what he heard from Weizmann, advising him that he could expect opposition from the assimilation-supporting Jewish community, and especially from the rising Liberal politician Edwin Montagu, who was, as it happened, Samuel's cousin. Weizmann also recollected that Samuel revealed the fact that he was preparing a memorandum which he was going to give to the Prime Minister.[13]

Although Samuel never actually joined the Zionist Organisation, he pressed ahead with his memorandum, which he first circulated to colleagues in January 1915, followed by a revised version in March. What he argued was that, lying as it did so close to the vital artery of the Suez Canal, Palestine should not be allowed to fall under the control of a major European power such as France or Germany. Instead, he suggested that it should become a British protectorate. On the question of Zionism, he admitted that the time was not ripe for the creation of a Jewish state in Palestine, but that under a British protectorate regulated Jewish immigration could lead in time to a Jewish majority which could be granted some form of self-government. It does not seem that Samuel's document excited any great degree of interest amongst his colleagues. Asquith, in particular, was totally dismissive, but, just the same, the idea of a future British administration in Palestine which could encourage Jewish aspirations had entered into political discourse at the highest level. Its time had

---

12 Weizmann to Vera Weizmann, Manchester, 10 December 1914; Weizmann to Charles P Scott, Manchester, 13 December 1914, in *LPCW*, Vol VII, 65, 67, pp 77–80.

13 Weizmann, *Trial and Error*, pp 192–3; Reinharz, *Chaim Weizmann: The Making of a Statesman*, pp 24–5.

not yet come, but it would, and Samuel made sure that Weizmann and Scott were aware of feelings in the Cabinet.[14]

What he learned from Samuel of the Cabinet's response prompted Weizmann to gather his thoughts together in a long letter to Scott on 23 March. He now believed that the mood in Cabinet was sympathetic to the realisation of Zionist aspirations in Palestine, and to their presentation at a peace conference, but that there was a reluctance to make the country a British responsibility. What he was referring to was a section of Liberal opinion which was opposed to a policy of annexation. On the other hand, there was the belief that Palestine should not come under another major power. That led him to the conclusion that Palestine should be a temporary British protectorate, to the mutual advantage of Britain and the Jews. Such an arrangement, he argued, would help guard the Egyptian border, earn Britain the thanks of Jews around the world, and enable the Jews to act as a bridge between East and West.

It is clear that both Weizmann and Samuel were working in the same direction. That this was the case was confirmed by Scott on 15 April when he related to Weizmann a dinner conversation with Samuel and Lloyd George in the course of which they had raised the question of Zionism. Samuel had spoken warmly about it, and Scott observed to Weizmann that Lloyd George was more important than Asquith, correctly as events were to demonstrate.[15]

The Ottoman Empire at war

These events in London took little account of the unfolding war in the Middle East, where the Turks were proving to be redoudtable fighters, despite some initial setbacks. In the winter of 1914/15, Enver led an Ottoman army to destruction in the snows of the mountains of eastern Anatolia on the Caucasian front, which stretched far from the nearest Ottoman railhead, but lay conveniently close to the Russian broad gauge rail network. In the south, Cemal pushed to the Suez Canal, which some of his units managed to cross, but the Egyptians failed to rise against

---

14 Weizmann to Yehiel Tschlenow and Nahum Sokolow, London, 20 March 1915, *LPCW*, Vol VII, 141, pp 178–9; Stein, *The Balfour Declaration*, pp 107–11.
15 Weizmann to Charles P Scott, Manchester, 23 March 1915; Weizmann to Yehiel Tschlenow and Nahum Sokolow, London, 15 April 1915, *LPCW*, Vol VII, 147, 154, pp 183–5, 190–1.

their British overlords who drove the Turks back into Palestine. Unsuccessful in their attacks, the Turkish army then scored two notable victories in defensive battles. It beat back the British-Anzac and French attempt to break through the Gallipoli peninsula to Istanbul in 1915, and checked a British advance from Basra to Baghdad the following year, surrounding a British force and forcing it to surrender at Kut al-Amara. It was the high point of the Ottoman war effort, which had an effect on Allied perceptions. The British army came to respect 'Johnny Turk' as a good fighter, but Allied governments and diplomats vowed revenge: the Turks' successful defence of Gallipoli and their dogged resistance in Mesopotamia and Palestine had prolonged the war and vastly increased its cost in casualties and resources. Allied statesmen, whose miscalculations had been exposed, became determined to eliminate once and for all the danger which, they believed, the Turks posed to their empires. This difference in perceptions between soldiers and civilians was to play an important part in post-war developments, which showed that the soldiers had the more realistic view of Turkey's strength.

The bloody battles in Gallipoli, in which each side lost a quarter of a million men dead and wounded, laid the foundations of the career of the young and ambitious Colonel Mustafa Kemal. Staff Colonel Mustafa Kemal was now 34 years old. He had with some difficulty secured the command of a Turkish division held in reserve on the peninsula when the British and Anzacs landed on 25 April 1915. When the First World War broke out, he was known as an independent-minded Unionist and a critic of Enver and of the subservience of the Ottoman army to the Germans. Nevertheless his initiative and personal courage, which helped contain the first Allied landings, impressed Field Marshal Liman von Sanders,[16] the German commander of the Ottoman troops at Gallipoli, and when the British made a second landing on the peninsula at Souvla Bay, Kemal was appointed commander of the forces that held the line against them. Later legend has it that Kemal's rising star was noticed immediately by friend and foe alike. In fact, the British did not distinguish him from other Ottoman commanders, and Enver denied him publicity in Turkey. But he won appreciation where it mattered – among other Turkish commanders.

---

16 German officers seconded to the Ottoman army were promoted one rank. Hence Generals Liman von Sanders, Erich von Falkenhayn and Colmar von der Goltz were styled Field Marshal during their service in Turkey.

Mustafa Kemal resisted German interference in Turkish military disposi-
tions and left Gallipoli in a huff before the Allied withdrawal in December 1915. Promoted Brigadier – the highest rank he was to achieve during
the war – he was given command of an army corps which was being
laboriously transferred to the Eastern Front in order to halt the Russian
advance. He arrived in an area devastated by the fighting and by the
deportation of the Armenians who had dominated it economically.

The Armenian question

Armenian nationalist revolutionaries had originally joined the Young
Turks in the ranks of the opposition to Abdülhamid II, but after the
reintroduction of the Constitution in 1908 their ways parted. While the
Young Turks' ideal was equality in a centralised state, the demands of
Armenian, as of other Christian nationalists, ranged from the recognition of special rights through autonomy to outright independence for
their community. Unlike Ottoman Greeks and Bulgarians, Ottoman
Armenians had no existing national state which they could join. But
when the Russians conquered the Caucasus, and particularly after the
Russian gains at the expense of the Ottomans in 1878, the number of
Armenian subjects of the Tsar increased, as Armenians long resident
in the Caucasus were joined by immigrants from Turkey, who found
greater scope for their energies under Christian Russian rule.

According to Armenian sources, in 1912 there were some 1.3 million
Armenians in 'Russian Armenia' (the Caucasian provinces) against 1
million in 'Turkish Armenia'.[17] True, there were tensions between the
Armenians and their Tsarist rulers, who favoured their own version of
Eastern Orthodox Christianity over the Armenian (Monophysite) Gregorian Church, and who fitfully pursued a policy of Russifying their subjects. Even so, as Christians, the Armenians had more in common with
the Russians than with Muslim Turks, and although by the end of the
19th century they did well in both the Ottoman and the Tsarist empires,
the latter was more advanced and opportunities in it accordingly more
promising. The decision of the Young Turks to throw in their lot with
the Germans against the Russians was a tragedy for the Armenians who

17 Justin McCarthy, *Muslims and Minorities: The Population of Ottoman
Anatolia and the End of the Empire* (New York University Press, New York: 1983)
pp 50, 52.

found themselves divided between the two combatants. The majority kept their heads down. But for nationalist Armenian revolutionaries who had used terrorism first against their own kinsmen to gain control over them, then against the Ottoman state and occasionally against Tsarist officials they disliked, the Ottomans' calamity was the Armenians' opportunity.

Disaster threatened to overwhelm the Ottoman state in 1915 when the Western Allies landed in Gallipoli and the Russians advanced deep into eastern Turkey. Armenian revolutionaries had been preparing for that day. They had infiltrated fighters and stockpiled arms in eastern Turkey; they had formed volunteer units to help the Russian army. As the Russians advanced, Armenian nationalist revolutionaries organised uprisings and acts of sabotage behind the Ottoman lines.[18] This compromised the Armenian community as a whole. In April 1915, the Young Turk leadership – and Talât in particular – became convinced that the removal of all Armenians from the war zone and from the vicinity of the railways leading to it was a military necessity. It would also remove once and for all the threat of losing yet another portion of the Turkish homeland to local Christians who, as experience showed, would, if successful, get rid of their Muslim neighbours by fair means or foul. For centuries Muslims and Christian Armenians had lived in reasonable amity side by side to their mutual benefit. Now fear and hatred gripped both communities, many of whose members became convinced that they were faced with a stark choice: kill or be killed.

Large-scale deportations have not been rare in history. The Ottomans had transferred their unruly kinsmen, the Turcoman tribesmen, from Asia to their new conquests in the Balkans; they had also moved Christian Armenians and others to repopulate Istanbul after the conquest. They had received Jews and Arabs deported from Spain after the reconquista, and then from the 18th century onwards, hundreds of thousands of Muslims forced out of the Balkans, southern Russia and the Caucasus.[19]

In the 19th century, more than a million Circassians were expelled by

---

18 Justin McCarthy et al, *The Armenian Rebellion at Van* (University of Utah Press, Salt Lake City, UT, 2006) pp 162–4, 180–5.

19 See Justin McCarthy, *Death and Exile: The Ethnic Cleansing of Ottoman Muslims, 1821–1922* (Darwin Press, Princeton: 1995). For the Circassians and other Muslim refugees from the Caucasus, see pp 32–6, 47–9.

the Russians from the Caucasus. Hundreds of thousands of them perished before they could start a new life in the Ottoman Empire. Many of the survivors were resettled in eastern Anatolia, which Armenian nationalists were claiming for themselves. The Circassians were a martial people: some of the refugees preyed on settled Ottoman subjects, others found employment in the Ottoman army and gendarmerie. In 1915, as the Russians threatened them again in their new homes, discipline could not restrain the Circassian gendarmes. In some instances, instead of protecting Armenians during the deportation, they killed them. In any case, the best-trained gendarmes had been sent to the front and their duties in the Ottoman countryside had been taken over by raw recruits, including released convicts. In some cases gendarmes escorting columns of deported Armenians sold them to Kurdish tribesmen who robbed, and then killed, the Armenians and raped their women. Undisciplined gendarmes, Kurdish tribesmen and bandits of all sorts, whose numbers had been swollen by deserters, took a heavy toll of the deportees. Others died of malnutrition and disease, which affected even larger numbers of Muslims, for as Armenian civilians were driven south to Syria, at least as many Muslim civilians – Kurds and Turks alike – were fleeing west from the advancing Russians and their Armenian auxiliaries.

In absolute numbers more Muslims than Armenians perished in Anatolia, but while Armenian deaths from all causes accounted for more than a third of their community, the Muslims lost one-fifth, and remained in possession of the land. Moreover, the sufferings of the Armenians were well documented. There were American missionaries and consuls in the area, as the United States was not at war with the Ottoman Empire; German officers and civilians also witnessed atrocities. The sufferings of the Muslim population passed largely unnoticed by Western observers. Even so, the fate of the Armenians was a gift to Allied propagandists, and could be used to counter Austro-German accusations of Russian atrocities against the Jews, who had similarly been deported from the war zone in their hundreds of thousands.

Britain and the Hashemites
The failure of the Gallipoli campaign, and the overriding demands of the Western Front, meant that the British had to look for potential allies against the Turks, and fortunately for them links already existed. In February 1914, Sherif Hussein's second son Abdullah, who was a member of

the Ottoman parliament, had paid a visit to the British High Commissioner in Egypt, Field Marshal Lord Kitchener. The visit was, to all intents
and purposes, a courtesy call. However, Abdullah took the opportunity
to tell Kitchener that there was a growing crisis in the Hejaz between
the Sherif and the new Turkish *Vali*. He requested British support in the
event of an attempt to depose his father. Specifically he asked that they
use their influence with Istanbul and block Turkish troops from being
transported through the Suez Canal.[20]

This support, which was unlikely to have been granted, was not
needed. It was soon reported that the differences between Hussein and
the Turks had been settled amicably.[21] However, the British continued
to hear of persistent rumours of dissatisfaction in the Ottoman Arab
world. At a subsequent meeting in April 1914 with the Oriental Secretary
to the British Residency in Cairo, Ronald Storrs, at the Khedive's palace
in Cairo, Abdullah reported that negotiations in Istanbul had not gone
well and his father had requested that he ask the British government
to enter into a quasi-protectorate with the Emir of Mecca that would
forestall any Turkish aggression. There was no prospect of this in April
1914. Britain's relations with the Ottoman Empire, while not having
the warmth of hitherto, remained fundamentally correct. The following
day, after consulting Kitchener, Storrs told Abdullah he could not expect
any British support, although Elie Kedourie suggests that the rejection
was not as categorical as it seemed.[22] However, Storrs, Kitchener, the
Governor-General of the Sudan Reginald Wingate, and the intelligence
department in the British-run Egyptian War Office all appear to have
recognised that the situation in Arabia in 1914 afforded opportunities
for the British government to exploit should the Ottomans go to war
against the Entente.

In September 1914, Kitchener ordered Storrs to reactivate contacts
with Abdullah, as it became increasingly evident that Turkey was likely
to enter the war on the side of the Central Powers. He was to ascertain
the attitude of Sherif Hussein should hostilities break out between the
Entente and Turkey. Abdullah, in a guarded reply, confirmed that the

---

20 Lord Kitchener to Sir Edward Grey, 6 February 1914 cited in *British Docs*, Vol
X, p 827. See also Kedourie, *In the Anglo-Arab Labyrinth*, p 5.
21 Kitchener to Grey, 14 February 1914, *British Docs*, Vol X, p 827.
22 Kedourie, *In the Anglo-Arab Labyrinth*, p 7.

Hashemite position was essentially favourable to the British, though it appeared that there would be no outright rebellion against the Ottomans unless they struck first to circumscribe the independence of Hussein. The British replied that they would protect Hussein against aggression, but also raised the tantalising possibility that a favourable outcome of the war might include the replacement of the Ottoman Sultan as Caliph by an Arab figure.[23] Storrs, who was ordered to transmit the reply, may have greatly exceeded his instructions from London, promising much more wide-ranging support to Hussein and the Arab cause than he was authorised to give.[24] Hussein, on 8 December 1914, replied that he could not break with the Ottomans at present but would do so should a suitable moment arrive. He also stated that 'there no longer exists a Caliphate … for their [the Ottomans'] rule projects … deeds that are all contrary to religion. The Caliphate means this, that the rule of the book of God should be enforced, and this they do not do.'[25]

Storrs seems to have taken further local initiatives without referring to London, which committed Britain almost completely to the general cause of Arab nationalism and an Arab Caliphate. Most notably, in December 1914 he issued a sweeping proclamation from the government of Great Britain to the natives of Arabia and the Arab provinces, pledging support for Arab independence and declaring that the Caliphate was the right of a member of the Prophet Muhammad's tribe, the Quraysh, i.e. someone like Sherif Hussein.[26] This was followed in April 1915 by a pledge to support Arab independence, declaring British opposition to annexations by any of the Great Powers in the Holy Places or the Arabian Peninsula. These British assurances appear to have done enough to keep Hussein in play.

---

23 C Ernest Dawn, 'The Amir of Mecca Al-Husayn Ibn-'Ali and the Origin of the Arab Revolt', *Proceedings of the American Philosophical Society*, Vol 104, No 1 (15 Feb 1960) p 22; Kedourie, *England and the Middle East*, pp 19, 52.

24 Kedourie, *In the Anglo-Arab Labyrinth*, pp 21–1.

25 Joshua Teitelbaum, 'Sherif Hussein ibn Ali and the Hashemite vision of the post-Ottoman order: from chieftaincy to suzerainty', *Middle Eastern Studies*, Vol 34, No 1 (1998) p 106.

26 Kedourie, *In the Anglo-Arab Labyrinth*, pp 20–5.

The evolution of British policy towards the Arabs

By the spring of 1915, the British were beginning to think seriously about the ultimate fate of the Ottoman Empire. Kitchener, in a remarkably prescient paper in March, proposed that 'it is to our interests to see an Arab Kingdom established in Arabia under the auspices of England, bounded in the north by the Valley of the Tigris and Euphrates and containing within it the chief Mahomedan Holy Places, Mecca, Medina and Kerbala'. Kitchener believed that in the aftermath of victory, Russia's position in the Middle East would be immeasurably strengthened and that Britain needed to think of acquiring territory or influence from the Mediterranean to the Persian Gulf to protect the route to India. Indeed, he gave serious consideration to the construction of a railway from Alexandretta on the Mediterranean coast to Basra at the head of the Gulf on which British forces could be rapidly deployed to reinforce the India garrison. There was a general disagreement in the Cabinet as to what Britain should seek. Asquith, while sharing Sir Edward Grey's disquiet about a territorial carve-up, concluded that if a scramble for Ottoman possessions took place, Britain would be neglecting its duty if it did not seek something for itself.[27]

In April 1915, the government appointed a committee chaired by Sir Maurice de Bunsen to examine what Britain's likely interests would be in the event of a Turkish defeat, particularly since France and Russia would also be eyeing up the possibilities. While its work had no practical effect, its deliberations do indicate the direction of British thinking on the region, even at this stage of the war. One possibility was of an empire reformed along federal lines, which would give national self-expression to Turks, Arabs and Armenians. The British liked federal schemes, as they had shown in Australia, and were to try them in other parts of their empire, mostly without success. But in the event of a break-up of the Ottoman Empire, de Bunsen's committee recommended that Britain should acquire Mesopotamia from Basra at the head of the Persian Gulf to Mosul, her oil interests in that part of the Middle East being paramount. This area would be connected to the port of Haifa. The French would have their interests recognised in the districts around Damascus

---

27 Kitchener's paper is cited in Jukka Nevakivvi, *Britain, France and the Arab Middle East 1914–1920* (Athlone Press, London: 1969), p 18; Asquith is cited on p 17.

and Beirut, while the Straits would go to Russia, fulfilling a long-standing ambition for access to the Aegean and Mediterranean. Palestine would require special agreement amongst the three Christian allies, Protestants, Catholics and Orthodox each having interests there. Muslim and Jewish interests were of less importance, it seems.[28]

Meanwhile, in January 1915, Sir Henry McMahon had become High Commissioner in Egypt in succession to Kitchener. He began taking tentative soundings on how to encourage the Arabs to split with the Ottomans. In the east and centre of the Arabian Peninsula the British were enjoying considerable success in acquiring support from the smaller Arab tribal rulers: the Emir of Kuwait, Ibn Saud, then ruler of Nejd, and the Idrisi of Asir had all been brought firmly into the British orbit by mid-1915. At the same time, Hussein was coming under growing pressure from the Turks openly to support the Caliph's call for jihad. Indeed, he was showing considerable support for it in theory, though in practice this amounted to little more than the staging of a few demonstrations. Instead, Hussein emphasised to the Turks the vulnerability of the coast of the Hejaz to British attacks from Egypt and the Sudan. In secret, though, Hussein was plotting bolder moves – an alliance with the British. The motivation for this is unclear. It is claimed that Hussein's main ambition was to become Caliph, yet there is little evidence of his Arabism at this point.[29] Rather, a key factor in motivating his disillusion with the Ottomans appears to have been his uncovering in January 1915 of a plot to unseat him by the CUP. Only the outbreak of war had prevented its implementation.

In March 1915, Hussein, still inclined to seek compromise with the Turks, sent his son Feisal with the incriminating documents about the attempted plot to the Grand Vizier in Istanbul. This may have been an elaborate subterfuge to allow Feisal to make contact in Damascus with the Arab nationalist groups *al-Fatat* and *al-Ahd*. However, Feisal's initial impressions of these were that they were insufficiently strong to revolt against the Ottomans without the support of outside powers.[30]

28 T G Fraser, 'The Middle East. Partition and reformation', in Seamus Dunn and T G Fraser (eds), *Europe and Ethnicity: The First World War and Contemporary Ethnic Conflict* (Routledge, London: 1996) p 163.
29 Kedourie, *England and the Middle East*, pp 48–56.
30 Dawn, 'Ottomanism to Arabism', p 28.

Feisal proceeded to Istanbul, where he stayed for a month attempting to reach agreement with the Turkish government over the issue of the plot against his father. The leading figures in the government, the Sultan, the Grand Vizier, Talât and Enver all disavowed any knowledge of the plot and promised to transfer the Turkish governor. However, the Turks also made clear that they would not go any further to strengthen Hussein's position until he fully endorsed and declared jihad against the British. Feisal promised loyalty to the Sultan and agreed to provide forces to help the upcoming Turkish attack on Suez. However, this was a tissue of lies. In reality, he was deeply dissatisfied with the Turks and confirmed his view that the present situation could not continue.

On his way back to the Hejaz in May 1915, Feisal stopped off again in Damascus to consult with the nationalists. They had been grievously weakened by a Turkish crackdown since the last meeting. Many of the Arab-manned Ottoman divisions in the Fertile Crescent had been broken up and their troops sent to the fronts at Gallipoli and the Caucasus. There was little or no prospect of a successful rebellion centred on dissident army officers in Syria. The nationalists urged the Hashemites to seek an agreement with the British on the basis of terms they had agreed and drawn up in the document referred to by Antonius as the 'Damascus Protocol' and to go into open revolt against the Sultan.[31] The document set out the terms under which the Arabs would form an alliance with Britain and take up arms against the Turks. It was a wide-ranging demand for independence of all the Arabic-speaking territories of the Ottoman Empire. Feisal was sceptical that it would be acceptable to the British. He also had little hope that a revolt would succeed. In spite of his doubts, however, this document formed the essence of Hussein's first letter in July 1915 to McMahon.[32]

Feisal continued to hedge his bets at every stage: again promising support from the Hejaz to Cemal, who had been Turkish commander in Syria since December 1914, and who frequently and forcefully beseeched Hussein to declare jihad. Feisal, while an advocate of revolt at some stage, was cautious about the timing. When he, his father and his brother Abdullah met for a council of war in June 1915, Feisal stated that he was anxious to see Turkey significantly weakened before the Arabs took the

---

31 Antonius, *The Arab Awakening*, p 79.
32 Fromkin, *A Peace to End All Peace*, pp 174–6.

field. Abdullah, however, was anxious to proceed with all possible haste. He seems to have been motivated by a fear that, unless the Arabs moved quickly, they would lose any rights at the Peace Conference:

> The war could have only one consequence for the Arabs: they would remain in the noose of [tyrannical] government whether the Turks and Germans or the French and British won; it was necessary to proclaim the Arab movement and [thus] escape through war the necessary consequence of submission to alien rule.[33]

Abdullah was the Hashemite most committed to rebellion. This had come to the notice of the Ottoman authorities who, he claimed, tried to buy him off with offers of high office (the position of *Vali* in Yemen). He later confided in T E Lawrence that even without the war there would have been an uprising, started by Hussein and his confederates taking pilgrims hostage during the *haj*. This action was intended to draw in the Great Powers, including Britain and France, to force a compromise, which would gain Hussein immunity from Turkish pressure in the future. This rather fanciful plan was mooted to take place in 1915, but the war had forced its postponement.[34]

Hussein backed Abdullah's reasoning that now was the time to make a claim for a seat at the post-war peace conference. It was decided to offer the British an alliance in return for their acceptance of the demands in the Damascus Protocol. An unsigned letter from Hussein was sent to Sir Henry McMahon with a letter from Abdullah to Ronald Storrs dated 14 July 1915 enclosed.

Some historians are sceptical of Hussein's sudden espousal of Arab nationalism. Mary Wilson, for instance, sees it as essentially self-serving. Hussein's main motivation was his dislike of the secularising and centralising impulses of the CUP.[35] Indeed, suspicion of the secular CUP leadership in Istanbul was a key motivating factor for many in the Hejaz.

---

33 Dawn, 'The Amir of Mecca Al-Husayn Ibn-'Ali and the Origin of the Arab Revolt', p 24.
34 T E Lawrence, report, 13 May 1917, 'Notes on Hejaz Affairs', *Arab Bulletin* (13 May 1917).
35 Mary C Wilson, 'The Hashemites, the Arab Revolt, and Arab Nationalism', in Khalidi et al, *The Origins of Arab Nationalism*, p 214.

Hussein believed the Ottomans had forfeited their right to the Caliphate and he was the most suitable leader to assume the position. However, to have emphasised Islamic zealotry as the primary motivation for rising against the Ottomans might have led the British, who had the empire with the greatest Islamic population, to have had second thoughts about backing Hussein. It was much safer to wrap the Hashemite cause in the banner of Arab nationalism, which at this time presented no threat to British interests. Efraim Karsh goes further; the Arab Revolt:

> was Hussein's personal bid for an empire. The Sherif was no champion of national liberation seeking to unshackle the 'Arab Nation' from the chains of Ottoman captivity: he was an imperialist aspirant anxious to exploit a unique window of opportunity for substituting his own empire for that of the Ottomans.[36]

Historical opinion is united in agreement that Hussein's motivations had little to do with Arab nationalism. However, there is dispute about what Hussein's ambitions actually were. Were they to build a personal empire or to win the Caliphate? The evidence remains unclear.

The McMahon-Hussein Correspondence

By July 1915, the British position in the Middle East had deteriorated substantially. The Anglo-French attack on Gallipoli, aimed at dealing a knock-out blow to Turkey, had clearly failed and the Expeditionary Force would withdraw by the end of the year. Hussein was now in a position to secure a premium from the British for leading a revolt against the Turks. Reflecting this, Hussein's opening gambit, his letter of 14 July 1915, was certainly a bold one. (This is the first in the sequence of letters that came to be known as the McMahon-Hussein correspondence.) He demanded that he be recognised as king of an Arab state encompassing the whole of the Arabian Peninsula (apart from Aden) as far north as Mersina and bounded by the Mediterranean, the Red Sea, the Persian Gulf and Persia. This would include all of modern-day Syria, a slice of southern Turkey, Israel-Palestine, Jordan, Iraq, Saudi Arabia, the Gulf States and most of Yemen. He also wanted Britain to approve the proclamation of an Arab

---

36 Efraim Karsh and Inari Karsh, 'Myth in the Desert, or not the Great Arab Revolt', *Middle Eastern Studies*, Vol 33, No 2 (1997) p 267.

Caliphate.[37] Unsurprisingly, British officials in Cairo thought Hussein's requests unrealistic. Ronald Storrs, the Oriental Secretary, later wrote: 'It was at the time and still is my opinion that the Sherif opened his mouth and the British Government their purse a good deal too wide ... We could not conceal from ourselves (and with difficulty from him) that his pretensions bordered upon the tragi-comic.'[38]

Nonetheless, the blow to British confidence caused by the setback at Gallipoli is surely evidenced by the decision not to reject out of hand what were in many respects the outrageous demands of a minor Arab potentate. Instead, via the High Commissioner to Egypt Sir Henry McMahon, the British government decided to engage in a lengthy sequence of correspondence (some ten letters) with Hussein.[39] The McMahon-Hussein exchange culminated in a military alliance between Britain and the Hashemites that was to be maintained for more than 40 years. However, the exchanges were less clear-cut and more ambiguous regarding the political agreements that were made. In essence, the questions left unresolved revolved around the degree of Arab independence and the territorial extent of this Arab state.[40] Why was this the case? Elie Kedourie argues that the British replies were 'at once deliberately vague and unwittingly obscure'.[41] McMahon believed his task was to tempt 'the Arab people onto the right path, detach them from the enemy and bring them on to our side'.[42] He perhaps crafted the correspondence more carefully than he is sometimes given credit. It was in British interests that Hussein might think that more was on the table than was really being offered,

---

37 Amir Abdullah to Ronald Storrs, 14 July 1915. The correspondence can be found in Great Britain Parliamentary Papers, Misc. No. 3., 1939, Cmd 5957; hereafter Cmd 5957.
38 Ronald Storrs, *Orientations* (Ivor Nicholson & Watson, London: 1939) pp 160–1.
39 The correspondence can be found in Cmd 5957 or in Antonius, *The Arab Awakening*, Chapter 6.
40 The following draws on Kedourie, *In the Anglo-Arab Labyrinth*, Chapter 2; Monroe, *Britain's Moment in the Middle East*, Chapter 2; Isaiah Friedman, *The Question of Palestine 1914–1918: British-Jewish-Arab Relations* (Routledge & Kegan Paul, London: 1973) Chapter 6; and Briton Cooper Busch, *Britain, India and the Arabs, 1914–1921* (University of California Press, Berkeley: 1971) Chapter 2.
41 Kedourie, *In the Anglo-Arab Labyrinth*, p 4.
42 Kedourie, *In the Anglo-Arab Labyrinth*, p 120.

while at the same time, the vagueness of the correspondence meant that the British promises would contain so much ambiguity that no objective reader would be able to decipher what exactly had been promised. The words chosen allowed a certain degree of deniability.

McMahon's first response was sent on 30 August 1915. It was an understandably evasive reply supporting the liberation of the Arabs from Turkish rule and an Arab Caliphate. However, McMahon felt it was premature to discuss boundary details in the heat of war, while Turkey remained in occupation, and when there were increasing signs that Hashemite influence in Syria was very weak and the Syrian Arabs were tending to align themselves with the Ottomans. Hussein replied on 9 September demanding a precise delineation of the boundaries of the putative Arab state. He wrote, ominously, that a failure to deal with the matter might be taken 'to infer an estrangement or something of the sort'.[43]

It is possible the correspondence might have ended at this point in disagreement or that the British would have taken a stronger line with Hussein. However, new developments had occurred: primarily a secret mission to Cairo by Muhammad Sherif al-Faruqi, an Arab staff officer in the Ottoman army and apparently a leading figure in the Arab nationalist group al-Ahd. In an interview with Brigadier-General Gilbert Clayton, Chief of Military Intelligence in Cairo, in the autumn of 1915, he revealed that Syrian Arab nationalist societies would take up arms on the side of the British. In return for this they wanted explicit British support for an independent Arab state. If they did not get such an assurance, they would provide full support for Turkey and Germany in the war.[44] It is now generally accepted that al-Faruqi exaggerated the strength of Arab nationalism and his contacts with the Turks and Germans. There is no evidence that the Turks had any interest in appeasing Arab nationalism and the Germans would not lightly have undertaken negotiations behind the back of their ally. Nonetheless, the interview and the reports that were drawn from it appear to have led British officials and soldiers in Cairo to conclude that a deal acceptable to Sherif Hussein must be put on the table as soon as possible. Lord Kitchener in London was strongly supportive of keeping the Arabs on side. 'You must do your best to prevent any alienation of the Arabs' traditional loyalty to England', he stated

---

43 Sherif Hussein to McMahon, 9 September 1915, Cmd 5957.
44 Fromkin, *A Peace to End All Peace*, pp 176–80.

unambiguously.[45] He may well have believed that an Arab rebellion in Syria led by dissident army units might still save the Gallipoli campaign, which was teetering on the edge of collapse.[46]

McMahon was given considerable leeway in drafting a reply by Sir Edward Grey, who was reasonably well disposed to a strategy of wooing the Arabs. Grey, nonetheless, feared that promising too much to the Arabs might cause friction with the French, who would probably perceive Hussein to be a British proxy. McMahon, without fully consulting all the relevant Whitehall departments, especially India Office colleagues who were aghast when they learnt of what had been offered, dispatched his letter to Hussein on 24 October 1915. This key British pledge became so critical to the future course of relations with the Arabs, and especially to the debate over Palestine, that the key passage must be quoted:

> The two districts of Mersina and Alexandretta and portions of Syria
> lying to the west of the districts of Damascus, Homs, Hama and
> Aleppo cannot be said to be purely Arab and should be excluded
> from the limits demanded. With the above modifications, and without
> prejudice to our existing treaties with Arab chiefs, we accept these
> limits … Subject to the modifications, Great Britain is prepared to
> recognise and support the independence of the Arabs in all regions
> within the limits demanded by the Sherif of Mecca.[47]

What did McMahon mean, and what were the implications of what he said? Support for the independence of the Arabs seems plain enough, and was taken at face value. When, therefore, the post-war system of Mandates was put in place it was seen by the Arabs as reneging on an obligation, and treated as such. As for Palestine, on 12 March 1922, McMahon wrote to the Colonial Office, pleading that it had been his intention to exclude Palestine from his pledges to Hussein. He argued, somewhat limply, that the reason why he stopped with Damascus was that he could not think of anywhere further south that he could use for purposes of definition. A year later, Clayton, who had helped draft McMahon's letters, assured Samuel, by then High Commissioner to

45 Friedman, *The Question of Palestine 1914–1918*, p 72.
46 Fromkin, *A Peace to End All Peace*, pp 177–8.
47 McMahon to Sherif Hussein, 24 October 1915, Cmd 5957.

Palestine, that there had been no intention of including Palestine. On 23 July 1937, McMahon confirmed publicly in a letter to *The Times* that he had not intended to include Palestine in the area which was to be the independent Arab kingdom.[48] While these letters must be treated with some respect, it must be remembered that McMahon and Clayton were writing at a time when the future of Palestine had become a matter of acute concern, which it had not been in 1915.

It has been argued that if 'district' is taken as synonymous with *vilayet*, (Ottoman province) then Palestine was excluded, since it lay to the west of the *vilayet* of Syria. But this hardly stands up against the fact that there were no *vilayet*s of Homs or Hama, while there was a *vilayet* of Aleppo, which included Alexandretta. If McMahon could not think of anywhere south of Damascus, places such as Dara'a, a rail junction with a line leading to Haifa, Amman and Aqaba, could have been identified. Crucially, of course, neither Palestine nor Jerusalem was mentioned. It is hard to escape the conclusion that by identifying districts to the west of the four cities of Damascus, Homs, Hama and Aleppo, McMahon was looking to the future of the Christian, and possibly Druze, communities of what was to become Lebanon, where Britain's ally France had long-standing interests.[49] Whether or not Palestine was part of the area pledged to Hussein has been, and doubtless will continue to be, endlessly debated, but the essential point was that the Arabs believed it to be part of their inheritance from the British.

The Sykes-Picot Agreement and the Arab Revolt

It was in the knowledge of these negotiations, but unknown to Hussein, that Britain entered into an agreement with France in 1916, essentially dividing the Middle East between them. The Sykes-Picot Agreement, called after its authors, Sir Mark Sykes and François Georges Picot, reflected many of the ideas of the de Bunsen committee. France was to have the stretch of the Mediterranean coast north of the port of Acre, while Britain's area was to be oil-rich Mesopotamia together with an

---

48 Sir Henry McMahon to Sir John Shuckburgh, 12 March 1922, in Martin Gilbert, *Winston S. Churchill, Companion Volume IV*, Part 3: April 1921–November 1922 (Heinemann, London: 1977) p 1805, hereafter Gilbert, *Churchill Companion, IV*, Part 3; Samuel, *Memoirs*, pp 172–3.
49 Antonius, *The Arab Awakening*, pp 168–79.

enclave around Haifa. Other Arab areas were to become British or French protectorates. What this implied for the pledge of Arab independence hardly needs stating, but what was also significant was the emergence of an entity called 'Palestine', the boundaries of which were close to what later became the British Mandate, although without the Negev Desert in the south. Palestine was to be international, since Britain was conscious of Catholic and Orthodox concerns over the Christian Holy Places, but also wished to keep the French at a distance from the Suez Canal. Cutting as it did across any sense of a united independent Arab kingdom, the Sykes-Picot Agreement was to be excoriated by the Arabs once its terms were revealed in the aftermath of the Bolshevik revolution in Russia.[50]

Just five months later, on 5 June 1916, Hussein raised the standard of revolt, but it turned out to be rather a damp squib. Both he and Britain's Arab Bureau had greatly exaggerated the likely extent of the revolt. For example, in his letter to McMahon of 16 February 1916, Hussein implied that 100,000 Arab soldiers in the Ottoman army would defect to his revolt. The Arab Bureau strongly backed this supposition as well. However, it never happened. The vast majority of Arab troops remained scrupulously loyal to the Ottoman Empire.[51] It would appear that the Arab Bedouin forces, virtually all irregulars, that Hussein was able to field never exceeded 15,000 men. Moreover, the geographical extent of the Arab Revolt was limited as well. No rising took place in Syria or Palestine due to Cemal's pre-emptive action in crushing potential dissidents among the Arabs in the army. Indeed, to keep the rebellion going, Britain had to lavish large amounts of money and arms on the Arabs. Direct British military involvement was limited mainly to the provision of advisers and occasional naval and air support.

The limited nature of Hussein's revolt was a disappointment to the British though they were glad to see a revolt had at least occurred. After an initial success with the capture of Mecca, the Arab forces made little progress. Utterly lacking in any tactical ability and fearful of exposing themselves to Ottoman artillery, their only other initial success was the capture of the Red Sea port of Jeddah and that was only because the British provided naval and air support. Taif did not fall until September

---

50 Fraser, 'The Middle East: Partition and reformation', p 166.
51 Fromkin, *A Peace to End All Peace*, pp 218–9.

1916, while Turkish forces held Medina until early in 1919, months after the conclusion of hostilities. By mid-July 1916, the revolt was running out of steam. Hussein found it difficult to maintain a disciplined force in the field and desertion was rife. Feisal, the most militarily astute and the bravest of Hussein's sons, confided to Colonel Cyril Wilson in August 1916 that the Turks would prevail if they took the offensive. Soon afterwards Feisal requested British landings on the coast of the Hejaz to aid the revolt.[52] Hussein, apparently undisturbed by his growing military problems, proclaimed himself King of the Arabs in October 1916. However, the British had become deeply concerned and at the end of 1916 it was decided to step up aid to Hussein. His subsidy was increased from £125,000 to £200,000 a month. Large quantities of rifles were also supplied – far in excess of Hussein's requirements. The subsidy was vital for the Revolt since gold, rather than appeals to patriotism, was the key to recruiting Bedouin tribesmen. However, haggling over the price often hindered the timely execution of military operations as did the general lack of discipline of the Bedouins. Battles would be broken off due to fallings-out between apparently allied tribesmen and on one memorable occasion even to stop for coffee. T E Lawrence, who became the Arabs' key military adviser from the end of 1916, was often critical of the tendency of Bedouin forces to go home with plunder before achieving their objective.[53] The strategic direction of the Revolt was increasingly removed from Hussein's hands, with Colonel C E Wilson, commanding the British military mission to the Hejaz, and Clayton taking increasingly influential roles, Clayton coordinating much of British support for the Arab Revolt through the Arab Bureau.[54]

The Arab Bureau

In 1916, William Reginald ('Blinker') Hall, Director of the Intelligence Division, recruited David Hogarth, an eminent British archaeologist of the Near and Middle East, to join a group of British officers and officials who would co-ordinate British dealings with the Arabs – this was the Arab Bureau, which would have an influential role in forthcoming

---

52 See Karsh and Karsh, 'Myth in the Desert', pp 295–7.
53 Karsh and Karsh, 'Myth in the Desert', pp 295–7.
54 Howard Morley Sachar, *The Emergence of the Middle East, 1914–1924* (Allen Lane, Penguin Press, London: 1970) pp 134–5.

events. Hogarth subsequently recruited one of his protégés, T E Lawrence, and an Arabist, Gertrude Bell. Cairo became the base of the Arab Bureau from March 1916. Clayton headed up the bureau and Ronald Storrs had a role as well. The Arab Bureau provided information, reports and policy briefings on Syria, Arabia and Palestine for the British government. Its most notable publication was the *Arab Bulletin*, a confidential briefing book, which was circulated to senior British officials from spring 1916.

The Bureau is usually characterised as extremely francophobic. Clayton, Hogarth, Lawrence, Bell and the new British High Commissioner to Egypt, Reginald Wingate, certainly exhibited antipathy towards French aims in the Middle East. They viewed the Hashemites as a potential means of reducing or eliminating French influence in Syria. Some historians have tended also to view the Arab Bureau as a group of innocents and enthusiasts entirely taken in by the Arab cause and the Hashemites. They, it is claimed, were determined to see their protégés and their cause achieve at least some of their post-war goals at the expense of the French. Some historians reason that the cause of this was its members' guilt over the contradictions between the Sykes-Picot Agreement and the Hussein-McMahon correspondence. What the Arab Bureau was most interested in, however, was the expansion of British imperial interests in the Arab world. Its members saw a loose confederation nominally under Hussein but informally controlled by Britain as the best means of achieving this.[55] They also saw this as a means of reducing, if not eliminating, French influence in the Arab World. T E Lawrence, in an oft-quoted passage written after the war, suggested the possibility of formal constitutional links between Britain and the successor Arab state of the Ottoman Empire: 'My own ambition is that the Arabs should be our first brown dominion, and not our last brown colony.'[56]

Feisal and Lawrence

T E Lawrence, a young subaltern, the illegitimate son of an Anglo-Irish landowner, was perhaps the most important figure in the Arab Bureau,

55 Bruce Westrate, *The Arab Bureau: British Policy in the Middle East, 1916–1920* (Pennsylvania State University Press, University Park, PA: 1992) pp 6–9.
56 T E Lawrence to Lord Curzon, 27 September 1919, in David Garnett (ed), *The Letters of T E Lawrence* (Jonathan Cape, London: 1938) pp 291–3.

and certainly became the most celebrated. Both man of action and intellectual, his role in it was due primarily to a knowledge of the Middle East gained during his extensive travels there before the First World War. He had developed an enthusiasm for traditional Arab culture as well as a hostility towards modernisers, be they Young Turks or French missionaries and educators. Unsurprisingly, the anti-French views of the Arab Bureau influenced him as well. After a mission in early 1916 to Mesopotamia, where he witnessed the incompetent British campaign, he was ordered to Jeddah with Storrs in October 1916, with a brief to appraise the Arab Revolt. He would spend the next two years in Arabia playing a leading role in it.

Lawrence certainly had a major impact on the Revolt, which was struggling desperately by the time he arrived. It was clear by October 1916 that the Turks held the military initiative. There was no prospect of the Arabs being able to take Medina. Furthermore, there was no sign that Hussein was attracting support outside the narrow confines of the Bedouin tribes, and what support was forthcoming was entirely due to bribes funded by British subsidy.

Lawrence quickly concluded that the Revolt needed to focus around the most dynamic of Hussein's sons, Feisal: 'I felt at first glance that this was the man I had come to Arabia to seek – the leader who would bring the Arab Revolt to full glory', he wrote later.[57] Lawrence recognised that Feisal was not without faults – he viewed him as excessively tribal in his allegiances. The alternatives, his three brothers, were far worse: Ali suffered from ill health, Zeid was too young and callow, and Abdullah, the most obvious choice, was considered by Lawrence to be too much of a politician and not enough of a statesman.[58] In any case, Lawrence considered him militarily incompetent. He was able to persuade the head of the Arab Bureau, Clayton, of the merits of this despite some reluctance on his part. Feisal was not a universally popular choice for leadership among the Arab Bureau. Abdullah had been the most enthusiastic about launching the Revolt and, moreover, had initiated the contacts with the British. Feisal, on the other hand, had been the most reluctant to rebel. However, as the Revolt had developed, his attitude towards the

---

57 Lawrence, *Seven Pillars of Wisdom*, p 76.
58 See Lawrence, *Seven Pillars of Wisdom*, p 51, which questions Abdullah's sincerity.

Ottomans had hardened and while he remained open to the possibility of rapprochement (see below), he considered it increasingly unlikely that any acceptable deal could be reached.[59]

Clayton became increasingly dependent on Lawrence for information on the Arab Revolt and operations in the northern Hejaz and Lawrence went from being a minor figure to a major influence due to his ability to control the information that was reaching Cairo. From November 1916, he became liaison officer to the Arab Revolt. This gave him a central role in deciding on Feisal's strategy. His control and supervision of the British subsidy and arms deliveries gave him real power. However, his brilliance was in his ability to forge a working partnership with Feisal and other Arabs by adapting himself successfully to the sensitivities of Arab culture. His tact and diplomacy helped smooth over some of the serious problems that faced the Anglo-Hashemite alliance.

There seems to be little doubt that Lawrence's arrival proved to be a major spur to the Arab Revolt. His key tactical decision was to utilise the Arabs' great advantage: their mobility thanks to their skills with camels and horses. Their great disadvantage was their vulnerability to casualties, which could not be afforded as Arab morale was extremely fragile. It was better, Lawrence recognised, to use the open spaces of the desert to avoid a war of contact but instead fight one of detachment.[60] Attacks would only be pressed home when the Arabs had the tactical advantage. Lawrence, therefore, aligned Arab tactics and strategy with their military resources and capabilities as well the geography of the Hejaz. In his view, attacks should be generally confined to soft targets such as railway lines, infrastructure and supply convoys rather than frontal assaults on Turkish infantry, which tended to end in disaster. He saw little point in pressing home attacks on major Turkish concentrations such as at Medina. The inability of the Arabs to stand up to artillery bombardment precluded this. It was much better to leave the 25,000-strong garrison bottled up, where it remained impotent for the course of the war.[61] Instead, little pinprick attacks, similar to the raids that were a frequent occurrence in the early 20th century Arabian Peninsula during peacetime, would keep

---

59 James Barr, *Setting the Desert on Fire: T E Lawrence and Britain's Secret War in Arabia, 1916–18* (Bloomsbury, London: 2007) pp 102–3.
60 Lawrence, *Seven Pillars of Wisdom*, pp 183–4.
61 Lawrence, *Seven Pillars of Wisdom*, p 215.

the Arabs in the field and build up their confidence. He also allowed the Arabs to keep plunder from their attacks. It was simply pointless to enforce Western military discipline on nomadic Bedouins when they could simply up and leave if they were not happy with their conditions. In key engagements, including the capture of Akaba in July 1917, Lawrence demonstrated considerable tactical flair and the ability to exploit a military situation.

Feisal was now transformed from being one of a number of brothers to *primus inter pares*. He would eclipse his elder brother Abdullah and ultimately even his father. He became the driving Arab force behind the Revolt. Having spent much of his childhood in Istanbul, he and his brothers were not natural Bedouin. Indeed many Arabs would have considered them *effendi*, a term describing Arabs of noble rank who had received a modern secular education and had adopted Western clothing and concepts. As soon as they returned to Mecca, however, their father had insisted that they act like Bedouin. They were sent out into the wilderness without comforts to get back to their roots. However, their upbringing isolated them from their fellow Bedouin. As Lawrence noted, the four sons of Hussein 'were natives of no country, lovers of no private plot of ground. They had no real confidants or ministers; and no one of them seemed open to another, or to the father, of whom they stood in awe.'[62]

Lawrence and Feisal's relationship was the key to the successes that the Arab Revolt enjoyed. Feisal always gave the orders, while Lawrence merely advised. It was simply unrealistic for Lawrence to give orders to Feisal – he had to persuade him and then let Feisal direct his men. Both Feisal and his father were at times extremely difficult to deal with. Nonetheless, Lawrence and Feisal forged a useful partnership. Part of the reason for the closeness was that Lawrence was willing to confide some of the most secret aspects of British policy to Feisal. In February 1917, he explained to him that the McMahon correspondence had been superseded by the Sykes-Picot Agreement and France was going to have a major role in the post-war settlement in the region. Moving north and spreading the Revolt into Syria was the only way of forestalling French claims there. Lawrence's revelations appear to have been motivated by proposals of the small French military mission in the Hejaz to stage an

---

62 Lawrence, *Seven Pillars of Wisdom*, p 85.

attack on the port of Akaba. He persuaded Feisal that this was meant to bottle the Arabs up in the Hejaz and leave the French a free hand in Syria. Feisal now knew that it was vitally important for him to move north and take Damascus and the main Syrian cities.[63]

The first sign that the tactics Lawrence advocated would work was seen in the attack on the coastal town of Wejh, which was far to the north of Jeddah and Mecca and would provide a base from which operations against the Hejaz railway could be carried out. It also pointed to the extension of operations out of the Hejaz and into Syria itself. Supported by British naval forces, the town fell to Feisal's men on 23 January 1917. From here, the Arabs were able to conduct their hit-and-run operations against the Hejaz railway. The Ottomans, forced to divert ever more resources into keeping the railway open, stood on the defensive for the rest of the campaign. They were, as Lawrence had desired, bottled up in Medina.

Lawrence disappeared from view for much of the spring and early summer of 1917. He went far into Syria in an attempt to ascertain for himself the extent of support from tribal groupings for the Arab Revolt. This appears linked to his desire to drive Feisal northwards. Upon his return to the Hejaz in June 1917, he directed an operation against Akaba. The capture of the port convinced the British commander in the Middle East, General Sir Edmund Allenby, of Lawrence's talent and the usefulness of the Arab Revolt. He saw Lawrence's guerrilla attacks as a means of tying down large numbers of Ottoman troops at relatively little cost to the British. For the next year, from their base at Akaba, Lawrence and Feisal led operations against Turkish forces in the towns of Maan and Amman and on the Damascus–Medina railway line, though he was never able completely to sever that link and the Ottoman garrison at Medina remained intact until well after the armistice. When Allenby and the British forces began their advance into Syria in the summer and autumn of 1918, the Arab irregular army provided a useful distraction on the flanks of the advance, though its impact tended to be exaggerated by Lawrence and the Arab leadership.[64]

---

63 Jeremy Wilson, *Lawrence of Arabia: The Authorized Biography of T E Lawrence* (Heinemann, London: 1989) pp 361–2.
64 Two recent accounts of Lawrence and the Arab Revolt are Barr, *Setting the Desert on Fire*, and Wilson, *Lawrence of Arabia*, Chapters 13–26.

The Zionists and the British government

By 1916, then, certain key issues in the Middle East had become intertwined. At their heart was the ultimate fate of the Ottoman Empire, where Britain had entered into ill-defined commitments to their new Hashemite allies, while harbouring ambitions of its own and having to take into account the sensitivities of the French and the Russians. All of this held potential for trouble in the future, but there was, of course, the added dimension of Zionist hopes over Palestine, which had been heightened as the result of Turkey's entry into the war. In Palestine itself, the Jews were naturally fearful for their position, given the fact that most of the recent settlers were from Russia, with which Turkey was now at war. The governorship of Syria and Palestine was in the hands of Cemal, who distrusted equally the political ambitions of Armenians, Jews and Arab nationalists, so much so that he went down in Arab memory as 'Cemal the Butcher', and was assassinated in 1922 by an Armenian. The Jews of Palestine were spared some of the worst of his attentions by the American Ambassador to Constantinople, Henry Morgenthau, and the fact that the Germans did not wish to alienate Jewish opinion. Even so, Cemal cracked down hard on Zionist activity. By the end of 1915, over 11,000 Jews had fled or been deported, mostly to Egypt. While some Jews were accepted for service in the Ottoman army, in 1917 Cemal ordered the evacuation of the new settlement of Tel Aviv. As the economy started to collapse, hunger hit the Arab and Jewish population alike.[65]

The response of young Jews who had been expelled to Egypt had been to rally to the British cause, forming the Zion Mule Corps, a transport company, which served with distinction at Gallipoli in 1915. Its commanding officer was an adventurous Irish Protestant, Lieutenant-Colonel John Henry Patterson DSO, who in 1916 published his account in *With the Zionists in Gallipoli*. So convinced was Patterson of the potential of the men he had led, that on his return to London he campaigned for the recruitment of Jewish battalions, three of which subsequently fought under his command in Palestine. Patterson, who has a reasonable claim to be regarded as one of the founders of the future Israel Defence Forces, retained an interest in Zionism for the rest of his life.[66] The Jewish

65 Slutsky, 'Under Ottoman Rule (1880–1917)', pp 24–7.
66 L S Amery, *My Political Life, Volume 2: War and Peace, 1914–1929* (Hutchinson, London: 1953) pp 117–8; John Henry Patterson, *With the Zionists*

driving forces behind the Mule Corps were Joseph Trumpeldor, a one-armed veteran of the Russo-Japanese War who had become the first Jewish officer in the Tsarist army, and Vladimir, or Ze'ev, Jabotinsky. An Odessa-born journalist, Jabotinsky had begun to make his mark as an orator at the pre-war Zionist Congresses, and had already clashed with Weizmann over the proposed Hebrew University. In the 1920s he was to quarrel fundamentally with Weizmann, seceding from the Zionist Organisation in 1925 to form the right-wing Revisionist Zionists. He is generally acknowledged to be the founder and intellectual dynamo behind the Zionist right, which eventually came into its inheritance in 1977 with the election victory of Menachem Begin, and which has been a powerful force in Israeli politics ever since.[67]

Jabotinsky, and the tradition he later inspired, are important for any understanding of the evolution of Zionism, but another young man who found himself in Egypt at that time was to find his fortunes intertwined with those of Weizmann. This was David Ben-Gurion, originally David Gryn, from Plonsk in the Polish part of the Russian empire, who had emigrated to Palestine in 1906. Their passionate commitment to Zionism apart, he and Weizmann could not have been less alike. Whereas Weizmann was tall, urbane and familiar with the educational systems of Russia, Germany, Switzerland and Great Britain, Ben-Gurion was short and feisty, his higher education confined to a brief spell studying law in Istanbul, which had been cut short by the outbreak of war. Perhaps the clue to Ben-Gurion's attitude to the older man was his observation in old age that compared with draining the swamps of Galilee the lobbying of the well-dressed Zionists in Western Europe was futile.[68]

Notwithstanding these events, which were to change the political map of the Middle East, the main British front was in France and Flanders, where the war had taken on almost unimaginable dimensions with the small British Expeditionary Force, the famous 'Old Contemptibles' of

in *Gallipoli* (Hutchinson, London: 1916). Patterson is best known for *The Man-Eaters of Tsavo* (Macmillan, London: 1907). His African adventures are vividly portrayed in the 1996 film *The Ghost and the Darkness*.

67 Avi Shlaim, *The Iron Wall: Israel and the Arab World* (Penguin, London: 2000) p 11; Rose, *Chaim Weizmann*, pp 131–3.

68 David Ben-Gurion, *Recollections*, ed Thomas R Bransten (Macdonald Unit 75, London: 1970) pp 60–1.

1914, transformed into the first mass army in British history. But that brought problems, not least in the area of munitions where supply failed to match the needs of the army. This was particularly true of the artillery, and by the spring of 1915 what became known as 'The Great Shell Scandal' rocked British politics, playing no small part in the formation of a new coalition government in May. As a result, a new Ministry of Munitions was created, under the direction of David Lloyd George, charged with ensuring that the Army received the supplies it needed.[69]

A particularly pressing need was for a plentiful supply of acetone, an essential ingredient in cordite, the propellant for shells and bullets, and a substance on which, as it happened, Weizmann had worked in the course of his researches into fermentation. His findings attracted the attention of the research scientists at the large Nobel munitions works at Ardeer near Irvine in Ayrshire, but a major explosion at the factory in 1915 proved to be a setback. Weizmann had, however, already been approached by the Admiralty through Sir Frederick Nathan, who had particular responsibility for cordite, and this approach was confirmed, it seems, at a meeting with the First Lord, Winston Churchill. While the records relating to the key meetings are somewhat elliptical, Weizmann apparently met Lloyd George again through Scott's good offices in June 1915, and from then on he had the green light to work on the mass production of acetone from maize. Working for the government meant that he had to take leave of absence from the University of Manchester and move to London. There is no question but that his work contributed significantly to the British war effort. Moreover, it gave him a new-found financial security, and it was to be the road which took him from provincial obscurity in a northern town to the hub of British politics.[70]

It was no less a person than Lloyd George who gave currency to the link between Weizmann's work on acetone and the subsequent Balfour Declaration on Zionism. According to his account, he asked Weizmann what honour he would like to be recommended for in recognition of his

---

69 David Lloyd George, *War Memoirs*, 2 vols (Odhams Press Ltd, London: 1938) Vol I, pp 112–17.
70 Weizmann, *Trial and Error*, pp 218–22; Wilson (ed), *The Political Diaries of C.P. Scott*, p 128; Lloyd George, *War Memoirs*, Vol I, pp 347–8; Reinharz, *Chaim Weizmann: The Making of a Statesman*, pp 40–72; Rose, *Chaim Weizmann*, pp 152–8.

work. Weizmann's reply was that he wanted nothing for himself, but something could be done for his people who had aspirations of returning to their ancient homeland. Lloyd George's claim that this was the origin of the Balfour Declaration need not be taken at face value, since the dynamics were much more complex than that, but he returned to it in November 1944 when writing a foreword to a volume honouring Weizmann on his 70th birthday.[71] The rather more prosaic truth was that by 1916 Weizmann had rendered a significant service to the British state and was now a respected figure in the eyes of those at the heart of government. This assumed even greater significance after December 1916 when Lloyd George succeeded Asquith, whose interest in Zionism had never been great, as Prime Minister with none other than Balfour as his Foreign Secretary. But since Samuel had followed Asquith into political exile, an influential ally had also been lost.

Lloyd George's coalition brought into the War Cabinet Alfred, Lord Milner, one of the country's most fertile imperial thinkers, and a key figure in the Boer War and subsequent reconstruction of South Africa. Sensitive to political change, Milner's mission in life was to advance ways of preserving the British Empire through the principles of imperial unity and federation. In 1910, he had been instrumental in inspiring a new group known as 'The Round Table', which began to publish an influential journal of the same name. Amongst its members, Leo Amery, Conservative Member of Parliament for South Birmingham from 1911 and Assistant Secretary to the War Cabinet, and Lord Robert Cecil, Minister of Blockade from 1916 to 1918 and son of the late Conservative Prime Minister the Marquess of Salisbury, were to join Milner in providing crucial support for what became the Balfour Declaration, while another, Reginald Coupland, was to become a key influence on Weizmann's thinking in later years and would help to decide the future fate of Palestine.[72] In 1917, Milner's influence in the War Cabinet was at its height, with his acolytes well placed. In addition to Milner, Amery and Cecil, Weizmann was to find

---

71 Lloyd George, *War Memoirs*, Vol I, p 349; The Rt Hon The Earl Lloyd George of Dwyfor, OM, 'Foreword', in Goodman, *Chaim Weizmann*; Reinharz, *Chaim Weizmann: The Making of a Statesman*, pp 67–9.
72 Andrea Bosco and Alex May (eds), *The Round Table, the Empire/ Commonwealth and British Foreign Policy* (Lothian Foundation Press, London: 1997) pp i–xv.

two other invaluable allies at the heart of the bureaucracy which was now driving the war effort. The first was a man of diverse talents and connections, the Right Honourable William Ormsby-Gore, Conservative MP for Denbigh, heir to the 3rd Baron Harlech, and husband of the daughter of the Marquess of Salisbury. More pertinently, his knowledge of the Middle East had recently been gained as an intelligence officer in the Arab Bureau in Cairo, and in 1917 he held the influential positions of Parliamentary Private Secretary to Milner and an Assistant Secretary to the War Cabinet. Ormsby-Gore was to prove a staunch ally of Weizmann's over many years. The other was Sir Mark Sykes, also a member of the Cabinet secretariat. Sykes was a wealthy Catholic landowner, 6th Baronet and Conservative MP for Hull, who had become an expert on Turkish affairs, and a champion of its subject nationalities, the Arabs, Armenians and Jews. He was, of course, the British part of the Sykes-Picot Agreement, with which his name will always be associated, and by 1917 he had a particular brief with regard to Palestine. Weizmann was to describe him as one of Zionism's greatest finds.[73] Tragically, Sykes was to die of influenza in Paris in February 1919 when part of the British delegation to the Peace Conference, aged only 39.

The evolution of the Balfour Declaration

Before examining the negotiations leading to the Balfour Declaration, it is as well to consider the situation in which Britain and its allies found themselves during 1917. At sea, the Battle of Jutland in 1916 had not delivered the kind of Nelsonian victory tradition demanded, while in the course of 1917 Germany's strategy of unrestricted submarine warfare threatened to choke off Britain's essential supplies. On land, the great Somme offensive launched with such high hopes in July 1916 had finally spluttered to a halt, while the French army had only held Verdun at appalling cost. The disastrous French offensive of 1917, which provoked a mutiny in its army, and the British campaign at Passchendaele were to be no more successful. The overthrow of the Tsar in March 1917, and the subsequent turn of events in Russia which resulted in the Bolshevik seizure of power in November, threatened to free veteran German and Austro-Hungarian divisions for service elsewhere. On the Italian front, October saw the Italian army almost shattered by the Austrians

---

73 Weizmann, *Trial and Error*, p 229.

and Germans at Caporetto. The one positive development was the entry of the United States into the war on 6 April, but this tested the loyalty of large ethnic groups in the country, such as the Irish, with their memories of the Famine and the recent Easter Rising, or the Jews, who had no reason to support a Russian alliance. In short, the British needed support from wherever it could be found. Weizmann was clear that British motives behind the Balfour Declaration combined idealism with the pressures of war, especially with regard to what was happening in the Jewish communities of Russia and the United States.[74]

In January 1917, Sykes was anxious to make contact with the leaders of British Zionism, but needed to know who they were and what they wanted. His intermediary seems to have been an anglicised Armenian, James Malcolm, who sounded out Weizmann's old adversary from the time of the Uganda controversy, Leopold Greenberg of the *Jewish Chronicle*. Somewhat surprisingly, Greenberg pointed to Weizmann and Nahum Sokolow, who had come to London the previous year and was now active in Zionist affairs. On 28 January, Malcolm introduced Weizmann and Greenberg to Sykes.[75] What Sykes wanted was a statement of the Zionist position, which is exactly what Weizmann, Sokolow and others had been working on for some time. The memorandum which he was given was called an 'Outline of Programme for the Jewish Resettlement of Palestine in Accordance with the Aspirations of the Zionist Movement'. It dealt with the future of Palestine under a suzerain government, which was not named but could be inferred. It called for the present and future Jewish population of Palestine to be recognised as the Jewish nation with full civic, national and political rights. Jewish immigrants would be encouraged and helped to purchase land. The suzerain government was to establish a Jewish company to foster Jewish settlement. The document also introduced a new term, coined by Sokolow, to the effect that Palestine was to be recognised as the Jewish National Home.[76] Here were the bare bones of what Weizmann was to present to the Peace Conference two years later.

Events took a decisive step forward at a meeting held on 7 February

---

74 For a discussion see Schneer, *The Balfour Declaration*, p 366.
75 Stein, *The Balfour Declaration*, pp 362–9.
76 Weizmann, *Trial and Error*, pp 235–6; Stein, *The Balfour Declaration*, pp 368–9.

1917 at the home of Dr Moses Gaster, a long-standing English Zionist. Insisting that he was there in a private capacity, which probably fooled no one, Sykes met a group of leading Zionists, including Weizmann, Sokolow, Samuel, Lord Rothschild, James de Rothschild, Joseph Cowen, Herbert Bentwich and Harry Sacher. They were concerned to put to Sykes that what they wanted was a British protectorate which would operate under the terms of the memorandum he had received. What they did not want was for the country to be put under some form of internationalisation, which was really code for an Anglo-French condominium. Sykes assured them he was sympathetic to the idea of a Jewish Palestine and that he did not anticipate a problem with the Russians, but was wary of French intentions in the area, even though he did not consider that they had any claims. The Italians would simply follow the French, he said. He was not, of course, in a position to reveal his own recent agreement with the French over the future disposition of the Turkish lands.

It was agreed that Sokolow should argue the Zionist case with the French. Sykes openly put it to the Zionists that they would be challenged by the growing strength of Arab nationalism, and advised that if they obtained Jewish support in other matters then he felt that the Arabs could be managed. This was to form an important element in Weizmann's subsequent negotiations with Feisal. From a letter to Jabotinsky sent the following day, it is clear that Weizmann was well aware of the meeting's significance, although his enthusiasm for Sykes was tempered somewhat by the feeling that the Arabs, and not the Zionists, were his priority.[77] Four days after this historic meeting, Weizmann was elected president of the English Zionist Federation, enabling him to negotiate with the government on these crucial issues from a recognised position.

From this tentative beginning, momentum built in the spring of 1917. What seems to have exercised the British most at this stage was the likely attitude of the French to any move over Palestine. Weizmann was warned of this by Balfour at a meeting on 22 March. It seems that Balfour took some convincing of Palestine's value to the British. His suggestion was

---

77 Weizmann to Vladimir Jabotinsky, Hazeley Down, 8 February 1917; Weizmann to C P Scott, Manchester, 20 March 1917, *LPCW*, Vol VII, 306, 321, pp 328–9; Weizmann, *Trial and Error*, pp 238–40; Stein, *The Balfour Declaration*, pp 370–4.

that if they could not get an agreement with France, then the Zionists should aim for an Anglo-American condominium, an idea which did not greatly tempt Weizmann. This theme was also taken up by Lloyd George when he breakfasted with Weizmann and Scott on 3 April.[78] The real significance of these meetings was that Weizmann and Zionism were being taken seriously at the highest level, important because large British forces were poised to advance into Palestine, but they also put into context the somewhat prolonged mission Sokolow undertook in Paris and Rome in April, May and June. It was far from a waste of time, however, since on 4 June Jules Cambon of the French Foreign Ministry wrote to him expressing sympathy with his cause. This was an invaluable document to have.[79] Sokolow's lengthy absence, of course, meant that in London the spotlight fell on Weizmann.

It was at this point that Weizmann at last got wind of the Sykes-Picot Agreement through the good offices of Scott. The proposal that France should acquire part of northern Palestine, and that the rest should be internationalised ran directly counter to Zionist hopes for a British protectorate. It was clearly vital to explore this, and make it clear where the Zionists stood. Weizmann did this on 25 April at a meeting with Lord Robert Cecil, who was running the Foreign Office during Balfour's absence in the United States. There were three options for Palestine, he explained; namely, a British protectorate, an Anglo-French condominium and internationalisation. What the Jews wanted was the first of these. They trusted Britain to allow Jewish development, and grant self-government at the appropriate time. Joint rule with the French would simply lead to confusion and intrigue. Moreover, he pointed out that French colonial policy was one of assimilation to French, and Catholic, values. Internationalisation would pose a strategic threat to Egypt. Weizmann then turned to the Sykes-Picot Agreement, which he outlined with remarkable accuracy. This, he said, would combine the faults of internationalisation and a condominium, as well as partitioning Palestine. Cecil appears to have been convinced, and he

78 Weizmann to C P Scott, Manchester, 23 March 1917, *LPCW,* Vol VII, 323, pp 346–7; Weizmann, *Trial and Error,* pp 240–1; Stein, *The Balfour Declaration,* pp 378–85.

79 Cambon's letter of 4 June 1917 is cited in Sokolow, *History of Zionism,* Vol II, p 53; Friedman, *The Question of Palestine 1914–1918,* pp 161–2.

advised Weizmann to mobilise world Jewish opinion in support of a British protectorate.[80]

Clearly, the key to such a strategy lay with the large American Jewish community, whose leader Justice Louis D Brandeis had the ear of President Woodrow Wilson. Born in Kentucky in 1856, in 1916 Brandeis had become the first Jew to be appointed to the Supreme Court. In 1914, he had accepted the presidency of the Provisional Executive Council for General Zionist Affairs, and as such was the acknowledged leader of American Zionism. Two days before his meeting with Cecil, Weizmann had contacted Brandeis, emphasising that from the Zionist perspective it was imperative that Palestine should become a British protectorate. Amongst other things, what was concerning him were anti-annexationist views coming from the American administration. It was vital that Brandeis should meet Balfour to impress this upon him. Brandeis met Balfour on several occasions during his American visit, and the two men seem to have agreed on the need for a future British administration in Palestine.[81]

It was Brandeis in June 1917 who warned Weizmann that an American mission was coming to the Middle East, and that he should contact it. From Sykes and Ormsby-Gore he learned that this was an initiative of Henry Morgenthau, former Ambassador to Constantinople, in an attempt to negotiate a separate peace with Turkey. The idea of some kind of deal which would leave the empire intact was as unwelcome to the British as it was to Weizmann, and it was Balfour who suggested that he intercept Morgenthau's party at Gibraltar and persuade him to drop the idea. In a somewhat cloak-and-dagger operation, Weizmann travelled to Gibraltar, accompanied by an armed intelligence officer, but he need not have worried, since Morgenthau soon saw the futility of the idea. In any case, the United States and Turkey were not at war. The real significance is the extent to which Weizmann was now trusted by the government, and the success of his mission certainly did his credibility no harm.[82]

---

80 Note of Interview with Robert Cecil at the Foreign Office, 25 April 1917, *LPCW*, Vol VII, pp 375–8; Weizmann, *Trial and Error*, pp 241–2; Stein, *The Balfour Declaration*, pp 392–3.

81 Weizmann to Louis D Brandeis, Washington, 23 April 1917, *LPCW*, Vol VII, 351, pp 371–3; Dugdale, *Arthur James Balfour*, Vol II, pp 169–70.

82 Weizmann, *Trial and Error*, pp 246–51; Reinharz, *Chaim Weizmann: The Making of a Statesman*, pp 153–71.

While events were clearly moving Weizmann's way, his activities had rung alarm bells amongst his old adversaries in the Anglo-Jewish elite, expressed through the Conjoint Foreign Committee, which brought together the Board of Deputies of British Jews and the Anglo-Jewish Association. On 24 May 1917, they published a statement in *The Times* under the title of 'Palestine and Zionism – Views of Anglo-Jewry'. While they supported the concept of making Palestine a spiritual centre for the Jews, they were strongly opposed to Zionism's political programme, arguing that for Palestine to be regarded as a Jewish homeland would undermine what the Jews had achieved in their native countries. Their action brought to a head the latent tensions within British Jewry over the question of Zionism, with Weizmann and the Jewish peer Lord Rothschild writing letters of rebuttal to *The Times*. Weizmann's letter, which was published on 28 May, asserted in no uncertain terms that the Jews were a nationality, and added that Zionism was not seeking an exclusive position in Palestine.[83] The result of this controversy was that on 17 June the Board of Deputies voted, albeit by a narrow majority, to reject the 'Statement', and the Conjoint Foreign Committee was dissolved. This was far from the end of the campaign against a pro-Zionist policy, since a determined enemy was lying in wait in the one of the great offices of state. This was Edwin Montagu, Secretary of State for India, of whose hostility to Zionism Lloyd George had warned three years before.[84]

The Balfour Declaration

On 13 June, Weizmann wrote to Sir Ronald Graham of the Foreign Office pressing for a British declaration of support for the Zionist position on Palestine, which he claimed, with some exaggeration, they had been negotiating for the past three years. Weizmann was at pains to point out the recent expressions of support for Zionism in influential German and Austrian newspapers.[85] By coincidence, Balfour had just received a minute recommending that the government issue an assurance

---

83 Weizmann to the Editor of *The Times*, London, 27 May 1917, *LPCW*, Vol VII, 405, pp 418–19.

84 Weizmann, *Trial and Error*, pp 252–5; Stein, *The Balfour Declaration*, pp 442–61.

85 Weizmann to Sir Ronald Graham, London, 13 June 1917, *LPCW*, Vol VII, 432, pp 438–42.

of British sympathy for Zionism. He was, therefore, in a receptive mood when Weizmann, Graham and Lord Rothschild came to see him on 19 June. Balfour agreed that the time had come to issue a declaration of support, and asked them to submit a draft which he could put to the War Cabinet. He also assured them that he was opposed to an Anglo-French condominium, and that he favoured joint Anglo-American control, but felt that this would not find favour with Lloyd George or the Americans. In reporting this to his colleagues, Weizmann suggested that the draft should talk in terms of a Jewish National Home in Palestine, precisely the formula the War Cabinet ultimately agreed.[86] The drafting was done by a committee chaired by Sokolow while Weizmann was in Gibraltar.

Various versions were discussed, including one by Herbert Side-botham, a non-Jewish journalist on the *Manchester Guardian*, who was strongly pro-Zionist. His rather turgid version was not accepted, but is, nevertheless, well worth noting for his use of the striking phrase that the national character of the Jewish state should be as Jewish as the dominant national character of England was English. Weizmann was to utter a somewhat terser version of this when responding to a question at the Peace Conference, and its implications were to echo for years, not always to his advantage. In discussing this episode in his book *Great Britain and Palestine*, which he published in 1937, Sidebotham refrained from mentioning that he was most probably the *fons et origo* of the phrase.[87] Harry Sacher was also influential in the working of a draft declaration.[88] On 18 July 1917, the agreed draft was given to Balfour by Lord Rothschild. It was admirably brief, and would have committed the British government to reconstituting Palestine as the National Home of the Jewish People, and to discussing with the Zionist Organisation how this would be done.[89] If the Zionists had reason to hope for early action, then they had not reckoned on the Byzantine ways of the British decision-making process, nor on the opposition the draft provoked.

---

86 Weizmann to Harry Sacher, Manchester, 20 June 1917, *LPCW*, Vol VII, 435, PP 444–5.
87 Esco Foundation for Palestine, *Palestine: A Study of Jewish, Arab, and British Policies*, 2 vols (Published for the Esco Foundation for Palestine, Inc, Yale University Press, New Haven: 1947) Vol I, pp 102–3 (hereafter Esco, *Palestine*).
Herbert Sidebotham, *Great Britain and Palestine* (Macmillan, London: 1937) p 65.
88 See Schneer, *The Balfour Declaration*, pp 334–5.
89 Stein, *The Balfour Declaration*, p 470.

As the Zionist draft circulated, a number of suggested amendments were put forward, the most significant being one from Milner which proposed that the declaration should commit Britain to securing a home for the Jews in Palestine.[90] The matter came before the War Cabinet on 3 September, in the absence of Lloyd George and Balfour. While Cecil and Milner and the South African General Jan Smuts were supporters of the idea, a powerful opponent had also been asked to attend. This was Edwin Montagu, who had recently been appointed Secretary of State for India, entrusted with carrying forward the reform scheme which was to emerge under his name and that of the Viceroy, Lord Chelmsford. Since India's wholehearted participation was vital at this stage of the war, his views mattered. The Indian Army formed a large part of the imperial forces in both Palestine and Mesopotamia, and it recruited heavily amongst Indian Muslims. Montagu felt passionately that the idea of a Jewish National Home undermined his status as a Jewish Englishman, and he expressed this in no uncertain terms in a memorandum which he entitled 'The Anti-Semitism of the Present Government'. The War Cabinet had before it Lord Rothschild's letter, a suggested reply by Balfour, Milner's alternative version, and Montagu's philippic against the whole idea. Montagu spoke to his memorandum, emphasising his central belief that the proposal would undermine the position of Jews everywhere. Others argued that the idea of a Jewish state in Palestine would not affect the position enjoyed by Jews in countries like Britain, but would strengthen it in countries where they did not have equal rights. Cecil argued against any postponement of the matter, pointing to the enthusiasm of the Zionist Organisation, especially in the United States, and the value of having them on the Allied side. Even so, it was felt prudent to consult the other Allies, especially the Americans.[91]

With the proposed declaration seemingly hanging in the balance, Weizmann deployed all his diplomatic skills to help secure it. The first attempt to put Lord Rothschild's draft before President Woodrow Wilson through his aide Colonel Edward M House produced a rather tepid reply on 10 September, to the effect that a declaration of sympathy could be made but without any commitment. Wilson's problem was that his country

---

90 Friedman, *The Question of Palestine 1914–1918*, p 257.
91 War Cabinet 227, 3 September 1917, CAB 23/4, in Fraser, *The Middle East 1914–1979*, pp 13–14.

was not at war with Turkey. When Weizmann learned of the tone of House's message, he immediately contacted Brandeis, emphasising the urgent need to secure Wilson's endorsement. Brandeis met House on 23 September, and the following day he telegraphed to the effect that the President was entirely sympathetic to the proposed declaration.[92]

Frustrated and somewhat perplexed by the influence Montagu was having, Weizmann was also actively lobbying on the domestic front. On 19 September, he met Balfour, who promised to use his influence with the Prime Minister, and then, a week later, he was able to snatch a few moments with Lloyd George, who issued peremptory instructions that the matter be tabled at the next Cabinet meeting.[93] With the matter now due to come back before the War Cabinet, on 3 October he and Rothschild wrote to Balfour expressing their alarm that the proposed declaration was being opposed by a prominent Jew whom they did not actually name, but who was, of course, clearly identifiable. What they sought to drive home was that the declaration had been submitted on behalf of an organisation which represented the will of a people who had the right to be regarded as a nation.[94]

The day after receiving Weizmann's letter, the War Cabinet resumed its consideration of the matter. Balfour opened the discussion by warning his colleagues that the Germans were trying to woo the Zionists. Conceding that Zionism was opposed by some wealthy British Jews, he believed it had the support of American and Russian Jews. He saw no contradiction between a national focus in Palestine and the assimilation of Jews into other countries. His justification for a declaration was that the Jews passionately wanted to regain their ancient homeland. Finally, he read the letter of support Cambon had given Sokolow, and referred to Wilson's favourable attitude, although others noted the difference in tone between the telegrams sent by House and Brandeis. Montagu responded by asserting that he was a Jewish Englishman and that the Jews were a

---

92 Weizmann to Louis D Brandeis, Washington (?), 12 September 1917, *LPCW*, Vol VII, 496, pp 505–6; Weizmann, *Trial and Error*, pp 257–8; Stein, *The Balfour Declaration*, pp 504–7; Friedman, *The Question of Palestine 1914–1918*, pp 261–3.
93 Weizmann to Philip Kerr, London, 19 September 1917; Weizmann to Nahum Sokolow, Brighton, 30 September 1917: *LPCW*, Vol VII, 507, 513, pp 516, 520.
94 Weizmann to Arthur J Balfour, London, 3 October 1917, *LPCW*, Vol VII, 514, pp 521–2; Weizmann, *Trial and Error*, pp 257–8.

religious community, asking how he could negotiate with the Indians if it was announced that the British government believed that his National Home was in the Turkish empire. Most native-born Jews, he claimed, were hostile to Zionism; its supporters, on the other hand, were foreign-born Jews like Weizmann, a native of Russia.

Strong opposition was also voiced by George Curzon, Earl of Kedleston, former Viceroy of India and now Leader of the House of Lords. Widely travelled in the Middle East, Curzon knew Palestine and did not think much of its potential as a future home for the Jews. More importantly, he asked how it was proposed to get rid of what he called the country's Muslim majority. The government should have nothing to do with the proposed declaration, he concluded. Knowing where the arguments were likely to go, Milner had tried to square the circle in advance of the meeting. Just before the start of the War Cabinet meeting, he asked Amery to draft a formula which might satisfy both the Jewish and pro-Arab critics. Amery's hastily-composed text added to Milner's earlier draft that nothing should be done to prejudice the rights of the existing non-Jewish population of Palestine or those enjoyed by Jews in other countries. It was agreed to put this to Wilson as well as to the Zionists and their opponents.[95]

Faced with this fresh delay, Weizmann once again moved to secure the backing he needed. On 9 October, he cabled Brandeis with the new version of the proposed declaration, stressing the need to secure Wilson's endorsement as well as that of the American Zionists.[96] In fact, House had already received it from Balfour, and the American embassy in London had also sent it direct to Wilson. On 16 October, House informed the British of Wilson's approval, with the proviso that it not be made public, and on the following day Brandeis was able to confirm this to Weizmann. The American Zionists made two suggested amendments to the proposed text. These were concerned with the phrasing concerning the rights and political status of Jews in other countries and a preference for the term 'Jewish people' rather than 'Jewish race'. It seems that these

---

95 War Cabinet 245, 4 October 1917, CAB 23/4, in Fraser, *The Middle East 1914–1979*, pp 15–17; Amery, *My Political Life*, Vol 2, pp 116–17.
96 Weizmann to Louis D Brandeis, Washington, 9 October 1917, *LPCW*, Vol VII, 516, pp 530–1.

issues were already being addressed by the British Zionists.[97] Meanwhile, Weizmann was also mobilising Zionist opinion at home, with some 300 synagogues and societies registering their support for a declaration.[98]

When the War Cabinet met for what proved to be its final discussion of the topic on 31 October, Balfour met his critics head-on. He emphasised the propaganda they could conduct in Russia and the United States, since the majority of Jews in these countries were behind Zionism. Once again, he was dismissive of the assimilationist fear of double allegiance. Montagu was not there to counter this, since he had left for India. As to Curzon's point about the unsuitability of Palestine, he claimed that if the country were properly developed it could sustain a much larger population, an argument which Weizmann was to use in the years to come. As to what was meant by the term 'National Home', his argument is interesting in view of later developments, since he said it did not necessarily mean the early establishment of a Jewish state, but would be some kind of British, American or other protectorate which could become a focus of Jewish national life. Curzon, the only one who had actually seen the country at first hand, remained pessimistic, but was grudgingly prepared to acknowledge the political value of what was being proposed. The way was now open for the Cabinet to authorise the Declaration, which was issued in a letter from Balfour to Lord Rothschild on 2 November:

> His Majesty's Government view with favour the establishment in Palestine of a national home for the Jewish people, and will use its best endeavours to facilitate the achievement of this object, it being clearly understood that nothing shall be done which may prejudice the civil and religious rights of existing non-Jewish communities in Palestine, or the rights and political status enjoyed by Jews in any other country.[99]

Weizmann later recalled that at the conclusion of the Cabinet meeting,

---

97 Brandeis to Jacob de Haas, 17 October 1917, in Melvin L Urofsky and David W Levy (eds), *Letters of Louis D Brandeis*, Vol IV (1916–1921) (State University of New York Press, Albany: 1975) pp 318–9; Stein, *The Balfour Declaration*, pp 528–32; Weizmann, *Trial and Error*, p 261.
98 Stein, *The Balfour Declaration*, p 274.
99 War Cabinet 261, 31 October 1917, CAB23/4, in Fraser, *The Middle East 1914–1979*, pp 17–18; *Palestine Royal Commission Report*, Cmd 5479 (London: 1937) p 22.

Sykes brought the Declaration out to him with the exclamation that it was a boy. If it was not quite all that Weizmann had hoped for, its birth was more down to him than anyone else, and he knew that history was in the making, referring to it in a letter to Rothschild as the Magna Carta of the Jews.[100] That evening, his wife later recorded, the Weizmanns and some friends formed a circle at his home and danced a Hassidic dance in celebration. A month later, there was a large demonstration in London of Jewish gratitude for the Declaration, which was addressed by Cecil, Samuel, Sykes and Ormsby-Gore, as well as Weizmann. If the British government had hoped to influence the course of events in Russia, the Declaration might have succeeded, since Russian Jews were, indeed, stirred by it, but by then the second revolution had robbed it of any real potential.[101] The Declaration was followed, on 14 February 1918, by a letter from Stéphen Pichon of the Foreign Ministry to Sokolow, assuring him that the French were in agreement with the British over what he rather tepidly termed a 'Jewish establishment' in Palestine, a phrase which allowed later interpretation.[102]

The collapse of the Ottoman Empire

From the Zionist perspective the Balfour Declaration could not have come at a better time, since the Turkish positions in Palestine and Syria were about to fall to the British. The Turkish army still had fighting spirit in 1917, fending off two attacks on Gaza by Sir Archibald Murray's Egyptian Expeditionary Force. But in June 1917 the lacklustre Murray was replaced by Sir Edmund Allenby under whose leadership the strength of the imperial forces, Australian, British, Indian and New Zealand, together with their Arab and Palestinian Jewish allies, began to tell. Taking Gaza and Beersheba, on 11 December 1917 Allenby entered

---

100 Weizmann to Lord Rothschild, Tring, 2 November 1917, *LPCW*, Vol VII, pp 541–2.
101 Weizmann to Jacobus H Kann, The Hague, 6 December 1917, in Dvorah Barzilay and Barnet Litvinoff (eds), *LPCW*, Series A, Vol VIII, November 1917–October 1918 (Transaction Books, Rutgers University, Israel Univerisities Press, Jerusalem: 1977) 21, pp 19–20, hereafter *LPCW*, Vol VIII; Weizmann, *Trial and Error*, p 262; Vera Weizmann, *The Impossible Takes Longer*, p 78; Sir Charles Kingsley Webster, *The Founder of the National Home* (Yad Chaim Weizmann, Rehovoth: 1955) pp 30–1.
102 Sokolow, *History of Zionism*, Vol II, pp 127–8.

Jerusalem through the same gate the Kaiser had used, but in his case pointedly on foot.[103] From then on, Britain's was the decisive voice in the fate of Palestine. By this time, the Turkish war effort was faltering on all fronts.

Soon after the first Russian Revolution in February 1917, the Tsarist army had disintegrated. On the Caucasian front, territory seized by the Russians, who had made some attempts to prevent inter-communal killings, was taken over by Armenian militias. The militias avenged themselves on local Muslims for the fate of their kinsmen deported two years previously. Then, after the Bolshevik Revolution in November 1917, the Soviet government had sued for peace and been forced to accept the loss of the western portion of the Tsarist empire (from Finland through Poland to the Ukraine), and, subject to a referendum, territory the Russians had gained from the Ottomans in 1878.

The collapse of Russia, a full year before the collapse of Germany in November 1918, tempted Enver into another adventure. Ottoman troops had earlier been dispatched to Galicia (now divided between Poland and Ukraine) to reinforce the Austro-Hungarians against the Russians. Just as the front held by the Ottomans against the British in Palestine and Mesopotamia was about to crumble, Enver withdrew more troops from it and ordered them to move into the Caucasus beyond the 1878 Russian frontier. He overrode the objections of the Germans who had their own plans for a puppet government in Georgia and for control of the oilfields in Baku (held precariously by a British force after the Russian collapse). As he pursued his dream of a Turkic empire stretching all the way to central Asia and eyed territories about which he was woefully ill-informed, Enver weakened the defence of the Turkish core of the empire – Anatolia and eastern Thrace.

The elderly, weak-willed Sultan Mehmed V (Mehmed Reşad) died in July 1918. He was succeeded by his younger brother, the 57-year-old Vahdettin, who took the title of Mehmed VI. Mustafa Kemal had made a favourable impression on him earlier that year when he accompanied him on a tour of the Western Front. They were both critical of the Unionist leadership and their conduct of the war. Vahdettin thought he could use

---

103 Matthew Hughes (ed), *Allenby in Palestine: The Middle East Correspondence of Field Marshal Viscount Allenby June 1917–October 1919* (Sutton Publishing for the Army Records Society, Stroud: 2004) pp 7–11.

Kemal, while Kemal banked on the favour of his new sovereign for his own designs. While Vahdettin was vacillating, suspicious, ill-informed, woolly-minded and fearful for the safety of his throne, Kemal was clear-headed and realistic. This allowed him to turn the relationship to his advantage. It was also Kemal who had the clearer grasp of the Ottomans' military weakness, which he witnessed in August 1918 when he accepted a command on the Syrian front, this time under his old commander Liman von Sanders. A year earlier, when he had refused to serve another German commander, Field Marshal Erich von Falkenhayn, Kemal had urged on the Ottoman high command in Istanbul the urgent need to withdraw troops from Galicia, renounce Enver's Caucasian adventure, and concentrate all available forces for the defence of Anatolia. By the time Kemal returned to Syria, a month after Vahdettin's accession to the throne, the position of the Ottoman forces had become desperate. Jerusalem had been lost to General Allenby's British imperial forces the previous December, and a weakened Ottoman army was trying to hold a line in northern Palestine, with headquarters in Nazareth. The British broke through in September, a month after Kemal's arrival on the front. Thereafter his main concern was to escape capture and to save as many of his troops as he could for the defence of Anatolia.

By the autumn of 1918, out of the total of 2.85 million men con-scripted in the Ottoman Empire during the war, only 560,000 still bore arms, and of these only a quarter were available for combat. Some of the best troops – eight well-equipped divisions at full strength – had been dis-patched to the Caucasus and northern Persia, where they could not affect the course of the war. Half a million deserters roamed the interior of Anatolia.[104] As the military situation worsened, talk of a separate peace began to be heard in Istanbul. President Woodrow Wilson's peace pro-posals seemed to offer a way out. In a speech to Congress in January 1918 Wilson had formulated the principles which, he believed, should inspire the peacemaking. He set them out in the Fourteen Points, of which the Twelfth declared:

> The Turkish portion of the present Ottoman Empire should be assured
> a secure sovereignty, but the other nationalities which are now under

---

104 Gwynne Dyer, 'The Turkish Armistice of 1918', I, *Middle Eastern Studies*, Vol 8, No 2 (May 1972) pp 144–6.

Turkish rule should be assured an undoubted security of life and an absolutely unmolested opportunity of autonomous development, and the Dardanelles should be permanently opened as a free passage to the ships and commerce of all nations under international guarantees.

This was not a bad bargaining offer to the embattled Ottomans. Moreover, the rhetoric of President Wilson and of the Young Turks coincided in one important respect: disregarding the fact that they were fighting to save an empire, the Young Turks had posed as the champions of the peoples of the East against the imperialists. Wilson seemed to echo them. Although by then the United States was fighting on the side of the British and French empires, Wilson proclaimed loftily: 'In regard to these essential rectifications of wrong and assertions of right, we feel ourselves to be intimate partners of all the governments and peoples associated together against the imperialists.'[105] No wonder that as they tried to avert the impending catastrophe, many Ottoman patriots saw a lifeline in Wilson's principles. Moreover, Wilson's Twelfth Point echoed the statement made three days earlier by Lloyd George. The Allies, he said, were not fighting 'to deprive Turkey of its capital, or of the rich and renowned lands of Asia Minor and Thrace, which are predominantly Turkish by race'.[106]

In a first response in February 1918, the Ottoman foreign minister agreed that the diverse nationalities in the empire should be granted their own institutions.[107] In spite of reverses in the field and weakening morale, the Ottomans still wielded considerable bargaining power at the time. But the Unionist leadership was unable to make up its mind on how to end the disastrous war into which they had led the country. Enver still believed in a German victory and kept Talât Pasha's Cabinet in the dark about the worsening situation on the front. Even the defeat of the last German offensive on the Western Front in July 1918 did not shake the government out of its indecision. The opportunity to make peace on favourable terms was lost.

On 15 September, the Bulgarian army crumbled before the assault of the Allied forces in Macedonia. Four days later Allenby scattered the

---

105 <http://www.americanrhetoric.com/speeches/wilsonfourteen points.htm>
106 Dyer, 'The Turkish Armistice of 1918', p 342, n 2.
107 Dyer, 'The Turkish Armistice of 1918', p 147.

Turkish troops holding the front in northern Palestine. Talât Pasha had earlier gone to Berlin to discuss a united response of the Central Powers to Wilson's peace terms. Unable to agree among themselves, the Central Powers sued for peace separately. The first to collapse was Bulgaria. Passing through the Bulgarian capital, Sofia, on his way back home, Talât Pasha witnessed the disintegration of the army which had guarded the western approaches to Istanbul. The game was up. Talât acknowledged this with characteristic bluntness, saying 'We have eaten shit!'[108] Four years later, Sir Horace Rumbold, British High Commissioner in the Ottoman capital, was to use the same image, in a slightly more polite form. 'If the Greeks crack,' he wrote, 'we may expect to eat dirt to an unlimited extent and this is not a form of diet that has ever agreed with me, though Pellé [the French High Commissioner] and Garroni [his Italian counterpart] may flourish on it.'[109] But no one, and least of all Lloyd George, expected such a reversal of fortune when the Allies emerged triumphant from the First World War.

Talât's Cabinet finally resigned on 13 October. On the same day Enver sent a last message to all Ottoman forces urging them to prevent the loss of any more Turkish territory before the conclusion of an armistice.[110] The CUP was finally out of office. But it still held the majority of seats in parliament, which could once again exercise its powers under the Constitution. The CUP also controlled the security forces in the capital and dominated the provinces through its local organisations. In opposition, in power and then again in opposition, the CUP represented modernity. Nationalism was the dominant ideology in the world, and Wilson's advocacy of the self-determination of nations confirmed its legitimacy. In the crumbling Ottoman state, it was the CUP which championed Muslim nationalism as it melded into Turkish nationalism. There were few men of experience in politics, the administration or the army who had not collaborated with the Unionists in the ranks of the opposition to Sultan Abdülhamid. Later, most of them had served Unionist governments or been members of the CUP. In the circumstances, it was the critics of the leadership within the party, and particularly of its decision to side

108 Dyer, 'The Turkish Armistice of 1918', p 150.
109 Martin Gilbert, *Sir Horace Rumbold: Portrait of a Diplomat 1869–1941* (Heinemann, London: 1973) p 249.
110 Dyer, 'The Turkish Armistice of 1918', p159.

with Germany in the war, who took over from the defeated Unionist triumvirate.

Peace negotiations

Talât was succeeded by a distinguished soldier, Ahmed İzzet Pasha, an outspoken opponent of the war policy of the triumvirate, who had nevertheless served with distinction as overall commander of the Caucasian front before the Russian Revolution. Ahmed İzzet was a bluff German-trained officer of Albanian origin, born in Macedonia. His long-standing association with the Germans showed in his moustache in the style of Kaiser Wilhelm II. More importantly, he was attached to the Ottoman dynasty with all the strength of the Albanian ideal of *besa* – the tradition of total loyal commitment to a patron. When an Albanian state emerged in 1913 from the Ottoman defeat in the Balkan wars, he had been offered the position of head of state as Prince of Albania. Ahmed İzzet refused, saying that it would be a step down for a servant of the Ottoman Sultan. It was, as the Turkish saying had it, 'to dismount a horse in order to ride a donkey'.

Ahmed İzzet's Cabinet included three prominent Unionist critics of the triumvirate: Cavid, who as Finance Minister had extracted every penny he could from Enver's German allies, Fethi (who later took the surname Okyar), an early political patron of Mustafa Kemal, and a naval officer, Rauf (later Orbay), who had risen to fame during the Balkan Wars as captain of the Ottoman cruiser *Hamidiye*, evading capture as it raided the coasts of the Balkan allies. While German influence was strong in the army, the Ottoman navy, which had had British advisers before the war, was traditionally pro-British, and Rauf felt, as it proved, an exaggerated confidence in British good intentions.

Mustafa Kemal, who was busy reorganising the remnants of Ottoman forces on the Syrian front, had sensed that a change of government was necessary to end the hostilities. Presuming on his friendship with the new Sultan Vahdettin, he advised him to appoint Ahmed İzzet Pasha Grand Vizier, and asked for himself the post of War Minister. The telegram was delayed, and Ahmed İzzet was appointed without the benefit of Mustafa Kemal's advice. As a professional soldier, the new Grand Vizier preferred to keep the post of War Minister for himself.

The first job of the new Ottoman government was to establish contact with the Allies. The abject condition of the country showed through the

high-flown Ottoman chancery rhetoric of the decree appointing Ahmed
İzzet to the post of Grand Vizier:

> Whereas it is our most particular wish that the effects produced by the
> present war, which has been waged with extreme violence for more
> than four years, on the general affairs of our dominions and their
> good order and discipline should be rectified, and that concord and
> general amity should be established among all classes of our people, it
> is our expectation that you apply your well-known zeal and devote the
> greatest care to the choice of powerful and efficient measures to obtain
> the means to bring to a successful conclusion the political initiatives
> we have undertaken in order to achieve these aims and, at the same
> time, to secure the supremacy of religious and civil law, the stability
> of safe and orderly government, to make perfect the condition of ease
> and well-being of our people, supplying them with the necessities of
> life without further delay and facilitating the satisfaction of general
> needs.[111]

In other words, the country is prey to anarchy and lawlessness, people
are at each other's throats, they are at their wits' end with hunger and
privation. Please do something about it quickly, and make sure that the
Allies respond to our political overtures.

At the beginning of October, the Sultan had sent a personal representative to Bern who arranged that the agent of an Armenian Ottoman
dignitary Boghos Nubar Pasha should communicate his peace terms
to the British minister in Switzerland, Sir Horace Rumbold. Vahdettin
proposed that the Arab provinces should become autonomous under his
suzerainty, that the Greek islands off Turkey's Aegean coast should be
returned to the Ottoman state along with Bulgarian gains in the Balkan
Wars, and that the British should help him destroy the CUP and should
maintain him on the throne. In exchange he offered an alliance with
Britain and reforms under British control.[112] In other words, if the British
made good the territorial losses the Ottoman Empire had suffered under
the rule of the Young Turks, he was prepared to place himself under

---

111 Mahmud Kemal İnal, *Osmanli Devrinde Son Sadriazamlar*, 2nd edition
(Istanbul MEB: 1965) p 2004.
112 Dyer, 'The Turkish Armistice of 1918', pp 153–4.

British protection. What Vahdettin did not realise was that while he was ready to trade the independence of his state for its nominal territorial integrity and his survival as Sultan, his subjects had other ideas. So too did the British, who were already in possession of the Ottomans' Arab provinces. Nubar Pasha, on whose good offices the Sultan relied, was soon afterwards to demand from the Allies a large slice of Ottoman territory for an independent Armenian state.

A few days later, the British received a similar offer from an independent-minded Unionist, Rahmi, who had run İzmir and the surrounding country as his personal fiefdom during the war, had protected the large community of Allied subjects who lived and traded there and had prevented the deportation of Armenians from the area. Rahmi had one additional request – that Britain should replace Germany as Turkey's paymaster by guaranteeing the Ottoman currency. Where the Sultan had used an Armenian, Rahmi had used a Greek as an intermediary.[113] Neither realised that the days of the multi-ethnic Ottoman state were numbered, and that the employment of local Christians to represent the Ottoman state could no longer placate eiither the Allies or the local Christian communities. Both these attempts to initiate peace talks failed.

Ahmed İzzet had better luck. This time the intermediary was the British General Sir Charles Townshend, who had surrendered to the Turks after a six-month siege at Kut al-Amara in Mesopotamia in the spring of 1916. While 70 per cent of the 3,000 British rank-and-file who surrendered at Kut had died in captivity – many during death marches through the desert, others due to appalling conditions in POW camps[114] – Townshend had been held in a comfortable villa on the island resort of Büyükada (Prinkipo), the largest of the Princes' Islands in the Sea of Marmara near Istanbul. He had even been invited to tea by Enver. When he heard that Ahmed İzzet was forming a new Cabinet, Townshend offered to transmit the Ottoman peace proposals to Admiral Sir Somerset Calthorpe, commander of the British Mediterranean Fleet, who had his headquarters on the Greek island of Lemnos in the Aegean.

On 16 October, the Ottoman Cabinet decided to seek a separate peace, after hearing a report on the military situation. 'We have six or seven

---

113 Dyer, 'The Turkish Armistice of 1918', pp 154–6.
114 A J Barker, *The Neglected War: Mesopotamia 1914–1918* (Faber and Faber, London: 1967) pp 266, 296. Of the original 9,300 Indian troops, 2,500 perished.

thousand men left on each front [Syria, Mesopotamia and Thrace],' the Ottoman General Staff told Ahmet İzzet's Cabinet. 'It's so bad you could invade the country with a handful of bandits.'[115] The delay in facing military facts had bred an exaggerated pessimism which was to weaken the hand of Ottoman negotiators. The following day, Ahmed İzzet received Townshend and accepted his offer to go to Lemnos. But, first of all, the composition of the Ottoman delegation and its instructions had to be decided. This did not prove easy. The Sultan, fearful and suspicious as ever, complicated matters.

On 23 October, Admiral Calthorpe informed the Ottoman government that he had been authorised to sign an armistice on behalf of the Allies. On hearing this, Ahmed İzzet sought the Sultan's approval for a delegation led by the Ottoman army commander in İzmir, the port from which the Ottoman emissaries would set off for Lemnos. The Sultan disagreed and asked that the chief of the delegation should be his brother-in-law, Damad Ferid Pasha. (*Damad* means son-in-law, and the title was conferred on Ferid when he became the second husband of Mediha, the daughter of Sultan Vahdettin's father, Abdülmecid I.) 'The man is mad,' objected Ahmet İzzet.[116] He was not the first to say so.

Ferid's highest job in the Ottoman civil service had been that of First Secretary at the Ottoman embassy in London. When in 1888 Mediha had asked the reigning Sultan Abdülhamid II (Vahdettin's elder brother) to send Ferid back to London, this time as ambassador, he had replied, 'Sister, the London embassy is not a school, it's an important embassy and the appointment should go to somebody who has experience and understanding of international politics.'[117] Later, when the CUP came to power, Ferid extolled it to the skies. But as he failed to win promotion, he had joined the opposition Liberty and Concord Party (known in the West as the Liberal Union). Here, too, he had been unlucky. When the CUP was briefly out of power at the beginning of the Balkan Wars, the Sultan had proposed that Ferid should head the delegation to the peace talks in London. Ferid had refused, saying that he could not sign away any part of Ottoman territory, as this would violate the Constitution. 'The man is mad', said the elderly Grand Vizier Kâmil Pasha, who

---

115 Dyer, 'The Turkish Armistice of 1918', p 161.
116 Dyer, 'The Turkish Armistice of 1918', p 166.
117 Mahmud Kemal İnal, *Osmanli Devrinde Son Sadriazamlar*, p 2034.

had known that territorial losses were inevitable. Ferid had thereafter twiddled his thumbs in his wife's mansion on the Bosphorus. Where in Britain politics often revolved round the country houses of the aristocracy, in the late Ottoman Empire political decisions were taken and plots hatched in *yalıs*, wooden seaside mansions of princes and pashas on the shores of the Bosphorus. In later years many of these *yalıs* were burned down. A few survive in the hands of business tycoons. Damad Ferid's (or rather his wife's) *yalı* now houses a restaurant patronised by university professors.

At the Sultan's insistence, Ahmed İzzet called on Damad Ferid and heard out his views on the armistice:

> As soon as I see the Admiral [Calthorpe], I shall propose an armistice treaty based on the territorial integrity of the [Ottoman] state. If the Admiral won't accept this, I will ask for a cruiser immediately and go straight to London. On arrival, I will have an audience with the King and say 'I was an old friend of your father's. I expect you to accept my wishes.' Having thus ensured that our proposals are accepted, I'll rescue the state from the catastrophe into which the Unionists have plunged it.

However, he could not leave immediately as he had to pack his clothes. When he was ready, he would leave on the Sultan's yacht, taking with him the secretary of the Greek Patriarch.[118] A year later, the Patriarch was to sever all relations with the Ottoman state and demand that the Ottoman capital should come under Greek rule.

The above nonsense confirmed Ahmed İzzet's original estimate of Damad Ferid's capacity. Loyal to the Sultan as he was, Ahmed İzzet insisted that the Cabinet should be free to choose its own chief negotiator. Sultan Vahdettin gave way with bad grace, but insisted that the instructions to the Ottoman delegates should specify that 'the rights of the Sultanate, the Caliphate and of the Ottoman dynasty should be protected',[119] and that the autonomy to be given to some provinces should be administrative and not political. Ahmed İzzet objected that these were matters to be settled in the peace treaty and not in an armistice agreement. Once again

---

118 Dyer, 'The Turkish Armistice of 1918', pp 166–7.
119 Dyer, 'The Turkish Armistice of 1918', p 167.

the Sultan gave way, but asked that the armistice should at least ensure the safe return of an Ottoman prince who was cut off in Libya.

Having warded off – for a short period of time, as it proved – the Sultan's interference, Ahmed İzzet's Cabinet chose Rauf, the patriotic naval officer, as chief negotiator. He was told that he could agree to the opening of the Straits and to the reduction in size of the Ottoman army to peacetime strength. However, no Greek warships should be allowed through the Straits, which would be defended by the Ottoman army. British control officers would be allowed until the conclusion of peace, but no Allied forces should land anywhere in the territories that the Ottomans still controlled, and there should be no interference in the Ottoman administration. Any conditions incompatible with the honour of the Ottoman state should be rejected. German and Austro-Hungarian troops and officials should be given at least two months to leave the country, but civilians from these countries should be allowed to stay on, if they wished, lest Germany and Austria-Hungary decide to retaliate by expelling from their territories Ottoman students, whose number was estimated at 15–20,000.[120]

The insistence on decent treatment of the Ottomans' German and Austrian allies shows that, in spite of wartime friction between the Turks and their German advisers, there was little animosity against them. On the military level, the alliance had worked well. True, the importance of German commanders in the Ottoman war effort was often exaggerated in Britain and France. Their most important help had been in communications, staff work and, of course, supplies. The Germans had worked hard to maintain and extend Ottoman railways; the Austro-Hungarians had provided a motor transport unit on the Caucasian front.[121] In Turkish popular tradition, the Germans stood for precision in everything.

'How do you make a good pilaff?' a German officer asks a Turkish army cook in a well known joke. 'You need enough rice, enough fat, enough water, and cook the rice long enough' the cook replies. But the German wants precise information. 'What do you mean by enough?' he asks. 'It's obvious, Sir,' says the cook, 'enough to make a good pilaff.'

The Germans had their own stories of the happy-go-lucky attitude

---

120 Dyer, 'The Turkish Armistice of 1918', pp 168–9.
121 Edward Erickson, *Ordered to Die: A History of the Ottoman Army in the First World War* (Greenwood, Westport, Conn: 2001) pp 231–5.

of Ottoman officers. One day, a German officer was horrified to see that his Ottoman companions were using a map of Gallipoli while fighting the British in Palestine. 'It's the wrong map,' he cried. 'What do you mean by wrong map?' replied the Ottoman. 'It served us well enough all through the campaign in Galicia.' Later these good-natured stories gave way to angrier reminiscences, and today many Turks will tell you that in the First World War, the Germans evacuated their wounded by rail, but left the Turks to die in the desert. This is true, but there were many more Turks than Germans, and the Germans fought in a foreign country while the Turks were, at least theoretically, at home among the Arabs.

The Germans left the Ottoman Empire in good time, but the other conditions on which the Ottoman armistice negotiators were to insist were sacrificed. Rauf and his fellow delegates were acutely aware of the weakness of the Ottoman state and of its urgent need for peace. They did not realise that, late as it was to conclude a separate peace under favourable conditions, there was still room for bargaining. Germany had not yet surrendered and the Allies wanted above all to send their navies through the Turkish Straits in order to cut off German troops in south-eastern Europe and the Caucasus. What is more, they had conflicting ambitions in the Near East. The instructions communicated to Admiral Calthorpe after difficult consultations in London and Paris defined a first bargaining position, but the admiral was told that he could make concessions, provided the Straits were opened, its fortifications placed under Allied control, the Germans expelled and the Ottoman army demobilised. This Ahmed İzzet's government was, in any case, prepared to concede. But it did not have to agree to peace at any price. There was no domestic pressure for unconditional surrender. In spite of widespread hardships, there were no military mutinies or civil disturbances in the areas under Ottoman control. The Istanbul government did not fear the disaffection of the Sultan's Muslim subjects. What terrified it was the prospect of a rising by local Christians, above all by the numerous Greeks in the capital.

In Turkish eyes, Greece was a Johnny-come-lately in the ranks of the Allies. Greece was still neutral when Allied troops under French command landed in Salonica in October 1916. It was under the protection of the Allies that the Greek Prime Minister Eleftherios Venizelos had formed a provisional government in the city and declared war on Bulgaria and the Central Powers. Greek troops thereafter fought under French command against the Bulgarians and Germans on the Macedonian front, and the Allies made use of Greek territory to prosecute the war with the Ottoman state. But there had been no fighting between Greek and Ottoman troops. Greece was not consulted when Admiral Calthorpe sat down to negotiate an armistice with the Ottoman delegation. However, the Ottoman government was well aware that Greek nationalists, who had found a champion in Venizelos, coveted Constantinople (Istanbul) as well as Smyrna (İzmir) and the surrounding area. The Turks felt that they had been defeated by the British and not by the Greeks, and resented the idea that the latter should figure among the victorious Allies, particularly in the streets of the imperial capital.

Negotiations between Admiral Calthorpe and Rauf opened on 27 October on board HMS *Agamemnon*, which was anchored in Moudros Bay (Mondros in Turkish), a natural deep-water harbour on the island of Lemnos. The delegations met in the captain's large day cabin, comfortably furnished with Persian rugs, which opened on to a pleasant stern walk. Both sides behaved with impeccable good manners. Calthorpe made some concessions to the Turks. But these concerned conditions on which he had not been instructed to insist. Only one concession was to prove important. Where the Turks had originally been asked to withdraw all their troops from former Tsarist territory in the Caucasus (and northwest Persia, whose neutrality had been violated by both sides during the war), the final text stipulated that 'the remainder [of the Ottoman troops] [is] to be evacuated if requested by the Allies after they have studied the situation'. The Ottoman troops sent by Enver to the Caucasus and Persia had not affected the course of the war. But these fresh divisions, well-armed with weapons from Tsarist arsenals or handed over by the Germans, were to become the nucleus of the Turkish national army when the War of Independence started a year later. A condition in the armistice calling for consultations with the Turkish government to determine the strength and disposition of Ottoman troops which were to maintain internal order after the demobilisation of the bulk of the Ottoman army, allowed Turkish nationalists to keep this military nucleus in order to avert the final catastrophe – the occupation and partition of the whole of Turkey.

The way had been opened for this by the insertion into the text of the armistice of Article 7 which read: 'The Allies have the right to occupy any strategic points in the event of a situation arising which threatens

Allied security.' The condition that a threat should arise to justify occupation was included as a concession to the Turks. But it was of no practical effect, since it was the Allies who would decide whether they were threatened. Article 7 meant that the Allies could occupy any part or the whole of Turkey if they were so minded. Rauf had stood out against this clause, but he finally gave way when Calthorpe threatened to break off negotiations. The armistice agreement was signed late in the evening of 30 October.

Immediately after the signing, Calthorpe gave a letter to Rauf promising that only British and French troops would be used to occupy the Straits and that a small number of Turkish soldiers would be allowed to remain when the forts were occupied. This promise was kept. Calthorpe said also that he had passed on the Turkish requests that no Greek warships should sail to Istanbul or İzmir, and that Istanbul should not be occupied unless the Turkish government failed to maintain order there. The request was indeed passed on – but as the Turks were to discover before long, the Allies turned a deaf ear to it.

Calthorpe described the final ceremony in a letter to his wife:

> I had champagne on ice in readiness as I knew that all was going to be well and there was hand-shaking, toasting and polite speeches. Raouf Bey made me a very graceful little speech thanking me for my hospitality and consideration to him as a technical enemy, and he delighted me, and I am sure you, by saying that our twins [whose photograph decorated the cabin] had also taken an important part in this historic event. He said that their cheery smiling faces had been a source of inspiration and encouragement to him in his most difficult and anxious hours. He had often come in and looked at them and they had told him what to do for the cause of humanity. Wasn't that nice![122]

Rauf returned to Istanbul on 1 November, convinced that he had won the confidence of the British and had secured the best possible terms. 'Our country's rights and the future of the Sultanate have been wholly saved as a result of the armistice we have concluded,' he told journalists, adding:

---

122 Dyer, 'The Turkish Armistice of 1918', pp 336–41.

First, I discovered that the British are not aiming at the destruction
of the Turkish nation. Second, I saw that our country, contrary to
what was expected, will not be occupied. I assure you that not a single
enemy soldier will disembark in Istanbul … Yes, the armistice we have
concluded is beyond our hopes.[123]

The Grand Vizier, Ahmed İzzet, was pleased with what Rauf had
achieved. Rauf's main concern now was to avoid inter-communal clashes,
which would give the Allies grounds for occupying Ottoman territory.
He insisted, therefore, that irresponsible statements, likely to increase
tension between Muslims and non-Muslims, and in particular between
Turks and Greeks, should be avoided. One such statement was attributed
to Damad Ferid Pasha, who was reported to have said that Ahmed İzzet's
government was plotting to massacre Greeks in Istanbul. Damad Ferid
was clearly peeved at his exclusion from the armistice negotiations, but
his behaviour was symptomatic of the antagonisms which were breaking
out within the Ottoman ruling class. The CUP had made many enemies
during its six years in power. There were dissensions within its ranks
as well as between it and the ramshackle opposition represented by the
Liberal Union, which, disastrously for the fate of the monarchy, Sultan
Vahdettin supported.

Immediately on his return, Rauf went to the palace to report on the
results of his mission. But Vahdettin pleaded tiredness and said that he
would receive him a few days later. When the Sultan finally granted an
audience, Rauf took the opportunity to complain about Damad Ferid's
behaviour. 'I love Ferid Pasha as a good husband to my sister,' Vahdettin replied deceptively, 'but I do not share his views. I am particularly
opposed to his political opinions. That's why we disagree strongly.' Then
he blurted out: 'There is a nation out there, which is like a flock of sheep.
It needs a shepherd to look after it. I am that shepherd.'[124]

Events were to show that no one was less qualified to be a shepherd,
and that the Sultan shared the illusion of Damad Ferid and the publicists
of the Liberal Union that the Allies would allow the Ottoman state to
survive and keep its territory if only it made friends with the non-Muslim

123 Dyer, 'The Turkish Armistice of 1918', p 337.
124 Cemal Kutay, *Osmanlidan Cumhuriyete: Yüzyılımızda bir İnsanımız Hüseyin
Rauf Orbay (1881–1964)* Vol 3 (Kazanci, Isttanbul: 1992) p 174.

communities and made room for foreign business, schools and mission-aries. This illusion was fed by a nostalgia for the times of Abdülhamid II, when foreigners and local Christians, including the bulk of the Armeni-ans, prospered. A return to the golden age of Abdülhamid, coupled with the abandonment of the late monarch's pan-Islamism which had threat-ened Britain and France, was the bait that Vahdettin and the Liberal Union offered the Allies. But the Allies were not tempted.

Departure of the Young Turks

Before this became clear, the Istanbul press, which had been freed from censorship in June 1918, directed its anger at the CUP, including critics of the triumvirate who were now members of the Cabinet. The attacks redoubled when the CUP leadership – Enver, Cemal, Talât and a handful of close associates, including the former police chief in the capital – slipped out of Istanbul in the night of 1/2 November on board a German U-boat.[125] The following day they arrived in German-occupied Crimea. None of them was to see Turkey again.

In Istanbul, Ahmed İzzet's Cabinet was accused by the opposition of collusion in the flight or, at least, incompetence in failing to prevent it. This gave the Sultan the opportunity to press for the exclusion from the government of former members of the CUP. Rather than comply with what he saw as an abuse of the sovereign's prerogative, Ahmed İzzet submitted his resignation on 11 November 1918 after less than a month in office.

He was succeeded by an even older man, Ahmed Tevfik Pasha, who had been the last Grand Vizier of Sultan Abdülhamid. As he saw mon-archies tumble first in Russia, then in Austria-Hungary and Germany, Vahdettin feared betrayal by his own ministers. In the case of Ahmed Tevfik, he thought that he could count, at least, on family loyalty, as the new Grand Vizier's son was courting and was soon to marry Vahdet-tin's daughter. Thus with a fearful and suspicious Sultan on the throne, yesterday's men – Enver, Cemal and Talât – were replaced by the men of the day before yesterday. It was in their company that Sultan Vahdettin would preside over the demise of the Ottoman Empire. But if the historic

---

125 According to some reports they boarded a torpedo-boat the Germans had captured from the Russians. The date of their flight is given as 8/9 November in some sources. See Andrew Mango, *Atatürk*, p 190, n 21.

polity of the Ottoman Empire had been defeated, the nature of what would replace it at the hands of the victorious British remained to be seen. For the moment, however, Britain seemed to be the arbiter of the Middle East.

3

Arabs and Zionists in Paris

The formal ending of hostilities between the British and Ottoman empires on 31 October 1918 did not bring peace to the Middle East for very long. To the observer, Britain's power seemed paramount, its fleet anchored in the Bosphorus dominating the Turkish capital with its guns, and its victorious forces throughout the region, occupying such historic cities as Jerusalem, Baghdad, Karbala and Damascus. Of Britain's former rivals, Austria-Hungary had dissolved, Russia was in the grip of revolution and civil war, while Germany was defeated. Britain's allies, France, Italy and Greece, while all harbouring ambitions of their own at the expense of the defeated Ottoman Empire, had not played much of a part in its defeat, certainly not compared with the million-strong army Britain had mustered from across its empire. A new area of British imperial endeavour seemed to be opening up. The most powerful man in the Middle East was now Sir Edmund Allenby, judged one of the war's most successful British commanders, in a not exactly overcrowded field. In 1919, he was awarded his Field Marshal's baton, became Viscount Allenby of Megiddo and Felixstowe, and was appointed High Commissioner in Egypt and the Sudan, the former having been declared a British protectorate on the outbreak of war. Behind the impressive façade of British power lay other realities, however.

In international affairs, Britain's clear priority was the peace settlement with Germany, not the future of the Middle East. The British were also preoccupied with the situation in Russia, not least since the disruption caused by the war had brought industrial unrest at home, with fears for the spread of revolutionary ideas. Glasgow was a particular concern. Disturbances in India were to culminate in the Jallianwala Bagh tragedy at Amritsar on 13 April 1919. The murder of two unarmed members of the Royal Irish Constabulary in County Tipperary in January 1919 signalled the start of Ireland's war for independence. In Egypt, too, Allenby was soon confronted by disturbances demanding freedom from British rule. His problems were made no easier by the fact that his troops were understandably anxious to go home after long years of service and separation.[1] More important than all of these disturbing developments was the sober fact that Britain would now have to implement the web of agreements and promises entered into in the course of the war. High expectations had been raised amongst Arabs and Jews, who had thoughts of their own as to how these might be realised as the war was ending. Even in defeat, some Turks were also beginning to glimpse a way forward from the ruins of the Ottoman Empire, Mustafa Kemal not the least of them. It was soon all too apparent that the Middle East was far from being an open book on which the British, or the French, Italians or Greeks for that matter, could write their imperial decrees. Things had moved on from 1914, as the victors were soon to learn.

The Zionist Commission

Even before the war's end, the Zionists had been keen to explore on the ground the possibilities opened up by the Balfour Declaration. Their chance to do so came in December 1917 when the British government suggested that a Zionist Commission should go to Palestine. Weizmann was the obvious choice as chairman. The commission's purpose was to establish a link between the Jews and the British military authorities, but it was also to co-ordinate relief for the Jewish population, help with the rebuilding of Jewish institutions, much needed as a result of the war, and to make political connections with the Arabs. Its terms of reference were later expanded to include Weizmann's favourite project of a Jewish university. Although it was intended that the commission's membership should include Jews from the principal Allied countries, the situation in Russia precluded this, and the Americans declined to take part since they were not at war with Turkey. The Italian member

---

1   Hughes (ed), *Allenby in Palestine*, pp 13–14.

was Angelo Levi-Bianchini, a naval officer, and the French appointed the distinguished scholar Sylvain Levi, Professor of Sanskrit at the elite College de France, who, however, was not a Zionist. Weizmann's other colleagues were the veteran English Zionist Joseph Cowen, Dr David Eder, a former student of Sigmund Freud, and Leon Simon, a distinguished civil servant, while his old friend Ormsby-Gore acted as his liaison officer. This was also the opportunity for Weizmann to explore relations with the Palestinian Arabs, an ambition he had been harbouring for at least a year.[2]

Weizmann left for the Middle East in early March 1918, having first been received in audience by King George V, a mark of how far he had come since 1914. Given wartime conditions, it was a far from easy journey, and it was the end of the month before he arrived in Cairo *en route* to Palestine. His first contact with the High Commissioner in Egypt, Sir Reginald Wingate, and Clayton, now Chief Political Officer to Allenby's army, seemed positive enough, though the question of Arab attitudes to possible Zionist intentions was raised.[3] Weizmann finally arrived at Tel Aviv on 4 April, and was immediately welcomed by Allenby at his nearby headquarters. While Allenby impressed him, Weizmann quickly concluded that the military authorities had no real grasp of the Balfour Declaration, and that they were very conscious of the position of the Arabs.[4] With his army planning its next advance, it was obvious that Allenby would not want a restive Palestine at his back, and Weizmann was alive to that. Disquieting signs were there, as he soon found out. On 11 April, Storrs, now Military Governor of Jerusalem, attended a function in the city at which speakers asserted Palestine's Arab identity. Storrs later recalled the Arab reaction to the Balfour Declaration, which was that they had been relegated to the position of 'non-Jewish communities' and that there was in it no reference to their political rights.[5]

2 Weizmann to Jacob de Haas, New York, (12) December 1917; Weizmann to Sir Mark Sykes, London, 16 January 1918, *LPCW*, Vol VIII, 23, 69, pp 20–1, 62–3; Weizmann, *Trial and Error*, pp 266–7; Stein, *The Balfour Declaration*, p 622.
3 Weizmann to Vera Weizmann, London, 24–6 March 1918, *LPCW*, Vol VIII, 138, pp 106–9.
4 Weizmann to Vera Weizmann, London, 6 April 1918, *LPCW*, Vol VIII, 151, pp 118–20.
5 Weizmann to William G A Ormsby-Gore, Tel Aviv, 16 April 1918, *LPCW*, Vol VIII, 161, pp 128–30; Storrs, *Orientations*, p 366.

Weizmann became quickly aware of the political temper of the Palestinian Arabs, informing Ormsby-Gore on 16 April that they were not disposed to accept what the Zionists were saying.[6] Two days later, he wrote home, giving Vera his thoughts on what he had seen. Jerusalem had impressed him no better than it had on first acquaintance. Once again, he lamented its lack of Jewish institutions and the nature of its Jewish inhabitants. The Jewish colonies elsewhere, on the other hand, excited his keen admiration, despite the effects of over three years of war. What was obviously giving him real cause for concern was the partiality of the British military for the Arabs. He confided in Brandeis that the Arabs believed it was the British government's intention to set up a Jewish government and expel them, and that, as a result, they were highly suspicious of the commission.[7] With his pessimistic view of Palestinian Arab attitudes now uppermost in his mind, Weizmann responded positively to a suggestion from Clayton that he should meet Feisal, Britain's principal Arab ally.

The journey to the camp of Feisal's Arab army was something of an adventure, in the course of which Ormsby-Gore came down with dysentery. Weizmann was able to approach close to the Turkish lines, watch Feisal's army at work, and witness T E Lawrence's preparations for his raids on the Hejaz railway. The meeting with Feisal went well. Weizmann explained the nature of the Zionist Commission, said that it wished to allay the fears of the Arabs, and hoped for Feisal's support. Feisal's answers seemed to indicate that he looked favourably on what he had heard, and Weizmann made his way back to Palestine convinced that he had enlisted the sympathy of the real leader of Arab nationalism. He wrote to Vera that Feisal held no high opinion of the Arabs of Palestine.[8] There is no doubt that Weizmann came away from this meeting with the belief that here, at last, was the Arab leader with whom he could work. Subsequent events were to prove him both right and wrong. The fact

---

6 Weizmann to William G A Ormsby-Gore, 16 April 1918, *LPCW*, Vol VIII, 161, pp 128–30.
7 Weizmann to Vera Weizmann, London, 18 April 1918; Weizmann to Louis D Brandeis, Washington, 25 April 1918: *LPCW*, Vol VIII, 163, 175, pp 131–3, 158–67.
8 Weizmann to Vera Weizmann, London, 17 June 1918; Weizmann to Louis D Brandeis, Washington, 23 June 1918: *LPCW*, Vol VIII, 213, 215, pp 209–11, 212–3; Weizmann, *Trial and Error,* pp 290–5.

that he had engaged so positively with Feisal led to the conclusion of the Feisal-Weizmann Agreement of January 1919, which strengthened his hand at the Peace Conference. But events were to show that the leadership of the Arab national movement, and particularly of the Palestinian Arabs, did not lie with Feisal, and that Weizmann was building too many hopes on their relationship. In a letter to Balfour on 17 July, he enthusiastically set out the prospects should Feisal enter Damascus, dismissing the Arabs of Palestine as of merely local significance.[9] Before leaving Palestine, Weizmann was to see the realisation of a project which he had embraced and encouraged for many years. On 24 July, in a ceremony attended by Allenby, Weizmann spoke at the laying of the foundation stone of the future Hebrew University on Mount Scopus.[10]

The Hashemites, the Balfour Declaration and the post-war settlement

Dismissing as he did any potential for reaching an accommodation with the Arabs of Palestine, Weizmann set great store by his meeting with Feisal. There is little evidence, however, that Feisal or the Hashemites endorsed or even envisaged any kind of a Jewish state in Palestine. The public announcement of the Balfour Declaration had brought no response from Sherif Hussein. While many Syrian notables loudly complained about the Declaration, Hussein remained conspicuously silent. Indeed, he ordered his sons to calm the apprehensions of their followers about British intentions.[11] When David Hogarth, the head of the Arab Bureau, called on the king on 4 January 1918, Kedourie reports that Hussein 'enthusiastically assented' to Zionist settlement in Palestine and was '[unconcerned] over the Balfour Declaration and Zionist aims'.[12] This seems curious: Hussein had continued to argue that Palestine was part of the area to be made independent. Moreover, Hogarth's mission to Hussein appears to have deliberately downplayed the Declaration and emphasised that the commitments that the British had made to Zionism

---

9 Weizmann to Arthur J Balfour, London, 17 July 1918, *LPCW*, Vol VIII, 232, pp 228–32; Weizmann, *Trial and Error*, pp 290–5.

10 Weizmann to Vera Weizmann, 27 July 1918, *LPCW*, Vol VIII, 236, 237–40; Weizmann, *Trial and Error*, pp 295–7.

11 Antonius, *The Arab Awakening*, p 269.

12 Kedourie, *In the Anglo-Arab Labyrinth*, pp 190–1.

had to be 'compatible with the freedom of the existing [Arab] population both economic and political...'.[13] It can be argued that Hussein by no means endorsed the creation of a Jewish state or even an autonomous homeland for the Jews. However, Hussein appears to have been blind to the consequences of the Balfour Declaration.

Hussein also appears to have been ignorant, or pretended to be so, of the likely post-war settlement, which would see a considerable role for France in the administration of Syria. Mark Sykes, accompanied by Picot, had visited Hussein in April 1917 and given some details of their Agreement. It is a matter of dispute as to how much information was given to him.[14] If Hussein had been in any doubt as to what it contained, the *Manchester Guardian* had published it in full on 26 and 28 November 1917 following its leaking by the new Bolshevik government in Russia, and this had been circulated by Cemal, the Turkish Governor of Syria. Despite all this evidence, Hussein remained in denial. Wingate wrote that it is 'evident that King Hussein has in no degree abated his original pretensions concerning Syria and apparently still nourishes illusion that through the good offices of His Majesty's Government he may be installed, at any rate nominally, as overlord of [a] greater part of the country'. Wingate tellingly argued against disabusing Hussein of this notion as he might abdicate.[15]

Hussein appears to have believed that once the war ended in the Middle East, traditional Anglo-French rivalry would reassert itself and the British would take the side of the Arabs. Lawrence had convinced Feisal:

> that his escape was to help the British so much that after the peace they would not be able, for shame, to shoot him down in its fulfillment: while if the Arabs did as I intended, there would no one-sided talk of shooting. I begged him to trust not in our promises, like his father, but in his own strong performance.[16]

13 Friedman, *The Question of Palestine 1914–1918*, p 328.

14 Fromkin, *A Peace to End All Peace*, pp 288–9.

15 Teitelbaum, 'Sherif Husayn ibn Ali and the Hashemite vision of the post-Ottoman order', p 109.

16 Lawrence, *Seven Pillars of Wisdom*, p 551.

In other words, it was vital for Feisal to make significant military progress to ensure the Arab case was heard at the war's conclusion. As it was, Cemal had attempted to break the Anglo-Hashemite alliance by using the Sykes-Picot Agreement as evidence of British perfidy. Feisal had received communications from Cemal, and Lawrence had agreed that he should respond. Lawrence was aware that Britain was in secret negotiations with conservative elements in the Turkish leadership and did not see why Feisal should not do likewise. Also Lawrence appears to have allowed the correspondence because it was better that it happened with his knowledge than in secret.

Feisal continued to be open about corresponding with Cemal, and in the summer of 1918 Cemal's proposals grew more serious. He had been willing to concede independence to Arabia and autonomy to Syria in return for the Arabs changing sides. Lawrence had been particularly alarmed by correspondence in June 1918, which outlined Feisal's conditions for a rapprochement with the Turks, which included handing over Amman as well as the Hejaz to Hussein.[17] Lawrence, aware of all this, sent a warning telegram to Hussein, who ordered the ending of the correspondence.

The Occupation

The British government gave Allenby instructions to treat, so far as military exigencies permitted, the territories captured by the Arabs as Allied 'territory enjoying the status of an independent state (or confederation of States) of friendly Arabs … and not as enemy provinces in temporary military occupation …'.[18] When Allenby met with Feisal in Damascus in October 1918, it was explained that while Feisal was to have the administration of Syria, it was to be a French protectorate. Also the coastal areas from Palestine to the Gulf of Alexandretta were to be under direct French rule. Feisal objected strongly. He did not want to be protected or advised by the French. Lawrence had been told that Sykes-Picot was dead in the water; now it appeared to be alive and well.[19]

Meanwhile, the French had begun to arrive in the Levant. However, French numbers were puny in comparison with the British – only a few

---

17 Wilson, *Lawrence of Arabia*, pp 469–70, 511–12.
18 Wilson, *Lawrence of Arabia*, p 566.
19 See Wilson, *Lawrence of Arabia*, pp 566–8.

thousand soldiers against nearly a million British and imperial troops. It was Britannia's writ that ran through the Middle East. Lloyd George was aware of this. He informed the War Cabinet in October 1918 that the Sykes-Picot Agreement was outdated in the new circumstances of an overwhelming British contribution to the conquest of the Middle East.[20] France's influence in the Middle East was based solely on British sufferance. The British conquest of the Levant and the Balfour Declaration had more or less ensured that French aspirations in Palestine were not going to be met. Indeed by the summer of 1918, the French Foreign Office and at least some colonial opinion was of the view that Palestine was lost and the French would have to seek compensation elsewhere. There was also, for annexationists in both France and Britain, the ominous new diplomatic language of President Wilson. This talk of self-determination and open diplomacy made the implementation of secret deals in the Middle East immensely more complex.

As a result, Feisal was initially in a strong position in Syria. On 30 September 1918, the Allies had created a series of zones in occupied Turkish territory. These were: Occupied Enemy Territory Administration South, made up of Palestine, which the British controlled; Occupied Enemy Territory West, encompassing the coastal littoral of Syria and Lebanon, which French forces were to administer; and Occupied Enemy Territory East, made up of the interior of Syria, which Feisal's Arabs were allowed to control jointly with British forces.[21] In overarching, virtually dictatorial, control of all three sectors was General Allenby. In practice, as he controlled the military forces, the French or Feisal could do little of significance without his agreement. Allenby, though, was extremely concerned about the potential for trouble from the competing ambitions of the Arabs and the French. He confided in a letter to the new Chief of the Imperial General Staff, General Sir Henry Wilson, that he believed that only if the French exercised considerable tact would there be any prospect of placating Arab opinion. He foresaw that politics in the occupied territories, especially in Palestine and Syria, would be difficult because of the competing claims of the Jews, Arabs, the European powers and other

---

20 War Cabinet Meeting, 3 October 1918, UK CAB 23181482, The National Archives, Kew, London, (hereafter TNA).
21 Fromkin, *A Peace to End All Peace*, pp 338–9.

minorities.[22] Attached to this letter was a memorandum from Hogarth of the Arab Bureau. While Hogarth claimed to be happy to leave Syria to the French, he warned that Arab opinion believed that this was incompatible with political independence and that Britain would be accused of having tricked the Arabs into betraying Islam (i.e. the Caliph, the Sultan of Turkey). Britain would also be open to charges of hypocrisy in its repeated declaration of self-determination for small nations.[23]

The first crisis soon arose. Arab forces dashed from Damascus to Beirut and the other coastal towns as Turkish resistance collapsed in early October. An Arab government was proclaimed in these regions. The French, who had been allocated Lebanon as recently as 30 September 1918, were furious. This, in their mind, was a breach of the wartime agreements. It fuelled suspicions of Feisal and the British. Allenby was forced to accelerate the advance of his troops towards Beirut, as it became increasingly clear that there might be a Franco-Arab clash. He attempted to get Feisal to withdraw. Feisal warned that he might be forced to abdicate if he did not get assurances that the withdrawal would be only temporary and did not imply any abdication of Arab or Hashemite rights in Lebanon. He was reassured that the divvying up of the occupation areas was a temporary solution until the Peace Conference had made its decision. This allowed Feisal to give way to the French and let them take over Beirut and the other coastal towns.[24]

Feisal's problems were not simply confined to the Great Powers. The Syria and Lebanon that he occupied had suffered from widespread famine in the previous two years of war. Eyewitnesses spoke of emaciated, hungry children in Beirut 'dying in the gutters'.[25] Influential Damascenes remained suspicious and resentful of the imposition of Feisal upon them by force of arms. The large Christian minorities in both Lebanon and Syria viewed the Hashemites with distaste. An American report on Syria concluded that the country was deeply divided between

22 See John Fisher, 'Syria and Mesopotamia in British Middle Eastern Policy in 1919', *Middle Eastern Studies*, Vol 34, No 2 (Apr 1998) p 130.

23 Fisher, 'Syria and Mesopotamia in British Middle Eastern Policy in 1919', p 131.

24 Meir Zamir, 'Faisal and the Lebanese Question, 1918–20', *Middle Eastern Studies*, Vol 27, No 3 (Jul 1991) pp 404–26.

25 Zeine N Zeine, *The Struggle for Arab Independence: Western Diplomacy and the Rise and Fall of Faisal's Kingdom in Syria* (Khayats, Beirut: 1960) p 33.

those who were desirous of immediate annexation by France and those, mainly Muslim, who believed Arabs could rapidly evolve politically and did not require French tutelage. This last group could be driven into the arms of the Turks if the French were not careful.[26] Feisal and his followers attempted to win hearts and minds in the countryside by restarting Ottoman welfare schemes. They also invested some of their British subsidy in buying off Syrian notables. In spite of this, Feisal's authority in Syria was limited.[27]

The British did not ease Feisal's problems by asking him to remain in a military role rather than becoming involved in local politics, and making a Syrian political leader, Ali Riza Pasha, governor of all the occupied territories. Independent-spirited and with no loyalty to Britain, France or Feisal, Riza Pasha began to encroach on French-occupied areas in Lebanon. Feisal, knowing this was popular with the Syrian population, could not object. However, it significantly impacted on his own ability to get on with the French. The British realised their mistake and removed Riza Pasha at the end of October and transferred his powers to Feisal. However, the Emir remained 'largely a figurehead, which nationalist organisations manipulated for their own purposes'.[28] Indeed, they tended to limit his room for compromise. Feisal was also overburdened with responsibility. He not only had to try to keep control in Syria, he was also to represent the Arabs at the Peace Conference. He would spend a considerable amount of 1919 in Europe. His protégés in Syria, seemingly with little awareness of the political realities, undermined him by seeking political advances far too quickly.

The British and the French continued to appease Arab opinion in the last couple of months of 1918. Perhaps motivated by the continuing fallout from the revelation of the Sykes-Picot Agreement, the disquiet in the Arab world about the Balfour Declaration and the need to impress the Americans that they were committed to the new diplomacy of self-determination, two declarations were issued to the Arabs in 1918. The first was the Declaration to the Seven. The Seven were a small committee

---

26 Zeine, *The Struggle for Arab Independence*, pp 213–14.
27 James L Gelvin, *Divided Loyalties: Nationalism and Mass Politics in Syria at the Close of Empire* (University of California Press, Berkeley: 1998) p 13.
28 M S Anderson, *The Eastern Question, 1774–1923* (Macmillan, London: 1966) p 378.

of Syrian nationalists with whom the British had been in contact. Issued by Mark Sykes with official British government approval in mid-1918, the Declaration reiterated the recognition of Arab independence in the Arabian Peninsula. Sykes felt he could go no further without French agreement.[29] After discussions between London and Paris, a new Anglo-French Declaration was issued on 9 November 1918. It explicitly committed the British and French to 'the complete and definite emancipation of the peoples so long oppressed by the Turks and the establishment of national governments and administrations deriving their authority from the initiative and free choice of the indigenous populations'.[30] It carefully avoided the use of words like independence. As one commentator has put it, the declaration did not contradict the Sykes-Picot Agreement, 'it only concealed its most crucial details'.[31] Indeed, the Declaration was for British ministers not a conversion to the principle of national self-determination but a hard-headed decision to use this new Wilsonian language of diplomacy for traditional balance-of-power ends. In this case it would be used to weaken the French case for territory in the Middle East.[32] The Arab cause, therefore, appeared to be in a very strong position on the eve of Feisal's departure for the Peace Conference. When these promises turned out to be unfulfilled, the Arabs felt an understandable sense of bewilderment and betrayal.

Feisal leaves for Europe

Feisal realised that he was unlikely to gain the loyalty of the Christians of Syria and Lebanon if he associated the Hashemites and the Arab cause too closely with Islam. Therefore, on 11 November 1918, the day of the Armistice in Europe, he spoke to a large crowd in Aleppo, denouncing the rule of the Ottomans. He made it clear that he realised that the loyalty of the Revolt he led depended on it not being motivated by personal or familial aggrandisement and that he was not a tool of the

29 Fromkin, *A Peace to End All Peace*, p 341.

30 Cited in 'Report of a Committee Set Up to Consider Certain Correspondence between Sir Henry McMahon and the Sherif of Mecca in 1915 and 1916', 1939, Cmd 5974, pp 50–1.

31 Jukka Nevakivi, *Britain, France, and the Arab Middle East, 1914–1920* (Athlone Press, London: 1969) p 82.

32 John Darwin, *Britain, Egypt and the Middle East: Imperial Policy in the Aftermath of War, 1918–1922* (Macmillan, London: 1981) p 155.

Western Powers. Pointing to the Anglo-French Declaration, he noted that independence would come if the Arabs organised orderly and stable government. The most important emphasis of the speech was his declaration that he was an Arab before anything else. He decried religious sectarianism and declared all religions equal before the law. In the ten days that followed, Feisal toured Syria and Lebanon. He generally received a warm welcome, but in Beirut, with its large Christian population, it was mainly Muslims who welcomed him with enthusiasm, suggesting problems ahead.[33]

On 21 November 1918, Feisal left for Europe on a British warship. The British government, on the advice of Lawrence, had been convinced that it was in Britain's interests to invite him to the Peace Conference.[34] Feisal would make the Arab case for self-determination and the cause would have a chance of attracting American support. King Hussein had agreed that Feisal would act as his plenipotentiary at the Peace Conference. Feisal was accompanied by a small delegation of Arabs, including Nuri al-Said, an Arab nationalist officer in the Ottoman army who had joined the Arab Revolt in 1916, and had become Feisal's chief-of-staff. Lawrence also acted as Feisal's chief adviser.

The French were unhappy with Britain's decision to invite Feisal to the Peace Conference. They knew that Feisal coveted all of Syria and were therefore anxious to exclude him. They also knew that Feisal might prove to be an attractive figure to the Americans and their campaign for national self-determination. After their attempt to prevent Feisal coming failed, they tried appeasement. On his arrival in Marseilles, he was decorated with the Croix de La Legion d'Honneur prior to going on a tour of the recent battlefields of the Western Front. He was treated as a distinguished guest but not as a plenipotentiary with the right to speak on behalf of the Arab nation.

An Anglo-French gentlemen's agreement

Excluding France from Syria was precisely what many in the British government wanted; none more so than the Lord President of the Council, Lord Curzon. (Curzon ran the Foreign Office for most of 1919 as Arthur Balfour was busy with the peace treaties; he became Foreign Secretary in October

33 Zeine, *The Struggle for Arab Independence*, pp 49–51.
34 Wilson, *Lawrence of Arabia*, p 586.

1919.) He reflected the widespread view within British government circles that France should not be allowed to straddle British lines of communication to India and the British Empire in the Far East. With German ambitions destroyed, the essential bond between the British and the French was no longer present. Instead Anglo-French relations might revert back to the days of the Fashoda Crisis, when a colonial dispute in the Sudan in 1898 had brought the two powers to the brink of war. Other advocates of using the Arabs to keep the French out of the Middle East included the Arab Bureau in Cairo and Foreign Office officials such as Arnold Toynbee.[35] They were given plenty of opportunities to put their case.

T E Lawrence, on his return from the Middle East, addressed the British Cabinet's Eastern Committee. He put forward a bold proposal for the administration of the post-war Middle East: that Feisal should administer Syria, while Mesopotamia should be split into two areas under Zeid and Abdullah. The War Office and the Foreign Office were supportive of Lawrence's grand design. However, the India Office, long sick of what they considered the indulgence of the Hashemites by their departmental colleagues, was bitterly opposed.[36] A truncated version of this plan would eventually emerge in 1922. By then Syria would be lost both to the Hashemites and to the wider cause of Arab nationalism.

In the meantime, Lloyd George had become increasingly obsessed with the Middle East. He had begun to view it as a blank canvas on which a new order could be drawn. Greek claims in Asia Minor could be endorsed, as could Jewish demands for a homeland in Palestine. Armenians and Kurds could carve out nation states. Arab states could be established under the tutelage of the British. Egypt would be made a kingdom under British supervision. Local client states could be cheaply brought under an umbrella of British power. In such a scenario only small forces would be required to maintain British power and influence in the region. What role the French would play in all of this was unclear.

The British would have liked to exclude the French from Middle Eastern arrangements completely. However, this proved impossible. France's involvement in the East had been circumscribed by the need

---

35 Kedourie, *In the Anglo-Arab Labyrinth*, p 213.
36 Timothy J Paris, 'British Middle East Policy-Making after the First World War: the Lawrentian and Wilsonian Schools', *The Historical Journal*, Vol 41, No 3 (Sep 1998) p 773.

to focus virtually all of its military efforts on the Western Front. Why should French sacrifices against the Germans at the Marne, Verdun and in Champagne be counted as less worthy of reward than the relatively easy victories won by the British in the Middle East? The British, especially Lloyd George, were aware of this claim, though as Britain had borne the brunt of the hardest fighting on the Western Front from mid-1917 this in itself carried little weight. However, the future peace of the world was more likely to be determined by cordial relations between Britain and France than by keeping the Arab cause happy. Lloyd George was to spend the first ten months of 1919 torn between his desire to rearrange the Middle East entirely on British terms and the requirement to keep France as an ally. At times, which goal was the priority was not entirely clear.

On 1 December 1918, Lloyd George and the veteran French Premier Clemenceau met in London where they made a 'gentlemen's agreement' that was to cement France's rights in the Levant and Syria. In return, Lloyd George secured enhanced gains for Britain. He was determined that Britain's share of the Middle Eastern spoils secured at such great cost in lives and money would be increased. There were more than a million British Empire troops in the Middle East at the end of 1918. Allenby's advance into Syria had been one of the few glorious British victories of the war. Lloyd George made clear to Clemenceau that he wanted control of Palestine and the area around Mosul. Mosul was wanted because of its large deposits of oil and the securing of future oil supplies had become an important aim of British policy, though by no means overarching.[37] Clemenceau was amenable. While acknowledging the problems he might have with his colonial lobby, the French leader replied phlegmatically to Lloyd George's demands. 'You shall have it', he declared. In truth, Clemenceau did not care much for the French Empire. His main, perhaps sole, interest was in maintaining British support for French demands against the Germans. His submission to Lloyd George's demands was partially in exchange for the Prime Minister's apparently clear backing for Clemenceau's request for a unified French administration for Syria. There were also promises of a share in the spoils of any Middle Eastern oil. There was no formal paper outlining this gentlemen's agreement. Clemenceau

37 See the discussions in Marian Kent, *Oil and Empire: British Policy and Mesopotamian Oil, 1900–1920* (Macmillan, London: 1976) pp 124–6, and Darwin, *Britain, Egypt and the Middle East*, pp 258–65.

had made his concessions. He now wanted to be assured that France's Middle Eastern ambitions would not be wholly thwarted.[38] Lloyd George and the British government, however, were to continue to play the Feisal card, alienating the French and perhaps encouraging their Arab protégé to be more obstinate in his dealings with the French than was wise.

On 4 December, the Eastern Committee met, with Lawrence attending again. Curzon fulminated against the Sykes-Picot Agreement, which he now believed had been completely superseded by the new facts on the ground. He saw the Agreement as storing up trouble in the future with Arab opinion. However, the Foreign Secretary Arthur Balfour, aware no doubt of Lloyd George's secret understanding with Clemenceau, declared that Britain could not revisit and amend Sykes-Picot. He took the view that the Agreement could only be scrapped if the Americans pressed for it. As Lawrence's biographer notes, the conclusions of this meeting were that the British Cabinet 'was not prepared to offer Feisal anything more than sympathy'.[39]

Undoubtedly, the British government viewed President Wilson's doctrine of national self-determination as a potentially useful tool to keep the French out of Syria. It suited British policy for the time being at least that Feisal get American help rather than British. Their policy was 'to back Feisal and the Arabs as far as we can, up to the point of not alienating the French'.[40] Curzon was also aware that channelling the Hashemites towards Syria rather than Mesopotamia or Palestine had the potential to aid, if not save, British ambitions in the Middle East.[41] At the same

---

38 There is no actual official government note of this conversation. See S W Roskill, *Hankey, Man of Secrets, Volume 2: 1919–1931* (Collins, London: 1972) pp 28–9. In August 1919 Clemenceau relied on the meeting to accuse Britain of perfidy: E L Woodward and Rohan Butler (eds), *Documents on British Foreign Policy, 1919–1939*, First Series, Volume IV (1919) (Her Majesty's Stationery Office, London: 1952) Doc 242, (hereafter *DBFP*, Vol IV, references are to Document numbers). See also Lloyd George, *The Truth about the Peace Treaties* (Victor Gollancz, London: 1938) p 1038.

39 Wilson, *Lawrence of Arabia*, p 591.

40 Paris, 'British Middle East Policy-Making after the First World War', p 779. See also Timothy J Paris, *Britain, the Hashemites, and Arab Rule, 1920–1925: The Sherifian Solution* (Frank Cass, London: 2003).

41 John Fisher, *Curzon and British Imperialism in the Middle East 1916–19* (Frank Cass, London: 1999) p xv.

time, the French attitude on Syria was hardening. They made clear that they wanted no British discussions with Feisal regarding Syria. Syria, as far as they were concerned, was now a French responsibility and not really a matter for the Peace Conference. When Balfour met Feisal on 12 December, the latter warned him that the Arabs would go to war against the French over Syria even if the chances of success against a Great Power were negligible. Balfour assured him that his suspicions regarding French plans for Syria had little basis in fact.[42]

Weizmann and the Zionist preparations for the Peace Conference

Weizmann's return from Palestine on 5 October allowed him no respite, rather the contrary since the war was clearly entering its final phase at bewildering speed, especially in the Middle East. With the future of Palestine now likely to be at Britain's disposal, he formed a small group chaired by Herbert Samuel, consisting of Sir Alfred Mond, a member of Lloyd George's government, Sokolow and himself, charged with producing a scheme whereby the Jewish position in the country could go forward under British trusteeship. Ormsby-Gore was also associated with its work.[43] Weizmann also embarked upon a flurry of meetings with leading politicians, including Balfour, Cecil, Sykes, Ormsby-Gore, Samuel and the influential General Smuts, as well as key figures in British intelligence and Lawrence and Hogarth. The focus of his discussions with Cecil, Lawrence and Hogarth seems to have been the need to maintain close relations with Feisal, which clearly needed a sensitive touch. The level of access he enjoyed at this pivotal time was, once again, of incalculable value to the Zionist movement.[44]

Also anxious to keep his American colleagues in close step with what he was doing, Weizmann explained the position at some length to Brandeis on 29 October 1918. What clearly concerned him was that in view of the rapid turn of events in the war, Zionism was hardly a priority

---

42 Wilson, *Lawrence of Arabia*, pp 592–3.
43 Weizmann to Aaron Aaronson, Washington, (22–23) October 1918; Weizmann to Gilbert F Clayton, GHQ, Palestine, 27 November 1918, in Jehuda Reinharz (ed), *LPCW*, Series A, Vol IX, October 1918–July 1920 (Transaction Books, Rutgers University; Israel Universities Press, Jerusalem: 1977) 1, 38, pp 1, 40–3; hereafter *LPCW*, Vol IX.
44 Weizmann to Gilbert F Clayton, Palestine, 5 November 1918; Weizmann to David Eder, Tel Aviv-Jaffa, 5 November 1918: *LPCW*, Vol IX, 7, 8, pp 9–20.

for the Allied leaders. Even so, the situation in the Middle East had its own momentum. Weizmann naturally viewed the establishment of Feisal's position as a positive development, explaining to Brandeis how the Hashemite leader had been prepared to acknowledge Palestine as a Jewish sphere of influence in return for technical and economic assistance to the Arab states. What he portrayed as a division of the Middle East between the Hashemites and the Zionists, he feared was being undermined by the details, which were now emerging, of the Sykes-Picot Agreement, resented as it was by the Arabs. But he was also concerned by reports of growing Arab hostility to the Jews in Palestine, and by the extent of pogroms in the disintegrating empires of central and eastern Europe. In a letter to his friend David Eder in Tel Aviv, he confided his fear that if they did not secure Palestine these communities might be exterminated.[45] His concern that the American Zionists should put their full weight behind any representation to a peace conference was repeated in a message to Brandeis sent on Armistice Day. On that historic day he had lunch with Lloyd George, arranged, it seems, by his old friend C P Scott.[46]

Meanwhile, what was of the essence was an agreed statement of what the Zionists wanted to come out of any Peace Conference, and given the disparate nature of the movement, stretched as it was across several jurisdictions, this was not as straightforward as it might have seemed. In the circumstances, it was vital to put down a marker about what the Zionists felt should happen during this crucial interim period. After meetings with Balfour and Cecil, on 1 November 1918 Weizmann submitted to the latter a ten-point document setting this out. Acknowledging that control would be in the hands of the British, the document requested that the work of the Zionist Commission be allowed to continue and that it be made the advisory body to the military administration on matters relating to the Jewish inhabitants. In addition, the military was to assist the Zionist Commission in organising the Jewish population and encouraging Jewish participation in administration. In a matter close to Weizmann's heart, the commission was also to be permitted to

---

45 Weizmann to Louis D Brandeis, Washington, 29 October 1918; Weizmann to David Eder, Tel Aviv-Jaffa, 26 November 1918: *LPCW*, Vol IX, 4, 37, pp 2–8, 39–40.

46 Weizmann to Louis D Brandeis, Washington, 11 November 1918; Weizmann to C P Scott, Manchester, 1918: *LPCW*, Vol IX, 11, 18, pp 22, 26–7.

carry out preparatory work for the Hebrew University on Mount Scopus. Crucially, a land commission was to be created, including Zionist Commission members, with a view to reviewing land tenure and ownership, including an examination of land registers and a possible modification of existing land law.[47]

Significant as this statement was, it could be nothing more than a holding document until Samuel's committee had completed its work on a definitive statement of Zionist aims which would be placed in the hands of the Peace Conference. A draft was ready by the end of November, and Weizmann, understandably anxious to sound out British reactions to what they would be proposing, sent copies to Clayton in Palestine and, crucially, to Balfour. At a meeting with Balfour on 4 December, Weizmann proposed that the Peace Conference should declare Palestine to be a Jewish country under a trustee. He then revealed that they would be asking for Britain to be that trustee, and confirmed that they would want to see a Jewish population of some 4 to 5 million being built up over the next 25 years. The interview was positive, with Balfour indicating his broad agreement with what was going to be proposed, and assuring Weizmann that it did not deviate from his November 1917 Declaration.[48]

However reassuring this might be, Weizmann still needed to secure other flanks, not least with Feisal who was also expected to press his claims before the Peace Conference. The two leaders met in London on 11 December 1918, with Lawrence acting as interpreter. Feisal began by denouncing the Sykes-Picot Agreement, a sentiment with which Weizmann concurred. He then asked for an outline of the Zionist programme. Weizmann's reply was remarkably candid, saying that they expected the Peace Conference and Feisal to acknowledge the rights of the Jews to Palestine. They would request that the country be put under British trusteeship, with a government in which the Jews would share. He also confirmed that they would request a reform of the land laws in order to permit the colonisation of 4 to 5 million Jews, while

47 Weizmann to Lord Robert Cecil, London, 1 November 1918: Appendix 1: 'Proposals submitted by the Zionist Organisation to the Secretary of State for Foreign Affairs regarding matters affecting the Jewish population of Palestine during the Military occupation of that Country', LPCW, Vol IX, 5, pp 8, 389–90.
48 Weizmann to David Eder, Tel Aviv–Jaffa, 4 December 1918; Weimann to Nahum Sokolow, Paris, 5 December 1918: LPCW, Vol IX, 52, 53, pp 53–6.

safeguarding the rights of the Arab peasantry, and reassured Feisal that there was no intention to interfere with the Muslim Holy Places. For his part, Feisal responded that he would seek to reassure the Peace Conference that the Zionist and Arab movements were in harmony, and that he would support the Jewish position.[49] The essence of this conversation was embodied in a document drawn up between the two leaders and signed on 3 January 1919. In what was to become known as the Feisal-Weizmann Agreement, the two agreed to promote the close cooperation of the Arab State and Palestine, the boundaries of which would be defined after the Peace Conference. The Constitution and administration of Palestine would allow for the implementation of the Balfour Declaration. Large-scale Jewish immigration into Palestine was to be encouraged, while the rights of the Arab farmers would be protected. Provision was to be made for the free exercise of religion, and the Muslim Holy Places were to be under Muslim control. A commission of experts sent to Palestine by the Zionist Organisation was also to report on how the Arab State might be developed. Finally, the parties pledged to work together on all these matters before the Peace Conference. Feisal did, however, enter an important caveat, of which there are two rather different versions. In the rather opaque translation made by Lawrence, Feisal recorded that if changes were made to the establishment of the Arabs then he could not be answerable for any failure to carry out the agreement. In the version published in 1938 by George Antonius, Feisal was more specific, making the agreement absolutely dependent upon the implementation of Arab independence. In fact, the meaning is clear enough, and the subsequent collapse of Feisal's hopes in Syria rendered the agreement meaningless; but it is interesting that Feisal made it, just the same.[50]

In anticipation of the forthcoming Peace Conference, Weizmann went to Paris at the beginning of January 1919 as part of the Zionist Mission which had been invited to present the movement's case, staying at the Hotel Plaza on the Avenue Montaigne.[51] An early sign that things might

49 Weizmann to Sir Eyre Crowe, London, 16 December 1918, *LPCW*, Vol IX, 70, pp 69–71.
50 'Feisal-Weizmann Agreement', 3 January 1919, *LPCW*, Vol IX, between pp 86 and 87; Antonius, *The Arab Awakening*, pp 437–9.
51 Rose, *Chaim Weizmann*, p 200.

go his way came at a meeting with the President's aide, Colonel House. Weizmann left with the clear impression that the Americans were sympathetic to the Zionist position, not least since House assured him that he had recently been briefed on the issues by Balfour. In a letter to his wife, he confided in her that the Americans favoured a Jewish Palestine under British auspices, the essence of the position he was preparing to put to the Conference. House also promised to arrange a meeting with President Wilson, which took place on 14 January. The fact that Weizmann had this level of access was in itself significant, and must have done his credibility no harm in his uneasy relations with the American Zionists.[52] His chief concern was ensuring that the statement of policy which was to be presented to the Conference was as realistic as possible, especially given the rather different perspectives of the various Zionist groups and his contacts in British government circles. Reconciling these views was by no means straightforward, as it turned out.

For some time Weizmann had been uneasy about the attitude of the British military administration in Palestine, which he felt was too inclined to take the Arab side. It was, therefore, important to seek the views of General Sir Arthur Money, Chief Administrator in Palestine, who was then in London. Money's reaction was that the Arabs would react against the proposals in the draft document, not least where they would affect distribution of the land. In reply, Weizmann argued that unless the Jews secured a home they would be faced with a catastrophe. He also asserted the historic right of the Jews to Palestine, which, he said, was not invalidated by the fact that their expulsion had happened 2,000 years before. On the land question, he claimed that what they wanted was to break up the large estates in favour of small farmers, by implication Jewish, though this was not stated.[53] Nevertheless, by 3 February 1919, the final text of this key document had been agreed. Much would turn on it, and its content was to underpin, in no small measure, the nature of the subsequent British Mandate for Palestine.

The 'Statement of the Zionist Organisation regarding Palestine' was signed by Lord Rothschild, by Weizmann and Sokolow on behalf of the

---

52 Weizmann to Vera Weizmann, London, 8 January 1919, *LPCW*, Vol IX, 100, pp 92–4; Reinharz, *Chaim Weizmann: The Making of a Statesman*, p 296.
53 Weizmann to Sir Arthur Wigram Money, London, 26 January 1919, *LPCW*, Vol IX, pp 104–7.

Zionist Organisation and of the Jewish population of Palestine, by Israel
Rosoff for the Russian Zionist Organisation, and by Julian Mack, Stephen
Wise, Harry Friedenwald, Jacob de Haas, Mary Fels, Louis Robison and
Bernard Flexner for the Zionist Organization of America. There was a
noticeable absence of any French Jewish signatory. In its preamble the
document asked that the Conference recognise the Jews' historic title to
Palestine and their right to have their National Home there. The newly
formed League of Nations was to have sovereignty over Palestine, governed by Great Britain as its Mandatory.

The choice of Britain rested on what the document claimed was the
special relationship it had with Zionism, as evidenced by the 'Uganda
Offer' and the Balfour Declaration. Moreover, the Jews liked the way in
which Britain had approached colonial government. The British were to
create the necessary conditions for the creation of the National Home,
but, in an interesting move beyond the terms of the Balfour Declaration, the document also looked forward to the eventual creation of an
autonomous commonwealth. In order to do that, Britain was to promote
Jewish immigration and settlement while safeguarding the rights of the
non-Jewish population, work together with a Jewish council, and give
that council priority where public works and natural resources were concerned. On the critical question of land, the Mandatory was to appoint
a commission, with Jewish representation, which would have the power
of compulsory purchase, as well as making available state land and what
it described as inadequately cultivated land, though the position of the
existing population was to be protected. There was to be no discrimina-
tion on racial or religious grounds. The boundary of Palestine was to lie
east of the river Jordan close to the line of the Hejaz railway, and include
the river headwaters on Mount Hermon in the north.

The document was at pains to justify the nature of the Jews' claims
to Palestine, notably that it was their historic home from which they had
been violently expelled, but to which they had always hoped to return.
In addition, Palestine would provide a refuge for Jews living under harsh
conditions in Eastern Europe, even though it was conceded that the
country was unable to take in more than a minority of them. Finally,
the document pointed to what it claimed was the desolate condition of
the land, which could only be developed through Jewish enterprise, as
evidenced by the success of the existing settlements. These Jewish claims
to Palestine had been recognised in the Balfour Declaration, and then

supported by the French, Italian, American, Japanese, Greek, Serbian, Chinese and Siamese governments.[54]

'Much the most dignified presence at the peace conference'

The Conference opened in Paris on 18 January 1919 under Clemenceau's presidency. While a wide variety of countries was present in Paris, the Council of Ten represented the principal victors; namely, the heads of government and foreign ministers of the United States, United Kingdom, France and Italy, as well as two Japanese members. Although Palestine was far from the top of its agenda, it was to the advantage of Weizmann and the Zionists that the British representatives on the Council were Lloyd George and Balfour. The Conference's dominant personalities were Clemenceau, Lloyd George and Wilson.[55]

A British proposal that the Arab territories captured from Turkey should be subject to what was euphemistically called advice and assistance from the Mandatory Power until they were able to stand on their own two feet was agreed by the Council of Ten. The native populations would receive the right to choose which power would hold the Mandate over them. The Mandatory system would also be subject to League of Nations supervision. Stéphen Pichon, the French Minister of Foreign Affairs, proposed in February that France wanted its sphere of influence and area of direct control as proposed under the Sykes-Picot Agreement to be amalgamated into a single Mandate. He argued that France's long-standing economic, political and cultural links with the region made it the most suitable Mandatory power. France also expressed a willingness to work with Feisal provided he was willing to accept a large degree of French control over his government. The French had clearly decided that the Mandate system was not significantly different from French colonial practice in Morocco.

Feisal presented his case on 6 February 1919.[56] By then he had already made a favourable impression on many of the assembled delegates. The

---

54 'Statement of the Zionist Organisation regarding Palestine', 3 February 1919, *LPCW*, Vol IX, Appendix II, pp 391–402.

55 See Temperley, *A History of the Peace Conference of Paris*, Vol I, pp 249–50.

56 Unless otherwise stated, what follows is based on *Papers Relating to the Foreign Relations of the United States, 1919: The Paris Peace Conference*, 13 vols (Washington, DC: 1942–7), Vol 3, pp 889–94, hereafter *FRUS PPC*.

American Secretary of State Robert Lansing, writing a couple of years later, was lavish in his praise. To another observer, he was 'much the most dignified presence at the peace conference'.[57] Lloyd George was of the view that Feisal's 'intellectual countenance and shining eyes would have made an impression in any assembly'.[58] The American journalist and Wilson's confidential translator Stephen Bonsal declared that Emir Feisal, Nuri Pasha and Lawrence 'were certainly the most resplendent figures that had ever entered the Quai d'Orsay'. Feisal had come not as a 'supplicant but to demand the rights of his people and the observance of solemn agreements which, as the emergency was over, some were inclined to forget'.[59]

Feisal was well aware that his case had to be strong to attract the sympathy of the United States in particular. He had to prove that Allied plans for the Middle East drawn up during the war were injurious to the right of national self-determination. He also had to prove that the Hashemites were the true leaders of the Arab cause. On this last point he was adamant:

> My father has a privileged place among Arabs as the head of their
> greatest family and as Sherif of Mecca. He is convinced of the ultimate
> triumph of the ideal of unity, if no attempt is made now to thwart it
> or to hinder it by dividing the area as spoils of war among the Great
> Powers.[60]

Feisal had prepared his case in a memorandum of 29 January, pointing out how the region had been the home of ancient civilisations and held potential for the future. His basic demand was straightforward – independence for all of the Arabs from the line Alexandretta–Persia southwards, which, he argued, had been promised by the Allies during the war. The basis for this demand was that the area constituted a unit suitable for national self-determination. All the inhabitants spoke Arabic and came

---

57 Sir James Headlam-Morley, *A Memoir of the Paris Peace Conference, 1919* (Methuen, London: 1972) pp 30–1.

58 Lloyd George, *The Truth about the Peace Treaties*, p 1038.

59 Stephen Bonsal, *Suitors and Supplicants: The Little Nations at Versailles* (Prentice Hall Inc, New York: 1946) p 32.

60 Bonsal, *Suitors and Supplicants*, p 33.

from the one Semitic stock; there were few nations so homogenous. Furthermore, the Arabs had fought with the Allies, fulfilling their part of the bargain.[61] Now it was time for the Allies to do likewise. Feisal's presentation did contain some exaggerations, however. There were never the 100,000 warriors that he claimed were fielded by the Arabs. While Lloyd George picked some holes in the military contribution of the Arabs, comparing it unfavourably to Britain's commitment of more than a million troops, he remained broadly positive about their case. Pichon's attempt to assert that France had played a major role in the Middle East campaign backfired as Feisal, in the nicest possible way, accurately outlined the insignificant numbers of French troops that had fought in the region.

The Reverend Howard S Bliss, President of the Syrian Protestant College in Beirut, addressed the Council of Ten a week after Feisal. Bliss was Syrian-born, but of American ancestry. He urged that a commission be sent at once to Syria in order to allow Syrians 'to express in a perfectly untrammelled way their political wishes and aspirations, viz: as to what form of Government they desire and as to what power, if any, should be their Mandatory Protecting Power'.[62] Clemenceau was hostile. The French had organised the attendance of a Lebanese Christian delegation, which decried any attempt to impose a primitive Bedouin emir as leader of the advanced races of Syria. Chekri Ganem, the chairman of the pro-French Central Syrian Committee, was brought forward to argue that Syria desperately needed French tutelage.[63] Ganem argued for the separation of Syria from Arabia, as it was a different country and that to 'annex Syria to Arabia would be to do violence to the very soil from which the race and its history have sprung'.[64] The delegation warned of the dangers of allowing the fanatically religious Hejaz to gain control of Syria because its popularity was based on Syrian Muslims, seeing this as 'the first foundations of a great Moslem (not Arabian) Empire, with the Hedjaz [sic] dynasty at the head'. Presumably for the benefit of the British, it was pointed out that certain Muslims were seeking 'a further extension of the Empire of Islam,

61 *FRUS PPC,* Vol 3, pp 889–90.
62 *FRUS PPC,* Vol 3, p 1016.
63 *FRUS PPC,* Vol 3, pp 1024–38.
64 *FRUS PPC,* Vol 3, p 1029.

towards Africa and towards India'.[65] Ganem had a point; the various Christian sects concentrated in Lebanon were wary of Hashemite rule. Indeed the monolithic Arab nation which Feisal referred to was much more diverse than he claimed. Feisal had made considerable attempts to woo Lebanese Christians since he had taken Damascus, offering eminent Christians high-ranking ministerial and diplomatic posts. But these efforts to bring the Lebanese, and for that matter Syrian, Christians on side did not work. No more than a small group of Christians actively supported the Hashemite cause.[66]

However, the French were not simply satisfied with the protection of this minority – they wanted all of Syria. However, Wilson was informed, during the course of this presentation, that Ganem's credentials as an objective observer were somewhat undermined by the fact that he had been resident in France for more than three decades. Wilson reacted by pacing the room.[67] He was far more impressed by the Arab case and Feisal in particular. Bonsal heard him say at the end of February 1919: 'Listening to the Emir I think to hear the voice of liberty, a strange, and, I fear, a stray voice coming from Asia.'[68]

Arguments continued to rage between the British, the French and the Americans. Britain's Colonial Secretary, Lord Milner, handled much of the negotiations with the French. Milner attempted to get the French to negotiate with Feisal. He pointed out the impossibility in the context of a Peace Conference committed to the ideal of self-determination for the French to be imposed on the Arabs of Syria as a Mandatory Power. Clemenceau, who was quite detached from the French colonial lobby, was amenable to agreeing some sort of deal with Feisal. Milner explained to Lloyd George on 8 March 1919 that the British position should be to put pressure on both sides to come to some kind of equitable solution. In a letter to Lloyd George, Milner came up with a proposal to resolve the impasse between France and Feisal: France would be given a Mandate over Syria. However, this was to be 'the mildest form of Mandate' and the

---

65 *FRUS PPC*, Vol 3, p 1030.
66 Meir Zamir, 'Faisal and the Lebanese Question, 1918–20', *Middle Eastern Studies*, Vol 27, No 3 (Jul 1991) p 408.
67 See M MacMillan, *Peacemakers: the Paris Peace Conference of 1919 and its Attempt to End War* (John Murray, London: 2001) p 402.
68 Bonsal, *Suitors and Supplicants*, p 45.

native population would exercise most of the powers, while France would have control over foreign policy and development. Milner, however, was not confident that the French would accept anything short of the 'virtual ownership of Syria'.[69]

The Zionists before the Council of Ten

The Zionist delegation was scheduled to present its case before the Council of Ten on 28 February 1919, but on the 26th Weizmann and Sokolow were informed that their meeting was being brought forward to the following day. The practical effect of this was that Jacob de Haas, who was to represent the American Zionists but who was still in London, was unable arrive in time. Much worse from Weizmann's perspective was the unwelcome news that the French Foreign Ministry was inviting two representatives of the French Jewish community. The first of these, André Spire, was a distinguished civil servant of noted Zionist sympathies. But his colleague, Sylvain Levi, was much more problematic. Not only did Levi come from a strongly assimilationist background hostile to Zionism, but he and Weizmann had crossed swords the previous year on the Zionist Commission. Members of the British and American delegations professed ignorance over Levi's invitation, but an attempt by Weizmann to lobby against him was unsuccessful. According to Weizmann's account, however, Levi was annoyed at not being trusted, and promised to say nothing against Zionism.[70]

The Zionist Mission which presented itself before the Council of Ten in the Quai d'Orsay on the afternoon of 27 February 1919 consisted of Weizmann, Sokolow, Ussishkin, Spire and Levi. Present to hear them were the Foreign Ministers Stéphen Pichon of France, Baron Sonnino of Italy and Baron Makino of Japan, as well as the American Robert Lansing. The British Empire was represented by Balfour and Milner, who, of course, had the arguments at their fingertips, while Ormsby-Gore was also present for this particular session. The Zionists could be assured of a sympathetic hearing and reception from the British members, while Pichon, too, was familiar with the issue, having signed the French government's declaration of 14 February 1918, and personally assured Sokolow

---

69 Lloyd George, *The Truth about the Peace Treaties*, pp 1048–9.
70 Weizmann to Vera Weizmann, London, 28 February 1919, *LPCW*, Vol IX, 123, pp 116–19.

of its support for the British government's position. In his autobiography, Weizmann recollected that Clemenceau was present for the early part of the hearing, and it seems that he did stay for a short time.[71]

The Zionist case was opened, with his customary gravitas, by Sokolow, who requested that he submit to the Council the 'Statement of the Zionist Organisation regarding Palestine', adding that the delegation had come to assert the historic rights of the Jews to Palestine, where they had created their civilisation prior to the Dispersion. Conceding the comfortable position of the Jewish communities of France, Britain, Italy and the United States, a key point in view of the nature of his audience, he nevertheless argued that they represented only a minority of a much greater world Jewish population whose needs could only be met through the establishment of a home. Sokolow then rehearsed the principal recommendations of the 'Statement' he had distributed; namely, that the Jews' historic title to Palestine be recognised together with the right to have a National Home there; that the League of Nations be granted sovereignty over Palestine with Britain as the Mandatory Power; and that Palestine be governed in such a way as to secure the Jewish National Home with the possibility of this leading to an autonomous commonwealth which would have due regard to the rights of the country's non-Jewish population and the status of Jews in other countries. Weizmann's recollection was that his colleague made a real impression on his listeners.[72]

It was now Weizmann's turn. While he was experienced in dealing with senior British politicians and public servants, this was his debut before such an international gathering, and his main concern was to convince them of the practicalities of the Zionist endeavour. He brought with him his recent experience as president of the 1918 Zionist Commission in Palestine. Beginning by highlighting the pre-war sufferings of the 6 to 7 million Russian Jews, he argued that these had continued under the new regime. This would result in an increase in Jewish emigration, but he

71 Weizmann, *Trial and Error*, p 304.

72 M Dockrill (ed), *British Documents on Foreign Affairs: Reports and Papers from the Foreign Office Confidential Print, Part II: From the First to the Second World War, Series I, The Paris Peace Conference of 1919*, General Editors Kenneth Bourne and D Cameron Watt, *Volume 2: Supreme Council Minutes, January–March 1919* (University Publications of America, Frederick, Maryland: 1989) pp 260–1, hereafter Dockrill, *Supreme Council Minutes*; Weizmann, *Trial and Error*, p 304.

predicted that the capacity of Western Europe and the United States to absorb immigrants would bring them under increasing scrutiny; in view of what was to happen to American immigration legislation in the early 1920s, which introduced strict ethnic quotas, he was accurate enough. He then turned to the crucial question of Palestine. Acknowledging that there were between 600,000 and 700,000 existing inhabitants, he argued that this represented a population density of 10 to 15 per square kilometre, which he compared with 160 per square kilometre in Lebanon. As a result, he argued that some 4 to 5 million could be settled without detriment to the rights of the existing population. Such was the essence of his case. In order to promote this settlement, the proposed Mandatory Power would promote Jewish immigration and settlement, while safeguarding the rights of the existing population; work to develop the National Home in cooperation with a council representing the Jews of Palestine and elsewhere; and give that council priority in the development of Palestine's natural resources. Weizmann concluded by referring to the 1 million Jews who, he claimed, were waiting to come to Palestine, emphasising that the support of the Great Powers would be needed for this to be done.[73]

Ussishkin, who spoke as President of the South Russian Jewish National Assembly representing some 3 million Jews, was brief, and contented himself with supporting what Sokolow and Weizmann had said. He was followed by Spire, who, while saying that he spoke on behalf of the French Zionists, conceded that they were a minority of French Jews. So far, all four had been remarkably succinct. Not so Levi, who addressed the Council for some 20 minutes, managing to undermine much of what the others had said. From the start he made it clear that he was not a Zionist, and that while a Jew by origin he was French. Even so, the first part of what he had to say did not seem greatly at odds with what had gone before. He, too, stressed the suffering of the Jews of Central and Eastern Europe, insisting that they dreamt of Palestine as the one place where their sense of nationality could be developed. He then proceeded to demonstrate that the Zionist movement had already created a foundation for further development through the fostering of the Jewish settlements which Rothschild had encouraged, as well as the opening of schools. Zionism's task, he argued, was to direct Jewish migration from Eastern Europe to Palestine.

At that point the tone of his submission changed abruptly. He said

---

73 Dockrill, *Supreme Council Minutes*, pp 261–2.

that he would now address the practical difficulties with the frankness of an historian. In the first place he pointed to the size of Palestine compared with the millions of Eastern European Jews who might go there. The country's present population was 600,000 to 700,000 Arabs, and he did not feel that an equal number of Jews could be accommodated at the standard of living they had experienced in Europe. He then turned to the nature of the prospective Jewish settlement, drawn as it would be from countries where they had been persecuted. They would, he warned, bring dangerous passions to Palestine, which, in a curious turn of phrase, he said would become a concentration camp for Jews. A further problem would be the merging of Jews from such a diverse group of countries into a single nationality, something with which the Peace Conference would be familiar. The Zionist solution to this dilemma was to be the formation of an International Jewish Council with responsibilities for Palestine, but as a Frenchman of Jewish origin he feared the dual citizenship that this might imply. Turning to the principles of the French Revolution, he then argued that as the Jews had campaigned for equal rights in the countries they inhabited, it would be shocking if they claimed an exceptional position in Palestine. The most he would concede, it appeared, was the creation of a Jewish committee to organise immigration and look after economic and social affairs in Palestine but with no political function. Notwithstanding the fact that his lengthy discourse had gone far to undo much of what had gone before, he ended by reminding the Council of the Jews' contribution to civilisation and the further contributions they might make by the shores of the Mediterranean.[74]

There is no doubt that the nature of Levi's submission threw the rest of the delegation into confusion, but after a hasty consultation they decided against entering into a public debate with him before the Council.[75] They were rescued from their dilemma by Lansing, who asked Weizmann whether the term 'Jewish National Home' meant an autonomous Jewish government. He replied that they did not want the latter but rather an administration, which, under a Mandatory, would be able to build up Jewish institutions. Over time, a sense of nationality would grow so that, in his striking phrase, Palestine would become as Jewish as America was American or England was English.

---

74 Dockrill, *Supreme Council Minutes*, pp 262–4.
75 Weizmann, *Trial and Error*, p 205.

Made impromptu in reply to Lansing's question, this concept was to enter the political lexicon over the next few years, not always to Weizmann's advantage. Weizmann then seized the opportunity to refute Levi. Since the International Jewish Council would have no political function, the matter of dual allegiance to which the Frenchman had alluded would not arise. Conceding Levi's point that Palestine as it then existed could not absorb large numbers, he made the obvious riposte that it was their purpose to transform the country in the manner of California or the French colony of Tunisia. In the latter, he instanced that there were 8 million olive trees compared with 45,000 in 1882. To achieve this kind of change would be difficult, he admitted, but not as bad as the problems of the Jews of Eastern Europe. Finally, in a clear stroke against the assimilationist position Levi had represented so vigorously, he claimed that he spoke for 96 per cent of the Jews of the world.[76] The delegation then left. Balfour's secretary came out to pass on his congratulations. Weizmann pointedly refused Levi's proffered hand, and accused him of betrayal. The two men never spoke again.[77] An exultant Weizmann confided in his wife that it had been the most triumphant moment of his life.[78]

The day after his appearance before the Council of Ten, Weizmann sought to reinforce his message in an interview with the British journalist Walter Duranty, which appeared in the *New York Times* on 3 March. He repeated what he had said about the Jews' right to reconstitute their National Home in Palestine under British trusteeship, but he also used the interview to refine his reply to Lansing with regard to the future shape of a Jewish polity in the country. There would not, he emphasised, be the immediate creation of a Jewish state or commonwealth; rather, he conceded that for some time to come the Jews would be a minority in Palestine and they would not be imposing their will on the majority.[79]

Generally, reaction to what had happened was positive. The French press was overwhelmingly supportive, and Clemenceau's principal adviser André Tardieu issued a statement to the effect that France would not oppose a British trusteeship for Palestine nor a Jewish state, a term

---

76 Dockrill, *Supreme Council Minutes*, pp 264–5.
77 Weizmann, *Trial and Error*, p 205.
78 Weizmann to Vera Weizmann, London, 28 February 1919, *LPCW*, Vol IX, 123, pp 116–19.
79 Esco, *Palestine*, Vol I, pp 161–2.

which the Zionist delegation had not used. A meeting between Weizmann and his colleagues and Lansing on 29 February clearly went well.
The only immediately discordant note came in a newspaper interview
with Feisal, which Weizmann and his colleagues sought to counter. The
result was a letter sent by Feisal on 3 March 1919 to the American Zionist
Felix Frankfurter. He recalled his earlier contacts with Weizmann, assuring Frankfurter of his deepest sympathy with Zionism, whose proposals
he described as modest. He did allude to difficulties which were arising
in Palestine, but dismissed these as matters of detail rather than of principle. The Jews would be welcome, he claimed.[80] Two days later, Weizmann gave a very full account of his meeting with the Peace Conference
at a Zionist meeting in London. His speech included his spat with Levi
and his response to Lansing's intervention to the effect that Palestine
would become as Jewish as as America was American or England was
English. He also read verbatim Feisal's letter to Frankfurter. Overall,
his speech was one of reassurance, even euphoric in tone, and he concluded by declaring that in principle the Jewish National Home was a
fait accompli.[81]

Establishment of a Commission of Inquiry into Syria

The decisive meeting was held on 20 March 1919 when Wilson, Pichon,
Lloyd George, Allenby and Clemenceau attempted to thrash out the issue
of Syria. The French were adamant that Sykes-Picot still stood and that
they should receive both Lebanon and Syria. Feisal could be accommodated under this arrangement. Lloyd George took the view that this was
based on a misreading of the Agreement. Only Lebanon was to be subject
to direct French control and France was bound first to accept that there
would be an independent Arab state in the area in the interior of Syria.
Lloyd George would not accept direct French control of Syria. Syria, he
said, had been promised to the Arabs and British forces had won the war
in the Middle East with their help. Allenby warned that the Arabs would
revolt if the French attempted to seize Syria, which could destabilise the
British position in Palestine, Mesopotamia and Egypt. At this point
Wilson intervened. He declared that the Sykes-Picot Agreement was a

---

80 'At the Peace Conference: Report on March 5th 1919 to the International
Zionist Conference held in London', in Goodman, *Chaim Weizmann*, pp 158–9.
81 'At the Peace Conference', in Goodman, *Chaim Weizmann*, pp 155–60.

dead letter since one party to it, the Russian empire, no longer existed. He now followed up the suggestion of Bliss and called for an inter-Allied commission to be dispatched to Syria to consult the population. Clemenceau was forced to accept the proposal. The danger of alienating the Americans was too great. He also had to pay lip service to the principle of self-determination. He did, however, insist on the expansion of the commission to look at the wishes of the peoples of Mesopotamia and Iraq, presumably to irritate the British.[82]

However, Clemenceau remained aggrieved towards the British and the following day bitter rows continued over the Syrian question. At one stage, the French leader challenged Lloyd George to a duel.[83] It never took place but Lloyd George, who had two trump cards, the huge British military presence in the Middle East and France's desperate need for a security guarantee from Britain and the United States, was able to win the war of words. Terms of reference for an inter-Allied Commission of Inquiry were prepared on 25 March. These emphasised the need to discover the sentiments of the Syrians and recommend what territorial divisions would promote peace and development in Syria, Palestine and Mesopotamia.[84] On 29 March, Feisal confided in House that the commission was the best thing that he had heard of in his life. He asked if it were possible for the United States to take over as the Mandatory Power in Syria. House was doubtful that America would accept the Mandate.[85]

Feisal's breach with the French

The British were not altogether happy with the Commission of Inquiry, since it might find that the British presence in Mesopotamia and Palestine was unwanted. Indeed, the British High Commissioner in Mesopotamia, Sir Arnold Wilson, was hostile to both Arab nationalism and the Hashemites. He had already carried out a survey, of admittedly dubious authenticity, which had found British direct rule was the preferred

---

82 This meeting is described in Lloyd George, *The Truth about the Peace Treaties*, pp 1057–73 and *FRUS PPC*, Vol 5, pp 1–14.

83 Christopher M Andrew and Alexander Sydney Kanya-Forstner, *France Overseas: The Great War and the Climax of French Imperial Expansion* (Thames and Hudson, London: 1981) p 197.

84 *FRUS PPC*, Vol 7, p 747.

85 Notes of a conversation between Colonel House and Emir Feisal, 29 March 1919, in Garnett, *The Letters of T E Lawrence*, p 275.

option and little support in Mesopotamia for a Hashemite as king. Lloyd George sought to have Mesopotamia excluded from the Commission of Inquiry on this ground on 27 March.[86]

It would appear that pressure was now put on Feisal and the French to come to an agreement that would eliminate the need for an inquiry. The British proposed the Milner formula of 'a mild form of Mandate'. In spite of their concern that Feisal was little more than a British proxy, by this point the French had run out of options. But Feisal now made a disastrous tactical error. Through Lawrence and presumably under considerable British pressure, Feisal told the French that he was willing to accept a French Mandate. He would accept French aid and advisers and cede control over foreign policy, but he wanted Lebanon to be included in a Greater Syria. His motivation for this was that he suspected that the Lebanese Christians would inform the forthcoming commission that they wished to be protected by France. Feisal feared that he would be left with a land-locked kingdom.

The French now began to see a use for Feisal. Having him on their side would improve Anglo-French relations and, most importantly, Feisal had conceded that France had a role in all of Syria, not just the coastal region. The French calculated that once they had got their way into Syria, it would be very difficult to remove them. Once French troops were in place, Feisal could either be a puppet or could be expelled at a time of French choosing. France put forward its counter-proposals. While France would accept Greater Syria under Feisal's nominal rule, it was to be federation of tribes and the various religious groups and be subject to the advice of French advisers and soldiers.[87] The French guessed that they would be able to manipulate tribal and sectarian divisions in Syria. They could pursue a policy of divide and conquer.

Clemenceau and Feisal met on 13 April 1919. The former conceded that France would agree to the independence of Syria subject to French

---

86 P Mantoux, *The Deliberations of the Council of Four, March 24–June 28, 1919: Notes of the Official Interpreter, Paul Mantoux, Vol I: To the Delivery to the German Delegation of the Preliminaries of Peace, Vol II: From the Delivery of the Peace Terms to the German Delegation to the Signing of the Treaty of Versailles* (Princeton University Press, Princeton, NJ: 1992) Vol I, pp 41–57.
87 Jan Karl Tanenbaum, 'France and the Middle East, 1914–1920', *Transactions of the American Philosophical Society*, New Series, Vol 68, No 7 (1978) pp 29–30.

troops being admitted to Damascus. Feisal refused. He believed it was a ruse to allow in a French military presence that would be very hard to dislodge. Feisal decided to return to Syria the next day. He had come to the conclusion that he would have to rely on the forthcoming inter-Allied commission to protect the independence of Syria. Feisal had been put under pressure from the British to compromise, but he would not trust the French. He rightly believed that they would betray him once they had established a military presence in Damascus.

The French still believed that Feisal was a British puppet. They remained of the view, not entirely without justification, that their erstwhile allies were reneging on the December 1918 Anglo-French Declaration under the spurious excuse of supporting self-determination for the Arabs. They noted that the British did not seem overly keen on allowing it in the Middle Eastern areas that they themselves controlled. Moreover, the French also considered Feisal to be a dangerous nationalist intent on carving out a large Arabian empire for himself. Clemenceau complained to Colonel House that Lawrence had apparently influenced Feisal's decision to reject the agreement and that a massacre of Christians was being planned by Arab nationalists in Syria.[88] American delegates had caught sight of a French memorandum on Syria which revealed that the French expected the commission to back French goals and the Middle East to be divided on the basis of the Sykes-Picot understanding. An American official commented: 'The Near East is the great loot of the war. The fight on the question of division and mandates must be fought out here in Paris – and the sooner the better.'[89] It would, however, take another year before the Peace Conference would make its final decisions on the settlement of the Middle East.

The emerging politics of Palestine

Notwithstanding the tone of Feisal's assurances to Frankfurter, there were distinct signs that the Arabs of Palestine were becoming increasingly uneasy about Zionist intentions. At a meeting on 1 April and in a subsequent letter, Balfour seemingly warned Weizmann that the

---

88 Colonel House Diary, 14 April 1919, in Woodrow Wilson and Arthur Stanley Link, *The Papers of Woodrow Wilson* (Princeton University Press, Princeton, NJ: 1986–92) Vol 57, pp 334–5; hereafter *Wilson Papers*.
89 Westerman memo, *c.* 17 April 1919, in *Wilson Papers*, Vol 57, p 444.

activities of the Zionists in Palestine were creating tensions with the Arab population. In reply, Weizmann conceded both that he was worried by what was happening, which he believed was being directed from Damascus, and by what some Zionists had been saying about the nature of the National Home. He tried to reassure Balfour of Feisal's continuing support, and that the movement was committed to the terms of the 1917 Declaration, which promised to safeguard the rights of the non-Jewish population. He argued that the unrest in the country would continue until the Mandate was decided. But he was also worried by the attitude of the British military administrators in Palestine, who, he implied, did not share the pro-Zionist sympathies of Balfour and Allenby, and asked that new men be put in place.[90] That British concerns over the situation in Palestine were not confined to Balfour was confirmed on 12 April at meetings with Lloyd George and with the influential diplomat Sir Eric Drummond. The Prime Minister's suggestion was that Weizmann should go to Palestine. In the discussion with Drummond, Weizmann asserted that Palestine was a Jewish rather than an Arab country, and must have been reassured when told that Balfour shared this view, but he was warned that they had to be careful.[91]

In the weeks and months that followed, the affairs of Palestine inevitably receded, since the terms of the German settlement were uppermost in the minds of the Allied leaders. It was inevitably a frustrating time for Weizmann, since it was still uncertain whether a Mandate for Palestine would be awarded to Britain, or, indeed, if it would accept it. French ambitions in the region were still active, and Feisal was apparently working hard to consolidate his position in Damascus, where he returned in April. Events on the ground had their own momentum, far removed from the rarefied atmosphere of Paris. It was soon clear that cracks were appearing in Feisal's apparent entente with Weizmann. On 16 May, Lieutenant-Colonel Cornwallis, Deputy Chief Political Officer at Damascus, reported that Feisal was beginning to realise that the question of relations between the Palestinians and the Zionists was not as simple as he had thought. Cornwallis also forwarded a translation of Feisal's

---

90 Weizmann to Arthur J Balfour, London, *LPCW*, Vol IX, 135, pp 128–32, also footnotes 1, 2 and 3.
91 Weizmann to Israel Sieff, Manchester, 12 April 1919, *LPCW*, Vol IX, 136, pp 132–4.

speech to Syrian notables in Damascus on 9 May, in which he had rallied support for Arab independence, expressions of solidarity coming from, amongst others, a delegate from Palestine.[92]

Weizmann's suspicions about the sympathies of the British military in Palestine were also far from groundless. On 5 May, Clayton forwarded a report from Arthur Money in which he stressed the degree of opposition to the Zionist programme which had been presented to the Peace Conference, concluding that as a result the population would prefer an American or French Mandate to that of Britain. Endorsing Money's appreciation, Clayton added that 'fear and distrust of Zionist aims grows daily and no amount of persuasion or propaganda will dispel it'. On seeing this, Balfour suggested to Curzon that Samuel be consulted on how the hostility to Zionism could be allayed by the administration.[93]

Where this new-found activism was coming from was explained in a report entitled 'The Arab Movement and Zionism', which was compiled by Major J N Camp, Assistant Political Officer in Jerusalem, on 12 August and forwarded to Curzon. Camp listed six Arab societies in Palestine, some of whose members he dismissed as 'ruffians and cut-throats', but others he knew were men of substance. With hindsight, what he had to say about al-Nadi al-'Arabi (The Arab Club), which he identified as being dominated by the Husayni family and strongly opposed to Zionism, is particularly interesting. Haj Amin al-Husayni, who was soon to come to prominence, was identified as among the leaders, though not, in Camp's view, as violent as some others. His overall conclusion was that 'practically all Moslems and Christians of any importance in Palestine are anti-Zionists, and bitterly so', and that 'Dr Weizmann's agreement with Emir Feisal is not worth the paper it is written on or the energy wasted in the conversation to make it'. So far his analysis might be held to sustain Weizmann's growing suspicion that the British military in Palestine was pro-Arab, but Camp's conclusions were rather more nuanced than that. He recommended that trouble might be averted by peaceful Jewish penetration, 'without the blaring of trumpets and without any special privileges such as Dr Weizmann and other official Zionists desire'. Britain could adopt a Mandate for Palestine, but not a Zionist Palestine. Immigrants could come in on a yearly basis as long as the land could sustain

---

92 *DBFP*, Vol IV, Doc 182.
93 *DBFP*, Vol IV, Docs 183 and 196.

them, a policy Britain was to adopt before too long. If this occurred, the Arabs could not object if the Jews gained supremacy in 20 or 30 years, he felt.[94]

Feisal's concerns

Before he returned to Syria in April 1919, Feisal wrote to Clemenceau. Robert de Caix, a senior French official known for his strong pro-colonial views, rejected Feisal's initial letter, which outlined the demands of the Syrian people and the basis on which he was willing to reach agreement with France.[95] The French, according to British accounts, had become increasingly exercised by what they considered British perfidy against them in Syria. Curzon regretfully reported 'the passionate intensity' with which France meant to stick to 'her Syrian pretensions'.[96] Feisal, too, was understandably concerned about the situation. He cabled Allenby in late May about rumours that the international commission was being cancelled and that a large French army was on the way to Syria. He warned that he could not be held responsible for what would happen in such an eventuality, but that much blood would be spilt. Allenby, as a result, warned his superiors in London that unless he could reassure Feisal that the commission would proceed, it was certain that he would raise the Arabs against the French and the British. This would endanger the whole position in Syria and Palestine and Allenby would be unable to handle the situation with the troops at his disposal.[97] These concerns were echoed in a cable from Clayton in Cairo to Curzon, in which he warned that 'violent local disturbances may combine into a general Anti-Christian and Anti-Foreign Movement'.[98] In British-occupied Mesopotamia the view was somewhat different. The commission was now considered a dangerous initiative and its arrival could 'undermine de facto position of European powers in the Middle East, where are [sic] military is not so strong that it can afford [to] neglect popular sentiment'.[99]

---

94 *DBFP*, Vol IV, Doc. 253.
95 *DBFP*, Vol IV, Chapter II Introductory Note, p 253.
96 *DBFP*, Vol IV, Doc 173.
97 *DBFP*, Vol IV, Doc 174.
98 *DBFP*, Vol IV, Doc 183.
99 Political Officer Baghdad to High Commissioner Egypt, 30 May 1919, TNA Fo4I158 119130/3.

Feisal placed far too much faith in the power of the Commission of Inquiry to give him control of all of Syria. He also completely overestimated the risks that the British and the Americans were prepared to take to protect him from the French, though he sometimes appeared to lurch into despair about his fate and that of Syria. One of his recurring motifs was that he could not understand 'why England should be so afraid of doing anything to offend the country [France], which should logically be prepared to make almost any sacrifice to avoid alienating England'. The result, as one British observer noted, was a lurking suspicion in the Emir's mind 'that the Arabs were being sold'.[100]

Allenby visited Damascus to meet Feisal on 12 May. His arrival was greeted by organised groups of schoolchildren and patriots demonstrating for independence in an attempt to persuade him of the mass popular appeal of Syrian nationalism. Feisal addressed a gathering of notables of Syria. They endorsed a programme of independence, and voted to grant him full powers. He referred to a plan to have a pan-Syrian conference that would declare independence without reference to the Peace Conference. Allenby persuaded him not to do so. According to the British political liaison officer, the 'politicians have only two convictions: firstly they want independence, and secondly that they do not want France. Anti-French feeling is surprisingly strong amongst the people who count, and it is very doubtful whether Feisal would be permitted to bring about a rapprochement even if he wanted to.'[101]

The King-Crane Commission

The Commission of Inquiry nearly did not get off the ground. Increasingly concerned about who garrisoned Syria, Clemenceau demanded that French troops take over from the British in advance of the commission. Lloyd George refused on the grounds that it would lead to widespread trouble in Syria. However, to stave off a complete collapse in Anglo-French relations and also possibly to forestall the commission from investigating British rule in Mesopotamia, he agreed that Britain would withdraw from the commission if France stayed out.[102] Wilson, who had first proposed the idea had, according to one source, 'clean forgotten'

---

100 *DBFP*, Vol IV, Doc 189, Annex B.
101 *DBFP*, Vol IV, Doc 182, Enc I.
102 *DBFP*, Vol IV, Doc 176.

about it.[103] After an appeal from Feisal, however, he ordered the American appointees, Dr Henry C King, President of Oberlin College in Ohio, and Charles R Crane, a Chicago businessman, and their staff to proceed with the mission.

The French appear to have viewed the commission as worthless even before it reported. Picot confided to Clayton in Cairo that it was a cover 'to keep him [Feisal] in the dark while the partition of Syria is being arranged'.[104] He later told Feisal that the commission had no standing with the Peace Conference and was a private initiative of President Wilson. Feisal refused to accept this interpretation.[105] King and Crane were predisposed to support the French claim for a Mandate, informing Wilson that the need for harmony between Britain and France was more important 'than the will of the people of Syria'.[106]

The commission spent April and May gathering information regarding the region before finally arriving in Jaffa in Palestine in mid-June 1919 and proceeded to travel through Palestine and Syria over the next six weeks. They left for Istanbul on 21 July.[107] The British were informed that they intended to make their stay as short as was possible 'consistent with adequate investigation of the problems before them'.[108] Feisal and his Syrian allies made great efforts to sell the Arab cause to the commission. Since the establishment of the Arab government in Syria at the end of the war, nationalist elites made up of urban notables and a middle stratum of intellectuals, army officers and professionals had been used to administer Feisal's Syria. They designed their greeting of the King-Crane Commission to present 'an image of a sophisticated nation eager and prepared for independence'. However, it is argued that they failed to win the allegiance of the masses.[109] A Syrian Congress was hastily put together. The intention was that this would demonstrate the absolute rejection of French rule by the Arabs of Syria. It was a somewhat

103 James L Gelvin, 'The Ironic Legacy of the King-Crane Commission', in David W Lesch, *The Middle East and the United States: A Historical and Political Reassessment* (Westview Press, Boulder, CO: 1996) p 16.

104 *DBFP*, Vol IV, Doc 181.

105 *DBFP*, Vol IV, Doc 192.

106 Gelvin, 'The Ironic Legacy of the King-Crane Commission', p 16.

107 The full itinerary is in *FRUS PPC*, Vol 12, pp 753–4.

108 *DBFP*, Vol IV, Doc 199.

109 Gelvin, *Divided Loyalties*, p 35.

imperfect and unrepresentative body. Delegates from French-controlled areas were unable to attend and minorities, be they Shias or Christians, were under-represented.

Nonetheless, King, Crane and their delegation fanned out across the countryside of Syria and Palestine taking soundings from people. They visited more than 30 towns and received thousands of petitions and delegations from villages. There was no ambiguity in the evidence that was presented to the commission: it was all anti-French. Contrary voices, such as the Maronite Christians from Lebanon, were excluded mainly by intimidation. The commission was firmly of the view that there was practically no appetite for a French Mandate in Syria. It also believed that within Syria, 'there is raw material here for a much more promising state than we [the USA] had in the Philippines'.[110] They stated baldly: 'In our judgment proclamation of [a] French Mandate for all Syria would precipitate warfare between Arabs and French, and force Great Britain to dangerous alternative.'[111] Furthermore, 'England would be obliged to choose between Arabs and French with Egypt and India in background'. The only support for a French Mandate came from 'strong parties of Lebanese who demand complete separation of Lebanon with French collaboration'. The commission was in no doubt that Feisal was the key figure:

> Emir Feisal despite limitation of education has become unique outstanding figure capable of rendering greatest service for world peace. He is heart of Moslem world, with enormous prestige and popularity, confirmed believer in Anglo-Saxon race; real[ly] great lover of Christians [Christianity]. Could do more than any other to reconcile Christians [Christianity] and Islam and longs to do so.[112]

It is argued that Feisal's manipulation of the commission to exclude contrary views was a tactical blunder. Furthermore, by placing too much faith in the commission to the exclusion of accommodation with France, Feisal, according to one hostile critic, 'effectively signed away his imperial

110 *Wilson Papers*, Vol 61, p 442.
111 *FRUS PPC*, Vol 12, p 749.
112 *FRUS PPC*, Vol 12, p 750.

dream'.[113] His faith in the power of the commission to influence the Peace Conference had been encouraged by the British.[114]

The committee reported to the Peace Conference on 28 August 1919. Its recommendations were a serious problem for the policies of the Great Powers. In the most explicit terms imaginable, it made clear that only a small fraction of opinion in Syria favoured a French Mandate. It proposed that America instead take the Mandate, and if it were unwilling that Britain do so. Since it was quickly pigeonholed, the report might have merited a brief footnote, if that, but for what it revealed about the political temper of Syria and Palestine. Comparing the Balfour Declaration with what they had heard from the Zionist Commission in Palestine, the two commissioners reported that a National Home was not the same as a Jewish state, nor could the latter be brought about except by trespassing on the rights of the existing non-Jewish communities. The Zionist representatives, they said, were looking forward to the dispossession of the non-Jewish inhabitants through purchase. Referring to Wilson's speech of 4 July 1918, in which he had emphasised the need for the acceptance of any settlement by the people concerned, they reported that nine-tenths of the population were opposed to Zionism. British officers they had consulted had said that the Zionist programme could only be carried out by force of arms. They also dismissed the Zionist claim to Palestine on the grounds that the Jews had lived there 2,000 years before. While it has been suggested that the two men were the victims of propaganda, their report broadly confirms what was being heard from other sources.[115]

The evolution of the British Mandate for Palestine

While such investigations were ongoing, the task before Weizmann and his colleagues was clearly to ensure that the British moved swiftly to confirm their commitment to a Palestinian Mandate and implementation of the Balfour Declaration. On 31 May, Curzon followed Balfour's advice and communicated to Samuel the gist of Clayton's pessimistic analysis of the situation in the country, and asked him how he thought

---

113 Karsh and Karsh, *Empires of the Sand*, p 278.
114 See *DBFP*, Vol IV, Doc 178, and Karsh and Karsh, *Empires of the Sand*, p 279, who are critical of Feisal's illusions and the British role in encouraging them.
115 Esco, *Palestine*, Vol I, pp 213–22; Antonius, *The Arab Awakening*, pp 443–58.

the administration in Palestine could counter the opposition to Zionism. Samuel, Weizmann and Sokolow conferred, and on 6 June Weizmann submitted their reply in Samuel's name. It accused the administration in Palestine of not conducting its policies in accordance with the Balfour Declaration, and that, as a result, the Arabs had been encouraged in the belief that they could force the British to abandon it through agitation. The answer, it was argued, was to convince them that the matter was 'a *chose jugée* and that continued agitation could only be to the detriment of the country and would certainly be without result'. Hence, the government should send definite instructions to the local administration that Britain would accept the Mandate for Palestine and that its terms would include the substance of the Balfour Declaration.[116]

Balfour, previously preoccupied with the principal peace treaty terms, seems to have taken the point that something now needed to be done, especially since the Conference was winding down, and Wilson and Lloyd George would be leaving Paris shortly. On 26 June, two days before the signing of the Treaty of Versailles, Balfour addressed a memorandum to the Prime Minister, outlining his views on the shape of a Turkish settlement. This document stated that all the Arab territories should be separated from the empire and put under Mandates. France should get the Mandate for Syria, Britain that for Mesopotamia, and Palestine should be awarded either to the United States or Britain. Curzon endorsed this, with the proviso that he did not think Congress would permit any American Mandates.[117]

With his business before the Conference concluded, Weizmann left for London. There he kept up the pressure on Whitehall, meeting Graham at the Foreign Office on 2 July. Denouncing the current administration in Palestine in no uncertain terms for its pro-Arab bias, he accused Allenby of taking no interest in the country and Clayton of being weak, while particularly castigating Storrs, the Governor of Jerusalem. In his minute on Graham's report, Curzon sourly observed that the Zionists were reaping the harvest they had sowed.[118]

Weizmann was also conferring with Cecil with a view to pushing ahead with the Mandate. On 24 July, a somewhat mystified Philip Noel Baker,

---

116 *DBFP*, Vol IV, Doc 197.
117 *DBFP*, Vol IV, Doc 211.
118 *DBFP*, Vol IV, Doc 213.

Secretary to the Commission on Mandates, wrote to the Foreign Office that Cecil and Weizmann had agreed that a draft Mandate should be drawn up and published. Balfour was non-committal, minuting that any draft Mandate should be referred to him.[119] Even so, Weizmann's campaign seems to have succeeded, since on 4 August Curzon telegraphed Colonel John French, Acting Chief Political Officer, instructions for the guidance of the administration:

> His Majesty's Government's policy contemplates concession to Great Britain of Mandate for Palestine. Terms of Mandate will embody substance of declaration of November 2, 1917. Arabs will not be despoiled of their land nor required to leave the country. There is no question of majority being subjected to the rule of minority, nor does Zionist programme contemplate this.

Echoing the memorandum which Samuel and Weizmann had submitted, the Arabs were to be told that the establishment of a Jewish National Home was a *chose jugée* and continued agitation would be useless and detrimental.[120]

On 11 August, Balfour felt compelled to pen a major analysis on the affairs of Syria, Palestine and Mesopotamia. Palestine was not really its main focus, since what was clearly exercising him were the continuing Anglo-French differences over Syria. Even so, what he had to say about Palestine reveals a great deal about his true feelings towards Zionism and the Arabs. Conceding that there was no intention of even going through the motions of consulting the wishes of the inhabitants, he wrote: 'The four Great Powers are committed to Zionism. And Zionism, be it right or wrong, good or bad, is rooted in age-long traditions, in present needs, in future hopes, of far profounder import than the desires and prejudices of the 700,000 Arabs who now inhabit that ancient land.' The Powers, he concluded, had made 'no declaration of policy which, at least in the letter, they have not always intended to violate'.[121]

That autumn, the Weizmanns travelled to Palestine. It was Vera Weizmann's first visit, but she found it a sore disappointment. In particular,

---

119 *DBFP*, Vol IV, Doc 227.
120 *DBFP*, Vol IV, Doc 236.
121 *DBFP*, Vol IV, Doc 242.

the trained doctor in her was appalled by what the pioneering Jewish women were doing. Their physical labour, she felt, was undermining both their health and their prospects for future motherhood. In building up the National Home, they were sacrificing their homes and diet. Before leaving for England, she sent them some flowers to thank them for their hospitality.[122]

The Turks and European imperial ambitions

While the victorious powers had wrestled with the nature of the peace settlement with Germany and the future shape of much of Europe, they had also seen something of the emerging shape of the Middle East as a result of the representations made by Feisal and Weizmann. Otherwise, the affairs of Turkey had barely featured in the discussions in Paris, but that did not mean that events were not unfolding on the ground. Italian troops had landed in Antalya, on Turkey's Mediterranean coast in January 1919, and had begun to fan out north and west. The Turkish population did not resist them. The occupied areas had faced starvation and the lifting of the Allied blockade and the arrival of supplies brought welcome relief. But there was a more important reason for Turkish acquiescence. Many Turks, including leading nationalists, felt that occupation by 'civilised' European powers would be temporary. Mustafa Kemal was not alone in claiming to have foreseen that the Western Allies would pack up and go. Another Turkish nationalist commander, General Kâzım Karabekir, wrote in his memoirs that he had always argued that the Turks would have to fight not the Western Allies, but only the Greeks and the Armenians who wished to oust them from their homeland. The thought of their former subjects lording it over them, at best, and, more likely, killing and driving them out, as Muslims had been killed and driven out from the Balkans, was bound to galvanise Turkish resistance. 'Are you willing to be ruled by your Greek grocer?' Turkish nationalists asked as they tried to rally Turkish villagers to their cause. The threat became concrete in May 1919.

Faced with reports that Italian warships were steaming towards İzmir and that the Italians were about to occupy the city they had been promised as a reward for their part in the war, Lloyd George persuaded Wilson and Clemenceau to authorise the Greeks to land there first. The decision

---

122 Vera Weizmann, *The Impossible Takes Longer*, pp 91–2.

by the Supreme Allied Council at the Paris Peace Conference was taken on 6 May in the absence of the Italian delegation. Venizelos, who had been assiduously cultivating the Allies in Paris, was informed immediately. The previous February he had set out Greek territorial claims which included western Anatolia – the shores of the Sea of Marmara and of the Aegean with a sizable hinterland – and the whole of Thrace up to the outskirts of Istanbul. When the authorisation to land Greek troops in İzmir was communicated to him, he was ready for it.

Greek soldiers landed in the flourishing cosmopolitan port of İzmir on 15 May 1919. Cheered to the echo by local Greeks, they were blessed by Chrysostom, the Greek Orthodox archbishop, who was of course an Ottoman subject. As a first column of Greek soldiers marched towards Government House, known as the Konak, a shot rang out. Greek troops responded by firing wildly as they attacked the barracks of the small Turkish garrison, which had no option but to surrender. Captured Turkish soldiers were kicked and bayoneted. Then a mob of the local Greek underclass looted the main Turkish neighbourhood, maltreating its inhabitants. Worse was to follow as Greek troops advanced inland. The town of Aydın (after which the province of İzmir was named) was destroyed, as a weak contingent of Greek soldiers was driven out by a local Turkish resistance band, which ransacked the Greek quarter, and then the Greeks returned in force and set fire to the Turkish quarter.

The Allies, who had tried to justify the Greek occupation on the grounds that it would ensure the security of the local population, were shocked into appointing a Commission of Inquiry under the American High Commissioner in Istanbul, Admiral Bristol. Its findings were highly unfavourable to the Greeks, whom it held responsible for the incidents which had followed the landings. More importantly, it noted that the occupation had 'assumed all the forms of an annexation', and recommended that the Greek troops should be replaced by Allied troops under the authority of the Supreme Allied Commander in Asia Minor. When the report of the commission was considered by the Supreme Allied Council in Paris on 9 November 1919, Clemenceau questioned the desirability of a Greek presence in Asia Minor. His doubts were ignored. But they presaged a division in the ranks of the Allies.

Venizelos tried to hasten a peace settlement with Turkey before he was left alone to face growing Turkish resistance. But the Allies had other priorities. As a temporary measure, at the suggestion of General George

Milne, the commander of British forces in Turkey, a line was drawn beyond which Greek troops were not to advance. The Milne Line, as it came to be known, also served to prevent friction between Greek forces and Italian troops which had landed south of İzmir and held the small port, known at the time in the West by its Italian name of Scala Nova,[123] and much better known to millions of tourists today as the flourishing resort of Kuşadasi, near the ruins of ancient Ephesus. An open clash between Greeks and Italians was indeed avoided, but the latter, having lost the prize of İzmir, retaliated by being the first of the Principal Allies to offer discreet help to Turkish nationalists. They were allowed to use the facilities of Scala Nova to enter and leave the country, and to obtain military equipment, as the Italians looked the other way. Count Carlo Sforza, who had served as an Italian diplomat in Istanbul and became Foreign Minister in 1920 (refusing two years later to serve the Fascists after Mussolini's march on Rome), was critical of Lloyd George's policy of supporting (and, at times, egging on) the Greeks in their expansionist ambitions. During the five months he spent in Istanbul between December 1918 and May 1919, Mustafa Kemal was promised Italian protection should the British try to arrest him. The intermediary was Mme Corinne Lütfi, the Italian widow of an Ottoman naval officer, who was young Mustafa Kemal's intimate friend and mentor in Western manners. In Turkey, as in other parts of the Middle East, the ambitions of the victorious powers were being challenged by the growth of local political aspirations.

---

123 Michael Llewellyn Smith, *Ionian Vision* (Allen Lane, London: 1973) pp 89–110.

4

San Remo and Sèvres: the Flawed Peace

Although the Allied leaders in Paris were understandably preoccupied with the settlement in Europe, affairs in the Middle East were developing their own momentum, since the Turks, in particular, were not long in taking matters into their own hands. By May 1919, the first stirrings of a new nationalism were already emerging across Anatolia, which, under the clear-sighted leadership of Mustafa Kemal, was to see an end to the Ottomans, the Caliphate and the Young Turks, confound the predatory ambitions of Armenians and Greeks, and within the space of a few years usher in a nation-state which bore scant resemblance to what had gone before. It was one of the most remarkable transformations of the period, not least since the Turkey which ultimately emerged proved more durable than some of the states which were being patched together in central and eastern Europe. Significantly, the focus of that nationalism was the Turkish heartland of Anatolia rather than cosmopolitan Istanbul. As this was developing far from the rarified negotiating chambers in Paris, the European powers were intent on pursuing their own agendas for the region. While they did so, Arab nationalists, their hopes for an independent kingdom still focused on Feisal, and the Zionists, pursuing their National Home in Palestine, nurtured and pursued their own aspirations.

The Turkish resistance

Traffic swirls past the statue of Hasan Tahsin in Konak (Government House) Square on the impressive newly rebuilt waterfront of İzmir.

Hasan Tahsin was the pseudonym of the journalist who shot dead the standard-bearer of the first Greek detachment of occupation troops in İzmir on 15 May 1919 (and was himself killed soon afterwards). The statue, which shows Hasan Tahsin raising the Turkish flag (rather than shooting at the Greek flag) is known as the monument to The First Shot in the Turkish War of Independence. Few passers-by know that Hasan Tahsin was a member of the CUP Special Organisation, set up to conduct unconventional warfare. Hasan Tahsin's first shot had been less successful: in Bucharest in October 1914, he shot but failed to kill Noel Buxton and his brother Charles, two prominent British liberals associated with the Balkan Committee in London, who had championed Slav Macedonians against the Turks in the opening years of the 20th century and then tried in vain to enlist Bulgaria in the ranks of the Allies.

However, the first organised resistance to the Greek occupation took place not in İzmir city on 15 May 1919, but a fortnight later, on 29 May, in the seaside town of Ayvalık, further north along the eastern shore of the Aegean. Ayvalık was at the time inhabited largely by Greeks (and was then, as now, famous for its olive oil presses, rather than for the quince trees which gave the town its name). On that day, Lieutenant-Colonel Ali (Çetinkaya) ordered his regiment, quartered in the town, to open fire on the Greek troops which were moving in to occupy the area. The Greek landing was not thwarted, and Çetinkaya's regiment retreated to the interior. It had little choice in the matter. As a result of demobilisation and desertions, the regiment numbered only 150 men armed with two machine-guns. The whole area in and around İzmir, which the Greeks occupied, had been held by 4,400 Turkish soldiers commanded by 143 officers.

Hasan Tahsin, a civilian, and Ali Çetinkaya, a soldier, had in common that they were both active members of the CUP. Çetinkaya survived the war and had a colourful career. Elected a member of the Turkish National Assembly, in 1925 he shot dead a fellow MP, Halid Pasha (known as 'Mad Halid'), a general who had distinguished himself against the Armenians on the eastern front, and later become an outspoken critic of Mustafa Kemal. The following year Çetinkaya presided over the notorious Independence Tribunal (the revolutionary court), which sentenced to death the prominent Young Turk politician Cavid Bey, Ottoman Finance Minister during the First World War, who was unjustly accused of being an organiser of a plot to kill Mustafa Kemal.

Today Çetinkaya is commemorated less controversially by the university which bears his name in his native town of Afyonkarahisar in western Anatolia, the first town to be regained by the Turkish army which drove out the Greeks in 1922.

The political trials and executions in 1926, which sealed the break between Mustafa Kemal and the CUP, have overshadowed the important part played by the CUP in organising early Turkish nationalist resistance after the armistice of Mudros, signed by the Ottoman Empire at the end of the First World War. As recent research shows, the CUP leadership had laid plans for resistance in Anatolia in anticipation of defeat in the First World War. But although most of Turkey's nationalist leaders after the war had been active members of the CUP, they had another, and more important, common bond. Most of them were professional soldiers who, as front line commanders, had personal experience of the deficiencies of Enver's leadership during the war and were well aware of the downside of the alliance with Germany. The CUP had been the standard-bearer of Turkish nationalism which had arisen as a response to the claims of other national communities in the Ottoman Empire. When the defeated CUP leaders fled the country discredited in November 1918, the standard passed to other hands – the hands of their erstwhile companions and rivals.

The nationalist officers who organised Turkish resistance to the partition of their country had hoped that the armistice would be a prelude to peace with honour. Nevertheless, they had taken the precaution, wherever possible, of moving troops and weapons to the interior of Anatolia out of reach of the Allied armies. When hostilities ended, their main concern was to retain command of those troops that were still under arms and to frustrate Allied efforts to disarm them. By and large they retained control of the War Ministry in Istanbul until Damad Ferid, the trusted man of the Sultan and of the Allies, became Grand Vizier in March 1919.

After the Young Turkish revolution of 1908 and particularly after the disastrous defeat of Ottoman armies in the Balkan Wars, the CUP had carried out a thorough purge of the senior command. They also put an end to the inflation of senior ranks to which Sultan Abdülhamid had had recourse to win the army's loyalty. Commanders who survived the CUP purge had their ranks reduced, and promotion during the First World War had to be won on merit and was, in any case, slow. Mustafa Kemal

was a colonel when he commanded a key sector in Gallipoli, and a brigadier when he was put in charge of whole armies on the eastern and southern fronts. İsmet (İnönü), who was his chief-of-staff on the eastern front
in 1916, was still a colonel when he was appointed under-secretary at the
War Office a week before the armistice. It was this policy which Damad
Ferid tried to reverse when he assumed office. Unsuccessful elderly generals purged by the CUP before the outbreak of the war were reinstated. A
glaring example was the appointment as Military Governor of İzmir, just
prior to the Greek occupation of the city, of the Ottoman commander
who had surrendered Salonica to the Greeks in 1912.

The fate of İzmir strengthened the resolve of Turkish nationalist officers to retain control of the War Ministry and through it of appointments
in the interior. By the time the Allies realised the key role of the War
Ministry in Istanbul and moved to occupy it, Turkish military resistance had taken shape out of their reach. Three young generals, Mustafa
Kemal (Atatürk), Kâzım Karabekir and Ali Fuad (Cebesoy) had hood-
winked the Sultan and his Grand Vizier and secured command of forces
which became the nucleus of a new Turkish national army. The first to
leave Istanbul was Ali Fuad, a close friend and companion of Mustafa
Kemal from their days as cadets in the Istanbul War College. He took up
command of the army corps in central Anatolia which had its headquarters in Ankara, the eastern railhead of a branch line of the incomplete
Istanbul–Baghdad railway. Ali Fuad was followed by Kâzım Karabekir
who was appointed commander of the army corps in the eastern Anatolian fortress town of Erzurum. This was the largest concentration of
Turkish troops after demobilisation. But it numbered only some 18,000
men.[1]

The gathering forces in Anatolia

Mustafa Kemal left Istanbul on 16 May, the day after the Greek landing
in İzmir. He was armed with wide-ranging powers as inspector of all the
Ottoman troops in eastern Turkey with additional jurisdiction covering
most of unoccupied Anatolia where he could issue orders both to military commanders and to the civil administration. A few days later, Rauf
(Orbay), who had resigned his commission in the navy, left Istanbul for
the eastern shores of the Sea of Marmara. Himself of Caucasian origin,

---

1 Kâzim Karabekir, *İstiklâl Harbimiz* (Yapi Kredi, Istanbul: 2008) Vol I, p 24.

Rauf rallied to the Turkish resistance the warlike Circassians who had been settled on the eastern approaches to the capital in the second half of the 19th century when they were expelled by the Russians from their ancestral lands in the western Caucasus. The commander of the Turkish division stationed in the area was also a Circassian, and was ready to resist foreign occupation.

After his return from the Syrian front in November 1918, Mustafa Kemal had made use of all his political contacts to secure the post of War Minister in the governments which were formed in quick succession after the armistice. In several audiences he tried to reinforce the favourable opinion which the Sultan had formed of him during their trip to Germany in the last year of the war. But although he was known as a critic of the CUP leadership, he had been a member of the CUP, and the perennial losers of the Liberal Union, who came to power when Damad Ferid became Grand Vizier, did not trust him fully. Moreover, Mustafa Kemal was notoriously ambitious and, therefore, a threat to those who had finally achieved office. But suspicious as they were, the Sultan and Damad Ferid needed a commander who had influence with the remnants of the Ottoman army. The superannuated generals they rescued from obscurity were clearly incapable of ensuring the loyalty to the throne of serving officers.

The Allies had threatened to occupy areas where public order was disturbed. There had been some bandit activity in the hinterland of İzmir, although the disturbance this caused was minor in comparison with what would follow the Greek occupation. Greeks lived also in considerable numbers along the shores of the Black Sea, with prosperous Greek communities in most coastal towns, while the interior was dominated by Muslims. Many of these Pontic Greeks (named after the Euxine Pontus, the name by which the Black Sea was known in classical antiquity) had emigrated to Russia, particularly after the Russian conquest of the Caucasus, and were now in flight from the Bolsheviks. Returning to the Ottoman shores of the Black Sea, they swelled the number of local Greeks who, with their clergy in the lead, were now clamouring for a Christian Pontus state which would recreate the kingdom of the Comnenes, the last Byzantine dominion to be captured by the Ottoman Turks. Venizelos, with his eyes fixed on Aegean Turkey and ultimately on Constantinople (Istanbul), thought it more practicable to have a Greek-Armenian state around Trabzon (Trebizond), on the assumption that local Armenians deported from the area would return. In either case, local Turks felt threatened. Known as Lazes, although the Laz, properly speaking, lived only in the eastern portion of the Ottoman Black Sea coast, where they preserved their ancestral tongue, akin to Georgian, they were late converts to Islam, and, after the fashion of late converts, passionate in defence of their faith. Living in a narrow strip squeezed between the mountains and the sea, they found an outlet for their energy as seamen, but also as bandits moving in and out of their mountain hideouts.

In April 1919, the Sultan's government sent out 'Commissions of Admonition' led by Ottoman princes to persuade its subjects of different faiths to live peacefully together. It was a vain attempt, as the leaders of Christian communities, Greeks and such Armenians as survived or had returned, were determined to break away from the Ottoman state and refused to have anything to do with the imperial princes. Nor were the Muslims impressed. The princes sent out on safari looked down on the natives. On his arrival in Trabzon, Prince Cemalettin found the boys of the local high school too noisy and complained to the headmaster. 'Your school,' he wrote, 'is as noisy as a synagogue full of Jews chanting their prayers. Is this row a premonition of a rebellion in the country? Or is it that you are not in control of the school? We would like to know.'[2]

The prince, and his master the Sultan, were soon to find out. But in the meantime, the Sultan and his Grand Vizier understood that it was not enough to send out princes to admonish rebellious subjects. Only the army could re-establish order and, the palace hoped, thus deprive the Allies of an excuse to intervene. Receiving Mustafa Kemal on the eve of his departure for eastern Anatolia, the Sultan said to him: 'Pasha, you have already rendered many services to the state. They are now part of history. Forget about them, for the service you are about to render will be more important still. You can save the state.'[3] Apologists for the Sultan claim that this suggests he sent out Mustafa Kemal for the express (and secret) purpose of organising resistance to the partition plans of the Allies. The claim is disproved by the Sultan's own proclamation in exile when he accused Mustafa Kemal of breaking his oath of allegiance and of becoming an unbearable source of trouble for the nation.[4]

---

2 Karabekir, İstiklâl Harbimiz, Vol I, p 21.
3 Mango, Atatürk, p 216.
4 Murat Bardakçı, Şahbaba (Pan Yaymcilik, Istanbul: 1998) p 449.

It was not an accusation that weighed heavily on Mustafa Kemal's conscience. But many of his fellow commanders found it difficult to break with centuries of Ottoman imperial tradition. The Muslim inhabitants of Anatolia were even less ready to abandon their sovereign. Some, like the Circassians, were pulled both ways. They had experienced foreign oppression in the Caucasus and were determined not to be subjected to it in their new home. But they were passionate in their loyalty to the Sultan-Caliph. There was no Turkish popular revolt against the monarchy as there had been in Russia, Germany and Austria-Hungary. Most Muslims did not blame the Sultan, who had been largely powerless since the rise to power of the Young Turks, but rather the CUP leadership which had involved the country in a catastrophic war. The division between the largely illiterate, conservative Muslim masses and a ruling class schooled in Western culture, which had developed gradually since the introduction of the first reforms in the 19th century, had deepened as a result of the miscalculations of the Young Turks. In the eyes of the mass of Muslims, the Unionists, as the Young Turks were known in the country, were impious bunglers. The fact that resistance to foreign occupation was led by Unionists, however critical these may have been of the CUP leadership, had to be downplayed. Moreover, the Muslim population had been decimated by the war. The survivors were hungry and largely destitute. It was widely believed that the Young Turk leaders, or at least their friends, had enriched themselves while the country suffered.

The accusations were false as far as the CUP leaders were concerned. Outside their ranks as well there were probably fewer war profiteers in Turkey than in other belligerent countries. One reason was that Muslim Turks were new to trade, which had been the preserve of foreigners and of native Christians and Jews. In industry, Turks provided only 15 per cent of the capital and of the workforce.[5] The CUP had tried to redress the balance through their 'national', or more accurately nationalist, economic policy. But this was in its early stages. The political power of the Young Turks had not yet translated into wealth. Such little wealth as there was in the countryside was in the hands of individual landowners or, particularly in the Kurdish areas, of tribal leaders, some of whom doubled up as sheikhs – leaders of Muslim fraternities. Sixty-five per cent of the total agricultural area belonged to feudal lords and large

5 Doğu Ergil, *Milli Mücadelenin Sosyal Tarihi* (Tarhan, Ankara: 1981) p 60.

landowners,[6] but their holdings yielded little revenue because of lack of investment and an acute shortage of manpower.

Popular resistance to the country's partition was ideological only in the sense that Muslim religious sentiment was important in animating it. However, the main stimulus was fear of dispossession at the hands of Christian minorities, which had been richer than their Muslim neighbours. During and immediately before the war, some 113,000 Turkish families, most of them refugees from the Balkans, had been settled on the Aegean coast, mainly around İzmir, in the property of deported Greeks. When Greek troops occupied the area in 1919, the original owners returned and some 80,000 Turkish settlers fled to the interior.[7] This was exactly what Venizelos wanted. In a memorandum to Lloyd George, the Greek Prime Minister had suggested that intermigration should be encouraged between Greeks who lived outside the area in western Turkey which he claimed and Turks within it.[8] His aim was not the continued co-existence of Greeks and Turks in a mixed society but the creation of new nationally homogeneous states.

In eastern Anatolia most of the 860,000 Armenians who lived in the area before the war had been deported.[9] The Muslims who took over their property, and who were themselves destitute as a result of the war, resisted restitution. In the parts of southern Anatolia bordering on Syria, which the French had occupied at the end of 1918, some of the 150,000 or so Armenians who had been deported began to return and reclaim their property. It was in these areas that popular resistance to Allied occupation arose spontaneously.

Even before nationalist commanders took charge, Muslims began to form societies which campaigned against the extension of foreign rule. The first was the National Defence Society in eastern Thrace founded in December 1918. Paradoxically, there were more Greeks in Turkish eastern Thrace than in western Thrace, an area with a Muslim majority which had passed from the Ottomans to the Bulgarians and then to the Greeks. The chief city of eastern Thrace was Edirne (Adrianople), the second capital of the Ottoman Sultans, who had built some of their

6 Ergil, *Milli Mücadelenin Sosyal Tarihi*, p 54.
7 Ergil, *Milli Mücadelenin Sosyal Tarihi*, p 65.
8 Llewellyn Smith, *Ionian Vision*, p 71.
9 McCarthy, *Muslims and Minorities*, p 77.

most splendid monuments there. All Turks were bound to resist its loss. In the Aegean area, when the first Greek advance stopped at the Milne Line, Turkish resistance took shape outside it and found expression in a congress of anti-annexation societies. In the east, similar societies were formed in Trabzon (Trebizond) and in Erzurum, areas coveted by local Greeks and Armenians. They joined forces in the Society for the Defence of Rights of the Eastern Provinces, a title which came to be adopted by civilian nationalist organisations throughout the country.

The title derived from the 'rights of nations' which President Wilson had proclaimed in a speech to the US Congress. But it also had a deeper, revolutionary resonance, echoing the third article of the *Declaration of the Rights of Man*, voted by the French National Assembly in 1789. This proclaimed that 'the principle of all sovereignty resides essentially in the nation'. The slogan of national rights pointed to the leading role of the Young Turks in these civil self-defence organisations. They were joined by local clerics, usually muftis, who in Ottoman times, as now, were civil servants, and by local Muslim notables, usually landowners. The societies were the civilian base on which nationalist commanders relied to mobilise resistance to the foreigner and provide a semblance of legitimate authority to their efforts to enlist men and requisition supplies.

Even with local support, nationalist commanders needed time to assemble the remnants of the Ottoman army and lay hands on sufficient weapons to take the field. While they were preparing for a renewal of the armed struggle, armed resistance came from a traditional quarter. Throughout most of its history, and particularly when central authority was weak, Anatolia was prey to bandits. After the First World War, bands which had formed around renowned local outlaws were joined by tens of thousands of army deserters seeking refuge in the mountains and in the vast areas of abandoned countryside in the peninsula.

In western Turkey, the outlaws were known as *zeybek*, and their leaders as *efe*. They wore characteristic clothes – bandoliers slung over colourful jerkins and baggy trousers – and they had developed their own forms of folk dance, which passed also to their Christian neighbours and survive in the popular *zeybekiko* music in Greece. Revered today as folk heroes to whom monuments are erected, the *zeybeks* and their *efe* leaders protected and preyed upon the settled population in equal measure. Local Christians and the foreign troops (Greeks in the west, French south of the Taurus mountains) with which Ottoman Christians made common cause, knew them simply as *çete* (usually spelled [*t*]*cheté* in contemporary documents) or bands. Turkish nationalist commanders renamed them 'national (meaning popular) forces' (*kuva-yı milliye*). They tried to control them, stiffening them with regular army officers whenever they could.

Local Turkish administrators, threatened with the loss of their jobs, and landowners, who feared the loss of their land, helped the militias. Landlords were, in any case, used to employing outlaws or raising their own militias in order to hold their own against rivals, bandits and tax-collectors. The numbers of militia bands varied, as between raids many of their members returned to their villages where they were indistinguishable from other peasants. The best-known militia or outlaw leader was Demirci (Blacksmith) Mehmet Efe in the hilly country round the valley of the Menderes (Great Meander). There were some 1,800 armed men under his command divided into a dozen or so detachments.[10] Local Christians also had their militias, the best-known among which was the Greek *Mavri Mira* (Black Destiny) band, operating in the area of İzmit (Nicomedia) on the eastern approaches to Istanbul. But as the Greeks had a regular army in the field, the role of their militias was more limited.

The building-blocks of Turkish resistance were thus in place when the war ended. But they could only be assembled when the danger of dispossession at the hands of local Christians and their foreign protectors overcame the weariness of the Turkish population whose first care was to keep body and soul together. This danger became acute first in the east and south as the Armenians began to move in and then in the west when Greek troops landed in İzmir on 15 May 1919. Elsewhere, in central Anatolia round the city of Konya (known as the centre of the Whirling Dervishes and of intense Muslim piety), in the countryside round Ankara, and also in some Kurdish mountain areas, which were not directly threatened, people feared that the nationalists might compromise their precarious survival, which they thought might be secured more effectively if they chose obedience to the Sultan and his Grand Vizier. The nationalists therefore had to mobilise support where they could, persuading reluctant peasants in some places, and suppressing resistance to their plans in others. Nationalist commanders told the Kurds that if they made common cause with the British they would fall prey to the Armenians

---

10 Ergil, *Milli Mücadelenin Sosyal Tarihi*, pp 94–5.

rather than achieve self-rule. Where persuasion failed, nationalist leaders had recourse to the violence of punitive expeditions and of revolutionary courts. Resistance which lacks the cover of a recognised government has to fight on several fronts and needs both to elicit support and to inspire fear. But before all else, it needs leadership and organisation. This is what Mustafa Kemal provided.

The rise of Mustafa Kemal

On 19 May 1919 Mustafa Kemal arrived in Samsun, a port lying at the centre of Turkey's Black Sea coast. Informed of his arrival, Kâzım Karabekir invited him to proceed eastwards to his headquarters in Erzurum where the Defence of Rights societies of the Eastern Provinces were about to meet. Instead, Mustafa Kemal travelled inland south to Amasya, a picturesque town situated in a narrow river valley, where a Turkish regiment was quartered. At the height of Ottoman power, Amasya was where imperial princes were sent as governors to learn the art of state-craft. Mustafa Kemal chose it because he could act as host there to a meeting of nationalist leaders. He was joined by Ali Fuad from Ankara and Rauf who had travelled from the shores of the Sea of Marmara. Military commanders were contacted throughout the country and their agreement was obtained to a statement declaring that the Ottoman government in Istanbul was incapable of defending the national interest, and summoning delegates from every Turkish province to make their way to a congress in Sivas in order to take the country's destiny into their own hands. In the meantime nationalist commanders and civil governors were not to surrender their posts to the Istanbul government's appointees. It was a first step to the formation of an alternative government in Anatolia, and, although none of the commanders dissented, some had reservations.

Mustafa Kemal had arrived in Anatolia as the Sultan's representative. It did not take long for British control officers in Anatolia to realise that instead of overseeing the disarming of Turkish troops and preventing attacks on local Greeks, Mustafa Kemal had set about organising Turkish national resistance to the Allies. At the insistence of the British High Commissioner, the Sultan's government recalled Mustafa Kemal to Istanbul. But he was now outside their control. From Amasya he travelled east to Erzurum where he arrived still wearing his uniform as an Ottoman brigadier with the cordon of honorary ADC to the Sultan. As the Sultan moved to sack him, Mustafa Kemal resigned his commission. Although he was not himself prepared to break free from Istanbul right away, Kâzım Karabekir stood by Mustafa Kemal and eased the way to his election, first, to the chair of the Erzurum Congress of the Eastern Provinces' Defence of Rights societies, and then to the presidency of its permanent executive (called the Representative Committee), which became the nucleus of an alternative government in Anatolia. The Erzurum Congress adopted the first text of what became known as the National Pact which proclaimed the sovereign independence and indivisibility of Ottoman lands within the armistice lines of November 1918.

Leaving Karabekir in Erzurum, Mustafa Kemal made his way to Sivas where enough provincial delegates had assembled to justify the claim that they represented the whole country. After a desultory discussion of the possibility of accepting an American Mandate, which the US Congress was in any case unwilling to take on, the Sivas Congress re-affirmed the National Pact, and demanded that the nation should be consulted before the conclusion of a peace treaty, and that the Ottoman government should be represented at the Peace Conference by delegates enjoying the people's trust.

While the nationalist congress was in progress, a British officer, Captain Edward Noel of the Indian Army, made his way from Istanbul to the town of Malatya in south-eastern Turkey where he tried to mobilise the Kurds against Turkish nationalists. Kurdish tribal leaders who aspired to independence had formed in Istanbul a Society for the Advancement of Kurdistan, which sought British support for its ambitions. Captain Noel took up their cause, but his efforts, far from undermining Turkish nationalist resistance, provided Mustafa Kemal with a propaganda weapon. The Kurds were incapable of united action, and when Mustafa Kemal ordered a detachment of Turkish troops to march on Malatya, Captain Noel and his Kurdish contacts fled to Syria. Mustafa Kemal then made maximum use of the episode to discredit Damad Ferid's government. The charge that the Grand Vizier had sought to incite wild Kurdish tribesmen to march on patriotic Turkish Muslims assembled in Sivas caused indignation in the ranks of the Ottoman ruling class. More than a century earlier, the revolutionary fervour of colonists in British North America had been similarly stiffened by the accusation that King George's generals had incited the 'Redskins' against their kith and kin.

The Ottomans and the Allies

Damad Ferid had resigned in the aftermath of the Greek occupation of İzmir. The Sultan immediately asked him to form a new Cabinet into which respected elder statesmen – the former Grand Viziers Ahmet İzzet and Tevfik – were co-opted. The imperial decree re-appointing the Grand Vizier declared in ringing tones:

> At this crucial moment, when all members of the nation led by their Caliph and Sultan, the head of the six-and-a half-centuries-old dynasty, sprung from the nation's bosom, who is himself ready for any sacrifice, are united in the single aspiration to safeguard the nation in its entirety, we demand that you should devote all your energy to this sacred national cause.[11]

The Sultan was indeed ready for any sacrifice except that of his throne.

Originally the Allies had not intended to invite Ottoman representatives to the Peace Conference before they had agreed the terms of the settlement among themselves. But the French did not want Damad Ferid to look exclusively to the British for protection. They promised that he would be heard in Paris and arranged transport for him and his delegation on board a French warship. On 17 June, a month after the landing of Greek troops in İzmir, Damad Ferid presented a memorandum to the Allies in which he blamed the CUP leadership for Turkey's entry into the war, and likened the Unionists to the Bolsheviks. 'Now,' he said, 'just as the Allies are trying to liberate the Slav people, so too they should extend their help to the Turkish people in kindness and humanity.' He then outlined his proposals, which he filled out in a second memorandum on 23 June. Even as a first bargaining position, Damad Ferid's proposals were pitched high. Not only did he ask for the territorial integrity of the Ottoman Empire to be respected, but he claimed also the Greek islands close to the Turkish coast and western Thrace which had been lost in the Balkan Wars. The Arabs could have self-rule under princes appointed by the Sultan who would also remain patron of the Muslim shrines in Arabia.

The Allies rubbed their eyes in astonishment and delivered a stinging riposte. The Turks, they said, had proved themselves incapable of ruling

---

11 Mahmud Kemal İnal, *Osmanli Devrinde Son Sadriazamlar*, p 2040.

other races. Wherever they went, they caused destruction and the loss of prosperity and cultural vitality, which recovered only after their departure. The Allies respected Islam, but the Turks would do better in 'appropriate conditions' – in other words, cut down to size. The reply was as absurd in its insulting generalisations and national stereotypes as Damad Ferid had been in his expectations. The Allies then told Damad Ferid that they had other pressing business to attend to, and that his continued presence in Paris would serve no useful purpose. He would be informed in due course when the Allies had decided among themselves the terms of the Turkish peace settlement.[12] Damad Ferid returned to Istanbul empty-handed and discredited, just as Mustafa Kemal was rallying the forces of Turkish nationalism and Muslim resistance in Anatolia.

As the Allies were still busy with the European peace settlement, and with Greek occupation troops corralled behind the Milne Line, the Sultan gave way to Turkish nationalist pressure. Damad Ferid resigned on 2 October 1919, barely three weeks after the conclusion of the nationalist congress in Sivas, and was replaced by Ali Rıza Pasha, a 60-year-old field marshal who had been the unsuccessful commander of the Ottoman Western Army in the Balkan War. In line with the demands of the nationalists, the Sultan decreed that parliamentary elections should be held before a peace settlement was negotiated. The new Grand Vizier made an effort to reaffirm Ottoman sovereignty in the capital, demanding that local Greeks who were Ottoman subjects should not fly the Greek flag. He tried to heal the breach with Mustafa Kemal and dispatched his Navy Minister, Salih Hulusi (another superannuated general) to negotiate with him. Nothing came of the attempt. Local Greeks refused to have anything to do with the elections, held in December 1919, which were won handsomely by Turkish nationalists.

The deterioration of Feisal's position

In late 1919 Feisal's position was weakening. The call by the King-Crane Commission on 28 August for an American Mandate over Syria had simply not been in the realm of practical politics. By the end of the summer of 1919, it was becoming increasingly clear that Wilson, thanks to his alienation of his political opponents, would have great difficulty

---

12 Sina Akşin, *İstanbul Hükümetleri ve Millî Mücadele* (Cem, Istanbul: 1992) Vol I, pp 396–402.

in getting the Treaty of Versailles passed by Congress, controlled since the November 1918 election by the opposition Republican Party. Wilson had precious little political capital left. In July 1919 he returned to Washington and in September he began a national campaign for the Treaty of Versailles and the League of Nations. On 26 September 1919, in the midst of an extraordinarily demanding whistle-stop tour promoting the League and the Treaty, he suffered a paralyzing stroke. His political influence essentially ended. Ironically, the next day the King-Crane Commission report arrived in the White House. It is unlikely that Wilson ever saw it. The Wilsonian internationalist tide was ebbing. In November 1919 and March 1920, the Senate rejected the Treaty of Versailles. It also declined to take a Mandate over Armenia. Syria, and the idea of an American Mandate over it, was not even discussed by the US Congress. Indeed, General Tasker Bliss, a US delegate to the Peace Conference, had by November 1919 come to the conclusion that American arbitration of Turkish and Middle East problems was 'futile'.[13] The report of the King-Crane Commission was never looked at by the Peace Conference and remained unpublished until 1922.[14]

The strongest British card for defending Feisal – an emphasis on Wilsonian national self-determination – was now essentially a dead letter. Unsurprisingly, the autumn and winter of 1919 saw the British retreat in the face of French demands over Syria. This was in many ways motivated by the demands of the Chief of the Imperial General Staff, Sir Henry Wilson, and the Secretary of State for War, Winston Churchill, for realism by Lloyd George in military affairs.[15] To put it simply, Britain could not afford to maintain its occupation of Syria. Balfour as early as 19 August, and in advance of the King-Crane recommendations, bemoaned the impact of the Syrian question on Anglo-French relations despite Britain's already well-publicised renunciation of any interest in taking a Mandate in Syria.[16] The French press continued to denounce what they considered British attempts to deny France's rights in Syria throughout the summer.

---

13 *Wilson Papers*, Vol 64, p 27.

14 Harry N Howard, *The King-Crane Commission: An American Inquiry in the Middle East* (Khayats, Beirut: 1963) p 258.

15 Darwin, *Britain, Egypt and the Middle East*, p 171.

16 *DBFP*, Vol IV, Doc 242.

Feisal was also disturbed when Britain made clear to him that it was going to take the Mandate over Palestine and implement the Balfour Declaration. Feisal argued that this was a return to the 'Unjust Agreement of 1916' i.e. the Sykes-Picot Agreement.[17] Arguing that the majority of Arabs had asked for a single Mandate over Mesopotamia and Syria, he warned that if 'there is any possibility of [the] Peace Conference making a decision which is contrary to this desire and which involves a division of country, [he] cannot remain in his present position which would render him liable to the accusation that he consented to the ruin of his country'.[18]

The British, on the basis of hard-headed political calculation, had decided to cut their losses and withdraw their support for Feisal. Since the beginning of the year, one of the more pressing problems for the British government had been the expense of the vast military forces that it had deployed both in Europe and the Middle East. Syria was, quite simply, a far lower priority than Egypt, India, Mesopotamia and Ireland. Secondly, the British had every intention of enforcing their own Mandate in Mesopotamia. How then, as Balfour noted on 9 September, could Feisal expect a larger measure of independence from the French? He further remarked, 'Neither of us want much less than supreme economic and political control to be exercised no doubt (at least in our case) in friendly and unostentatious co-operation with the Arab – but nevertheless, in the last resort, to be exercised.'[19] Lloyd George consulted with Allenby and the Conservative Party's most influential Cabinet Minister, Andrew Bonar Law, in a series of meetings in Deauville from 9 to 11 September 1919. A decision was taken to evacuate British forces from the Syrian coast westwards to the Sykes-Picot line. The British subsidy to Feisal would be cut in half and France should take this up. This would all be done by 1 November 1919. Feisal was also instructed to come to France immediately.[20] This was communicated to Clemenceau at a meeting on 15 September. Feisal received the news in person from Lloyd George at 10 Downing Street four days later. Feisal warned that the consequences would be bloodshed.[21]

---

17 *DBFP*, Vol IV, Doc 236.
18 *DBFP*, Vol IV, Doc 256.
19 *DBFP*, Vol IV, Doc 265.
20 *DBFP*, Vol IV, Doc 278.
21 *DBFP*, Vol IV, Doc 283.

Feisal was now desperate for some way of avoiding a French occupation. He proposed three alternatives to the British: namely, that Allenby remain in control of the evacuated areas; an international commission to consider temporary arrangement until the Peace Conference had decided; or that the Peace Conference make an immediate decision on the fate of Syria. He also contemplated sending a mission to the United States. In spite of the fact that Arab opinion according to most British reports and the King-Crane Commission had turned very strongly against any significant Jewish settlement in Palestine, Feisal met again with Weizmann, who proposed that in exchange for Feisal's backing of the Zionist project, the Zionist movement could provide advisers and money to the Arab government. Feisal was inclined to accept the agreement provided the Zionists joined with the Arabs against the French, but Weizmann was reluctant to break with the French, arguing that they could be squeezed out of the coastal parts of Syria later.[22]

It was inevitable that Feisal, under considerable British pressure, would once more turn to the French. Lloyd George asked Clemenceau to avoid treating 'Feisal and the Arab problem with a high hand. If this were indeed the policy of the French Government, the British Government are afraid that it would inevitably lead to serious and long continued disturbances throughout the Arab territories which might easily spread to the whole Mohammedan world.'[23] Clemenceau took note of Lloyd George's views and began to moderate French aims. The objective remained to protect French imperial designs but now, crucially, an attempt would be made to satisfy Feisal and the British. Notably, Clemenceau prevented the French commander in Syria, General Henri Gouraud, from occupying the Bekaa Valley.[24] However, when Feisal and Clemenceau met in October and November there was no meeting of minds between them on the issue of sovereignty over Syria. Clemenceau was determined that French troops would occupy Syria and French administrators would have virtual carte blanche to run the country as they pleased. Feisal rejected this proposal.

However, Clemenceau and the French decided to make significant concessions, and new proposals were presented to Feisal on 16 December. Now, in return for the French having the sole monopoly over provision

22 *DBFP*, Vol IV, Doc 295.
23 *DBFP*, Vol IV, Doc 334.
24 *DBFP*, Vol IV, Doc 383.

of military and civilian advisers, who would be responsible to the Syrian government, and Feisal's acknowledgment of France as the Mandatory Power, Syria would have an independent parliament with the right to levy taxes and make laws and Feisal would be recognised as head of the new Syrian state. Additionally, France agreed not to station troops in the Arab part of Syria without the consent of the government. Feisal agreed these terms on 6 January 1920. However, Feisal had to secure popular support within Syria for the French Mandate before Lebanon would be handed over.[25] The agreement was kept secret. A French official who communicated the terms to the British claimed the French 'were rather nervous as to whether Feisal would be able to maintain his position on his return to Syria and for this reason the agreement was to be kept secret at present and Feisal was to return with an ostensibly clear hand'.[26]

Undoubtedly, Feisal was extremely unhappy with the agreement. He almost certainly realised that it would be difficult to sell to the radical nationalists, whose influence in Syria was steadily increasing. Conversely, Gouraud saw the new agreement as a defeat for France. He foresaw that the agreement would be interpreted by the Arabs as providing for their complete independence without any French influence.

The situation in Syria

Feisal's political influence in Syria was never all that strong. There were nationalist undercurrents there over which he had little control. His second trip to Europe at the end of 1919 reduced even this limited influence. Gertrude Bell, a member of the Arab Bureau, identified some of these problems when she visited Syria in October 1919. In her view things were falling apart as the Arab government had refused help or advice from the French while at the same time the British could not help for fear of damaging relations with the French. Therefore, she noted 'they go their own way and their way is not good'.[27] The main centres of power were three nationalist groups: the mainly Palestinian Arab Club

---

25 Karsh and Karsh, *Empires of the Sand*, p 281; Sachar, *The Emergence of the Middle East*, pp 272–3.
26 *DBFP*, Vol IV, Doc 412.
27 Gertrude Bell to Family, 12 Oct 1919. Gertrude Bell's Diaries and Letters have been digitized by the University of Newcastle and are available at <http://www.gerty.ncl.ac.uk>. All references to Bell's Diaries and Letters are to that source.

(al-Nadi al-'Arabi), the Syrian-led *al-Fatat*, which controlled the Arab Independence Party (Hizb al-Istiqlal al-'Arabi), and *al-Ahd*, which was made up of Iraqi members of the Ottoman army who had defected to the Arab Revolt. These organisations sometimes worked together for the Arab cause. Often though, they displayed more loyalty to their regional or tribal interest. In such a factional atmosphere there was also a tendency for these groupings to attempt to outbid each other with displays of nationalist fervour, which limited Feisal's room for compromise with the French.

The men left in control by Feisal and who dominated his brother Zeid were mainly from *al-Ahd*, whose key figure was Yasin Pasha al-Hashimi.[28] In Bell's view they were 'violent Nationalists and are out for an independent Syria and Mesopotamia without any foreign control'.[29] Her summary of the state of opinion in Damascus was that Feisal had lost ground.[30] In a dispatch written at the end of her visit she noted the sense of growing despair about the future in the Syrian capital:

> Damascenes are exceedingly anxious at the prospect which lies before them. At the end of the year the subsidy to the Sherif will cease and the financial position of the Arab Government will be extremely precarious but even if it can contrive to keep itself in existence and succeed in preventing open disorder it is anticipated that the French in the coast provinces will foster disturbances, either by the continuance of propaganda within the Arab State, or by provocative acts towards Moslems in the area under their administration, and that on the first breach of the peace their troops will cross the frontier on the plea of restoring order.[31]

When Feisal returned with his deal, he found that it commanded little popular support among nationalists. Another problem was the resignation of Clemenceau as French Prime Minister soon after the agreement was put into practice. The French elections at the end of 1919 had produced a conservative majority that had little interest in appeasing Arab

---

28 Bell Diary, 8 Oct 1919.
29 Gertrude Bell to Family, 12 October 1919.
30 Bell Diary, 13 Oct 1919.
31 'Syria in October 1919', November 1919, TNA Fo371/4152.

opinion. The new French Prime Minister, Alexandre Millerand, was of the view that France had already conceded too much to Feisal. There was also the problem that Syrian nationalists and independent bandits were stepping up attacks on French forces, which angered the French government. Gouraud had no confidence in Feisal and believed that he was in the hands of the most radical nationalist elements in Syria. The British were positive about the agreement but saw little prospect that Feisal would be able to implement it. As Lloyd George noted at an Allied conference in February 1920, Feisal was not in 'a consenting frame of mind'.[32]

Events bore out this gloomy assessment. Feisal was caught between the demands of the French and the Syrian nationalists. He desperately sought more concessions from Millerand. Specifically, he sought increased independence in foreign policy and a reduction in the size of the Lebanese state, but Millerand rebuffed the approach. On the contrary, the French Premier wanted the accords of 6 January to be amended to grant France even greater influence and control in Syria. His preference was for the division of Syria along ethnic and tribal lines, leaving it with a powerless centre. Feisal was now left with an ever-decreasing set of options. He either had to go completely over to the French and sanction the use of their troops to crush Syrian nationalists or he had to abandon all dealings with them and go over to active opposition. British reports noted the enormous pressure he was under from the extremist party. His father Hussein, perhaps out of envy of Feisal's successes, warned he would repudiate any agreement with France that did not safeguard Arab independence.

Yasin Pasha al-Hashimi, who exercised considerable influence over Feisal, had strongly opposed any pact with the French and led street demonstrations in January 1920 against the Feisal-Clemenceau agreement. Feisal's appeals for moderation fell on deaf ears. The nationalist cause meanwhile had given every nationalist but also every bandit licence to carry out attacks, especially in the coastal area.[33] Christians and other minorities in Damascus lived in fear of being massacred. On 6 March 1920, Feisal was obliged to reconvene the Syrian National Congress that had been formed for the visit of the King-Crane Commission. It

---

32 *DBFP*, Vol VII, Doc 12.
33 Malcolm B Russell, *The First Modern Arab State: Syria Under Faysal, 1918–1920* (Bibliotheca Islamica, Minneapolis: 1985) pp 166–8.

remained absolutely uncompromising in its nationalist views. It declared Feisal's accord with the French null and void and declared independence with Feisal as head of state. Palestine was proclaimed part of the new kingdom. Some time later Abdullah, Feisal's elder brother was proclaimed King of Mesopotamia. Feisal, as he had warned the British, had to go along with the nationalist tide or be overthrown.[34]

Appeals were made to other governments for recognition. The French saw the declarations by the Syrian nationalists as conclusive evidence that Feisal had endorsed the views of the extremists. In Lebanon, Christian groupings, no doubt with the encouragement of the French, proclaimed their independence from this new Syrian state. The British also suggested that Feisal's support in Damascus among Christians and the Druze was quite weak.[35] Millerand was determined that the declarations of the Syrian National Congress would not stand. The British were now very much in step with the French; Curzon, Foreign Secretary since the autumn of 1919, told them that the declarations were 'an unwarranted and intolerable exercise of authority' by the Syrian National Congress. However, Curzon also took the opportunity to berate the French for imperiling the British and French positions in the Middle East by 'forcing themselves into areas where the French were not welcomed by the inhabitants'.[36] The British were especially concerned by the Syrian National Congress's claims in Palestine and Mesopotamia. Lloyd George, though, seemed to be favourable to this and Allenby argued that Britain and France should recognise Feisal as sovereign over a confederation of Syria, Palestine and Mesopotamia while tying them administratively to Britain and France. Curzon, though, felt the plan was unclear and that consultations in Mesopotamia in 1919 had suggested that there was little appetite for a Sherifian ruler.[37]

Feisal appears not to have been concerned enough by the warnings issued by the British and French. Instead, the French were brusquely

34 Rohan Butler and J P T Bury (eds), *Documents on British Foreign Policy 1919–1939*, First Series, Vol VIII (Her Majesty's Stationery Office, London: 1958); hereafter *DBFP*, Vol VIII, Doc 214.

35 *DBFP*, Vol XIII, Doc 219.

36 *DBFP*, Vol IV, Doc 221.

37 Martin Gilbert, *Winston S. Churchill, Companion Volume IV*, Part 2: 1917–1922, (Heinemann, London: 1977) p 1050, hereafter Gilbert, *Churchill Companion, IV*, Part 2; *DBFP*, Vol XIII, Docs 217, 223, 224.

informed that they must recognise Syrian independence and withdraw their forces from Lebanon before he would return to Europe. Superficially, Feisal's position remained strong. The French appeared to have insufficient troops on the ground to drive the nationalists out. The British remained reticent about an assault on Feisal and the French also had the problem of Cilicia to the north of Syria, which Mustafa Kemal and his nationalist Turkish forces were beginning to menace. In early 1920, a French force was routed. Until these problems were resolved, there was no prospect of moving against Feisal.

However, in reality, Feisal's position was much weaker than it seemed. According to his own testimony, he was more or less forced into acceding to the independence declaration or face losing his crown. Indeed, he hoped the declaration would sate popular opinion in Syria and provide a breathing space in which he could negotiate a deal with the British and French. There were many in Syrian nationalist circles who would like to have made common cause with the Kemalists.[38] Furthermore, the military and economic position was desperate.[39] There were food riots in Hama just four days after the declaration of independence. Food shortages, rising prices and currency problems became increasingly acute. Politically, Feisal's position was weak. His ability to compromise with the French, which he almost certainly favoured, was constrained by extreme nationalists who brooked no compromise.

The San Remo Conference

The Treaty of Versailles came into force on 10 January 1920, even though on 19 November 1919, the American Senate had failed to ratify it. While the Treaty set the complex terms of the peace settlement with Germany, important issues remained to be resolved, not least in the Middle East. In the light of the forthcoming conference at San Remo in Italy, which would at last move forward the peace settlement with Turkey, Weizmann sought to reinforce his message with Robert Vansittart of the British Foreign Office. He was concerned to drive home that Palestine's position as the Jewish National Home should be embodied in the peace treaty with Turkey. What was perturbing him, it seems, was the possible nature of the Mandate system. The Mandates for the other areas of the former

38 Russell, *The First Modern Arab State*, pp 138–9.
39 Russell, *The First Modern Arab State*, pp 142–6.

Turkish empire were to be administered in the interests of their inhabitants, while the overriding purpose of that for Palestine, as far as the Zionists were concerned, was to be the creation of the Jewish National Home, the rights of the inhabitants being safeguarded.[40] He need not have worried, as it happened, but before the Conference took place he was to have an experience which gave him even more reason to be concerned about the future.

What Weizmann encountered at first hand was the growing strength of Arab opposition to the Jewish presence in Palestine, which he had been aware of for some time. In March 1920, he made a return visit to the country in the company of his elder son. The timing was bad, since the anger of the Arab population had been rising on a number of counts. There was growing frustration that promises they believed had been made over Arab independence were not being honoured. There was fear that the Balfour Declaration would lead to Arab subordination to the Jews as a consequence of massive Jewish immigration. Finally, there were hopes of an Arab state embracing both Syria and Palestine, ruled by Feisal from Damascus.[41] During his temporary stopover in Egypt, Weizmann became aware of growing unrest in parts of Palestine, which had resulted in the death of, amongst others, Joseph Trumpeldor, who had been organising Jewish defence groups. On 25 March, Weizmann summed up his impressions of the current situation in Palestine in a deeply pessimistic letter to the Zionist Executive in London. In this he castigated the military authorities for what he believed was their open hostility to the Jews and partiality towards the Arabs. The prevailing view amongst the officers, he reported, was that the Balfour Declaration had been a mistake. Such British attitudes were encouraging the Arabs, and, he confided, he had lost faith in Feisal.[42]

What then happened was tragic, but also a grim portent of what was to come in the affairs of Palestine. The proclamation of Feisal as King of Syria on 8 March 1920 by a Syrian Congress in which Palestinians were

---

40 Weizmann to Robert Vansittart, London, 1 March 1920, *LPCW*, Vol IX, 294, pp 320–2.
41 *Palestine Royal Commission Report*, Cmd 5479, Chapter II, 'The War and the Mandate'.
42 Weizmann to the Zionist Executive, London, 25 March 1920, *LPCW*, Vol IX, pp 325–30.

represented stirred demonstrations of support in various parts of Palestine, leading the British to ban further such events. Nevertheless, such a demonstration did take place in Jerusalem on 4 April on the occasion of the Muslim festival of Nabi Musa, which coincided with the Christian Easter and Jewish Passover. Amongst the organisers were the Mayor of Jerusalem, Musa Kasim al-Husayni, the newspaper editor Arif al-Arif and the young man who was soon to become the *bête noire* of both the Jews and the British, Haj Amin al-Husayni. Both Husaynis belonged to Jerusalem's most prominent Arab family. Once again, support for Feisal was the focus of the demonstration. In the violence which then followed, 5 Jews were killed and over 200 wounded, while 4 Arabs were killed and 21 wounded.[43] Weizmann, who had gone to Haifa to celebrate Passover with his mother, who had settled in Palestine after the Russian Revolution, returned with his son to Jerusalem to find the city under military occupation. Although he had been out of the city when the violence had broken out, there is no doubt that what had happened deeply shocked Weizmann, for whom these events were all too reminiscent of the Russian pogroms, only this time under the British.[44] Apart from what it revealed about Arab hostility, the outbreak also exposed the limitations of British power, which was far from reassuring to the Jews. Weizmann was fiercely critical of the actions of the British forces in disarming Jews. It was also alarming to the Jews that while Arif al-Arif and Amin al-Husayni were given ten-year sentences *in absentia*, Vladimir Jabotinsky, who had sought to mobilise young Jews, was sentenced to 15 years. However, what deeply worried Weizmann was the possible impact of these events on the deliberations and decisions of the forthcoming San Remo conference, which would settle the nature of the Middle Eastern Mandates as well as prepare the way for an overall Turkish settlement.[45]

Both Feisal and Weizmann, and the movements they led, were to be profoundly affected by the Conference's decisions. Interestingly, though, Feisal refused to attend, sending instead his chief-of-staff, Nuri al-Said, who was unable to influence the deliberations. Weizmann fared much

---

43 *Palestine Royal Commission Report*, pp 50–1; Mattar, *The Mufti of Jerusalem*, pp 15–18.

44 Weizmann to (Lady) Emma Caroline Schuster, Twyford, Montreux, 3 May 1920, *LPCW*, Vol IX, 318, pp 343–4.

45 Weizmann, *Trial and Error*, pp 318–21.

better even although he arrived in San Remo disheartened, apprehensive, and by his own account somewhat grimy. Since the Conference lasted from 18 to 26 April, and the future of Palestine was one of the last items under discussion, he did not have much to do. It was, perhaps, a measure of the toll that recent events had taken that in the course of his train journey to San Remo, he confided in Vera his distrust of the British.[46] He was clearly seeing clear water between the British he knew in London and those he was encountering in Palestine. Once there, however, several things occurred which relieved his anxieties. Balfour was able to reassure him that he and Curzon were agreed that the recent events in Jerusalem would not affect British policy, which had been Weizmann's main concern. He also learned that Lloyd George and Balfour were agreed that Samuel should be the first British High Commissioner to Palestine.

The future of Palestine came before the Supreme Council on 24 April 1920, chaired by the Italian Premier Francesco Nitti. Lloyd George, Curzon and Robert Vansittart were present for Britain, Prime Minister Alexandre Millerand and Philippe Berthelot of the Ministry of Foreign Affairs represented France, and Matsui Keishiro spoke for Japan. They were joined by the American Ambassador to Italy, Robert Underwood Johnson. Curzon opened by referring to the Balfour Declaration, which he grandly, if somewhat inaccurately, claimed had promised Palestine as the National Home of the Jews of the world, and which he said had been accepted by the major powers. What he wanted was that the Declaration as it stood should be incorporated into the treaty, claiming that he had resisted attempts by the Zionists to have its terms expanded. Curzon had clearly got wind of the fact that the French still had reservations. A lengthy debate with Berthelot confirmed this to be the case.

Berthelot countered by questioning several of Curzon's assertions. There had not, he stated, been any official acceptance of the Balfour Declaration by the Allied governments. While the French did not wish to thwart Britain's desire to give the Jews a National Home in Palestine, he queried what this meant. If it were to be different from other states, then it would create difficulties in the Muslim and Christian world. He was clearly thinking of France's large stake in Muslim North Africa, as well as its plans for Syria. The Christian dimension would emerge in

---

46 Weizmann to Vera Weizmann, Launay, 19 April 1920, *LPCW*, Vol IX, 306, pp 336–7.

the course of the ensuing debate. It would be best, he said, to refer the matter to the League of Nations. Curzon then treated Berthelot to a brief history lesson. He was not quite accurate in saying that Balfour had issued the Declaration on behalf of the Zionists, he said, but then went on to claim that it had been accepted by Pichon, then head of the French Foreign Office, by President Wilson, and by the governments of Greece, China, Serbia and Siam (now Thailand). The two men then wrangled for some time over exactly what Pichon had, or had not, agreed to.

Millerand adopted a rather softer line, while Nitti tried to bring the two sides to an understanding. Berthelot eagerly pounced on a statement by Matsui that his government had never accepted the Declaration as confirmation of his point that it was not official Allied policy. It then emerged that what was really troubling the French, and to an extent Nitti, was the position of the Catholic community in Palestine. The Vatican had made public its view that the French, and not the British, should be the protector of Catholic interests in the country. Lloyd George was adamant that there could not be two Mandatory powers in Palestine. The French were also keen to assert the political, as opposed to the civil and religious, rights of the non-Jewish communities of Palestine, which had been expressed in the Balfour Declaration, but Millerand conceded that he would be satisfied if this were placed on record.[47]

The following day, the Conference returned to the question of Mandates, especially the question of boundaries. There was no repetition of the prolonged wrangling of the previous day. The border of Palestine was linked to where that of the Mosul region would be, which had been a point of contention between Britain and France. The main issue between them was where the northern border of Palestine was to lie. The Zionist hope was that it would be along the Litani River, which would include the headwaters of the river Jordan. While acknowledging their case, Lloyd George was prepared to concede that this area had never formed part of Palestine, and that, as a result, the border should be focused on the town of Dan. On hearing this concession, Berthelot asked whether the Conference could now decide that the Mandates for Mesopotamia, or Iraq as it was to be known after 1921, and Palestine should be given to Britain, and Syria to France. Nitti agreed. The formal agreement regarding Palestine was that the country's administration be entrusted to a Mandatory to be

47 *DBFP*, Vol VIII, Doc 15.

chosen by the Principal Allied Powers. The chosen Mandatory Power was Britain. The Mandatory was charged with putting into effect the Declaration of November 1917, and it was confirmed that this instruction had been adopted by the other Allies.[48]

As the Conference ended, Lloyd George emerged to inform Weizmann of the decision to award the Palestine Mandate to Britain, with the incorporation of the Balfour Declaration as an essential proviso. He was also told that Samuel would be appointed High Commissioner, and that there would be changes in the Palestine administration. In Weizmann's view the outcome was of equal significance to the Balfour Declaration, and in his letter to Vera telling her of what had been agreed he heralded it as the dawn of a new Palestine.[49] With a British Mandate based upon the Balfour Declaration now in his pocket, Weizmann's stature within the Zionist movement was unique and unassailable, or so it seemed.

For their part, the French viewed the Conference as a means of clearing away the obstacles to intervention against Feisal, and indeed the problem with Britain was largely dealt with at San Remo. Curzon had tried to fight a rearguard action on Feisal's behalf. His suggestion that if Feisal came to the Peace Conference, agreed to accept a proper Mandate and came to a final agreement with the French and British regarding the status of Syria and Palestine, the Allies should recognise him as King of Syria, was, however, unacceptable to Millerand. He was not willing to concede that France would have a weak Mandate in Syria, while Britain would have much greater freedom of action in Palestine and Mesopotamia. Britain was resigned to France dealing with Syria as it pleased.

The San Remo Conference had set a template for the post-Ottoman Middle East, with results that were to resonate for decades to come. France had Mandates for Syria and Lebanon, while Britain had Iraq and Palestine in its charge. Weizmann and the Zionists now had what they had hoped and worked for, namely, a British Mandate for Palestine charged with implementing the Balfour Declaration. For Feisal and Arab nationalism the outcome could not have been more different, as events were soon to show.

---

48 *DBFP*, Vol VIII, Doc 16.
49 Weizmann to Vera Weizmann, London, 26 April 1920; Weizmann to the Zionist Bureau, London, 27 April 1920: *LPCW*, Vol IX, 313, 315, pp 340–2; Weizmann, *Trial and Error*, pp 324–5.

The end of Feisal's kingdom

After San Remo, Millerand moved to prepare the ground for an assault on Syria. General Gouraud was ordered to encourage the development of local autonomy in the country. He had advocated such a strategy earlier in the year. Gouraud also sent Robert de Caix to parley with Mustafa Kemal. A ceasefire was secured at the end of May, giving Gouraud a free hand to concentrate his forces against Feisal and the Syrians. The French plan was simple. Feisal was to be presented with an ultimatum to end all attacks on the French by Arab groups. Should this not be immediately complied with, French forces would occupy Damascus and Aleppo, disarm the Syrian forces and depose him. It would appear Millerand relished the opportunity to finish with Feisal once and for all. Substantial reinforcements were sent to Lebanon to prepare for a military solution. Gouraud was equally enthusiastic to end the 'phoney war'. French agents also sought allies among the Syrians. There were a number of groups in Syria that were anxious to see the back of Feisal's regime, the Druze and Christian populations being the most notable collaborators with the French.

On 18 May, Curzon appeared to abandon any pretense of support for Syria. While still asking that the French show moderation in their treatment of Feisal, for fear that they would drive him into the hands of the Turkish nationalists, it was recognised that France was the best judge of the 'military measures' needed to meet the local situation and that it had the right to use such measures.[50] The following day, the French government resolved to crush Feisal and the Syrian nationalists by force. Appropriate orders were issued to General Gouraud on 22 May. He was promised considerable reinforcements that would arrive in time for a military strike in July.[51] All other French aims in the Middle East became subordinated to gaining control of Syria. Gouraud was instructed to renounce or put on hold French rights in Cilicia in order to secure his flank from attack by the Turks, and a truce with Kemal was concluded on 1 June. By the end of June, the French had assembled sufficient forces in the Levant for a strike at Damascus.

---

50 *DBFP*, Vol XIII, Doc 251.
51 Dan Eldar, 'France in Syria: The Abolition of the Sharifian Government, April–July 1920', *Middle Eastern Studies*, Vol 29, No 3 (Jul 1993) pp 487–504, esp pp 492–5.

Feisal was by now aware of French forces massing on the frontier of Syria and that France was seeking allies among Syrian notables and tribal leaders. He again sought to compromise and began to rein in the activities of the guerrillas. Similarly, the Damascus press and political parties were brought under tighter supervision. This repression was put in place to prevent any incident that would provide an excuse for the French to march on Damascus.[52] Feisal also sent Nuri al-Said to parley with Gouraud.

Gouraud, with his forces in place and anxious to force the issue, wanted Feisal isolated in Damascus. He feared that Feisal might prevent an attack by either making a deal with Paris or securing another British intervention. Either occurrence might cheat him of the final reckoning that he now desired. Gouraud sent Nuri back to Damascus on 11 July with new and unpalatable demands including French occupation of the Rayaq–Aleppo railway, acceptance of the Mandate and the end of military conscription. Feisal rejected the demands. In response to Arab reinforcement of the border with the French zone, Gouraud moved forces into Rayaq. On 14 July, he sent a written ultimatum to Feisal demanding he accept the 11 July terms and outlining how Feisal and the Syrian nationalists had failed to comply with previous agreements. Feisal had five days to respond or face invasion and French military occupation. He made last desperate appeals to Britain to intervene. The British urged caution on the French but as Lord Hardinge, the Permanent Under-Secretary at the Foreign Office, noted, it was impossible for Britain to intervene as a result of the San Remo agreements. In his view, if the French treatment of Feisal led to trouble in the future it would be better that the responsibility should lie solely with them and that the British were not implicated.[53]

War fever now spread through the unoccupied part of Syria. Despite some desertions, the bulk of the military officers around Feisal remained steadfast and determined to fight. However, the army was an army in name only. It was desperately short of heavy weapons, and while rifles were plentiful, ammunition was in very short supply. Feisal's attempts at negotiations with Gouraud yielded a few concessions but the French commander still made demands for the punishment of extremists, which included high-ranking officials in the army. Feisal agreed to virtually the

---

52 Russell, *The First Modern Arab State*, pp 179–80.
53 *DBFP*, Vol XIII, Doc 284.

entire French ultimatum. He began to make preparations for a military crackdown against extremists who would almost certainly oppose his capitulation. Feisal suppressed the Syrian Congress when it opposed his acceptance of the French terms, leading to an outbreak of street fighting in Damascus, which troops loyal to Feisal crushed with great force.

Gouraud, however, appears to have been playing Feisal along. On 20 July he declared that Feisal had not complied sufficiently with French demands despite desperate efforts to do so. French forces moved against Syria just after midnight of that day. Feisal, after a final and fruitless attempt to negotiate, decided to stand and fight. Arab forces attempted to block the French advance at Maysalun near Damascus. The French had more troops as well as tanks, aircraft and superior artillery. The result was the inevitable rout of the Arab forces.

Feisal returned to Damascus. Gouraud and the French now had no use for him and he was told to leave. On 1 August, Feisal and his entourage left for Europe via Haifa. Syria was now completely in French hands. Gouraud immediately implemented a divide-and-rule strategy by creating autonomous areas in Syria that would emphasise tribal, religious and ethnic divisions so as to facilitate French rule. The dream of an Arab kingdom in Syria was now gone forever. Feisal appeared to be just another nationalist that the Western Powers no longer had any use for – destined to be forgotten.

Weizmann at high tide: the Palestine Mandate

Despite Weizmann's undoubted success at San Remo, the International Zionist Conference, the first truly representative Zionist congress since 1913, which was held in London in early July 1920, proved to be far from harmonious. Weizmann's address opened with what can only be described as a paean of praise for the British leaders, Balfour and Lloyd George, of course, but also Curzon for the way in which he had defended the Zionist position at San Remo. He reminded his audience that the conditions for creating the National Home had been established, and that a sympathiser, Samuel, had been given responsibility for Palestine. If they were to make Palestine as Jewish a country as quickly as possible, then the work had to be set in hand over the next few years. Not to do so would raise a question mark against the Zionist enterprise. His hope was to settle some 30,000 to 50,000 Jews in the first year. Such a level of immigration would require land purchases which did not infringe the rights of the Arabs. A major objective, he argued, was to secure the good-will of the Palestinian Arabs; failure to do so would poison their efforts. Echoing his earlier contacts with Feisal, he argued that Jewish expertise could assist with the development of the Arab world. In his peroration he returned to the theme that the conditions for the re-creation of the Jewish nation had been secured. It was now up to the Jews themselves to achieve it.[54]

Despite his fine oratory and recent triumph, the conference was a far from happy experience for Weizmann, who found himself criticised by, amongst others, Ben-Gurion, who now made his debut in the world of international Zionism. Ben-Gurion's power base was starkly different to that of Weizmann; namely, the Achdut ha-Avodah, the Socialist-Zionist Association of Workers of Palestine, which had been formed in the spring of 1919. His attack on Weizmann was both bitter and personal, accusing him of creating a barrier between the administration and the Jews of Palestine. Moreover, his concessions had led to hostility on the part of the government that had helped incite Arab violence. Finally, he claimed that the Jews had been better served under the Turks than under the British, a curious notion given the Balfour Declaration. Weizmann had little difficulty in rebutting this intemperate assault on his leadership, but it did not bode well for his relationship with the Jews of Palestine, who were, after all, pivotal to the movement's success. Ben-Gurion had made his mark, and his influence was to grow significantly with the years. It was an inauspicious start to a relationship between the two men which would ultimately end on a bitter note.[55]

More serious at the time was Weizmann's rift with Brandeis and the leadership of the large American contingent which had come to London. With his base in the Olympian atmosphere of the Supreme Court in Washington, Brandeis had always been a somewhat improbable Zionist leader, and his punctilious legal mind was repelled by what he saw of the somewhat scatty preparations for the London conference. At root, however, was a clash between how the two men saw the future of Zionism. Brandeis and his followers believed that by securing the

---

54 'At the First International Zionist Conference after the San Remo Decision, held in London, July 7th, 1920', in Goodman, *Chaim Weizmann*, pp 160–5.
55 Shabtai Teveth, *Ben-Gurion: The Burning Ground 1886–1948* (Robert Hale Ltd, London: 1987) pp 161–4.

Balfour Declaration and the British Mandate, Zionism had achieved its political purpose and objectives, and hence should now turn its hand to the economic development of Palestine. For Weizmann, the political struggle was only just beginning. Brandeis's proposal that the Zionist Organisation should focus on economic activity was clearly defeated on the floor of the conference. But Brandeis believed, seemingly with justice, that Weizmann had lobbied against his ideas for a reorganisation of the Zionist leadership, and the two leaders also quarrelled over the size of the American contribution to the budget. The breach between these two gifted men was never to be repaired. The conference concluded with Brandeis's appointment as Honorary President of the World Zionist Organisation, with Weizmann as its President. At last, Weizmann had a position of strength from which he could operate, but it had been purchased at a price, both in Palestine and the United States.[56]

When Sir Herbert Samuel, as he had become, assumed office as High Commissioner and Commander-in-Chief in Palestine on 30 June 1920 it seemed to herald the fulfilment of Zionist dreams. Not only was his one of the main voices which had led to the Balfour Declaration, but after nearly two millennia a Jew stood at the head of Palestine's affairs. But it was not as simple as that. The achievement of the Zionist dream, at least as it had evolved under Weizmann, rested on two external conditions: sustained British commitment to the idea of a National Home and Arab, especially Palestinian Arab, acquiescence in it. Samuel's arrival in Palestine was not reassuring on either count. His journey from Jaffa to Jerusalem had to be changed to take account of rumours of plots on his life, and he had to be given an escort of armoured cars for his journey from the Jerusalem railway station to the government house on the Mount of Olives, where the outgoing Chief Administrator, Major-General Sir Louis Bols, persuaded him to sign a receipt for Palestine. It was hardly a triumphal entry, although he did receive a 17-gun salute.[57]

---

56 Weizmann, *Trial and Error*, pp 326–8; Laqueur, *A History of Zionism*, pp 458–9; Reinharz, *Chaim Weizmann: The Making of a Statesman*, pp 327–33.
57 Samuel, *Memoirs*, p 154; Storrs, *Orientations*, p 349; Norman and Helen Bentwich, *Mandate Memories 1918–1948* (The Hogarth Press, London: 1965) p 59.

Britain and the new Turkish nationalism

Mustafa Kemal had in the meantime left Sivas for Ankara, which had direct railway communications with Istanbul. He stood for election, but refused to go to Istanbul when elected to the new parliament. However, most of his companions, who were also successful in the elections, travelled there, in spite of Mustafa Kemal's insistence that the new parliament should meet in unoccupied Anatolia, just as the German parliament had met not in Berlin, but in Weimar. Left alone in Anatolia, Mustafa Kemal's control over his sympathisers in the new parliament became tenuous. Although some disagreements surfaced, parliament reaffirmed the National Pact, stiffening it with the demand that popular referendums should also be held in western Thrace and in the three provinces which the Ottomans had regained from Tsarist Russia, to determine whether local people wanted to be part of an independent Ottoman state. On 17 February 1920, parliament voted to communicate the National Pact to all Allied parliaments.

The nationalist stand of the Ottoman parliament under the complacent eyes of the Ali Rıza government was too much for the British occupation authorities, which were not mollified when Ali Rıza resigned and was replaced by Salih Hulusi Pasha, the go-between chosen to bring Mustafa Kemal back into the Ottoman fold. On 16 March 1920, with the reluctant assent of the other Allies, British troops occupied the Ottoman War Ministry and the barracks of Ottoman troops in the capital. There was some firing and a few Turkish soldiers were killed. A Turkish telegraph clerk, a refugee from Macedonia called Hamdi, achieved national fame by keeping open the line to Ankara and informing Mustafa Kemal's headquarters of the progress of the British occupation. He then made his way to Ankara and, many years later, when it was decreed that all Turks should have surnames, he chose the surname 'Sixteenth March'.

British troops moved to arrest the leading nationalists in the newly elected parliament, which immediately adjourned without fixing a date for a new session. Rauf, who had returned to Istanbul as a Member of Parliament, was among the exiles sent to Malta. The forcible entry into a freely elected Ottoman parliament of the troops of a country which prided itself on being the mother of parliaments provided Turkish nationalists with useful propaganda ammunition. There were to be no further sessions of the Ottoman parliament. The Sultan dissolved it, and his government could not organise new elections as its authority did not extend much beyond the capital. Salih Hulusi resigned and was replaced yet again by Damad Ferid, a man utterly incapable of rallying the country round him.

In the confusion caused by the British occupation and the change of government, those Turkish nationalists who had not been rounded up made their way to Ankara. They included not only Members of Parliament, but also military commanders, notably General Fevzi Çakmak, the most senior Ottoman officer to side with Mustafa Kemal, and Colonel İsmet (İnönü), Mustafa Kemal's faithful, but careful, lieutenant, who always looked before he leapt. Fevzi had earlier tried to turn Kâzım Karabekir against Mustafa Kemal, but this was not held against him. Mustafa Kemal shared the esteem in which Fevzi was held in the Turkish officer corps and made him chief-of-staff of the new Turkish national army.

The Allied occupation of Istanbul sealed Mustafa Kemal's leadership of the Turkish nationalist movement and allowed him to take the next step. This was to summon a national assembly in Ankara as a prelude to the formation of a fully fledged alternative government. The assembly called itself the Grand National Assembly and its executive became known as the Government of the Grand National Assembly. The adjective 'Turkish' was to be added later: at first the fiction was maintained that it was the Ottoman nation which was represented.

Kemal in power: the Grand National Assembly

Mustafa Kemal saw to it that his parliament and government appealed to all and sundry, Muslims and Turks. The Assembly was made up of those deputies of the last Ottoman parliament who had managed to make their way to Istanbul and of new members elected ad hoc, or, more accurately co-opted by nationalists in Societies for the Defence of Rights or by provincial notables. Some of the members of the new assembly were deemed to represent occupied areas where no elections could be held. All the members were united in their determination to resist foreign rule. But they were not of one mind when it came to tactics, and were ready to criticise the nationalist leadership when things went wrong, and to limit as far as possible the power of Mustafa Kemal, who was suspected of nurturing dictatorial ambitions.

The Assembly held its first meeting on 23 April 1920 under the slogan 'sovereignty belongs unconditionally to the nation'. This revolutionary sentiment was reflected also in the powers which the Assembly arrogated to itself, combining the functions of the legislature, executive and judiciary. Elected President of the Assembly, Mustafa Kemal was also head of government, which took the title of Committee of Executive Commissioners. The commissioners were elected singly by the Assembly, which could also dismiss them. The inspiration came from the French National Convention after the 1789 Revolution, but also from the Bolshevik Committee of Executive Commissars (known by the Russian abbreviation *ispolkom*). From the start, Mustafa Kemal (and to a lesser extent Kâzım Karabekir in Erzurum) tried to secure the support of the Bolsheviks, while keeping them out of the country. Ideologies were fluid, misconceptions flourished, and contradictory views were held, genuinely or for tactical reasons.

The opening of the revolutionary Assembly was marked with an Islamic ritual, excessive even by late Ottoman standards. It took place on a Friday when all male adult Muslims are meant to pray as a congregation. After prayers in the main Ankara mosque (which was also a shrine to a local holy man), members of the Assembly walked in procession preceded by a cleric holding a relic – one of the many supposed hairs from the beard of the Prophet Muhammad, venerated in the country. Imams throughout unoccupied Anatolia were ordered to recite not only the whole of the Koran, but also a lengthy compendium of the sayings attributed to the Prophet. Sheep were sacrificed in Ankara and the provinces to invoke divine blessing.

After these preliminaries, the Assembly met in the building which had served as the premises of the club of the Young Turks. It was built in what became known in Turkey as the 'national style', although Western colonial architecture, from French North Africa to the British Federated Malay States, was a more obvious source of inspiration. Refurbished and enlarged, the building was later used by the Turkish parliament for many years, then by the Republican People's Party, which Mustafa Kemal founded; it is now preserved as a museum.

The first act of the revolutionary Assembly was to send a message of loyalty to the Sultan, who was deemed to have become the captive of the Allies and to be surrounded by evil ministers who kept him ignorant of his subjects' concerns. But while the fiction was maintained, Mustafa Kemal made sure that even those members of the Ottoman dynasty who were sympathetic to the nationalist cause were kept out of Anatolia. In April 1921, Prince Ömer Faruk, son of the heir apparent Abdülmecid, eluded Allied controls and travelled secretly to the small port of İnebolu on the Black Sea which the nationalists controlled and which served as the point of entry to unoccupied Anatolia. At Mustafa Kemal's instructions, he was sent back to Istanbul and told that the time to make use of his services would come later.

Mustafa Kemal was a master tactician who used fictions when they served his purpose. He sought support wherever he could find it. In order to obtain help both from the Bolsheviks and from foreign Muslims, he went along with the argument that the Muslim world and Bolshevism had a common enemy in imperialism, and that they were, at least to some extent, compatible. Misconceptions reinforced useful fiction. Addressing a Bolshevik envoy, Mustafa Kemal declared: 'Turkey is engaged in a determined and vital endeavour, because it is battling in the cause of all oppressed nations, of the whole Orient.'[58]

There was at the time of the Russian Civil War a ragged armed band, led by the anti-Semitic peasant bandit Makhno, which styled itself the Green Army. As green is the colour of Islam, some supporters of Turkish national resistance believed that the Green Army had been formed by Muslim Communists, and they set up a similar organisation in unoccupied Anatolia. Also called the Green Army, it attracted the Circassians who resisted control even by their fellow Muslims. But in addition to undisciplined rebel fighters, there was also a small group of Marxists in Turkey, usually rebellious children of the ruling class who had been impressed by the Spartacist movement in Germany and had pinned their hopes on the worldwide revolution preached by the Bolsheviks.

The Treaty of Sèvres

While Mustafa Kemal was consolidating his power in Ankara, the Allies continued to dither. But a peace settlement with Turkey could not be put off for ever. The Treaty of Versailles with Germany was followed by treaties with Austria, Bulgaria and Hungary. All left a legacy of bitterness which erupted in the Second World War, when the nationalist leaders of defeated nations made common cause with Nazi Germany. The Turkish settlement was more difficult, but when it finally came it proved more durable. The rise of modern Turkey provides a perfect illustration of the law of unintended consequences – in this case the beneficial

---

58 Cited in Taha Akyol, *Ama Hangi Atatürk* (Dogan Kitap, Istanbul: 2008) p 156.

consequences of Lloyd George's ill-advised policy. But an immense price in human suffering had to be paid before the benefits finally emerged.

The government which Damad Ferid formed on 5 May 1919 after the British had raided the Ottoman parliament did all it could to strangle at birth the nationalist movement in Anatolia. A week into its tenure of power, it procured from the Sheikh al-Islam, the head of the official clerical establishment in Istanbul, a fatwa declaring that the nationalist forces were rebels against the faith and that it was the duty of all Muslims to kill them. The nationalists responded by obtaining a counter-fatwa from the muftis of Anatolia, with the mufti of Ankara in the lead, saying that, on the contrary, it was the duty of all good Muslims to resist foreign occupation and free the Sultan-Caliph from foreign captivity. (Throughout Ottoman history fatwas were issued with the ease of vending machines: you put in a coin and got your fatwa.) The National Assembly in Ankara passed a law declaring that those who resisted its authority would be guilty of high treason. In Istanbul a court martial passed death sentences on Mustafa Kemal and his companions.

The war of words was reflected by clashes on the ground, as rebellions broke out in nationalist-held territory. Damad Ferid's government formed a 'disciplinary force', known also as the Army of the Caliphate, to suppress the nationalists. The pay it offered attracted a ragbag of none-too-enthusiastic volunteers, whom the nationalists had little difficulty in putting to flight. The rebellions behind the lines held by the nationalists posed a greater problem, but these too were suppressed, often by militias. Circassians who supported the nationalists routed their fellow tribesmen loyal to the Sultan. Similarly, Kurdish tribes fought each other, and those which sided with the nationalists helped the weak national army to establish the authority of the National Assembly. Nevertheless Mustafa Kemal felt personally threatened when the feudal clan which dominated the district of Yozgat, just east of Ankara, rebelled against his authority. The army was unable to suppress the rising, and the nationalists' Circassian allies had to be rushed from their territory west of Ankara to do the job. Their leader, Edhem, commander of the 'mobile force' of horsemen, and patron of the Green Army, got ideas above his station and strutted around like a bully when he showed up in Ankara with his fighters. He got his comeuppance a few months later when the new regular national army took over the command of militias. Refusing to submit to the discipline of the new nationalist regime, Edhem and the remnant of his forces sought refuge with the Greeks. He ended up in Transjordan, where fellow Circassians provided the guard of Abdullah, whom the British had installed as emir.

On the ground, the military situation remained frozen for a year after the Greek occupation of İzmir and the surrounding area in May 1919. But while the wheels of diplomacy slowly ground forward, the Allies demobilised in response to domestic discontent. When the Paris Peace Conference opened, Lloyd George made much of the fact that there were more than 1 million British troops occupying Ottoman territory.[59] A few months later their numbers fell to little over 300,000, and these were fully occupied holding Mesopotamia and Palestine, with only a weak force guarding the Turkish Straits and occupying Istanbul. This led to the next step in the destruction of Anatolia.

On the night of 14/15 June 1920, Turkish nationalist detachments outside İzmit (Nicomedia) clashed with a weak British force guarding the town, which controlled access to Istanbul from the east. The British commander, General George Milne, asked London for reinforcements. None were available, and the Chief of the Imperial General Staff proposed that a Greek division should be used to defend the Ottoman capital. The Greek Prime Minister Venizelos was only too ready to oblige with a division stationed in western Thrace. His reward was permission for Greek troops to occupy eastern Thrace, including Edirne (Adrianople), and to cross the Milne Line to seize the whole of western Anatolia, south of the Sea of Marmara.[60]

The first steps leading to the disastrous decision to impose draconian peace terms on Turkey were taken at Allied consultations in London between 12 February and 10 March 1920. At a meeting on 16 February, Venizelos pressed his claims to İzmir and the surrounding area on the basis of population statistics, which exaggerated the number of Greeks and undercounted the Turks. He was supported by Lloyd George. The London conference was followed by the extension of British military control in Istanbul on 16 March, but not before the British High Commissioner in the Ottoman capital had outlined his fears. 'The terms are such that no Turks ... can very well accept,' wrote Admiral de Robeck. He warned that the Allies would have to be prepared 'for a resumption

---

59 Fromkin, *A Peace to End All Peace*, p 385.
60 Llewellyn Smith, *Ionian Vision*, pp 123–5.

of general warfare'. Moreover, they would 'do violence to their own declared and cherished principles ... and perpetuate bloodshed indefinitely in the Near East'.[61]

The French had similar reservations. On 12 February 1920, the day that the London conference opened, their troops had been forced by a local uprising to evacuate Maraş in southern Turkey. The uprising was led by an imam, known as 'the Milkman'. The memory of this episode has been kept alive. Today, the town is known officially as Kahramanmaraş (Maraş the Heroic), and it boasts of the University of the Milkman Imam. Some of the Armenians who had accompanied the French troops were killed during the evacuation, giving rise to reports of an Armenian massacre. Having experienced Turkish resistance, the new French Prime Minister Alexandre Millerand persuaded the Allies to commission a report from the military commission chaired in Versailles by Marshal Ferdinand Foch, the victorious commander on the Western Front. Foch concluded that no less than 27 divisions would be required to impose the terms demanded by Lloyd George and his protégé Venizelos.[62] Although he was warned by Lloyd George that he could expect no help, Venizelos promised rashly that his army could do it alone. The Italians, who had been cheated out of their main prize, expressed their doubts. Nevertheless, the final plan to partition Turkey was agreed at the San Remo Conference, just as Mustafa Kemal's nationalist government was taking shape in Ankara. There was only one way of enforcing the Allied peace terms. On 21 June at a meeting in Boulogne, the Allied leaders allowed the Greek army to occupy eastern Thrace and the whole of western Anatolia.

An Ottoman delegation was summoned to Paris to sign the peace treaty. It was led by the elderly Tevfik Pasha, the Sultan's man for all seasons. On 25 June, the Ottoman delegation submitted its reply to the partition project on which the Allies had agreed at San Remo. Tevfik Pasha had already advised his government that the Allied peace terms were incompatible with the continued existence of an independent Ottoman state. This was strongly argued in the Ottoman reply, which made the point that the Allied peace settlement imposed on the Ottoman government obligations while depriving it of the means to carry them out. The desire to tie down the Turks had been pushed to absurd lengths. Under the

---

61 Llewellyn Smith, *Ionian Vision*, p 122.
62 Llewellyn Smith, *Ionian Vision*, p 121.

Allied plan, there would be eight separate jurisdictions in Istanbul: the Sultan's government, the proposed Straits Commission (with its own flag), the military authorities of the Allied occupation forces, the political authority of the High Commissioners of Britain, France and Italy, the Allied commission for supervision and organisation, the international financial commission, the board of the foreign-owned Ottoman public debt and foreign consular courts applying their own laws. But the Allies were in no mood to listen to reason. Rather than wait for their response, which he could guess in advance, Tevfik turned to the Grand Vizier Damad Ferid, who had joined the delegation, much to the displeasure of the other members, and said, 'There is no point in staying on for there is nothing more we can do. Let us at least save money by returning home and leaving our junior colleagues here.'[63]

On 11 July the Allied leaders met in Spa in Belgium, where the Kaiser had his headquarters during the First World War. Millerand, Curzon, the Italian representative Count Sforza, Viscount Chinda of Japan and Venizelos were there. Sforza was an ironic observer; the Japanese were not really interested; Curzon stuck to Lloyd George's line, in spite of his reservations; and Venizelos made sure that a crushing reply was sent to the Ottoman government. He succeeded. Whatever they might think in private, the Principal Allies agreed on a text that was both uncompromising and insulting.

The Ottoman decision to enter the war on the side of Germany, they declared, was an act of treachery. It prolonged the war by two years and caused the Allies the loss of millions of men and billions in money. After 1914, the reply thundered, the Ottomans had murdered 800,000 Armenians, and deported another 100,000 as well as 200,000 Greeks. The Allies had to guard against further treachery in deciding the regime of the Straits. The accusations led to a final threat: if the Ottoman government did not sign the Treaty, or if it was unable to impose its authority in Anatolia, the Allies reserved the right to review their terms and drive the Turks out of Europe for ever. The Ottoman government was given ten days until 27 July to reply to this ultimatum.[64] Prejudice against Turks could go no further. In Britain today this forgotten text would fall foul of

63 Mahmud Kemal İnal, *Osmanli Devrinde Son Sadriazamlar*, pp 1731–2; Baskin Oran, *Türkiye'nin Dış Politikası*, Vol I, pp 119–23.

64 Baskin Oran, *Türkiye'nin Dış Politikası* (İletişim, Istanbul: 2001) Vol I, p 123.

the Race Relations Act. But in Turkey it is remembered as the expression of abiding anti-Turkish prejudice, and it has left a mark on attitudes to the outside world.

By the time the Allied ultimatum was received in Istanbul, the whole of coastal Anatolia, with the exception of the shores of the Black Sea, was under foreign occupation. Turkish troops on the ground were too weak to prevent the advance of the Greek army. Isolated in eastern Thrace they had no option but to surrender. In Anatolia, the Greeks swept north and west out of their enclave round İzmir. On 8 July 1920, they occupied Bursa, the second capital of the Ottomans, at the centre of the rich Bithynian plain south of the Sea of Marmara. This was a bitter blow to the Turks, for whom Bursa, like Edirne (Adrianople), symbolised the glories of the Ottoman Empire. As a sign of mourning, the rostrum of the National Assembly in Ankara was draped in black.

Arnold Toynbee, who had earlier worked for the government and helped compile the British *Blue Book* designed to rally the American public to the Allied cause, with stories of Armenian atrocities, took time away from his duties as Professor of Medieval and Modern Greek at King's College, London in order to report for the *Manchester Guardian*, then as now the voice of British liberalism, on the progress of the Greek occupation of Anatolia. From the eastern approaches of Istanbul, he could see the flames of Turkish villages torched by the Greeks on the eastern shores of the Gulf of İzmit. The experience changed his outlook. In *The Western Question in Greece and Turkey*, the book he published in 1922, he came to the conclusion that Greece was 'as incapable as Turkey (or for that matter any Western country) of governing well a mixed population containing an alien majority and a minority of her own nationality'.[65] The Greek shipowners who had funded the chair at King's College were furious. Toynbee was forced to leave. He devoted himself to the development of the Royal Institute of International Affairs and to writing his ten-volume *Study of History*, in which his pessimistic view of Western civilisation found expression in the theory that all civilisations arise as a challenge to a response and that they are all destined to die. Historical, and generally cultural, relativism was a response to Allied triumphalism at the end of the First World War. Eventually, Toynbee gained the admiration of Turks who, unlike him, had no doubts about

---

65 Mango, *Atatürk*, p 329.

the values of Western civilisation, whatever the misdeeds committed in its name.

The Allied threat to drive the Turks out of Europe forever cut no ice with the Turkish nationalists who had, in any case, left European Turkey to carry on the fight in Anatolia. But the Sultan was determined not to compromise the prospect of staying on in Istanbul, as a shadowy sovereign claiming to be Caliph of all Muslims. Even so, he decided to summon a council of the throne before agreeing to the Allied demands. His Grand Vizier, Damad Ferid, argued that to reject the terms would be equivalent to committing the sin of suicide. The Ottoman dynasty was like an ancient tree. So long as its roots remained in its native soil, it was capable of new growth. Summoned to choose between a shadowy survival and extinction, the grandees summoned to the council voted in favour of accepting the peace settlement in spite of its 'terrible conditions'. There was only one dissenting vote. It was cast by Rıza Pasha, a retired artillery general.

Armed with the authority of the throne council, an Ottoman delegation went to Paris to sign the peace treaty imposed by the Allies. Two of its members – a diplomat and a senator – were inconspicuous. But the third had a considerable, although controversial, reputation. He was the poet Rıza Tevfik, known as 'the philosopher', philosophy being the subject he taught at the university of Istanbul. He had been a member of the CUP before joining Damad Ferid in the Liberal Union. A liberal and a patriot after his fashion, who believed in the doomed ideal of 'the union of all elements' (the peaceful co-existence of the constituent communities of the Ottoman state), he was listed among the 150 opponents of the nationalists who were exiled after 1923. Together with the surviving exiles, he was pardoned in 1938 and returned to Turkey where he is remembered as an eccentric idealist out of tune with the times.

On 10 August 1920, the Ottoman delegation signed the peace treaty at Sèvres, outside Paris. Critics were not slow to observe that the Treaty was as brittle as the porcelain made there for the French court. But it was certainly nothing like as beautiful. On the same day, Britain, France and Italy signed a pact on their respective zones of influence in what remained of Turkey. The Italians were to enjoy preferential treatment in south-western Anatolia, the French in the south and the British in the extreme south-east, north of Iraq. The pact was a British sop to the French, who had given up Mosul, promised to them in the Sykes-Picot

Agreement, and particularly to the Italians, who lost İzmir and who did not add to their territorial gains – the Dodecanese and Libya – acquired on the eve of the war. But the Italians were not satisfied, and became the first Allies to befriend the Turkish nationalists. The French preferred to wait on events before making their own arrangements. Thus, right from the beginning, two of the Principal Allies did not share Lloyd George's enthusiasm for the Treaty of Sèvres. Even Curzon had misgivings. He asked Lloyd George to 'think seriously' about Anatolia and the Greeks. He was, he said, 'the last man to wish to do a good turn to the Turks', but he wanted to achieve 'something like peace in Asia Minor, which was impossible so long as the Greeks were marching about inside it'.[66]

The Treaty of Sèvres died 'intact, though dead, whole though unratified' in the words of Andrew Ryan, the Dragoman at the British embassy in Istanbul.[67] Greece was, in fact, the only signatory to ratify it. Six months after the signature of the Treaty, a conference had to be arranged in London to amend its more outrageous provisions. But this proved impossible.

Under the Treaty of Sèvres, the Ottoman state was to lose eastern Thrace to Greece, the territory of which would extend right up to the suburbs of Istanbul. Istanbul would remain nominally under Ottoman sovereignty, but as the Ottoman delegates had already pointed out, this would be diluted to vanishing point. The area around İzmir, known to Greek nationalists and Western Philhellenes by the classical name of Ionia, would also remain under nominal Ottoman sovereignty, but only for five years, after which its fate would be decided by a referendum. The deportation and flight of Turks which followed the Greek occupation had made certain in advance that the referendum would result in the annexation of Ionia to Greece. In the south, French-Mandated Syria would gain a large slice of adjacent Turkish territory. In the east, the Kurds would gain autonomy immediately and independence if they opted for it a year later and the Council of the League of Nations thought they had the capacity for it. Further north, there would be a greater independent Armenia with access to the sea, within borders which were to be decided by President Wilson. Wilson announced his award on 22 November 1920, in the dying days of his administration after Congress had refused to

---

66 David Gilmour, *Curzon* (John Murray, London: 1994) p 532.
67 Andrew Ryan, *The Last of the Dragomans* (Bles, London: 1951) p 173.

ratify the Covenant of the League of Nations. The outgoing president generously gave the Armenians the port city of Trabzon, the fortress town of Erzurum, and all the country round Lake Van. Wilson's letter announcing his decision was touching in its optimism. 'It is my confident expectation,' he wrote that:

> the Armenian refugees and their leaders ... will by refraining from any and all form of reprisals give the world an example of that high moral courage which must always be the foundation of national strength ... surpassing in the liberality of their administrative arrangements ... even the ample provisions for non-Armenian racial and religious groups embodied in the Minorities Treaty.[68]

Woodrow Wilson's faith was misplaced. When the newly established Armenian republic took over the frontier provinces of Russian Transcaucasia from the British, which Turkish troops had evacuated after the armistice, Muslim villages were torched and many of their inhabitants killed. In September 1920, a month after the signature of the Treaty of Sèvres, the nationalist government in Ankara authorised Karabekir to cross the old Tsarist frontier. On 30 October he captured the fortress of Kars. This time Armenian civilians fled or were killed. It was the fourth wave of human wretchedness washing over the eastern Anatolian plateau since 1914: Muslim Turks and Kurds escaping the advancing Russians in 1915, while Armenians were being deported and killed in the Turkish rear; Turks fleeing from Armenians who took over from the Russians in February 1917; Armenians escaping from advancing Turks later the same year; and, finally, the two rounds of ethnic cleansing in 1919–20, with Muslims suffering first and Armenians second. No Armenians were left thereafter on the Turkish side of the frontier except for those who sought refuge with their Muslim neighbours and converted to Islam. On the Russian side, ethnic cleansing stopped and was replaced by the cleansing of class enemies with the advent of the Bolsheviks, and then resumed and was completed after the dissolution of the Soviet Union some 70 years later.

---

68 <http://wilsonforarmenian.am/Report/007Letter.pdf>, pp 10–11. It is not surprising that the full text of the Treaty of Sèvres should be available on the internet courtesy of the Hellenic resources network and the Wilson Award thanks to an organisation of Armenian nationalists, 'Wilson for Armenia'.

As its army collapsed, the Armenian government sued for an armistice. On 2 December 1920 the government of the Grand National Assembly signed a peace treaty with Armenia, and Turkey regained the three frontier provinces which it had lost to the Russians in 1878. Soon afterwards the Bolsheviks took over in what remained of Armenia, which was thereafter ruled from Moscow as the Armenian Soviet Socialist Republic. Its coat of arms showed Mount Ararat (Ağrı Dağ in Turkish), but the mountain now lay in Turkish territory. It did not take long for Wilson's award to be mocked by history. Armenian nationalists are still hoping that somehow or other they will regain what Wilson had given them. But if there is, in their eyes, an unredeemed Armenia, there are no unredeemed Armenians, and they are finding it difficult enough as it is to repopulate the territory which they seized from Azerbaijan and ethnically cleansed in the 1980s.

Neither Sultan Vahdettin nor his hated Grand Vizier Damad Ferid signed the Treaty of Sèvres. Forgetting conveniently that he had done his best to stifle opposition to the Treaty, the Sultan claimed later that his only motive was to gain time until the balance of external forces moved in Turkey's favour. In Ankara, the Grand National Assembly, under Mustafa Kemal's determined leadership, did not prevaricate. On 19 August, nine days after the signature of the Treaty, it declared that the Ottoman signatories and all those in the throne council who had voted in favour of signing were guilty of high treason.

Ineffective as it was, the Treaty of Sèvres left a legacy of bitterness which persists to this day. Its authors looked down on the Turks as a people incapable of progress who had to be civilised by external force. They had to make sure that the brakes on their railway carriages were in order (Article 358), that only qualified archaeologists were allowed to dig for antiquities (Article 421, add.7), that the white slave trade was effectively banned (Article 273/6), that obscene publications were banned (Article 273/7) and that birds useful to agriculture were protected (Article 273/11).[69] If to this day it is a criminal offence in Turkey to denigrate 'Turkishness', the reason should be sought in the memory left by the Treaty of Sèvres.

---

69 Examples given in Bardakçı, *Şahbaba*, p 162.

The impact of San Remo and Sèvres

These events of 1919–20, which culminated in the Treaty of Sèvres, had attempted to set a new path for the Middle East based on the ambitions of the victors, and for a time they seemed to have succeeded. It was now clear that the centuries-old Turkish dominance of the Arab lands was at an end. In its place were four new entities under Anglo-French Mandates, Palestine, Iraq, Lebanon and Syria, within boundaries which were to remain in place even though they took little account of the wishes of the inhabitants at the time, let alone established economic patterns or geographical realities. These Mandates confirmed the ambitions of the British and French to replace the Turks, which had emerged by 1916 in the Sykes-Picot Agreement. The Zionists, guided by Weizmann, had secured their major objective of having Palestine placed under a British Mandate, with Britain charged with implementing the Balfour Declaration. They had the added bonus, or so it seemed, of having Samuel as first High Commissioner. By any reckoning it was a triumph for the strategy Weizmann had been pursuing, even though he had his critics within the Zionist movement, both in Palestine and the United States. Feisal's dream of a Hashemite Arab kingdom based upon Damascus had perished on the altar of France's colonial ambition which the British were willing to indulge, despite the fact that the French had contributed virtually nothing to Allenby's victories. Both the British and the Zionists were coming to realise, however, that Arab nationalism was a growing force as disturbances across the Middle East, not least in Palestine, were showing all too clearly. Even more of an immediate challenge to the victorious powers was the fast-emerging Turkish nationalism, which had found its voice in 1919–20, and its leader in Mustafa Kemal. If the Treaty of Sèvres had humiliated Turkey, as it clearly did, those who imposed it had not reckoned with Mustafa Kemal and the strength of the forces he was now leading.

5

The Middle East Rebels and the Peace Settlement Revisited

The consolidation of Kemal's authority

The Treaty of Sèvres was buried on the battlefields of western Turkey. The casualties suffered by the new regular Turkish army in these battles were comparatively light – 13,000 men killed and 35,000 wounded.[1] The combined losses of the Greek and Armenian armies were much heavier – more than twice as many. But it was the civilian population which suffered most, with hundreds of thousands dying and some 3 million uprooted. It took a generation before these losses were made good, and when they were, another mistaken assumption which underlay the rickety edifice designed at Sèvres was made manifest. The Greek territorial claims put forward by Venizelos and the Armenian claims accepted by President Wilson were both based on demographic projections which assumed that the Greek and Armenian population would increase fast enough to fill the territories wrenched from Turkey, and faster in any case than the Turkish population. This was the case when Greeks and Armenians were more prosperous and, therefore, healthier than their Turkish neighbours. But peace and medical services reversed the trend.

---

1 Mango, *Atatürk*, p 345. A single battle – Enver's unsuccessful assault on the Russians in the winter of 1914/15 – cost the Ottoman army 110,000 casualties (Hikmet Özdemir, *The Ottoman Army 1914–1918* (Utah University Press, Salt Lake City, UT: 2008) p 52).

Today the population of Turkey is five times larger than that of Greece and Armenia combined, and there are not enough Greeks and Armenians to realise the dreams of such unreconstructed nationalists as survive in their midst.

Diplomacy and armed resistance went hand in hand under Mustafa Kemal's guidance. The immediate task after Sèvres was to suppress the risings in the Turkish nationalist rear fomented by the Sultan's government in Istanbul. This was done between August and December 1920. Faced with the failure of his attempts to liquidate the nationalist movement in Anatolia, Damad Ferid resigned on 17 October, and left the country for a rest cure in the spa of Karlsbad (now Karlovy Vary in the Czech Republic). He was to return to Istanbul once only, very briefly in September 1922 when he collected his wife Mediha (the Sultan's sister), other members of the family and such belongings as he could carry away, and slipped off to permanent exile in France. Sultan Vahdettin, who was himself about to follow him, was informed in an impersonal note which read: 'At her husband's insistence, the Princess Mediha left for Europe for treatment two hours ago, as her rheumatism was getting worse here.' Put out, the Sultan remarked pathetically, 'The naughty boy! He got the State into this mess and then walked away.'[2] Vahdettin was, of course, himself responsible for bringing the 'naughty boy' to power over and over again. When he had appointed Damad Ferid for the last time after the signature of the Treaty of Sèvres, he was warned by the former Deputy Speaker of Parliament that the appointment would be calamitous for the country and the dynasty. Vahdettin was not dissuaded. 'If I so desired,' he said, 'I could name as Grand Vizier the Greek or Armenian Patriarch or even the Chief Rabbi.' 'You could, Sir,' the Deputy Speaker replied, 'but it wouldn't do you any good.'[3] After Damad Ferid's precipitate final departure, his name never again passed the lips of his exiled sovereign.

Damad Ferid was succeeded once again by the veteran statesman Tevfik Pasha, who was to be the last Grand Vizier of the Ottoman Empire. Tevfik's son was married to the Sultan's daughter, and he was, therefore, trusted as a relative. Nevertheless, in the proclamation which he issued from exile in Mecca in order to exculpate himself, Vahdettin claimed that his actions had always been guided by public opinion or by

2 Mahmud Kemal İnal, *Osmanli Devrinde Son Sadriazamlar*, p 2067.
3 Mahmud Kemal İnal, *Osmanli Devrinde Son Sadriazamlar*, p 2053.

other 'considerations which could not be resisted', and went on, 'The best proof is that I kept Tevfik Pasha in power for more than two years, solely because public opinion was not opposed to him, even although he allowed Kemalists, whose bad intentions towards my person and my position were manifest, to establish their influence in Istanbul.'[4]

The Soviet dimension

In July 1920, a month before the signature of the Treaty of Sèvres, Mustafa Kemal had dispatched to Moscow his Foreign Minister Bekir Sami (a Turkish nationalist of Caucasian stock). But, just like their Western foes, the Bolsheviks were loath to put their money on Mustafa Kemal before they could see his form. At first they offered unacceptable odds, demanding a slice of eastern Turkey for the Armenians as the price of their support. In any case, there were other Turkish competitors for Moscow gold.

The CUP war leader Enver, who had sought refuge in Germany at the end of the war, managed to get to Moscow with the help of his German friends and canvassed Bolshevik support for a plan to mobilise Muslims worldwide against the British. He was opposed by Turkish Communists subservient to Moscow. Their leader was a Paris-trained radical journalist, Mustafa Suphi. An opponent of the German alliance, he had sought refuge in Russia where he was detained as an enemy alien. Set free after the Bolshevik Revolution, he recruited Turkish prisoners of war in Russian camps to help the Red Army, and formed the Turkish Communist Party which was admitted to the Communist International. The three groups contending for Bolshevik support – the delegates of the government of the Grand National Assembly in Ankara, Enver and his fellow exiles and Mustafa Suphi and his Moscow-line Turkish Communists came face to face at the First Congress of the Peoples of the East which opened in Baku on 1 September 1920.

In April that year the Red Army had invaded Azerbaijan, which became a Soviet Socialist Republic. But while the short-lived nationalist government of Azerbaijan was thus removed from power in Baku, 'bourgeois' nationalists were still in control of Armenia and Georgia to the west. Moreover, Bolshevik control was incomplete elsewhere in the Tsar's former possessions in Asia. The collapse of the Tsarist regime had

---

4 Bardakçı, Şahbaba, p 450.

brought to the fore indigenous revolutionaries in non-Russian communities. But these tended to be National Communists – nationalists first, Communists second. In the eyes of Moscow they were useful idiots, like Western apologists for the Bolsheviks, who could be liquidated at a later date. The purpose of the Baku congress was to form an Eastern popular front of Moscow-line Communists, National Communists, radicals and anti-imperialists of various persuasions, in order to further the aims of the Bolsheviks.

The three competing groups of Turkish delegates kept in touch with each other, while eyeing each other with suspicion. Enver, who had formed a shadowy League of Islamic Revolutionaries, which existed largely in his imagination, took part as the self-appointed representative of the Muslims of north Africa. He had prepared a speech in which he argued that, had the Soviets been in power in 1914, he would have made common cause with them rather than with the Kaiser's Germany, but that, in any case, he had hastened the advent of the Russian Revolution by closing the Straits to the Allies in the First World War. However, Turkish Communists prevented Enver from reading his own speech, shouting, 'His place is not on the rostrum, but in the dock of a people's tribunal.' More realistically, Mustafa Kemal warned Enver against frightening the Bolsheviks with the spectre of pan-Islam.[5]

Mustafa Kemal had to tread delicately to achieve his objective. He wanted to win material support from the Bolsheviks, while keeping them out of his country, and at the same time regain territory lost to the Russians in 1878, which the Bolsheviks wanted for themselves. What he offered in return was Turkish acquiescence in the establishment of Soviet power in Azerbaijan, whatever was left of Armenia and a slightly reduced Georgia. To pacify the Bolsheviks further and pre-empt Turkey's own Marxist revolutionaries, he went through the motions of creating a 'people's government' in Ankara. In Marxist jargon, a 'people's republic' is an acceptable stage in the transition from capitalism to socialism. Having opened the National Assembly with elaborate Islamic ritual and proclaimed the nationalists' loyalty to the Sultan, Mustafa Kemal presented to his deputies the programme of the 'people's government', as he

---

5 Şevket Süreyya Aydemir, *Makedonya'dan Ortaasya'ya Enver Paşa* (Remzi, Istanbul: 1972) Vol 3, pp 549, 574.

called his government on that occasion only – and then never again.[6] The programme, which set out the objective of 'liberating the Turkish nation from the domination of imperialism and capitalism ... with the help of God', was endorsed unanimously and enthusiastically by the National Assembly on 18 October 1920. It was, of course, never implemented, but it served its purpose domestically and internationally, and it has left some traces.

At home, the 'people's programme' helped Mustafa Kemal establish control over the People's Group, which consisted of some 60–70 Assembly members, and was the political wing of the Green Army. When the time came for Mustafa Kemal to form his own party, he called it the People's Party. After the proclamation of the republic, it became the Republican People's Party, a name which it has retained to this day. For a long time, it ruled the country single-handed, but it has never achieved power single-handed in a free election. Abroad, there was of course no question of pulling the wool over the eyes of the Bolsheviks, but Mustafa Kemal's dealings with Moscow frightened the Principal Allies with the spectre of Communism.

Kâzım Karabekir, the nationalist commander in eastern Turkey, wrote in his memoirs that when he took up his command in May 1919, the British control officer, Colonel Alfred Rawlinson, confided in him that the Allies were in no position to stop the spread of Bolshevism by military means, for that would require calling up once again men who had just been demobilised. Karabekir thought that Rawlinson wanted him to provide an anti-Communist barrier in the Caucasus.[7] In the event Mustafa Kemal wrote off the Caucasus, while preventing the spread of Communism to Turkey.

In December 1920, after the Turkish nationalists and the Bolsheviks had partitioned the territory claimed by Armenian nationalists, Mustafa Suphi, the leader of Turkish Communists loyal to Moscow, left Baku for Turkey. As Karabekir did not allow him to enter Erzurum, he made his way to Trabzon (Trebizond). Harassed on the way and despairing of success, he found a boat for the return voyage to Bolshevik territory. He never made it. Thugs, organised by the Unionist boss of the guild of boatmen, embarked with him. Off the Turkish coast, they murdered

6 Taha Akyol, *Ama Hangi Atatürk* (Doğan Kitap), Istanbul: 2008) pp 274–80.
7 Karabekir, *İstiklâl Harbimiz*, Vol I, p 24.

Mustafa Suphi, his wife and 13 companions and threw their bodies overboard. Some time later, the perpetrators of the crime were themselves killed by the nationalist authorities. Ankara's relations with Moscow were not affected.

Kemal and the Greeks

Just as Mustafa Kemal's diplomatic position was beginning to improve, the position of Greece weakened dramatically. Venizelos had sought to capitalise on his illusory gains at Sèvres by calling a general election. On the eve of the election, on 25 October 1920, King Alexander of Greece died of blood-poisoning after being bitten by a monkey in the palace grounds. Alexander had been brought to the throne as the unwilling successor to his father Constantine, an opponent of Greek entry into the war on the side of the Allies. Greeks living within the country's pre-war boundaries were war-weary. Venizelos, who knew this, employed questionable tactics to win the election. Greeks in the newly acquired province of eastern Thrace, who were Venizelist to a man, were given the vote; so, too, were the armed forces, where Venizelist officers not only put pressure on their comrades, but falsified results. An opposition leader was murdered in Athens. Constantine's policy of neutrality appeared attractive in retrospect. Accused of tyranny, Venizelos was roundly beaten on 14 November by supporters of Constantine. On 2 December 1920, at French prompting, Britain, France and Italy issued a joint warning that 'the restoration to the throne of Greece of a King, whose disloyal attitude … towards the Allies during the war caused them great embarrassment and loss, could only be regarded by them as a ratification by Greece of his hostile acts'. In spite of this warning, the referendum held in Greece three days later yielded a massive vote for Constantine's return.[8]

Regime change could, at least in theory, have given Greece the opportunity to withdraw from Anatolia while trying to hang on to eastern Thrace. But withdrawal was not an easy option. Greeks who had been Ottoman subjects had compromised their position by siding with their country's enemies. What is more, Venizelos had convinced most metropolitan Greeks that he had settled 'the national question' – in other words that the annexation of 'Ionia' (western Anatolia) to Greece was an accomplished fact. Swayed by this unfounded belief, the new regime

8 Llewellyn Smith, *Ionian Vision*, p 166.

lost the opportunity to go for half a loaf. It was not the monkey's bite that changed the course of history. It was rather the decision of the new Greek regime under King Constantine to outbid Venizelos in expansionist zeal. Before long, the risks they had taken became clear on the ground.

The defeat of the Armenians and the understanding with Moscow allowed Mustafa Kemal to concentrate his forces on the western front against the Greeks. Karabekir stayed on in Erzurum, while the western front was entrusted to Colonel İsmet. In January 1921, Greek troops made a first attempt to move inland from the coastal areas they had occupied. Their main thrust was from the Bithynian plain, centred on Bursa, towards the town of Eskişehir, lying on the railway line between Istanbul and Ankara. On the edge of the Anatolian escarpment, near the small railway station of İnönü, they were met by İsmet's newly assembled troops and thrown back. As a reward for his victory, İsmet was promoted to brigadier by the National Assembly. The rank of one-star general carried with it the title of Pasha.

The Greeks claimed that their advance had been a probing manoeuvre rather than an offensive to defeat Turkish nationalists. Nevertheless, the setback had immediate political consequences. The Principal Allies called a conference in London to discuss a mutually acceptable revision of the Treaty of Sèvres concluded four months earlier. They invited to it both the Istanbul and the Ankara governments, thus conferring a measure of recognition on the latter. As soon as the conference opened on 21 February 1921, the chief Ottoman delegate, Grand Vizier Tevfik Pasha, withdrew to the background, saying that the Turkish case would be presented by Bekir Sami, the Foreign Minister of the Ankara government. Predictably, the conference failed: the Greeks stood out for all their gains at Sèvres, Bekir Sami insisted on the National Pact – the integrity of Turkey within the 1918 armistice boundaries. But while the conference produced no results, on its margins Bekir Sami struck separate bargains with the Principal Allies, tempting them with economic concessions if they came to an agreement with Ankara. After his return, the bargains were repudiated by the Turkish National Assembly, and Bekir Sami resigned. But they widened the cracks in the laboriously constructed Allied united front.

While Bekir Sami was holding off and then tempting the Western Allies in London, another Turkish nationalist delegation was negotiating in Moscow. On 16 March, four days after the London conference had broken down, a Turkish-Soviet friendship agreement was signed in Moscow. A few months later, it was supplemented by a friendship agreement between Turkey, on the one hand, and, on the other, Georgia, Armenia and Azerbaijan, which had all become Soviet Socialist Republics. Turkey regained its pre-1878 eastern frontier, with the exception of the port of Batum which became the chief town of Ajaria (or Adjara), theoretically an autonomous republic within Georgia. Apart from fixing the eastern frontier of the Turkish state, the agreement also provided for Soviet aid in gold and weapons. It was to prove crucial in sustaining the military capacity of Turkish nationalists.

The first shipment of 1.5 million gold roubles arrived in December 1920. Others followed at regular intervals: another 4 million gold roubles, more than 33,000 rifles, 50 heavy guns (some left by the British), 300 machine-guns, etc.[9] Characteristically, the shipments came after a second Turkish military success. On 23 March 1921, the Greeks returned in force, trying once again to scale the escarpment near İnönü. At first they succeeded in storming some commanding heights. But a Turkish counter-attack on 31 March dislodged them from their gains. İsmet gave the news to Mustafa Kemal. From the peak of Metristepe, he reported, he could see the Greeks fleeing to the plain below. Turkish history records the victory as 'the second Battle of İnönü'. Mustafa Kemal congratulated İsmet with a Churchillian phrase which every Turkish schoolboy is meant to know by heart: 'You have vanquished not just the enemy but also the ill fortune of our nation.'[10] Yet the country's destiny had to take another knock before it triumphed over adversity.

The Hashemite revival: Iraq and Transjordan

After the debacle in Syria, it would not have been any great surprise if the world had never heard of Feisal again. However, within a year, the British government had come to the conclusion that he was the only possible candidate to be ruler of strife-torn Iraq and his election as Iraqi king was arranged. This astonishing change of fortune was driven by the necessity of the British to create ruling structures in Iraq that would allow Britain to retain its influence there but at a much lower cost. More or less at the same time, Abdullah was allowed to establish himself as Emir of Transjordan. This occurred because of the same financial

9 Akyol, *Ama Hangi Atatürk*, pp 289–90. Figures vary in different sources.
10 Mango, *Atatürk*, p 311.

constraints on the British and the need to have some plan for the desert territory east of the Jordan that the British appear to have envisaged as forming part of Feisal's kingdom in Syria. By the mid-1920s, Feisal and Abdullah were firmly established as rulers in the British Mandates of Iraq and Transjordan. Hussein, however, who maintained lingering hopes that he would be ruler of a wider Arab entity in the Middle East was to lose the kingdom he had established in the Hejaz and was to end his life in bitter exile in Cyprus.

In October 1916, the *ulema*, the leading Muslim scholars, in Mecca had declared Hussein King of the Arab Nation and religious chief until Muslims were of one opinion concerning the fate of the Islamic Caliphate. Hussein's claim for leadership of all Arabs was not widely accepted by many Arabs, nor, indeed by his main sponsor, the British government. The British were disturbed by the hubris of his claims and would only recognise Hussein as King of the Hejaz.

During the Arab Revolt, power had begun to drain away from Hussein to Feisal, of whose successes Hussein became increasingly jealous. In August 1918 a furious row had broken out between them, with Feisal threatening to resign as military commander, and only Lawrence's mediation prevented this from developing into a full-blown crisis. During the Syrian crisis of early 1920, Hussein had undermined Feisal's attempts to compromise with the French, seemingly oblivious to the realities of the situation.

Within the Hejaz itself, Hussein's position was not that strong. His other rivals in the Arabian peninsula, especially 'Abd al-'Aziz Ibn Saud, had also been strengthened by the war. Ibn Saud had risen to prominence in 1902 when a force he led captured the city of Riyadh in central Arabia from Ibn Rashid. This success allowed him to make himself Emir of Nejd. He had continued to expand his territory and by 1914 he was the most significant power in Central Arabia and was essentially independent of the Ottomans. Ibn Saud was an adherent to the particularly austere Wahhabi sect of Sunni Islam, which was founded in the 18th century by Muhammad ibn 'Abd al-Wahhab (1703–92), who formed an alliance with the Sauds. By 1806, most of the Arabian Peninsula including Mecca and Medina had been conquered. Eventually forces from Egypt crushed the Sauds and the Wahhabis. The family's fortunes did not recover until the early 20th century when Ibn Saud launched his wave of conquest.

The religious zeal of the Wahhabis provided considerable societal cohesion in the Nejd. Any sort of cohesion, other than a universal willingness to accept Hussein's subsidies and bribes, was singularly absent in the Hejaz. Ibn Saud also forged a new instrument of state-building and military power with his creation of the quasi-military religious brotherhood called the *Ikhwan*. The *Ikhwan*, mostly former nomads, established settlements in the Nejd in which they founded *madrasahs* (religious schools) and cultivated land. However, they could quickly be mobilised to terrorise Ibn Saud's internal and external enemies.[11] Hussein and Abdullah were both well aware of the growing threat of Saud. While Ibn Saud had carefully husbanded the British subsidy he had received during the war, Hussein had lavished his on both the Arab Revolt and on bribing tribes to stay out of Ibn Saud's orbit. Abdullah's lack of participation in the Arab Revolt is partly explained by his fear that Ibn Saud would take advantage of Hussein's commitment to it to further his power.[12]

The Khurma dispute and the decline of Hussein[13]

In 1914, Emir Khalid of the Utayba tribe in the Khurma region, to the east of Jeddah, had converted to Wahhabism. He had remained under Hussein's political influence and had participated in the Arab Revolt. However, in 1917 Khalid had fallen out with Abdullah and begun to assert his independence by refusing to fight any more or pay taxes. He also sought aid from Ibn Saud, though Saud demurred from providing it. Hussein had also become increasingly concerned about British encouragement of Ibn Saud to attack the Ottoman supporter Ibn Rashid, which he saw as a threat to his pre-eminent position among the Arabs. At the root of it all was Hussein's desire to have Ibn Saud excluded from the war effort against the Ottomans. He wanted the British to be overwhelmingly dependent on him, but they, while leaning towards Hussein, also wanted to keep Ibn Saud as an ally and continued to cultivate him.

Hussein was determined to enforce his will in Khurma by military force. His first attempt to do so was rebuffed by Khalid and local forces

---

11 For background on Ibn Saud see Yapp, *The Making of the Modern Near East*, p 60.
12 Teitelbaum, *The Rise and Fall of the Hashemite Kingdom of Arabia*, p 103.
13 This section leans heavily on J Kostiner, 'Prologue of Hashemite Downfall and Saudi Ascendancy: A New Look at the Khurma dispute', in Susser and Shmuelevitz, *The Hasehemites in the Modern Arab World*, pp 47–65.

in July 1918. *Ikhwan* warriors began to move into Khurma to aid their co-religionists and Ibn Saud became increasingly committed to supporting its independence from Hussein. Leadership in the Arabian Peninsula in the early 20th century grew out of the barrel of a gun. If he could not suppress recalcitrant tribes such as the Utayba in Khurma, Hussein's claims to primacy would inevitably fail.

In May 1919, following the long-delayed surrender of the Ottoman garrison at Medina, Abdullah was sent with a Hejazi army to try to suppress Khurma once more. Abdullah had not gone north to Syria with Feisal because he viewed Hashemite ambitions in the Arabian Peninsula as more important than those in Syria and Mesopotamia. He had concluded that the end of hostilities with the Ottomans was merely a pause before a future conflict with Ibn Saud for supremacy in the Arabian Peninsula. However, on 25 May 1919, Abdullah's better armed and equipped army of 3,000 men was surprised by a night attack on their camp at Turaba spearheaded by *Ikhwan* warriors. The army, including its heavy equipment, was virtually destroyed; Abdullah only just escaped with his life.[14]

Hussein's power in the Arabian Peninsula was now severely diminished. Only British pressure on Ibn Saud prevented him pressing home his advantage. The British went so far as to prepare contingency plans to intervene. Ibn Saud, as usual, demonstrated commendable restraint and did not push his military advantage to its obvious conclusion. He remained anxious to remain on good terms with the British. As a British government memorandum written a couple of years later noted 'there is no doubt had he so desired, Ibn Saud could have taken Mecca and overrun the Hejaz'.[15] Feisal, in control of Syria at this time, fearful that France would take the opportunity to attack should he rush to his father's aid, was unable to help. Hussein, however, became ever more anxious after Turaba that Syria should be linked to the Hejaz, as the viability of the Hejaz as an independent kingdom was always doubtful. The limitations of Hashemite power and Hussein's lack of leadership skills had been all too evident in the Khurma affair.

---

14 Mary C Wilson, *King Abdullah, Britain, and the Making of Jordan*,
Cambridge Middle East Library (Cambridge University Press, Cambridge: 1987)
p 37.
15 Paper on proposed kingdom of Mesopotamia and the advantages and disadvantages of making Emir Faisal first King, War Office 32/5619.

The British government considered that Hussein had been the cause of most of his own troubles by failing to parley with Ibn Saud. Lord Curzon now saw Britain's erstwhile ally as 'a pampered and querulous nuisance'.[16] Hussein's sons, particularly Abdullah and Feisal, were estranged from him; Feisal, because of his success, and Abdullah as a result of the disaster at Turaba. His eldest son Ali, who remained at his father's side in Mecca, believed that the temperamental behaviour of his father was isolating him and was increasingly dangerous to the Arab cause.[17]

The consequences of the defeat at Turaba were exacerbated by a growing financial crisis for Hussein. Since 1916, Hussein had become utterly dependent on the British financial subsidy. The subsidy proved to be an additional Achilles heel for him, however, for such was the lavishness with which he bribed tribes, he created the expectation that such largesse would continue for ever. The bribes also only bought temporary loyalty. When the British government began to reduce the subsidy, Hussein found his ability to maintain tribal influence in the Hejaz and neighbouring parts of Arabia severely diminished.[18] Indeed, the financial crisis cost him support in the Hejaz as he was forced to tax the merchants and traders of Jeddah and Mecca in order to fund himself. The people of the Hejaz were used to receiving money from the Ottomans, not having to pay it out. By mid-1920 Hussein was receiving only £30,000 in gold a month from the British as opposed to over £200,000 at the height of the war.

In August 1920, the British requested that Hussein sign up to the Treaty of Versailles and the arrangements agreed at San Remo the previous April in return for further funding. Hussein adamantly refused. The British spent the next four years attempting to formalise their relationship with Hussein by means of a bilateral treaty. Lawrence met him in July and August 1921, tasked with persuading him to accept British terms. Hussein was his usual contradictory self. Lawrence commented: 'The old man is conceited to a degree, greedy and stupid, but very friendly, and protests devotion to our interests.'[19] The fact was that Hussein had

16 Busch, *Britain, India, and the Arabs, 1914–1921*, p 333.
17 Teitelbaum, *The Rise and Fall of the Hashemite Kingdom of Arabia*, p 198.
18 Teitelbaum, *The Rise and Fall of the Hashemite Kingdom of Arabia*, p 166.
19 Wilson, *Lawrence of Arabia*, p 656.

become increasingly convinced that the British had let him down over the post-war settlement and in his conflict with Ibn Saud. Despite Lawrence's entreaties, he refused to sign any treaty until the British recognised his kingship of Palestine and Iraq and priority over all rulers in Arabia. Lawrence eventually left.

The refusal to agree a treaty prevented Hussein receiving any further British support. It was a foolish decision and a fatal error.[20] While Ibn Saud had created a socially and militarily cohesive state in central Arabia, Hussein had relied for legitimacy on his diplomatic skill and ability to win international support. The combination of military failure, incompetent governance and the rejection of overtures from Britain, his main sponsor, left his kingdom extremely vulnerable to further attack from his great enemy, Ibn Saud.

Revolts in Egypt and Iraq

Because of its strategic importance for their imperial communications, Egypt was of vital concern to the British, but the disturbances which Allenby had faced in March 1919 exposed just how deep and widespread opposition to Britain's rule had become. The key seemed to be to find a formula which would secure Britain's strategic interests whilst recognising the reality of Egyptian national aspirations, and this lay behind the negotiations which Lord Milner conducted with nationalist leaders in the summer of 1920. Progress proved difficult, however, and in February 1922 the British government issued a unilateral declaration of Egyptian independence, but retained control of the country's defence and foreign affairs. Egyptian resentment continued, confirmed by the assassination in Cairo in 1924 of Sir Lee Stack, Governor-General of the Sudan.[21] Attempts to negotiate a treaty between the two countries in 1928 and 1930 were unsuccessful, and the state of Anglo-Egyptian relations continued to be unsatisfactory.

The situation in Mesopotamia, as it was still termed, was, if anything, even more volatile. The award of the Mandate to Britain at the San Remo Conference was followed by a widespread revolt which broke out in July 1920. The reasons for this outbreak were a matter of some controversy

---

20 Wilson, *Lawrence of Arabia*, p 656, 657–61.
21 Yapp, *The Making of the Modern Near East*, pp 340–45; Hughes, *Allenby in Palestine*, pp 13–15.

at the time. The Acting Civil Commissioner, the gifted but imperious Arnold T Wilson, viewed what happened in part as the result of incitement from Feisal's government in Damascus, although even he could not disguise the fact of opposition to the Mandate. In fairness to Wilson, he was doubtful whether the Shia Arabs or the Kurds could come to terms with a government dominated by Sunni Arabs, the issue which has been at the heart of the country's problems ever since.[22] Lawrence, on the other hand, put the matter with stark simplicity in a letter published in *The Times* on 23 July. The Arabs, he pointed out, had not fought the Turks simply to change masters, but for their independence. The insurrection, which lasted into 1921, claimed an estimated 8,450 Iraqi lives. It was a severe strain on the British and Indian Armies, overstretched as they were. At the outbreak of the rebellion, there were 9,800 British and 25,000 Indian soldiers, but over the summer of 1920 a further 20 battalions had to be sent from India. British and Indian Army casualties were 426 killed, 1,228 wounded, and 615 missing or prisoners. The Mandate for Iraq was proving a poisoned chalice.[23]

The pressure to cut military expenditure in Mesopotamia now required a reversal of policy. Direct rule from London or Delhi was no longer a feasible strategy and there was an urgent need to install a reliable Arab regime that would limit British expenditure in the country.[24] At the end of December 1920, the Cabinet discussed a proposal from Percy Cox, who had resumed his old job as High Commissioner in Mesopotamia, that Feisal be proposed as king of Mesopotamia to sate nationalist sentiment and allow a significant reduction in the British garrison.[25] Despite the disaster in Syria, Feisal still had considerable respect and numerous supporters within the upper echelons of the British government including the Prime Minister, Curzon and Hardinge, the Permanent Under-Secretary at the Foreign Office. Indeed Curzon would have activated the 'Feisal as King of Mesopotamia' option sooner had it not been for French objections.[26]

22 Sir Arnold T Wilson, MP, *A Clash of Loyalties: Mesopotamia 1917–1920. A Personal and Historical Record* (Oxford University Press, London: 1931) pp 310–14.
23 Keith Jeffery, *The British Army and the Crisis of Empire 1918–22* (Manchester University Press, Manchester: 1984) pp 150–1; John Marlowe, *Late Victorian: The Life of Sir Arnold Wilson* (The Cresset Press, London: 1967) pp 212–31.
24 Darwin, *Britain, Egypt and the Middle East*, pp 39–40.
25 Gilbert, *Churchill Companion, IV*, Part 2, p 1279.
26 Paris, 'British Middle East Policy-Making after the First World War', pp 773–93.

The alternative to this strategy was far more unpalatable. This was to withdraw British forces to Basra and leave the rest of Mesopotamia to Mustafa Kemal's Turkish nationalists or even anarchy.[27] Churchill's alternative strategy for reducing expenditure was to use air power. He succeeded in persuading Lloyd George that prescriptive (or perhaps more accurately, terror) bombing of recalcitrant Mesopotamian villages would allow significant savings in the number of troops required to hold the region. Combined with Cox's political strategy to provide an Arab government that would command the loyalty of the population and reduce the requirement for troops, massive expenditure savings could be made.

Churchill's coherent cost-saving strategy in Mesopotamia made him an obvious choice to deal with the crisis in the British Mandates in the Middle East. Therefore, when Milner indicated his desire to be relieved of the Colonial Office, Lloyd George decided to replace him with Churchill in January 1921. Churchill moved swiftly. He rapidly concluded that Feisal was the best man for the job of ruling Iraq. He also fast-tracked moves to streamline decision-making in the Middle East. Churchill was convinced that a single sub-department of the Colonial Office was the best solution, 'otherwise muddle, failure and discredit are certain'.[28] Since 1917, the British had wrestled with how to run their policy in the Middle East, which according to Mark Sykes had some 18 different organisations and groups providing input.[29] Now there was to be a single voice under the control of Churchill. While Curzon was irritated and suspected Churchill of a Middle Eastern power-grab, there must also have been a certain sense of relief that the troublesome area was now someone else's problem.

The Middle East Department of the Colonial Office came into being on 1 March 1921. It was given responsibility for the British Mandates, the Arabian Peninsula and Persia. The first Under-Secretary was John Shuckburgh, an India Office hand with significant experience of the Middle East. T E Lawrence agreed to be Churchill's Middle Eastern adviser.[30] Both Lawrence and Hubert Young, the head of the political and administrative branch of the new department, were pro-Hashemite

27 Darwin, *Britain, Egypt and the Middle East*, pp 35–6.
28 Gilbert, *Churchill Companion*, IV, Part 2, pp 1300, 1303–6.
29 Monroe, *Britain's Moment in the Middle East*, pp 35–6.
30 Wilson, *Lawrence of Arabia*, pp 641–2.

'partisans'.[31] However, their appointment reflected the need to have officials on board who would be able to woo the Hashemites and implement the new British strategy.

The key British link to Feisal remained, of course, Lawrence. He had been initially sceptical about helping the British government after what he felt was the betrayal of the Arabs at the Peace Conference. However, he met privately with Feisal to ascertain his views. The Emir was willing to work with the British though concerned that both Abdullah and his father might object.[32] His strategy having some prospect of success, Churchill now decided to hold a conference in early March 1921 of all of the British Middle Eastern experts in Cairo that would focus on what to do with the Mesopotamian Mandate. The objectives were: to formally endorse a new Arab ruler; to formulate a timetable for the reduction in size of the British garrison to a more economical peacetime establishment; to calculate future financial aid for the Mandate; and to decide which parts of Mesopotamia were worth retaining.[33] On his way to Cairo, Churchill met the French who reiterated their objections to Feisal being made king of Mesopotamia. However, the British no longer felt much beholden to the French on this issue.

The Cairo Conference[34]

The venue for the conference was the Semiramis Hotel. Beginning on 12 March 1921, for 12 days over the course of more than 40 secret sessions, some 40 British Middle Eastern experts and policymakers – including all of the High Commissioners, the senior regional military commanders, the political residents, and governors of territories such as Somaliland – worked through an agenda that would shape the Middle East to the present day. It was rapidly agreed that for Mesopotamia, which was to be renamed Iraq, Feisal offered the best and most economical chance of success. Percy Cox and Gertrude Bell were both supportive but they proposed that Feisal should be seen to be the choice of the Iraqi

---

31 Karsh and Karsh, *Empires of the Sand*, p 308.
32 Wilson, *Lawrence of Arabia*, p 643.
33 Gilbert, *Churchill Companion*, IV, Part 2, p 1334.
34 The best account remains Aaron S Klieman, *Foundations of British Policy in the Arab World: The Cairo Conference of 1921* (Johns Hopkins Press, Baltimore: 1970).

people rather than be imposed. A formula was agreed that Feisal would announce his availability to serve as king of Iraq and the British government would state that it would not stand in his way.[35]

The conference also considered the question of Palestine. Herbert Samuel, the High Commissioner, was still in favour of a Mandate encompassing all of Palestine and Transjordan, arguing that this was what the Balfour Declaration had stated and that the creation of a separate Mandate might lead to complications with the League of Nations. The question became more urgent when news reached the conference that Abdullah had advanced to Amman. It was now clear to Churchill that an agreement would have to be reached with him.

When Churchill and Lawrence went north to Jerusalem at the conclusion of the conference, a meeting was arranged with the Emir. Churchill told Abdullah that Transjordan would not be part of Palestine. Abdullah was offered a leadership role in Transjordan and a subsidy. In return he was to stop attacking the French. He would also receive British advisors and a promise of eventual progress towards independence.[36] Abdullah was also persuaded to waive his claims to Iraq. There was also an intimation that if he behaved well, the French might approach him and give him a role in Damascus, although Antonius suggests that this was a trick to keep him quiet.[37]

While in Jerusalem, Churchill addressed Arab and Zionist delegations on 30 March 1921. The Palestinians had already submitted a memorandum asking him to repudiate the Balfour Declaration and halt immigration. He made it clear to them that he had no intention of doing either. But of particular significance for the future was what he went on to say about the Balfour Declaration. Emphasising that Balfour had used the term *a* National Home rather than *the* National Home, he said that this did not mean a Jewish government that would dominate the Arabs. More ominously, from a Zionist perspective, he used the term 'national centre' when talking about the National Home, a term which was soon to take on some significance. Interestingly, this qualification did not feature in his response to the Zionist delegation. Rather he confirmed the British

---

35 Sachar, *The Emergence of the Middle East*, p 378.
36 Sachar, *The Emergence of the Middle East*, pp 402–3; Wilson, *Lawrence of Arabia*, p 649; Fromkin, *A Peace to End All Peace*, p 504.
37 Wilson, *King Abdullah, Britain, and the Making of Jordan*, pp 52–3.

government's commitment to the Balfour Declaration, while emphasising this had to be undertaken without prejudice to the country's existing majority. He also warned them that the Arabs were very much afraid for their future. Just exactly how the Arabs felt would soon be revealed.[38]

The most notable impact of the conference was that the 'Sherifian Solution' became the new British strategy for managing the Middle East. As Aaron Klieman notes, 'What had begun as an exercise in pragmatism had been expanded at Cairo into a principle to be applied wherever possible, beginning with Mesopotamia and then spreading to Arabia and Transjordan.'[39]

Events now moved swiftly as the British sought to implement their plan. Lawrence told Feisal to make his way to the Middle East. On 15 April, they had a long conversation in which Feisal agreed that he would not attack the French in Syria, and would seek to compromise with Ibn Saud provided he did not attack his father in the Hejaz. He also fully acknowledged that he would need British advice and support in Iraq as the population there was not yet ready for self-government.[40] The British agreed with him, Churchill envisaging that Iraq would be run 'much like an Indian state'.[41] Percy Cox and Gertrude Bell prepared for Feisal's arrival. She organised everything from the Emir's travel arrangements to the design of a temporary flag for the new state. The main potential domestic opponent of Feisal was Sayid Talib, an ambitious former deputy in the Turkish parliament from a leading Basra family, who had spent the war in exile and was probably the most prominent nationalist in the country.[42] After he was reported to have expressed displeasure at the turn of events, he was arrested and sent into permanent exile in Ceylon.

Feisal arrived in Baghdad on 23 June 1921. The Iraqi Council of Ministers, under Cox's direction, ratified Feisal as candidate and a plebiscite was arranged for August. Ninety-six per cent pronounced themselves in favour of Feisal, but there was no way that Feisal actually had that level of support. There were large numbers of pro-Turkish groupings who

38 Gilbert, *Churchill Companion*, IV, Part 2, pp 1419–22.
39 Klieman, *Foundations of British Policy in the Arab World*, p 124.
40 Wilson, *Lawrence of Arabia*, p 650.
41 Gilbert, *Churchill Companion*, IV, Part 3, pp 1553–4.
42 See Wilson, *A Clash of Loyalties*, pp 265–6.

wanted close links with Mustafa Kemal, Shias who wanted a theocracy and Kurds who desired independence. However, Feisal was probably the least worse option. As Phoebe Marr notes, 'there is little doubt that no other candidate had his stature or could have received anywhere near the acclamation he did'.[43] Feisal was crowned as Iraq's first monarch on 23 August 1921.

Tensions in the Zionist movement: Weizmann and Brandeis

While these events were unfolding in the Middle East, Weizmann briefly returned to Palestine prior to making his first visit to the United States in April 1921; the ostensible purpose of his trip to America was to stimulate interest in the Hebrew University, still a barren site on Mount Scopus, and to establish the Palestine Foundation Fund, the Keren Hayesod, in the country. Behind this journey, of course, lay his simmering feud with Brandeis and his supporters in the American Zionist movement, which had come into sharper focus at the annual congress of the Zionist Organization of America (ZOA) in November 1920. Here Brandeis's supporters had effectively downgraded the Keren Hayesod. Although he was, in a sense, entering the lions' den, Weizmann had brought with him a strong delegation, including Ussishkin, had enlisted the active support of Albert Einstein, and was welcomed on his arrival in the city by an ecstatic crowd of New York Jews.

It was not long before he locked horns with the ZOA's leadership. Even before he had disembarked, Judge Julian Mack, President of the ZOA, who came on board to meet him, handed him a memorandum setting out the views of Brandeis and his supporters. What it proposed amounted, in Weizmann's view, to nothing less than a disaggregation of the Zionist movement into its component parts. For his part, Weizmann was clear that a united Zionism was of the essence, and, as a result, he could not accept the terms of the memorandum. In not doing so, he was openly confronting the established leadership of the ZOA, Brandeis, Mack, Felix Frankfurter, Robert Szold, Jacob de Haas and Stephen Wise, as eminent a group of American Jews as could be imagined. In contrast, Weizmann's American supporters, such as Louis Lipsky, seemed lesser figures. But Weizmann's instincts told him that the sentiments of American Jewry

---

43 Phoebe Marr, *The Modern History of Iraq* (Westview Press, Boulder, CO: 2004) p 25.

were with him, and Ussishkin shared his view that they should not surrender to the American leadership.

Even so, attempts at a compromise were made, but they proved inconclusive. By the end of April, Brandeis was writing to his wife and to Frankfurter in bitter terms about Weizmann, whom he had evidently come to detest. For his part, Weizmann issued a statement as President of the World Zionist Organisation establishing the Keren Hayesod in the United States. This action brought the fraught relations between the two groups to a head, the confrontation coming at the 24th annual convention of the ZOA which met in the city of Cleveland from 5–8 June 1921. Weizmann and his delegation attended, but did not speak, although the deliberations and votes went decisively in their favour. Brandeis and Mack had been in contact prior to the convention about their positions should the decisions go against them, and they promptly resigned their offices, their main supporters leaving with them. On 19 June, Brandeis formally tendered his resignation as Honorary President of the World Zionist Organisation. Weizmann and his supporters within American Zionism were left in possession of the field, but at the cost of a bitter rift in the leadership of one of the world's most vibrant Jewish communities, the echoes of which would be heard for years to come.[44]

Samuel, Arab resistance and British policy in Palestine
Churchill's warning about the nature of Arab fears was realised to an extent that put the outbreak of violence in 1920 into the shade. When Samuel had been in office just a week, he proclaimed an amnesty for those who had been involved in the spring disturbances, which included Jabotinsky, for whose release Weizmann had been vigorously campaigning. In August 1920, this amnesty was extended to the two principal Arab fugitives, Arif al-Arif and Amin al-Husayni, thus opening the way for the latter's entry into active Palestinian politics. His opportunity came in March 1921 with the death of the Grand Mufti of Jerusalem, his half-brother Kamil al-Husayni. Amin immediately campaigned to

---

44 Weizmann, *Trial and Errror*, pp 326–36; Brandeis to Felix Frankfurter, 26 April 1921; Brandeis to Julian William Mack, 3 June 1921; Brandeis to the Executive Council of the World Zionist Organisation, 19 June 1921, in Urofsky and Levy (eds), *Letters of Louis D Brandeis*, Vol IV, pp 553–4, 562–3, 567–8; Reinharz, *Chaim Weizmann: The Making of a Statesman*, pp 344–50.

succeed him, apparently assuring the British of his good offices. Before this could happen, however, trouble broke out in a way that could hardly have been expected. On May Day, a quarrel occurred between communist and non-communist Jews in Jaffa, which, for reasons that are not entirely clear, sparked an Arab attack on the city's Jewish population, and then on five Jewish settlements. In the resulting violence, 47 Jews were killed and 146 wounded, while the police and troops killed 48 Arabs and wounded 73 others. In the aftermath, Amin al-Husayni was confirmed as Mufti, an appointment which saw him develop into one of Zionism's deadliest enemies.[45]

While the Mufti's activism lay in the future, more serious from the perspective of Weizmann and the Zionists was both the scale of the violence and what it revealed about the state of Arab opinion. The official inquiry into what happened, chaired by the Chief Justice of Palestine, Sir Thomas Haycraft, left little doubt as to the latter. It identified the principal cause as hostility towards the Jews, linked to Jewish immigration and Arab perceptions of Zionist policies. Dismissing as superficial Zionist claims that the violence had really been directed against British rule, Haycraft identified the basic cause as the Arab fear that the increasing Jewish immigration would result in the loss of their economic and political position. He further pointed to the lifestyle of the young Jewish immigrants which jarred with the Arab way of life. Hostility to the Jews also cut across class barriers and the Muslim-Christian divide. By any reckoning, it was a sober analysis for the British and a disturbing one for the Zionists.[46]

Samuel now turned to appease the Arabs. One of his first decisions following the outbreak of violence was to suspend immigration, an action which caused understandable consternation among the Jews. While he intended this to be temporary, Samuel indicated to Churchill that it should only be resumed if there were projects ready for the new immigrants. Part of his proposed solution was to create representative institutions through enlarging his Advisory Council with elected Muslim, Jewish and Christian members. He also confided in Churchill that the Zionist leaders had to recognise that their policies would not be possible in the face of the opposition of the greater part of the Palestinian population.[47]

---

45 Mattar, *The Mufti of Jerusalem*, pp 21–7.
46 *Palestine Royal Commission Report*, pp 51–2.
47 Gilbert, *Churchill Companion, IV*, Part 3, pp 1459–93.

The high hopes that Weizmann and the Zionists had placed in Samuel at the time of the San Remo Conference were now turning sour. The appointment as Mufti of Haj Amin, whom they identified with the Jerusalem riots of the previous year, was distinctly unwelcome.[48] The changing tone of British policy, already signalled in Samuel's letter to Churchill, could be clearly seen in his royal birthday speech in Jerusalem on 3 June 1921, in which he denied that Britain would countenance a Jewish government over the non-Jewish majority. He also introduced the concept of economic absorbability, which, he claimed, should govern immigration policy, and announced that the government was considering a partially elected legislative council.

Even before the Mandate had been formally endorsed by the League of Nations, qualifications of the Balfour Declaration were thus beginning to emerge. Given the fact that Churchill had been closely consulted on Samuel's speech, Weizmann was spurred into action.[49] Clearly alarmed by the speech's content and tone, Weizmann attended a meeting at Balfour's house, during which he confided his fears in Lloyd George, Churchill and Maurice Hankey. That he had such access to the Prime Minister and Colonial Secretary was a clear answer to his critics in the Zionist movement, since neither Brandeis nor Ben-Gurion could have brought together such key figures at that time. After discussing his visit to the United States, Weizmann cut quickly to the point, castigating Samuel's speech as a negation of the Balfour Declaration. Challenged on the point by Churchill, he then compared the two documents, claiming that the speech would prevent the creation of a Jewish majority, which the Declaration had sanctioned. At this point Lloyd George and Balfour both interjected, reassuring Weizmann that the Declaration had anticipated an eventual Jewish state. Turning to the defence of the Jews, Weizmann apparently secured covert approval for bringing weapons into Palestine. He then turned to the legislative council proposal. While Churchill argued that this was being undertaken in Iraq and Transjordan, Weizmann responded, with some justice, that it was only being proposed for Palestine because the British had been forced into it. Lloyd George, Churchill and Balfour were inclined to agree. Weizmann then came to what was clearly his main concern; namely, that to set up representative

48 Weizmann, *Trial and Error*, pp 342–3.
49 Esco, *Palestine*, Vol I, pp 274–5.

government would mean abandoning Palestine, at which point Lloyd George told Churchill that the country must not be given representative government. The Colonial Secretary responded that he might have to bring this idea to the Cabinet, but that the establishment of the Jewish National Home would be excluded from any discussion. Weizmann denied that such a thing was possible.[50]

The Palestinian delegation to London

Impressive though Weizmann's intervention in London was, it could not in itself halt the Arab offensive against Zionist aims. In May 1921, a Palestine Arab congress resolved to send a joint Muslim-Christian delegation, headed by Musa Kasim al-Husayn, of the powerful Jerusalem family, and the Christian Shibly al-Jamal, to Rome, where they were received by the Pope. The delegation then travelled to Paris, Geneva and London to lobby against the Balfour Declaration's incorporation into the proposed Mandate. In anticipation of their visit, Churchill felt the need to present his appreciation of the situation in Palestine to the Cabinet. His analysis was that the country was in ferment, with the Zionists' policies unpopular with everyone except themselves. He reported that elective institutions had been refused in deference to the Zionists, and that, as a result, the Arabs contrasted their situation in Palestine with that of Iraq. Nevertheless, Churchill said that if it were the wish of the Cabinet, he would implement the Balfour Declaration and the San Remo decisions. Reinforcing its chief's views, the Colonial Office advised that the Arabs objected to Zionist policy *per se*, and that, as a result, the British government's aims in Palestine could only be achieved by showing that Jewish immigration would not undermine the Arabs' existing position. The tactic to be followed should be that of allowing gradual Jewish immigration linked to the ability of the country to absorb it.[51]

The Palestinian delegation was in London for almost a year, in the course of which it became clear that the British government would not accede to their demands that it renounce the Balfour Declaration, end Jewish immigration, and grant self-government. A meeting with Weizmann, arranged by Churchill, was fruitless.[52] Churchill's advice to the

---

50 Gilbert, *Churchill Companion, IV,* Part 3, pp 1558–61.
51 Gilbert, *Churchill Companion, IV,* Part 3, pp 1585–90.
52 Esco, *Palestine,* Vol I, pp 277–9.

Cabinet was that there were two choices. It could revoke the Balfour Declaration, refer the Mandate to the League of Nations, set up an Arab government, and curtail or stop Jewish immigration. Alternatively, it could
pursue existing policy and arm the Jews. A draft announcement by Weizmann to that effect failed to find support, however. This was an unpalatable choice, and it is hardly surprising that the ministers failed to make
it. Discussion centred around two issues; namely, the fact that Britain
had made a pledge in the Balfour Declaration, and the growing power of
the Arabs in the territories around Palestine. While some argued that the
Arabs had no right to Palestine since they had not developed it, others
pointed to the inconsistency in the Balfour Declaration in promising
support for a National Home while respecting the rights of the Arabs.[53]

For his part, Samuel was increasingly worried by the situation in Palestine, especially given the pressure he was under to reduce the costs of
its garrison. On 14 October 1921, he wrote to Churchill expressing his
fears of repercussions should the Arab delegation to London return dissatisfied. In the first instance, he pressed for ratification of the Mandate,
the delay in which he identified as contributing to his political, economic
and financial difficulties. Secondly, he turned to the critical question of
Arab-Jewish relations. What he was concerned to drive home was his
belief that many Arabs would be prepared to accept the definition of
the National Home which he had set out in his speech of 3 June, as
long as this was held to be British policy. Again, however, he turned to
Weizmann's Peace Conference statement that Palestine would become as
Jewish as England is English, which, he said, was repeatedly quoted in
the press in Palestine, as being inconsistent with the idea that Arabs and
Jews could work together towards a common future. Samuel concluded
by saying that the Arabs should stop asking for the abrogation of the
Balfour Declaration, but also that, for their part, the Zionists should
acknowledge that they were aiming to build a democratic commonwealth
rather than a state in which they would be politically privileged, and that
the statement about Palestine becoming as Jewish as England is English
be amended to take into account that Palestine was a common home.[54]

---

53 Gilbert, *Churchill Companion, IV,* Part 3, p 1606.
54 Gilbert, *Churchill Companion, IV,* Part 3, pp 1650–5.

The evolution of the Churchill White Paper

Samuel's letter was poorly timed, since three days earlier negotiations for an Irish settlement had got under way in London, with Churchill as a key member of the British team. Compared with Ireland, Palestine was a peripheral British interest. Even after the treaty was signed on 6 December 1921, Churchill's involvement in Irish affairs increased since as a Dominion the emergent Irish Free State came under his portfolio as Colonial Secretary. When Sinn Fein split on 7 January 1922 between the supporters of Arthur Griffith and Michael Collins, who had signed the treaty, and those of Eamon de Valera, who rejected it, Irish affairs once again took on a dangerous dimension. With anti-Catholic riots in Belfast in the spring of 1922 and the outbreak of civil war in the Free State on 28 June, Ireland was never far from Churchill's mind. He was also engaged in a simmering, but increasingly acrimonious, dispute with Edwin Montagu over the rights of the Indian community in Kenya. While it would be going too far to say that Palestine was a distraction, its problems needed to be addressed.

If the purpose of the Arab delegation had been to seek a reversal of government policy, then they had clearly failed. What they had succeeded in doing was driving home that the Arabs of Palestine were adamantly opposed to British policies, something confirmed in November 1921 with the publication of the Haycraft Committee of Inquiry into the May disturbances. The measure of their success may be seen in a mounting campaign against the Balfour Declaration in sections of the British press, including those owned by the powerful newspaper barons Lords Northcliffe and Beaverbrook. Once again trying to square the circle, on 11 April 1922 John Shuckburgh wrote to the delegation on Churchill's behalf confirming that there would be no retreat from the Balfour Declaration, but that the government's purpose was to ensure that the section of the Declaration referring to the position of non-Jewish inhabitants was carried out.[55]

With ratification of the Mandate now imminent, confirming this became the purpose of British policy, and in May Samuel came to London to assist in reaching a formula that would achieve it. Weizmann, meanwhile, allowed himself to be diverted into visiting Rome, since he believed the Vatican was a key opponent of the Balfour Declaration, as well as

55 Esco, *Palestine*, Vol I, pp 279–80.

Berlin and Paris. On his return, he had to confront the uncomfortable fact that the House of Lords had voted to repeal the Balfour Declaration, although fortunately for the Zionists the House of Commons rejected a similar motion. While Balfour reassured Weizmann that the House of Lords vote was immaterial, it was yet another indication that British support could not necessarily be taken for granted.[56] It stands repeating that this was a time when Irish affairs were consuming Churchill's attention with the seizure of the Pettigo-Belleek Triangle in County Fermanagh in Northern Ireland by Republican forces, and that Conservative support for the Lloyd George coalition was fast eroding – the House of Lords vote on the Balfour Declaration a clear symptom of this, whatever its author might say.

This highly febrile political situation saw the publication, on 3 June 1922, of the *Statement of British Policy in Palestine*, commonly referred to as the Churchill White Paper. Here Weizmann's response to Lansing came back to bite him:

> Unauthorised statements have been made to the effect that the purpose in view is to create a wholly Jewish Palestine. Phrases have been used such as that Palestine is to become 'as Jewish as England is English'. His Majesty's Government regard any such expectation as impracticable and have no such aim in view.

Referring to the fears which the Arab delegation had expressed, the *Statement* denied that there had ever been any intention of subordinating the Arabs, pointing out that the Balfour Declaration had made it clear that the National Home was to be founded 'in Palestine' rather than being the whole of the country. Addressing the Zionists, it confirmed that the Balfour Declaration was not up for negotiation, affirming the 'ancient historic connection' of the Jews to the National Home and that they were in Palestine 'as of right and not on sufferance'. It was the definition of the National Home that was problematic for Weizmann and the Zionists, however:

> When it is asked what is meant by the development of the Jewish National Home in Palestine, it may be answered that it is not the

---

56 Weizmann, *Trial and Error*, pp 350–60.

imposition of a Jewish nationality upon the inhabitants of Palestine as a whole, but the further development of the existing Jewish community, with the assistance of Jews in other parts of the world, in order that it may become a centre in which the Jewish people as a whole may take, on grounds of religion and race, an interest and a pride.

Two other elements displeased and alarmed the Zionists. The first was the acceptance of the establishment of a legislative council, albeit gradually, which the Arabs had been demanding, but which the Zionists had opposed and which Weizmann had been given reason to believe Lloyd George had ruled out. The other was confirmation of the principle that immigration into Palestine should be dependant on its absorptive capacity, an unwelcome concept introduced by Samuel in his 3 July speech the previous year. To the Zionists it was a negation of their conviction that only through immigration could the economy of the National Home be developed.[57]

Weizmann rightly regarded the terms of the announcement as a considerable retreat from the Balfour Declaration, but since he had been told that confirmation of the Mandate depended on Jewish acceptance of the White Paper, he was left with no alternative but to do so. He was even prepared to argue that the idea of economic absorbability could work to the Jews' advantage, though he later had to confess that this had not been the case. Even so, on 18 June 1922, Weizmann wrote on behalf of the Zionist Organisation, confirming acceptance of the new policy as set out in the *Statement*. The previous day, the Arabs had rejected it, as they were to do with so many initiatives in the future, usually to their disadvantage, as it turned out.[58]

The way was now open for the Council of the League of Nations to confirm unanimously the Mandate, which it did on 24 July 1922. Weizmann's fear that the predominantly Catholic countries of Spain and Brazil would demur proved to be unfounded, and an attempt by the Papal Nuncio to defer the item was thwarted by the French.[59] In many respects, the terms of the Mandate were what the Zionists had been working to

57 *Statement of British Policy in Palestine*, 3 June 1922, Cmd 1700 (London: 1922).
58 Weizmann, *Trial and Error*, pp 360–2; Esco, *Palestine*, Vol I, pp 285–6.
59 Weizmann, *Trial and Error*, pp 363–4.

secure and the Arabs had hoped to prevent. Crucially, the Preamble formally incorporated the Balfour Declaration into the Mandate, and, in a sense, went even further by recognising 'the historical connection of the Jewish people with Palestine and to the grounds for reconstituting their National Home in the country'. Under Article 2 of the Mandate, Britain was to place Palestine 'under such political, administrative and economic conditions as will secure the establishment of the Jewish National Home, as laid down in the preamble, and the development of self-governing institutions, and also for safeguarding the civil and religious rights of all the inhabitants of Palestine, irrespective of race and religion'. Articles 4 and 6 of the Mandate sanctioned the creation of a Jewish Agency, and charged the Mandatory with facilitating Jewish immigration, while making sure that the rights and positions of others were not prejudiced. Finally, Article 25 permitted the Mandatory to make separate provision for the land to the east of the river Jordan, which was confirmed by the League on 16 September.[60] The campaign to secure the British Mandate for Palestine, which would include the implementation of the Balfour Declaration, was one which Weizmann had waged for five gruelling years. Now, at last, this key objective had been secured. But in the meantime events in Palestine and elsewhere in the Middle East had been gathering pace.

Turkey's war with Greece

As always, international politics were moving in response to the balance of forces on the ground. In May 1921, the British, French and Italian High Commissioners in Istanbul declared that the Straits would be treated as a neutral zone. Given that the Treaty of Sèvres had not been ratified, the Allies were officially still at war with the Ottoman state. But with their declaration of neutrality in the fighting between the armies of Constantine and those of Mustafa Kemal, the conflict which had started in 1914 between the Turks and the Allies was transformed into a Turkish-Greek war. This was underlined by the decision of the Italians in April and May to withdraw their occupation troops from Antalya and the area south of the Greek positions round İzmir. The Italians had arrived with supplies of food; they got on well with Turkish nationalists; and, finally, they left behind part of their equipment. The local Turkish population remembered them fondly.

---

60 *Palestine Royal Commission Report*, pp 34–40.

The French were soon to follow suit. But, like the Bolsheviks, they wanted to see first whether the Turkish nationalists would hold their own in the war with the Greeks. However, even before the issue became clear on the western battlefields of Anatolia, the French commander in southern Turkey agreed to a 20-day armistice in May 1920. This was prompted by the capture by Turkish irregulars of a French detachment which had tried to hold a railway station in the Taurus mountains, north of Adana. As clashes resumed between Turkish militias, commanded by regular officers, and French forces trying to hold the territory awarded to France under the Treaty of Sèvres, the French government sent an unofficial envoy to Ankara to reach an understanding with the nationalist authorities. The envoy, Henri Franklin-Bouillon, chairman of the Senate Foreign Relations Committee, arrived in Ankara on 8 June 1921. He got on well with Mustafa Kemal, who guessed that France was willing to trade Turkish territory, north of the 1918 armistice lines, against Turkish acceptance of French rule in Syria. The French gave a preliminary sweetener by withdrawing their troops from Turkey's Black Sea coast where they were protecting French investments in Turkey's main coalfield. However, before a comprehensive deal was struck, France had to make sure that the Ankara government would survive the Greek onslaught in the west.

Rejecting the offer of mediation by Britain, France and Italy, the new Greek government reinforced its troops in Anatolia and launched a general offensive against the new and as yet untried Turkish army. Venizelos, who had moved to France after losing power in Athens, argued that by turning down the Allies' offer, his successors had led their country into diplomatic isolation. He had worked tirelessly, he said, to secure Britain's support for Greek territorial claims. Now that support had been compromised by Constantine's government.[61]

At first this did not seem important, as the Greek army made spectacular gains. İsmet was out-manoeuvred. He expected the Greeks to renew their attack from the west. But the main thrust came from the south, and threatened to cut off his headquarters in Eskişahir. The morale of the Turkish troops was severely shaken and large numbers deserted. It was a critical moment for the Turkish nationalists. After visiting the crumbling front, Mustafa Kemal decided to sacrifice territory in order to save

---

61 Llewellyn Smith, *Ionian Vision*, p 166.

the core of his army, and ordered it to withdraw to the east bank of the river Sakarya, the last natural barrier before Ankara. The Greeks pressed on rapidly from Eskişehir, advancing deeper into the treeless Anatolian plateau in the heat of summer. On 23 August, they crossed a tributary of the Sakarya River and attacked Turkish positions on the heights over-looking the east bank.

In Ankara, the civil servants of the embryonic nationalist adminis-tration prepared to leave their ramshackle offices in the caravanserais and dilapidated private houses of their Anatolian capital, and move with their papers to Kayseri, the most considerable city to the east. The fami-lies of deputies in the National Assembly joined in the evacuation. Greek aircraft appeared in the sky and dropped bombs on Ankara's railway station. But for all its unruly and fractious nature, the Assembly stood firm. 'Have we come here to fight or to run away like women?' asked a bearded Kurdish tribal leader, whose loyalty to the Turkish resistance movement is remembered to this day.[62] Faced with disaster, the deputies rallied round Mustafa Kemal. His place, they declared, was at the front in command of his troops. Mustafa Kemal agreed, but on condition that he was given extraordinary powers as commander-in-chief. It was a radical move, for under the Ottoman Constitution it was the Sultan who was commander-in-chief. Nevertheless, the powers were granted, but only for a term of three months, renewable at the National Assembly's discretion, and on condition that that they affected only the military conduct of the war and did not impinge on the Assembly's political prerogatives. These distinctions were lost to most Allied observers, who habitually referred to Mustafa Kemal as the nationalists' all-powerful 'generalissimo'.

Mustafa Kemal wasted no time in meeting the Greek threat. Promising the nation that the enemy would be 'throttled in the inner sanctuary of the fatherland',[63] he ordered the requisitioning of supplies – food, horses, peasant carts, clothes – from an already impoverished population. Prov-identially, the first supplies of Soviet weapons arrived in the national-ist-held ports of the Black Sea in the nick of time. They were hauled by bullock-cart along dirt tracks to the front, often driven by peasant women. Turkish schoolchildren are taught to remember the heroic par-ticipation of Turkish women in their country's defence.

---

62 <http://www.tarihogretmeni.net/tarih/diyab-aga-t13218.html>
63 Mango, *Atatürk*, p 318.

A few months earlier, the nationalists had organised officer training courses in Ankara. Freshly commissioned officers and cadets were thrown into the battle, which Mustafa Kemal directed from the small railway station of Polatlı, west of Ankara. Repeating their earlier successful manoeuvre, the Greeks tried to cut off Turkish forces by attacking them from the south, while keeping up the pressure from the west. They were better equipped than the Turks, but they were fighting in an inhospitable, alien environment. The arid plateau was ideal country for the cavalry, and the Turks made full use of it by harassing Greek lines of communications.

The Greek army fought well. It stormed the main heights commanding the battlefield and advanced to within 30 miles (48 kilometres) of Ankara. Explaining the setback to the National Assembly, Mustafa Kemal made the memorable statement: 'We are not defending a line, but an area – the area that encompasses the whole of the fatherland. Not an inch of it is to be surrendered until it is drenched with the blood of our citizens.'[64] On 14 September he proclaimed a general mobilisation. This amounted to a final repudiation of the armistice agreement of 1918. Mustafa Kemal's strategy worked. The Greeks could not sustain their offensive. Sensing this, the Turkish army launched a counter-attack, forcing the Greek command to order a withdrawal to the west of the Sakarya River. Turkish troops were too exhausted to pursue them, and the Greeks returned to their starting point at Eskişehir, destroying everything in their path: villages, bridges, and the railway line to Ankara. It was a foretaste of what was to happen in much of western Turkey.

The Battle of Sakarya

On 17 September it became clear that the Turks had succeeded in throwing back the Greek offensive. The following day, Mustafa Kemal returned to Ankara. On 19 September a grateful Assembly promoted him to the rank of field marshal, and awarded him the title of Gazi. Its literal meaning is 'warrior for the faith (of Islam)', while in current usage it designates old combatants in general (soldiers who are killed are remembered as şehit, or martyrs), and heroic commanders, in particular.

The Battle of Sakarya is remembered in Turkey as 'the officers' battle'.

---

64 Sami Özerdem, *Atatürk Devrimi Kronolojisi* (Çankaya Belediyesi, Ankara: 1996) p 58.

The army of the National Assembly had some 5,000 officers in all. Of them 300 were killed and 1,000 wounded in the battle, as they led soldiers demoralised by the retreat from Eskişehir and raw peasant recruits who had just joined the ranks. Total Turkish casualties of 3,700 dead and 18,000 wounded roughly matched the Greeks' losses.[65] But Mustafa Kemal had greater reserves of manpower, and his fellow countrymen had their backs to the wall and pulled together, while Greek opinion was sharply divided on the wisdom of the invasion of Anatolia.

King Constantine had staked his throne on the success of the policy of waging war to the finish against the Ankara government. He had arrived in İzmir before the offensive began. It was not a successful visit: the Greek occupation authorities restricted his movements for fear of an attempt on his life; and the king was not impressed by the local Greeks who, he felt, expected their kinsmen from continental 'old' Greece to win the country for them. But Constantine's harshest remarks were reserved for the Turks. Moving to the newly occupied town of Eskişehir, where his younger brother Prince Andrew (the father of the Duke of Edinburgh) commanded an army corps, he wrote, 'It is extraordinary how little civilised the Turks are … It is high time they disappeared once more and went back into the interior of Asia whence they came.'[66] But the Turks had no intention of disappearing, and, as far as civilisation was concerned, as Constantine had to admit himself, both sides fought each other with the greatest cruelty. The term 'ethnic cleansing' had not been invented at the time, but the reality was practised by both sides. Greeks drove Turks out of their villages in their zone of occupation; Turks deported Greeks from the coastlands they controlled. The shelling of Turkey's harbours on the Black Sea by Greek warships provided an excuse for the deportation of Black Sea Greeks, but the long-term aim of the deportation was to pre-empt Greek-Armenian plans to establish a Christian state of Pontus.

The deportation worried the representative of the area in the National Assembly in Ankara. Well-to-do Greeks and Turks lived side by side in some coastal towns. One deputy asked that Turkish property should be protected from the looting which inevitably followed the deportation of Greek householders. The practice of looting and then setting fire to the houses of the ethnic adversary was widespread during the long process

65 Mango, *Atatürk*, p 321.
66 Llewellyn Smith, *Ionian Vision*, p 232.

of the dissolution of the Ottoman Empire. The deliberate destruction which the present generation has witnessed in former Yugoslavia had well-established historical precedents.

Militarily, Mustafa Kemal's success at the Battle of Sakarya was the turning point of the war. Unable to launch another offensive, the Greeks began to blame each other as they sought a way to cut short the conflict. It was a royalist, German-trained general, Ioannis Metaxas, the future dictator of Greece, who was the first to offer a realistic diagnosis:

> It is only superficially a question of the Treaty of Sèvres. It is really a question of the dissolution of Turkey and the establishment of our state on Turkish soil ... And the Turks realise what we want. If they had no national feeling, perhaps such a policy would be possible. But they have proved that they have, not a religious, but a national feeling. And they mean to fight for their freedom and independence.[67]

Politically, success at Sakarya saved Mustafa Kemal's position both domestically and internationally. As the outcome was being decided, Enver waited on the Soviet side of the border in Batum, ready to bid for the leadership of Turkish resistance if Mustafa Kemal fell by the wayside. After Sakarya, Enver gave up any hope of returning and made for Central Asia. Instead of joining with the Bolsheviks against the British, he drifted – without realising what he was doing – into the ranks of the *Basmachi*, or raiders, a disorganised popular movement of local Muslims who resisted the imposition of Soviet rule in Central Asia. It was his last adventure. He was killed in what is today the independent republic of Tajikistan, when the Red Army caught up with his band of irregulars and wiped it out. Having gambled with the lives of millions of his countrymen and lost, he gambled with his own life and lost again. Turks today remember his dashing courage and his patriotism, however wrong-headed. But for Mustafa Kemal he served as the counter-exemplar, who demonstrated the perils of adventurism.

Moscow understood that Mustafa Kemal had no time for pan-Islamic adventures, and caused him no difficulties when he got rid of Communists in his own country. Arrests of Communists in Anatolia began early in 1921 when Mustafa Kemal's army won its first successes at İnönü.

---

67 Llewellyn Smith, *Ionian Vision*, p 232.

After Sakarya, in October that year, Mustafa Kemal formed his own official Communist Party and ordered some of his generals to register as members. The official party was not admitted to the Communist International, but it served its purpose in weeding out such Turkish Communists as would not join it.

The most famous was Nazım Hikmet, Turkey's best-known and best-loved modern poet. Typically, he came from a family of high officials of Polish origin. He was greeted as a hero in Anatolia when he joined the nationalist movement in January 1921. But his romantic revolutionary zeal could not be accommodated in Ankara, and he was sent off to teach in a provincial school. Disappointed, Nazım Hikmet slipped off to Moscow where he moved in the circle of Mayakovsky, the leading poet of the Russian Revolution. He returned to Turkey after the nationalist victory in 1923, and was imprisoned time and again. He finally fled behind the Iron Curtain in 1951, just as Turkey became involved in the Cold War on the side of the West. Nazım Hikmet died in Moscow in 1963, leaving behind a body of work which has changed the course of Turkish poetry.

The most important diplomatic consequence of the Battle of Sakarya was the conclusion on 20 October 1921 of an agreement with France. Officially called an 'accord', it was in fact a preliminary separate peace treaty, which established the frontier between Turkey and French-ruled Syria. In exchange for French evacuation of southern Turkey, Turkey gave up – provisionally, as it happened – the district of İskenderun (Alexandretta). But the accord promised to establish a special administration there, which would protect the rights of its Turkish-speaking inhabitants. The Turkish government remained loyal to its implicit promise to desist from any interference in the internal affairs of Syria. Having frightened the French with the prospect of cooperation between Turkish and Arab nationalists, Mustafa Kemal turned away from the Arabs. As the last commander of Ottoman troops which had faced the disloyalty of Arab nationalists, he owed them nothing, and least of all the Hashemites, who had accepted British gold to harass the Turks. The French were to prove less meticulous than the Turks in carrying out their commitments. While anti-French Arab nationalists were denied facilities in Turkey, Kurdish exiles from Turkey, grouped round a tribal dynasty, were allowed to keep the feeble flame of Kurdish nationalism alive in Syria.

Apart from a free hand in Syria, France wanted to safeguard its network of schools, most of which were run by Catholic teaching orders in Istanbul. As ever, the promotion of French culture ranked high in French foreign policy. Kemal, who had been moulded by that culture, even if it was at second hand, did not object, for in his eyes, and in the eyes of most of his companions, France represented civilisation – not Western civilisation, but the one single civilisation of mankind. It followed that far from obstructing the development of an independent Turkey, French culture promoted it. However, Kemal resisted French pressure for economic privileges. France had been the major investor in the Ottoman Empire, including British-ruled Egypt, and it fought hard to keep the regime of capitulations, which allowed foreigners extraterritorial rights. The Ankara accord made no mention of the capitulations. They were left for the final peace treaty between Turkey and the Allies.

Lloyd George and the Greeks

The British were thus left as the sole defenders of the Greeks in Turkey. But cracks appeared in the British position too. While Lloyd George remained totally committed to the Greek nationalist cause, in spite of the fall from power in Athens of his fatal friend Venizelos, the Foreign Office under Curzon sought to lessen the damage done to British interests by Lloyd George's policy. The British High Commissioner in the Ottoman capital, Sir Horace Rumbold, believed that the future struggle for influence in Turkey would be fought between Britain and France. 'If this struggle comes,' he claimed, 'it will not be so much owing to any action taken by England but rather the direct result of French jealousy.'[68] Doubts in London were reinforced by the stalwart opposition of the India Office to any step that might antagonise Indian Muslims and shake their loyalty to the British Raj.

While civilian politicians argued and intrigued among themselves, it was the military who acted to avoid the risk of a clash with Turkish nationalists. In July 1921, on the eve of the Turkish victory at Sakarya, the Allied Commander-in-Chief in Turkey, General Sir Charles ('Tim') Harington, agreed to meet Mustafa Kemal on board a British warship off the Turkish-held Black Sea port of İnebolu. The plan had been hatched by a demobilised British officer, Major James Henry, who was trying to win a mining concession in Anatolia. He suggested to the Turks that the British were keen on such a meeting, while telling the British military that

---

68 Gilbert, *Sir Horace Rumbold*, p 243.

the Turks wanted it. The intrigue fell through. Told that Harington was willing to meet him, Mustafa Kemal replied that he would come only if the British general agreed in advance to the complete liberation of the national territory and Turkey's unqualified independence in the political, financial, economic, judicial and religious spheres.[69] Nevertheless, even if the initiative failed, it showed that the British military were ready to establish contact with Turkish nationalists.

In February 1922, the Ankara government sent its Foreign Minister Yusuf Kemal, who had succeeded Bekir Sami, to put its case directly to the French and British governments. On his way to France, Yusuf Kemal called on the British High Commissioner in Istanbul, and impressed him with his determination to accept nothing short of the sovereign independence of Turkey within the 1918 armistice lines. When Sir Horace Rumbold suggested that territorial concessions might be necessary, he replied that 'compromise must not always be at the expense of Turkey'.[70] At the end of March, the British, French and Italian Foreign Ministers meeting in Paris proposed an immediate armistice, followed by negotiations for a new peace treaty. The proposal fell on deaf ears: the Turks demanded a full Greek withdrawal as soon as the armistice was concluded; the Greeks turned this down, believing that the Turks were incapable of turning them out of İzmir and eastern Thrace.

The Greeks sought desperately to avert the disaster threatening their Anatolian adventure. But their attempt to force the issue resulted in uniting all the Allies against them. In mid-July 1922, the Greeks threatened to march on Istanbul in the belief that possession of the Ottoman capital would give them the leverage to impose their terms on the Turks. Portraits of King Constantine appeared in the front windows of Greek shops in Istanbul, surmounted by the one word '*Erchetai!*' – 'He is coming!'. But Constantine did not come to regain the city lost to the Turks by his namesake in 1453. For once, the Principal Allies acted in unison, and reinforced their warning to the Greeks to stay out of the neutral zone by assembling their troops and warships to resist a Greek march on Istanbul by force if necessary. The Greeks stopped in their tracks, having diverted to no purpose troops needed in western Anatolia for the final battle with the Turks.

---

69 Gilbert, *Sir Horace Rumbold*, p 243.
70 Gilbert, *Sir Horace Rumbold*, p 249.

Instead of counselling caution, Lloyd George hastened to undo the effect of the Allies' belated show of firmness. 'We are not allowing the Greeks to wage the war with their full strength,' he declared in the House of Commons on 4 August. 'We cannot allow that sort of thing to go on indefinitely, in the hope that the Kemalists entertain, that they will at last exhaust this little country, whose men have been under arms for ten or twelve years ... and which has not indefinite resources.'[71] But allow 'that sort of thing' was precisely what the Allies, including Britain, did. To paraphrase Henry Kissinger, one cannot expect a Great Power to commit suicide (or even to endanger its interests) in defence of an unwise ally.

As the Greek advance on Istanbul was being halted, the Greek procon-sul in İzmir, Aristeidis Stergiadis, tried another way to lighten the burden. On 31 July he issued a proclamation saying that 'the work of liberation' would be continued 'by the liberating people itself', in other words by the locals and not by the Greek government. The administration of the area held by Greeks troops under the terms of the Treaty of Sèvres would be reorganised accordingly.[72] But autonomy for Ionia made no sense. There were no Ionians, as there had been in classical antiquity, but only Greeks and Turks, and they were no longer able to live under the same roof. As the Greeks looked for outside help to hang on to their gains, the Turks took on 'the work of liberation' for themselves. The only effect of Stergi-adis's initiative was to demoralise Greek troops even further, for in effect they were being asked to fight for territory which was about to be given up in any case.

Kemal's victory and the fate of Levantine Smyrna

In Ankara, Mustafa Kemal came under increasing pressure to take the offensive. Nearly a year had passed since the Greeks had been stopped at the Battle of Sakarya. The Turkish national army had replenished its ranks with newly commissioned officers and recruits, and its arsenals with arms left behind by the French and the Italians, in addition to earlier shipments from Russia. What was the commander-in-chief waiting for? The answer was that Mustafa Kemal was keenly aware of the poverty of his domestic resources. His government controlled the most back-ward part of the country, without industry and with precious few skills.

---

71 Llewellyn Smith, *Ionian Vision*, p 283.
72 Llewellyn Smith, *Ionian Vision*, p 281.

The new strength of the nationalists could easily be dissipated in an ill-planned operation. Mustafa Kemal wanted to be sure that he would be able to deliver a decisive blow, and before that to exhaust all possibilities of achieving his objective without further destruction and bloodshed. He proceeded cautiously. He inspected the front in July under cover of a football match between two army teams, which he watched in the company of his commanders. Having satisfied himself that his army was ready, he returned to Ankara and persuaded his ministers to minute their agreement with his decision to launch an offensive. Failure would have not only military but also political consequences. He tried to guard against both. To preserve complete secrecy, an announcement was put out that the commander-in-chief would be staying in Ankara to host a tea party at his residence. Then all communications were cut between Anatolia and the outside world.

An army of 225,000 Greeks were deployed against 208,000 Turks along a front which stretched from the shores of the Sea of Marmara in the north to the valley of the river Menderes (Great Meander), south of İzmir (Smyrna). Like other successful generals, Mustafa Kemal took the strategically sound risk of concentrating most of his forces on a narrow sector, leaving the rest of his front uncovered. It was the strategy of the single knock-out blow, which became known as the *blitzkrieg*. He targeted his offensive on the pivot of the Greek line, the peaks which dominated the town of Afyon on the main railway line from Istanbul. The Afyon salient was where the Greek front line changed direction from north-south to east-west, and was therefore open to attack from two sides. The main blow was delivered from the south to the right flank of the fortified mountain positions held by the Greeks. The intention was to cut them off from their rear base in İzmir, where the Greek commander-in-chief General George Hatzianestis had his headquarters on board a ship. Hatzianestis was an eccentric disciplinarian, who, it was rumoured, believed that his legs were made of glass and could break at any moment. But it was his army that broke.

The issue was decided in the sector chosen by Mustafa Kemal. On 25 August 1922, he joined his battle headquarters on the 6,000-foot (1,829-metre) high peak of Kocatepe. The following day, the Turks let loose an artillery barrage on the Greek positions on the peaks facing them. Then the Turkish troops advanced, climbing up the slopes against determined Greek resistance. The first day the Greek lines held. But Turkish determination was not dented. A Turkish colonel committed suicide because he could not keep his promise to capture a position as quickly as he had promised. 'It is not because I approve his action that I am telling you this', Mustafa Kemal said in his report to Parliament a few days later. 'Such behaviour is unacceptable. But I wanted to illustrate the spirit in which our officers and our commanders discharged their duty.'[73]

The Turkish breakthrough came the following day, 27 August. Almost immediately, Greek morale collapsed. Their officers were bitterly divided into two rival camps, as Venizelists tried to undermine supporters of King Constantine. Troops had been exposed to Communist agitation about the imperialist nature of the war. Soldiers did not trust their officers, and the officers did not trust other ranks – or each other. Greek units retreating from their positions on the hills surrounding Afyon lost contact with each other. Many were surrounded. The retreat which started at Afyon extended to the whole front as far north as the Sea of Marmara. On 1 September, Mustafa Kemal issued his famous order: 'Armies, your immediate objective is the Mediterranean. Forward.'[74] On 2/3 September, two Greek corps commanders surrendered when they found they had fallen into a trap. One of them, General Trikoupis, learned after his capture that he had been appointed commander of the entire front.

It took Turkish front-line troops six days to cover the 250 miles (400 kilometres) from Afyon to İzmir. As the Greeks fled to the coast, they set fire to towns and villages, destroying all that lay on their path. Units that managed to make it slipped through İzmir, leaving behind its terror-stricken Greek, Armenian and foreign citizens, and embarked on ships waiting off the Çeşme peninsula further west. On 9 September, Turkish troops entered İzmir. Mustafa Kemal made his official entry the following day. Three days later there was not a Greek soldier left anywhere in Anatolia, except for prisoners. A few days later there was almost nothing left of İzmir – or more accurately of Levantine Smyrna – and its non-Muslim inhabitants.

There were sporadic incidents of violence as Turkish troops advanced through the prosperous suburbs, where English and other European merchants had their villas, and entered the city. The troops were commanded by Nurettin Pasha, known as 'bearded Nurettin', who was notorious for

---

73 Mango, *Atatürk*, p 340.
74 Mango, *Atatürk*, p 332.

his cruelty. He had been in command of the Ottoman troops which had besieged General Townshend's force in Kut in 1915 during the Mesopotamian campaign, but had been relieved of his command by von der Goltz, the German officer in overall command, before the British surrendered. At the end of the First World War, he was commander of the Turkish garrison in İzmir until the Allies insisted on his replacement just before the Greek landing. The Ankara government appointed him commander of the Central Army, whose task was to keep control of the nationalists' rear. It was this army which forced the Greek civilian population out of their homes along the Black Sea coast and then went on to suppress Kurdish risings. This was accompanied by so much bloodshed and destruction that the Grand National Assembly wanted to have Nurettin court martialled. But Mustafa Kemal was short of commanders and saved him from the wrath of the Assembly, transferring him to the command of the First Army under İsmet Pasha's overall command on the western front.

As commandant of a captured city, Nurettin had the duty of ensuring law and order in İzmir. But when the Greek Archbishop Chrysostom visited him to plead for the safety of his community, Nurettin handed him over to a mob of vengeful Muslims who tore the unfortunate prelate to pieces. Admittedly, it was difficult to restrain soldiers who had seen the destruction wrought by the retreating Greeks, and who found themselves in a prosperous city after years of hardship and grinding poverty. But no effort was made to prevent revenge killings and looting. And, as usual, once looting started fires followed, destroying the lives and property of ethnic adversaries.

The great fire of İzmir started in the Armenian quarter. In all, 20–25,000 buildings were burned down and an area of 2.4 million square yards (2.5 million square metres) was devastated.[75] It was later claimed that the trouble was caused by Armenian resistance and by explosions of ammunition hidden in Armenian homes. Hatred between the Turks and the Armenians was intense, and only the strictest measures could have prevented a murderous confrontation. But instead of reining in ethnic hatred, Nurettin encouraged it. He did nothing to stop the killings and looting. The depleted city fire service was incapable of controlling the fire which engulfed the town right up to the waterfront. Only the

---

75 Izmir Metropolitan Council, *The City that Rose from the Ashes* (Izmir Council, Izmir: 2003) p 15.

poverty-stricken Turkish quarter on the heights round the citadel, the Jewish quarter and the immediate surroundings of the French consulate near the quayside were spared, suggesting that disloyal fellow subjects of the Sultan were deliberately targeted.

Terrified Greeks, Armenians and other Christians crowded the quays, begging to be taken on board Allied warships and transports anchored in the harbour. At first, Allied officers tried to restrict evacuation to their nationals, but as the harbour filled with the bodies of refugees who had thrown themselves on the mercy of Allied seamen, they had to accept on board civilians of any nationality, including Ottoman subjects. Within a few days 213,000 men, women and children were evacuated from the ruined city and carried to safety on board Allied warships and merchantmen.[76] It was a remarkable achievement.

The Chanak Crisis

The occupation of İzmir by the Greeks had mobilised Turkish resistance to the partition plans of the Allies. The city was now to play an important part also in the consummation of the victory of Turkish nationalists. It was from İzmir that Mustafa Kemal decided to move Turkish troops north to press against the British-held perimeter of the neutral zone of the Straits.

During the four years which followed his return from the Syrian front at the end of the First World War, Mustafa Kemal had done his best to avoid a direct clash with the British, while he fought British protégés at home and abroad. He also encouraged contacts, however indirect and tentative, to convey his message that British policy towards his country was wrong-headed, and that if Britain accepted Turkey's full independence within the 1918 armistice lines, he would be only too happy to be its friend in the region and beyond. He had explained his position at a secret session of the National Assembly as early as 24 April 1920, the day after its official opening in Ankara:

Our nation is not opposed to the English. On the contrary it acknowledges and respects them as the greatest, the most just, most civilised and humane nation in the world . But after the armistice, the British entered our capital, and after establishing close contact with

---

76 David Walder, *The Chanak Affair* (Hutchinson, London: 1969) p 177.

our people, they oversaw and backed the Greek occupation of the province of Aydın [İzmir] .So we said 'Do something to correct [your policy] and our nation will once again turn to you [in friendship]'.[77]

Lloyd George was deaf to the message, but the British military were more receptive. And it was the attitude of the British (and Allied) commander-in-chief in Istanbul, General Harington, which prevented an armed clash between British and Turkish troops in September 1922.

Mustafa Kemal's aim in sending his troops to the perimeter of British positions at Çanakkale (Chanak), the fortress on the Asian side of the entrance to the Dardanelles, was to ensure that Istanbul and eastern Thrace up to the 1914 frontier came under the control of his government. With the exception of clashes with French occupation forces south of the Taurus mountains, officially attributed to popular resistance, he had succeeded from May 1919 onwards in achieving his objectives one by one without fighting British, French or Italian troops. Now, once again, he used the threat of force to avoid recourse to it. And once again the tactic worked. British policy changed in the way that Mustafa Kemal had suggested right at the beginning.

The painful, noisy and messy – but, in the last resort, effective – change in British policy was the essence of the Chanak Crisis, as it came to be called, which lasted for barely a month from mid-September to mid-October 1922. And it was not only British policy towards Turkey that changed. So, too, did the governments in London and Athens. The crisis affected also the relationship between London and the Dominions: the refusal of most of the Dominions to back a new conflict (New Zealand and Newfoundland were the two exceptions) marked the growing independence of the constituent parts of the British Empire. The change was bloodless for the British, bloody in Athens. But what came out of the Chanak Crisis was the birth of a new dispensation in that part of the Middle East, a dispensation which has lasted to this day. The peace treaty that was signed in Lausanne nine months later confirmed the outcome of the Chanak Crisis. Fortunately for the world, the crisis did not end, but merely interrupted, the career of one of the enemies of change, Winston Churchill.

Churchill was to describe his position with characteristic elegance:

---

77 *Atatürk'un Butun Eserleri* (Kaynak Yaymlari, Istanbul: 2002) Vol 8, p 83.

Defeat is a nauseating draught, and that the victors in the greatest
of all wars should gulp it down was not readily to be accepted. So
having done my utmost for three years to procure a friendly peace with
Mustapha Kemal and the withdrawal of the Greeks from Asia Minor,
and having consistently opposed my friend the Prime Minister upon
this issue, I now found myself wholeheartedly upon his side in resisting
the consequences of the policy which I had condemned.[78]

Churchill was an imperialist. He resisted the independence of India.
He guided the British Empire through the perils of the Second World
War and presided over its transformation into the Commonwealth. He
believed in the benefits of empire for all its subjects, just as the French
believed in their civilising mission in their empire and beyond. But
Mustafa Kemal too had been a loyal servant of his empire, the Ottoman
state, and had fought hard on three continents to defend its frontiers.
He also believed passionately in the value of the civilisation which had
developed in the West, and which Western empires were propagating
throughout the world. His success in establishing a Turkish national
state on the ruins of the Ottoman Empire, in the teeth of Western opposition, did not blind him to the merits of British or French administration for people who were as yet incapable of achieving and sustaining
civilised self-rule.

It was natural to fear for the safety of Istanbul, the cosmopolitan
capital of the Ottoman state, in the wake of the humanitarian disaster
which had just stricken Levantine Smyrna (İzmir). Non-Muslims, particularly non-Muslim Ottoman subjects, as well as those Muslims who had
sided with the Sultan and pinned their faith on the Allies, were terrified
at the prospect of the forcible entry of the Turkish nationalist army into
their city. But although Allied officials in Istanbul were keenly aware of
these fears, the main concerns of the British government were different.

There was, of course, the prestige of the victors to be considered. But
geopolitics was more important. Control of the Straits had been achieved
at the cost of great sacrifices in the First World War. Freedom of navigation was important for the great trading powers of the West, although
less important now that the Bolsheviks had seized control of Russia,
which ceased to be a significant trading partner of the West. Now the

---

78 Cited in Walder, *The Chanak Affair*, p 191.

pressing need was for a bulwark against Bolshevism. Mustafa Kemal had cooperated with the Bolsheviks, while Venizelos had sent Greek troops to Odessa to help the White Russian counter-revolutionaries. For the British government in particular, the rise of the Bolsheviks revived the fear of Russian expansion which had inspired the policy of supporting the Turks throughout the 19th century. That policy had been abandoned as the Kaiser's Germany came to present a greater threat to British (and French) interests, and, of course, as the Young Turks threw in their lot with the Germans. Lloyd George had been persuaded by Venizelos that Greece could replace Turkey as the defender of the northern frontier of the Middle East, an area long important to Britain as it lay across the route to India. Moreover, British and French rule newly established in the Arab lands had to be defended. But the defeat of the Greeks by Turkish nationalists had disproved the arguments of Venizelos. It was no use blaming the French, the Italians, the soldiers, the opposition and the press at home, as Lloyd George did, for the defeat of the Greeks and, consequently, of his policy. The policy had failed and an alternative had to be found.

When Turkish troops entered the neutral zone and pressed against the British positions round Çanakkale, the first reaction of the British government was to reinforce the troops on the ground and the warships patrolling the Straits. As there were no reserves available, appeals were sent to the Dominions to help guard the positions for which thousands of Anzacs had died. But Australia was unwilling to send its men back to Gallipoli. In fact none of the Allies was willing to fight the Turks.

This became clear when Curzon went to Paris to meet the French Prime Minister Raymond Poincaré. 'It was both a moral and physical impossibility for France to resist the Turks if they advanced,' Poincaré told Curzon, adding, 'French public opinion would not admit of a shot being fired against the Turk.' Curzon burst into tears, complaining: 'Never in my life have I had to endure such speeches.' It made no difference. On 23 September, ten days after the arrival of Turkish troops outside Çanakkale, Poincaré, Curzon and Count Sforza sent a joint note to Ankara which went a long way towards meeting Mustafa Kemal's objectives. The note declared that the Allies 'viewed with favour' the desire of Turkey to recover eastern Thrace, including Edirne (Adrianople), and the Turks could have Istanbul after the peace was signed. As a first step, they suggested a meeting between the Allied generals and Mustafa Kemal

– at Mudanya, south of the Sea of Marmara, or İzmit on the eastern approaches to Istanbul.[79]

The Mudanya armistice

Mustafa Kemal wanted – and needed – a more precise commitment. On 23 September, the same day that the Principal Allies sent their joint note to Mustafa Kemal, there was a military coup in Athens. King Constantine was forced to abdicate and a junta of Venizelist colonels seized power. Just as Constantine's return to the throne in 1920 had not halted the Greek invasion of Anatolia, but, on the contrary, had channelled more resources into it, so now the revolutionary colonels sought to prove their patriotic credentials by assembling troops in Thrace and hanging on at least to their country's gains in European Turkey. In the circumstances, the Allies' promise 'to look with favour' on the restoration of Turkey's 1914 frontier in Europe was not sufficient. What Mustafa Kemal wanted was for the Allies themselves to evict the Greeks. Urged by some nationalist politicians to extend the war to Europe, he replied that he would not sacrifice a single Turkish gendarme for an object he could achieve by peaceful means. Mustafa Kemal's popularity with his troops was well merited.

The Chanak Crisis showed also Mustafa Kemal's mastery of a very modern skill. Right from the beginning of his career, he had realised the importance of the press and made every effort to make friends of journalists. However, he also made sure that it was he and not the press who set the political agenda. During the First World War, Enver, the country's virtual military dictator, had deprived him of publicity. When Mustafa Kemal returned to Istanbul in November 1918 after the signature of the armistice, one of his first steps had been to start a newspaper that would propagate his fame and his views. The newspaper (which was managed by Fethi (Okyar), Mustafa Kemal's main political ally in the capital) was called *Minber* ('The Pulpit'). It served Mustafa Kemal's purpose in presenting him as a safe candidate for his crucial appointment to Anatolia.

Almost immediately after his move to Ankara, Mustafa Kemal set up a press agency. Called the Anatolian Agency and staffed by professional journalists, it helped raise morale at home by disseminating news and comment which favoured the nationalists, and made their views known

---

79 Walder, *The Chanak Affair*, pp 232, 235, 242.

abroad. But securing the friendship of foreign correspondents was a more effective way of influencing public opinion in countries where they had greater credibility. Here Mustafa Kemal was fortunate in his choice of contacts. The French journalist Berthe Georges Gaulis visited him in Ankara and her friendly articles earned her the thanks of the Turkish National Assembly. Later her books made Mustafa Kemal's reforms known and appreciated in the West. But it was the attention that Mustafa Kemal had paid to a British correspondent, George Ward Price of the *Daily Mail*, which was to prove particularly beneficial during the Chanak Crisis.

Ward Price had made his name as a war reporter when still in his mid-twenties during the Balkan Wars of 1912–13. Mustafa Kemal first met him in Istanbul in 1918 when he tried to persuade him of his friendly feelings towards Britain. Ward Price's reports from Turkey made him no friends among British officialdom: in the words of Neville Henderson, British Deputy High Commissioner in Istanbul, Ward Price 'dropped like a vulture from the sky' on a news story.[80] But what mattered was the effect of his reports on the editorial policy of his paper. Even though Ward Price praised the mettle of British troops that faced the Turks at Chanak, the *Daily Mail* concluded that Churchill's efforts to mobilise the Dominions against the Turks were 'bordering upon insanity'. On 21 September, the newspaper came out with the headline 'Get out of Chanak'.

Sir Horace Rumbold, the British High Commissioner, was enraged by the press which, he believed, had readily supported the Turkish nationalist cause. The *Daily Mail*, he wrote, was 'beneath contempt'. The *Morning Post* 'shuts its eyes to the bestialities of the Turks and slobbers over the French who don't deserve it'. As for the French press, it 'seems to be in the grip of the International financier or Jew who only cares for French financial interests and nothing else'.[81] The self-righteous diplomat raged in vain. Mustafa Kemal's handling of the press helped him achieve his objectives.

On 29 September, General Harington was instructed to deliver an ultimatum to the Ankara government demanding that Turkish troops withdraw from the neutral zone immediately. If they did not, the British would attack them. Fortunately, General Harington was as determined as

---

80 Walder, *The Chanak Affair*, p 176.
81 Gilbert, *Sir Horace Rumbold*, p 278.

Mustafa Kemal to avoid a resumption of hostilities. Instead of delivering the ultimatum, he continued negotiations with the Turkish nationalists' representative in Istanbul. The Greek fleet, he said, had been withdrawn from the Sea of Marmara on 27 September 'under the strongest British pressure'. The French unofficial representative, the indefatigable Franklin Bouillon, reported that the Ankara government was prepared to negotiate an armistice leading to a peace settlement. Harington called him 'a perfect curse', but believed that if the Frenchman helped the two sides to sit round a conference table, he would have performed a useful service.[82]

On 1 October, the Ankara government agreed to meet Allied representatives in Mudanya, the small port on the south shore of the Sea of Marmara which served the city of Bursa, now firmly under Turkish control. But Mustafa Kemal would not attend, just as he had earlier refused to meet Harington on board a British warship in the Black Sea, unless his terms were accepted in advance. The Turkish representative would be İsmet Pasha, the Turkish commander of the western front, and Mustafa Kemal's trusted lieutenant. Isolated politically at home and abroad, Lloyd George and Churchill gave way to the peace lobby, albeit with bad grace. Harington, who had earlier disobeyed instructions to confront the Turkish nationalists with an ultimatum, was instructed to be tough in the negotiations. He did not need advice from London to map out common ground for a satisfactory settlement.

The conference began on 3 October in a merchant's house on the waterfront, which had been used by the honorary Russian consul before the war. It was essentially a military meeting between equals: the British, French, Italian and Greek commanders in Istanbul on one side, and İsmet, the Turkish commander on the other. What was under discussion was the gradual transfer of Istanbul and of eastern Thrace to Turkish control. It was not an easy matter to arrange. The capital and its hinterland had a mixed population. Inter-communal relations had broken down, and the prospect of losing Allied protection terrified Christian communities, which had been led to believe that they would replace the Turks as rulers of the cosmopolitan heart of the Ottoman state. There were some 150,000 foreign nationals, most of them natives, who clung to their privileged status. As soon as they entered the First World War, the Young Turks had abrogated the capitulations, under which foreigners

---

82 Walder, *The Chanak Affair*, p 289.

came under the jurisdiction of their own consular authorities. The Treaty
of Sèvres had restored their extra-territorial status. It was no secret that
the Ankara government was determined to abolish this privilege. Suspicions and fears were rife on all sides.

In the circumstances, the delegates could congratulate themselves on
coming to an agreement after a week of tough bargaining. The terms
signed on 11 October were simple. The Greeks were to evacuate their
troops from eastern Thrace within 30 days, transferring civil authority
to the Allies, who would also interpose themselves between Greeks and
Turks on the frontier. The Allies would in turn hand over the administration to Turkish officials, who would be assisted by up to 8,000 Turkish
gendarmes. Allied troops would remain in their present positions, i.e.
would continue to occupy Istanbul and the Straits, until peace was signed.

The Greek delegate, General Mazarakis, saved face by absenting
himself from the signing ceremony. But three days later, on 14 October,
the Greek government announced that it would abide by the terms of the
armistice. It had no other option. Fighting had ended in effect a month
earlier when the last Greek soldier left Anatolia. Now, nearly four years
after the defeat of the Ottoman state, and eight years after it had entered
the First World War on the side of Germany, hostilities ceased officially.
The armistice of Mudros, imposed on the defeated multi-national
Ottoman Empire in November 1918, was replaced by an armistice negotiated with the victorious new Turkish national government. Mudros had
not ended the fighting; Mudanya did so.

Within a month, all the Greeks – soldiers from the mainland and local
civilians – had left eastern Thrace. Villagers loaded their belongings on
carriages and carts and drove their cattle with them to the western bank
of the Meriç (Maritza/Evros) River. The towns, including the frontier
city of Edirne (Adrianople), took years to recover the loss of most of
their skilled citizens. In Istanbul, Greeks who wanted to leave had longer
to make their arrangements. Within a year some 150,000 had left, including the wealthiest members of the community.[83] In 1914 there had been
between 2 and 2.5 million Greek Orthodox residents in Turkey.[84] By 1927,

83 Alexis Alexandris, *The Greek Minority of Istanbul and Greek-Turkish
Relations 1918–1974* (Centre for Asia Minor Studies, Athens: 1983) p 104.
84 There were some 1.8 million Greeks in Anatolia (McCarthy, *The Ottoman
Peoples and the End of Empire*, p 91). Greek sources put the number of Greeks in

when the first official census was held in the Turkish Republic, the Greek community was reduced to 150,000, all of them in Istanbul.[85] Today there are fewer than 5,000 Greeks in Turkey.

Eight days after the signing of the armistice at Mudanya, Lloyd George's coalition of Liberals and Conservatives fell apart. Meeting at the Carlton Club on 19 October the Conservatives decided to pull out of the government and fight the forthcoming general election as an independent party. Lloyd George resigned the following day and was replaced by the Conservative leader Bonar Law. Curzon deserted Lloyd George, whose interference in the conduct of foreign policy he had long resented, and stayed in charge at the Foreign Office. He kept his office when Bonar Law won the general election on 15 November. Lloyd George, unrepentant to the end, never saw office again. Churchill, who stood by him, put the leisure he had not sought to good use by writing his account of the war and much else besides, until his finest hour came in 1940.

In Greece accounts were settled in a more savage way. The junta court martialled the country's defeated leaders. After a travesty of a trial, six of them, including the Prime Minister Dimitrios Gounaris and the commander-in-chief General Hatzianestis, were sentenced to death on 28 November and shot without further ado. Prince Andrew escaped a similar fate thanks to British intervention. His sentence of exile was a lucky deliverance. Venizelos returned to the international scene, and became Greek representative at the Peace Conference in Lausanne.

If San Remo and Sèvres saw the imperial ambitions of the victorious powers touch their zenith, then the events of 1921–2 brought them back to earth. The Turks had demonstrated their ability to thwart the provisions of the Treaty of Sèvres, routing the Greeks and defying the British in the process. Lloyd George did not long survive the Chanak Crisis, and with him, of course, Weizmann and the Zionists lost one of their most consistent patrons. Nor could the Zionists be reassured by the drift of events in Palestine, Samuel's appointment as High Commissioner notwithstanding. The strength of Arab opposition saw Haj Amin

---

Istanbul in 1923 at 250,000 (Alexandris, *The Greek Minority in Istanbul*, p 104), and a similar number of refugees from eastern Thrace resident in Greece in 1928 (McCarthy, *The Ottoman Peoples and the End of Empire*, p 131).
85 Alexandris, *The Greek Minority of Istanbul and Greek-Turkish Relations*, p 141.

al-Husayni, who was to emerge as a deadly enemy, ushered in as Grand Mufti of Jerusalem, while the Churchill White Paper was an unwelcome qualification of the terms of the Balfour Declaration. For their part, Arabs could take some comfort from the installation of Hashemite rulers in Baghdad and Amman. If this was not yet independence then, arguably, events were to prove, as was said in defence of the Irish treaty, that it provided the means of achieving it.

6
From War to War

The Middle East had been at war, almost without a break, since 1911, the year the Italians invaded Libya. The First World War and the Turkish War of Independence, which followed, lasted eight years. But after the Turkish victory at the end of August 1922, the pace quickened. A fortnight later, the Greek army was out of Anatolia. A month after that an armistice was signed with the Allies. It then took another two weeks to sweep away the Ottoman monarchy, which had ruled the country for seven centuries. The Middle East now seemed set on a period of peace and reconstruction but while this became true for Turkey, once the Treaty of Lausanne had settled its future, for the rest of the region events were to be much less straightforward. The Arab world grew increasingly restive under the Mandates system, while the future of Palestine grew distinctly problematic as tensions grew between Arabs and Jews. Nor could the region be immune to the international tensions which steadily built up in Europe from 1933. The Middle East's critical importance as a strategic hub, as well as the need to have access to its oil, meant that it would not be left in isolation once hostilities broke out again in 1939. This time, however, Turkey was to be an exception, adhering to a clear policy of neutrality until virtually the end of the war. No such exception was to apply to the Jews of Europe, however, who were to become the victims of genocide.

Turkey and the Near East 1923

SOVIET UNION

Poti

Tbilisi

Batumi

Kars

Erivan

Trabzon

Araks

Erzurum

Caspian
Sea

Van

Lake
Van

Lake
Urmia

PERSIA

Tigris

lexandretta)

Euphrates

SYRIA
(French mandated)

Samara

Baghdad

Ctesiphon

Kut el Amara

IRAQ
(British mandated)

Basra

HEJAZ & NEJD

KUWAIT

Neutral
Zone

0 ⟺ 300 kilometres

The end of Ottoman rule

On 19 October 1922, a week after the signature of the armistice at
Mudanya, General Re'fet (Bele), one of Mustafa Kemal's original companions in the War of Independence, arrived in Istanbul at the head
of the force of Turkish gendarmes (in fact, soldiers in gendarmerie
uniforms) that was to take over eastern Thrace. Turks in the Ottoman
capital received him enthusiastically. The Ankara government had long
had a representative in Istanbul with whom Allied High Commissioners dealt. But with Re'fet Pasha's arrival the relationship changed, as
power in the old capital slipped out of the hands of the Allied authorities. Welcomed by the Sultan's ADC and the Grand Vizier, Re'fet made
it clear that he recognised Vahdettin as Caliph only and not as temporal sovereign, and his government not at all. Mustafa Kemal had
already decided to abolish the monarchy, even though the matter had
not been debated in the National Assembly. Re'fet waited ten days
before visiting Vahdettin in Yıldız Palace. The Sultan left this account
of the audience:

> This little man hid his true intention behind grand aspirations,
> and said that if I accepted a meaningless caliphate shorn of the
> constitutional sultanate, which we had all sworn to uphold, and if
> I sent a telegram to Ankara declaring that I recognised the law of
> fundamental organisation [the provisional Constitution voted by the
> National Assembly in 1921] and the Ankara government, I could save
> my person and position. I replied that I had to think it over. But the
> following day when I read Mustafa Kemal's insults against my person
> and our dynasty, the time came for a decision.

Re'fet was reported to have said later: 'I crossed my legs in front of
the Sultan and leaned back so far that the tip of my shoes nearly touched
his nose'.[1] According to the Grand Vizier, Tevfik Pasha, Re'fet told the
Sultan: 'Close the palace gates and don't allow anyone in. Unsuitable
people are coming and going, and this leads to gossip. You can go to the
mosque and nowhere else.' Nevertheless the Sultan received in audience
two trusted advisers who were hated in Ankara – Mustafa Sabri, a clerical politician who had served Damad Ferid as Sheikh al-Islam, and the

---

1 Bardakçı, *Şahbaba*, p 231.

journalist Ali Kemal, who had infuriated the nationalists with his fiery articles denouncing the resistance movement in Anatolia.[2]

It was not the Sultan, but the Allies who forced a decision. On 27 October, the Principal Allies – Britain, France and Italy – invited both the Istanbul government of Grand Vizier Tevfik Pasha and Mustafa Kemal's Ankara government to send delegations to a peace conference to be held at Lausanne in Switzerland. In response, Tevfik Pasha suggested to Mustafa Kemal that they should discuss the matter, but Kemal would have none of it. There was only one Turkish government, he insisted, the Ankara government formed by the National Assembly. He did not need the help or advice of Tevfik Pasha and his ministers. The Sultan's government was defunct and the time had come for him and his ministers to leave the stage.

On 30 October, Dr Rıza Nur, a maverick politician who had opposed the CUP before joining Mustafa Kemal in Ankara (and who was later to break with him and vilify him in his memoirs), tabled a bill in the Assembly, declaring that the Sultan's government had ceased to exist when the Allies forcibly closed down the Ottoman parliament on 16 March 1920. From that date, sovereignty, which had been appropriated by the Ottoman dynasty, had reverted to the Turkish nation. The Sultanate was now abolished, but the dynasty would continue to exercise the function of Caliphate at the discretion of the National Assembly. It was in Mustafa Kemal's mind a transitional arrangement, but he argued for it eloquently, saying:

On the one hand, the people of Turkey will become daily stronger as
a modern and civilised state, and realise increasingly their humanity
… and, on the other, the institution of the Caliphate will be exalted as
the central link of the spirit, the conscience and the faith of the Islamic
world.[3]

Modernity and civilisation were synonymous.

Mustafa Kemal reminded his audience that there had been shadowy Caliphs between the 10th and the 16th century when temporal government was exercised by Sultans in the Islamic world. The two functions

---

2 Mahmud Kemal İnal, *Osmanli Devrinde Son Sadriazamlar*, pp 2097–8.
3 Mango, *Atatürk*, p 364.

could, therefore, be separated. But the change of rhetoric was abrupt. When the National Assembly opened in Ankara on 23 April 1920, it had pledged loyalty to the Sultan and Caliph. Now it denounced the monarchy and praised a shadowy Caliphate. Inevitably, there was uneasiness in the ranks of the deputies. Could the wording of the bill perhaps be changed? Mustafa Kemal ended the argument the following day, when the matter came up in committee. In a speech in 1927 in which he gave his account of the genesis of the Turkish republic, Mustafa Kemal said that he stood on a bench in the committee room and told members:

> Sovereignty and kingship are never decided by academic debate. They are seized by force. Now the Turkish nation has effectively gained possession of its sovereignty. This is an accomplished fact. If those assembled here see the matter in its natural light, we shall all agree. Otherwise, facts will prevail, but some heads may roll.

Thereupon, a member said, 'Sorry, we had approached the matter from a different angle. Now you have set us right.'[4] On 1 November, the full Assembly passed the law abolishing the monarchy. There was only one dissenting vote.

The minutes of the committee have never been published, but whatever the exact words used by Mustafa Kemal, there was no doubt about his intentions. The Grand Vizier took the hint. On 4 November Tevfik Pasha submitted his resignation to the Sultan. Moving into his office, Re'fet informed the Allies that the administration of Istanbul was now in the hands of the Ankara government.

The first consequence was far from reassuring. The nationalists' hate figure, the journalist Ali Kemal (whose great-grandson Boris Johnson, also a polemical journalist and politician, was to be elected Mayor of London 85 years later) had tried to make amends by admitting that he had been wrong and the nationalists right. He had believed that salvation lay in cooperation with the Allies. The nationalists had proved that opposition to them was the right course. The tactics differed, but the objective was the same. The admission did not save him. He was kidnapped by nationalist agents in broad daylight in the European heart of Istanbul and taken to İzmit, where 'bearded Nurettin' now had his headquarters.

---

4 Mango, *Atatürk*, p 364.

After abusing him as a traitor, Nurettin handed Ali Kemal over to a lynch mob, which beat him to death. Mustafa Kemal made no secret of his disgust at the fate meted out to his opponent.[5] Soon afterwards Nurettin fell into disgrace. He came out as a political opponent of Mustafa Kemal, who denounced him at length in his 1927 speech, and belittled his military career. Henceforth, repression was left to the courts.

News of Ali Kemal's murder terrified Turks who had cooperated with the Allies in Istanbul, and they hastened to seek refuge in the embassies and consulates of Allied states. The following year the peace treaty provided for a general amnesty for political offences. At the same time, the Turkish government undertook to draw up a list of no more than 150 political opponents who were to be exiled from the country. Prominent critics of the nationalist cause could thus make their way to safety abroad. Survivors among them were allowed back into the country in 1938. This act of reconciliation was one of Mustafa Kemal's last political decisions. He died later that year.

Fear of the new regime was keenest in the Sultan's palace at Yıldız. 'The philosopher' Rıza Tevfik, one of the Ottoman signatories of the Treaty of Sèvres, reports in his memoirs that rumours had reached the palace that 'Mustafa Kemal Pasha will come to depose the Sultan and have him executed. After all, this Turkish revolution is a replica of the great French Revolution. What the French did to Louis XVI, the Turks will do to Vahdettin. Revolutionaries have no other way.'[6] The women and servants in the Sultan's private apartments were panic-stricken. 'Come what may, ensure the escape of our lord and master', they pleaded. But the Sultan had one more matter to settle.

It was a tradition that when the throne was vacated, every single person in the retinue of the late sovereign had to leave the palace. Women in the harem were either married off or entrusted to the care of their relatives. Only elderly servant women who knew the palace ceremonial were allowed to stay on. There had been 36 women in the harem of Vahdettin's brother and predecessor, Sultan Mehmed V (Mehmed Reşad). Vahdettin did not have a harem of his own before his accession, and he had allowed 12 women of his brother's harem to stay on. One of them was a young girl, called Nevzad, who celebrated her 19th birthday on 1 November

---

5 Falih Rıfkı Atay, *Çankaya* (Bateş, Istanbul: 1984) p 342.
6 Bardakçı, *Şahbaba*, p 225.

1922. Vahdettin married her before leaving the country. She was his third wife: the first had borne him two daughters, and the second his only son and heir, Mehmed Ertuğrul, who was ten years old in 1922, and was to die in Cairo in 1944. All three women joined Vahdettin in exile in Italy.

Vahdettin had always been fearful for his safety. Even before his accession to the throne he carried a handgun in his pocket, and he continued to do so to the end of his life. His audience was surprised one day when the gun fell noisily to the floor. Indecisive in most matters, he was, it seems, a good shot. But now safety had to be sought by other means. On 16 November Vahdettin wrote this letter to the Allied Commander-in-Chief, General Harington: 'I consider my life to be in danger in Istanbul, and I therefore take refuge with the noble British state and ask for transport from Istanbul to some other destination.'[7] He signed it Mehmed Vahdettin, Caliph of the Muslims, and not Sultan. Forewarned, Harington had already been authorised to make the necessary arrangements. The following day at dawn an ambulance drew up at the gate of Yıldız palace. Vahdettin was smuggled on board. There was a delay on the way to the harbour as a tyre had to be changed. Eventually, Vahdettin, his son, and a suite of ten courtiers arrived at the quayside. It was raining heavily.

Harington was waiting to see off the last Ottoman Sultan. Vahdettin took out a gold cigarette case and lit a cigarette with trembling hands. Harington is said to have expected to be given the cigarette case as a souvenir. But retentive to the last, Vahdettin put it back in his pocket, as he asked Harington to make sure that his wives joined him abroad. He then embarked on the British battleship HMS *Malaya* which was standing by in the harbour. Asked whether he would be happy to be taken to Malta, Vahdettin agreed. From Malta he made his way to Mecca, ruled precariously by the British protégé King Hussein, who had led the rebellion against the Ottoman state. Mecca, which was about to fall to Ibn Saud, did not provide an agreeable environment, and Vahdettin went on to take up residence in a villa at San Remo on the Italian Riviera. He died there in 1926, his young wife Nevzad at his bedside. It is said that the local Italian court took the unusual step of sequestering Vahdettin's coffin in an attempt to secure payments of his debts. Somehow a settlement was reached with his creditors, and the coffin was shipped to Damascus

7 Bardakçı, *Şahbaba*, p 244

where Vahdettin was finally buried.[8] HMS *Malaya* was to make a return visit to Istanbul in 1938. On board was the British guard of honour which was to take part in Mustafa Kemal's funeral procession.

Superstitious observers noted that Vahdettin had brought ill fortune on himself. He suffered from rheumatism and walked with difficulty. When he entered the old palace at Topkapi for his accession ceremony in 1918, he had asked for his ebony walking stick. Told that it had been left behind, he exclaimed 'What a disaster!' This word of ill omen, uttered at the beginning of the reign, was bound to bring bad luck in the end. The ebony walking stick was the last object Vahdettin took with him when he left his palace for ever.[9]

As soon as he left the country, Vahdettin issued a statement declaring 'I have not fled. I have migrated'.[10] It was a reference to the Prophet Muhammad whose move from Mecca to Medina in CE 622, known as the *hijra*, is the beginning of the Muslim era. Vahdettin insisted that he had not abdicated and that the Ottoman throne was still his by right. He pleaded in vain. On 18 November, the day after his escape, the chief cleric who acted as a minister of the Ankara government issued a fatwa ruling that it was lawful to depose the fugitive Sultan. The National Assembly immediately implemented the decision. It then proceeded to elect Vahdettin's cousin Abdülmecid, the heir apparent, to the newly defined position of Caliph.

Vahdettin had tried to rule as well as reign, like his eldest brother Abdülhamid II and unlike his other brother and predecessor Mehmed V. He claimed that he followed Abdülhamid's policy when he sought the friendship of Britain and France. Abdülhamid had in fact relied on Germany to offset Britain's political and France's economic power, and he used his title of Caliph to frighten European empires, worried about the loyalty of their Muslim subjects. The power equation had changed with the defeat of Germany and the triumph of Bolshevism in Russia. Britain and, to a lesser extent, France had a choice of Muslim puppets, and certainly by 1922 they had come to the conclusion that they could do without Vahdettin, either as Sultan or as nominal Caliph of all Muslims.

---

8 This account of Vahdettin's departure and the events leading to it is based on Bardakçı, *Şahbaba*, pp 239–54.
9 Mahmud Kemal İnal, *Osmanli Devrinde Son Sadriazamlar*, p 2103.
10 Bardakçı, *Şahbaba*, p 241.

True, the Ottoman Caliphate had supporters in India, but it was the survival of Turkey as an independent Muslim country rather than of the Ottoman dynasty that was the aim of the Khalifat movement in the subcontinent. That is why it sent money to the Turkish resistance movement, led by Mustafa Kemal, and opposed Lloyd George's design to partition the most important surviving independent Muslim country. After the First World War, decolonisation rather than pan-Islamism became the dominant ideology of elites among the Muslim subjects of European empires. Nostalgia was the only resource left to the Ottoman dynasty.

The shift in the ideological climate was beyond Vahdettin's grasp. He had trained himself in traditional Islamic culture during his long years of seclusion before his accession to the throne in 1918. The CUP had been modernist. Vahdettin turned away from the modern world. Abdülhamid II was interested in photography and had a photographic studio in his palace in Yıldız. Vahdettin's interest lay in Islamic calligraphy, classical Ottoman poetry and music. In all three he had ability, but not an outstanding talent. Abdülmecid, his successor as last Caliph, preferred Western arts. He composed Western palm court music, and was a competent portrait painter. Disregarding Islamic objections to the representation of the human form, he chose for his paintings subjects such as *Beethoven in the Harem* and *Goethe in the Harem*, as well as *Palace Concubine*. His interests did not endear him either to the elite or to the people. He practised Western arts, but thought of himself as a champion of Asia against Europe. One of his last political gestures in exile in German-occupied Paris was to send a telegram to the Japanese Emperor congratulating him on the success of his forces after Pearl Harbor.[11] Bad judgement was characteristic of the last days of the Ottoman dynasty.

In spite of his tactical praise for the institution of a spiritual Caliphate, Mustafa Kemal was beginning to show his real feelings towards religion. On 2 October 1922, when he made his triumphal entry into Ankara to announce the victory of his armies, he was met at the door of the National Assembly by a uniformed imam, who started reciting a prayer of thanksgiving in Arabic. Mustafa Kemal pushed him aside. 'There is no need for this here,' he said. 'You can say your prayers in a mosque. We

---

11 Philip Mansel, *Sultans in Splendour: The Last Years of the Ottoman World* (Andre Deutsch, London: 1988) p 125a.

have won the war not with prayers, but with the blood of our soldiers.'[12] He had mobilised Muslim religious sentiment at home and abroad to fight foreign invaders. He decided he could dispense with this now. But, at this stage, he took care not to confront Islam as such. In an off-the-record briefing he gave to leading Istanbul journalists in January 1923, he asked them not to describe the government as irreligious. That would be tantamount to an invitation to the public to attack him. The people, he explained, were not without a religion. They professed the Muslim faith. 'No one is rejecting religion, the way the Communists do', he said. Anyway, Communism was nonsense, and when Russia abandoned it, it would become stronger than it had been under the Tsars.[13] When a journalist asked whether the government itself would be religious, he was vague. 'Will it or won't it? I don't know. There is nothing in the laws today to prevent it.' However, he indicated his own position when he added, 'If you insist, call the government materialist, but not irreligious.'[14] He made no bones about his dislike of Muslim clerics, the *hocas* (pronounced hodjas). They were, he said, a worthless lot. The *madrasahs* (religious schools), where they taught, had been a resort of draft-dodgers during the War of Independence.[15] Talking to tradesmen in the southern city of Adana later that year, he made the claim that has dominated secularist discourse in Turkey to this day: 'The evils which have ruined and enslaved our nation have all been wrought in the name of religion', he said. There was no need to consult religious scholars (*ulema*). 'Whatever is rational, whatever is in the interest of the nation and of the Muslim community, is also in conformity with religion. For if our religion had not been rational, it would not have been the perfect and the final religion.'[16]

Mustafa Kemal had earlier addressed the faithful from the pulpit of a mosque in Balıkesir in western Anatolia. Preachers, he said, should use a language everyone understood, in other words, Turkish not Arabic. They should follow developments in science, politics, society and civilisation,

---

12 Taha Akyol, *Ama Hangi Atatürk*, p 345.

13 Mustafa Kemal, *Eskişehir-İzmit Konuşmaları (1923)* (Kaynak Yayinlari, Istanbul: 1993) p 96.

14 Mustafa Kemal, *Eskişehir-İzmit Konuşmaları*, pp 136, 148.

15 Mustafa Kemal, *Eskişehir-İzmit Konuşmaları*, p 144.

16 *Atatürk'ün Söylev ve Demeçleri* (Atatürk Araştirma Merkezi, Ankara: 1989) Vol 2, p 131.

and their sermons should be in conformity with scientific truths.[17] Then, step by step, religion was banished from the public sphere altogether. Truth was to be found solely in contemporary scientific civilisation. If Islam equalled rationalism, then rationalism was sufficient.

However, the full secularisation of the state could wait a little longer. The immediate job after the conclusion of the armistice was to prepare for the Peace Conference in Lausanne. Mustafa Kemal was pleased with the way İsmet had brought the armistice negotiations at Mudanya to a successful conclusion, and decided to appoint him chief Turkish delegate in the final peace talks. True, İsmet was a soldier, not a diplomat. At Mudanya he had acted within his competence, as he faced Allied military commanders. At Lausanne he would have to argue with foreign ministers. İsmet himself was nervous about his qualifications. Mustafa Kemal brushed aside his reservations. İsmet was loyal and he fully shared his leader's vision. That was enough.

The Lausanne Conference

As the Lausanne Conference was held at foreign minister level, the first step was to appoint İsmet Foreign Minister, and then to choose his delegation. He was given two assistant delegates (one of them the sharp-tongued Rıza Nur) and 25 advisers. Some were members of the National Assembly, others career civil servants who had served the Ottoman government. Inevitably, the new civil service was recruited largely from among members of the Ottoman bureaucracy. One of the advisers was the former Unionist minister, Cavid Bey, an acknowledged expert in financial affairs. There was also one eccentric but astute choice – the Chief Rabbi Hayim Nahum. Unlike the Christians, the Jewish community had remained loyal to the Ottoman state, and Hayim Nahum could be relied upon to make use of his foreign contacts to advance the interests of the new government in Ankara. That he was a critic of Zionism was an additional advantage. It meant that his loyalty was not divided. Nahum was described as a teacher of French, the official language of the conference.

When İsmet arrived in Lausanne, he was told that the opening would be postponed for a few days to await the results of the British general election. Was this a British trick?, he wondered. The French hastened to

---

17 *Atatürk'ün Söylev ve Demeçleri*, Vol 2, p 98.

reassure him. Prime Minister Poincaré invited him to Paris where he told İsmet that peace would definitely be concluded.[18] In Britain, the Conservatives won the election on 15 November. Curzon, happy to be rid of the constant interference of Lloyd George, stayed on as Foreign Secretary under the new Prime Minister, Andrew Bonar Law. Before going to Lausanne, he, too, met Poincaré and the newly installed Italian dictator Benito Mussolini. But the united Allied front which Curzon wanted to form against the Turks was shaky.

The Conference was opened on 20 November by the Swiss President Robert Haab in the Mont Benon casino. İsmet thought that after the inaugural speech the meeting would break up until the first working session the following morning. But when Curzon insisted on speaking on behalf of the Allies, İsmet gave an impromptu reply in his schoolboy French (as he himself said). The Peace Conference was to be held between equals, not between a coalition of victors and a vanquished country. Sir Horace Rumbold, the British High Commissioner in Istanbul who had been summoned to Lausanne as Curzon's assistant, believed that İsmet had a great advantage. 'In the last resort,' he wrote, 'the Turks will not shrink from the use of force, while the mere thought of hostilities is repugnant to Bonar Law's mind.'[19] Rumbold did not realise that Mustafa Kemal was just as averse to the resumption of hostilities. Both sides bluffed. But Mustafa Kemal had a clearer idea of his objective. This was the total independence of Turkey and, therefore, an end to foreign interference in Turkish internal affairs. The premise of the Treaty of Sèvres had been that the Turks were incapable of running their own state, whether in the management of the economy or in the administration of justice, or even in public health. Mustafa Kemal was determined that this judgment should be reversed at Lausanne. He was well aware of his country's backwardness, but he was convinced that his people had in them the capacity to run a successful state in the modern world.

The Peace Conference ranged far and wide. There were 12 national delegations – four host Allied countries (the fourth being Japan, which had little to say), five countries, including Turkey, invited to attend all sessions (one of them, the US, did not consider itself a party to the proceedings,

18 Ihan Turan (ed), *İsmet İnönü: Lozan Barış Konferansi* (Atatürk Araştirma Merkezi, Ankara: 2003) p 301.
19 Gilbert, *Sir Horace Rumbold*, p 281.

while pursuing its own interests), the Soviet Union, invited to take part in the discussions of navigation through the Straits, and, for some reason, Belgium and Portugal (but not Spain, which had represented Greek interests in Istanbul in the absence of proper diplomatic relations). The last two were asked to state their views on some topics only.

Curzon was determined to dominate this unwieldy gathering. Poincaré and Mussolini left after the opening, and Curzon declared himself chairman on behalf of the Allied hosts. This might have encouraged the Greeks, reliant as ever on British support, to make impossible demands. But Venizelos, who was the chief Greek delegate, had learnt his lesson. In his heart of hearts he had always believed in disengagement between Greeks and Turks, in what a Turkish observer called 'divorce total'. He had been unable to get it on his own terms, but this did not mean that peace between the two peoples could not be secured in any other way. Greece had been defeated and was bankrupt. But Turkey, too, was in dire straits: many of its cities lay in ruins; it was poor and backward. Both countries had a common interest in peace.

Turkey's frontiers with the Soviet Union and French-Mandated Syria had already been fixed by bilateral treaties. For the rest, the usual practice of *uti possidetis* prevailed: the final peace treaty was to legitimise facts on the ground. Eastern Thrace was already in Turkish hands; Mosul was occupied by the British as Mandatory Power in Iraq. The National Pact, voted by the last Ottoman parliament, had claimed İskenderun (Alexandretta) and the province of Mosul, and demanded referendums to determine the future of western Thrace and of the territory lost to Russia in the Caucasus in 1878. The treaties approved by the National Assembly during the War of Independence had already conceded İskenderun to the French, and Batum (but not the rest of the three districts originally lost to Russia) to the Soviet Union.

Mustafa Kemal was a realist: Turkish claims which were unlikely to succeed could be used as bargaining counters. But his political opponents in the National Assembly played the nationalist card and demanded that the Turkish delegation in Lausanne should insist on the full implementation of the National Pact. The opposition in the Assembly was joined by the Prime Minister Rauf (Orbay), the chief Ottoman signatory of the armistice signed at Mudros in 1918, and subsequently a principled nationalist supporter of Mustafa Kemal. Rauf had hoped to be the chief delegate in Lausanne, and was now determined to make İsmet's life difficult. İsmet played fair by asking the government's permission before departing in any way from the instructions he had been given. But he infuriated Rauf by copying his reports to Mustafa Kemal. He had other readers, unknown to him: the British had broken the code used by the Turkish delegation and were fully aware of his tactics. İsmet realised that there were leaks, but thought that these occurred in Ankara.[20]

Frontiers were not the main issue of contention, as Britain and Turkey agreed to set aside the fate of Mosul for subsequent negotiations and, ultimately, for arbitration by the newly established League of Nations. Curzon's admirers attributed Turkish concessions to the British Foreign Secretary's encyclopaedic knowledge which allowed him to argue convincingly that Kurds, who were the majority in the province of Mosul, were ethnically distinct from the Turks. This, however, was hardly news to İsmet. His point was that Turks and Kurds formed a single community, united by common interests. Curzon did not dispose of the argument that sorting out Kurds from Turks would not serve the interests of either people.

The Kurds would rather be ruled by Turks than by Arabs. Their resistance to incorporation in an Arab Iraq was broken by British aerial bombing, accompanied by the promise that the British would stay on until Kurdish rights were secured. This is what happened in theory. In reality, the Kurds of Mosul were better off than their kinsmen in Turkey so long as British influence was paramount in Iraq. The moment that influence ceased, the Arabs tried to impose their rule on the Kurds, who resisted at great cost to themselves. The conflict continues to this day.

While the fate of Mosul was left in suspense at Lausanne, a settlement was agreed on the status of the Turkish Straits. The zone of the Straits was to be demilitarised, and free navigation was to be ensured under the supervision of an international commission. Soviet Russia wanted the Straits to be closed always to warships of countries which did not border on it. It was disappointed and did not sign the text which was eventually agreed. However, friendly relations between Moscow and Ankara were preserved, as both governments had other priorities.

After long and laborious negotiations, the political problems between Britain and Turkey were largely overcome. Now it was France, with which Turkey had already signed what amounted to a preliminary peace treaty,

20 Kemal Atatürk, *Nutuk* (Atatürk Araştirma Merkezi, Ankara: 1989) p 513.

which delayed a final peace settlement. France stood out for the interests of its investors in the defunct Ottoman state. It believed that these could be safeguarded only if foreigners retained their extra-territorial privileges under the regime of capitulations. This meant setting a limit to Turkish sovereign independence. İsmet stood out for his country's untrammelled sovereignty. Special facilities could be granted to foreigners (and to non-Muslim communities in Turkey) only if they were reciprocated. Similarly, any settlement of economic claims should not impose impossible burdens on Turkey.

Mustafa Kemal probably overestimated the power of Britain, a country which he certainly admired, even though it had been his principal opponent. Like other Turks educated in the Western mould, he had a better understanding of the French, and this helped him to drive a wedge between the two Principal Allies. Curzon, bruised in earlier encounters with the French, tried his best to preserve a common Allied front. When İsmet refused to budge on capitulations, the settlement of Ottoman debt and compensation claims – where the French were particularly demanding – Curzon tried to twist his arm by appeals to self-interest. İsmet liked to tell the story that Curzon countered his insistence on Turkey's unconditional independence by saying:

> We are not happy. We've been unable to have our way on any point. But all the proposals you have rejected are still in our pockets. You're taking over a ruined country. You'll certainly need money to build it up. You'll come and kneel before us to get that money. That's when I'll present to you one by one all the demands you're now rejecting.[21]

Curzon may well have thought so, but he is unlikely to have been so crude. Whatever his exact words, İnönü's account enjoys universal credence in Turkey, and is frequently quoted by nationalists today as they denounce sales of Turkish assets to foreigners and the evils of globalisation.

Unable to make headway in the face of İsmet's stubborn resistance, Curzon issued what amounted to an ultimatum. On 30 January 1923, he asked İsmet to sign a text that, he argued, represented the final Allied position. But Curzon's stand was undermined by Poincaré who told the

---

21 Turan (ed), *İsmet İnönü*, p 305.

press that the Treaty, as it stood, formed only 'a basis for discussion' and no more. This made it easier for İsmet to refuse to sign. It was a dramatic moment. The British delegation had packed its bags, but the train which was to take them away was delayed in case İsmet changed his mind. He did not. There was no alternative to breaking off negotiations and adjourning the conference.

Curzon's superior airs were widely mocked behind his back. His discomfiture when his drunken valet stole all his trousers and hid them under his bed to cover up his hoard of empty bottles made the rounds of clubs in London. His assistant, Sir Horace Rumbold, was blimpish beyond parody. He thought that 'an uppish oriental' was 'an unpleasant animal', and was proud of the fact that he had never asked a Turk inside his house when he was High Commissioner in Istanbul. But his prejudices, which were shared by his colleagues, did not always impair his judgment. As the Lausanne Conference ground to a halt, he predicted in a private letter that the Turks would not sign the Treaty. He added that the French also were discontented with it, believing that it gave Britain what it wanted, but did not give France the economic benefits for which it had hoped.[22] He was right, but he disregarded one other factor.

The Americans, who did not take part in the negotiations, nevertheless watched them carefully to make sure that the open-door principle giving all states equal access to international markets was respected, except where their own interests would be served by privileged treatment. They were particularly interested in a project originally formulated before the First World War by the retired US admiral Colby Chester. In its revived form, the Chester Concession provided for the construction by an American company of railways and harbours on a vast scale in eastern Turkey in exchange for the exclusive right to exploit mineral resources lying within 12½ miles (20 kilometres) either side of the new railways. The Kirkuk oilfield in the province of Mosul was the prize coveted by the Americans. Competition between the Americans and the British, who wanted to retain control of Mosul, suited the Turks in their effort to regain the area, and the National Assembly approved the deal on 9 April 1923. But eight months later it rescinded its decision, after the US had distanced itself from the Near Eastern peace settlement, and it had become clear that it was not going to intervene in the Mosul dispute.

22 Gilbert, *Sir Horace Rumbold*, pp 282–3.

While a mass of unfinished business was left on the table, Greece and Turkey signed two important agreements on 30 January, the day the Conference was adjourned. The first met an urgent humanitarian concern by providing for the exchange of prisoners of war and civilian detainees. As a result, thousands of Greek prisoners did not have to wait for the final peace settlement to regain their freedom. The second agreement had more profound long-term implications. It provided for an exchange of populations, covering all Ottoman subjects professing the Greek (Eastern) Orthodox faith in Turkey and all Muslims in Greece. There were two exceptions: Greeks in Istanbul and on two islands off the entrance to the Dardanelles – Imvros (later renamed Gökçeada) and Tenedhos (Bozcaada) – which reverted to Turkey could stay on, provided they had been resident there when the First World War started. The same provision applied to Muslims in western Thrace, which Greece had gained from Bulgaria – its only prize for its involvement in the war. The numbers of the two communities were roughly equal at 150–200,000.

The Greek Patriarchate could thus stay on in Istanbul. The Greek Patriarch is accepted by all Eastern Orthodox Christians as Ecumenical (in other words, universal) Patriarch, the most senior prelate in their church. However, as far as the Turks are concerned, the Patriarch is simply the religious leader of the Greek Orthodox community in the country. It was therefore agreed in Lausanne that he should be a Turkish citizen. This remains the official position of the Turkish government to this day. İsmet wanted the exchange of populations to be total, with no exceptions for Istanbul and western Thrace. This would have prevented much trouble in years to come. However, there was value also in preserving this most important link with the city's imperial (and, therefore, multi-ethnic) past. Life might have been simpler, but Istanbul would have been poorer without it. It was a reminder of the destiny of Istanbul as a world city. The preservation of some traces of its cosmopolitan past held the promise of a cosmopolitan future built on new foundations.

For the rest, most Greeks had already left Turkey, fleeing with the Greek army. But there were two Greek communities which had been cut off. Many of the Greeks who lived along the coast of the Black Sea had been deported to the interior, and for them resettlement in Greece came as a liberation. The other isolated community was made up of the Turkish-speaking Greeks of central Anatolia, an area known as Karaman (Caramania in Western literature) before the rise of the Ottoman state. These

Caramanian Greeks (*Karamanlı* in Turkish; *Karamanlidhes* in Greek) found it difficult to adapt to life in Greece, where they were mocked as Christians 'baptised in yoghurt'. They retaliated by referring to natives of Greece as 'Vlachs' – Romanian-speaking shepherds. Initial difficulties fostered survival techniques, and the descendants of the *Karamanlidhes* gradually rose to prominence in their new homeland.

As for the Muslims who had lived in Greece during the centuries of Ottoman rule, many had migrated to Turkey before 1914, when independent Greece emerged in 1830 and then acquired Ottoman Thessaly in 1878, and most of Ottoman Macedonia in 1913. The exchange of populations of 1923 completed the process, except in western Thrace and for the small Turkish community in the Dodecanese islands, ruled by the Italians from 1911 to 1945.

The break in the Conference on 30 January 1923 was not an unmitigated disaster for the participants. But there were dangers, too. Rumbold, who returned to his post as High Commissioner in Istanbul, had to deal with fears that the Turks might seize the city by force. One contingency plan provided for the withdrawal of British troops from Istanbul to a fortified enclave in Gallipoli. In the fevered atmosphere of Istanbul, with its large population of panicky local Christians, British authorities found it hard to realise that Mustafa Kemal was a careful and patient statesman, averse to military adventures,

İsmet had his own difficulties, as critics in the National Assembly blamed him for making unnecessary concessions, which had not in the event saved the conference. Mustafa Kemal responded by touring the country to mobilise popular support. He returned to Ankara after he had outlined his reconstruction policy at the economic congress in İzmir, and made sure that the Assembly approved reasonable counter-proposals for the resumption of the Peace Conference.

As soon as the Allies agreed to send their delegates back to Lausanne, Mustafa Kemal prevailed on the Assembly to dissolve itself and fix a date for new elections. He then drew up a party manifesto and vetted all the candidates his embryonic party was to put forward. However, Rauf was still Prime Minister when the Peace Conference resumed in Lausanne on 23 April, exactly three years after the opening of the Turkish National Assembly in Ankara. Curzon, who had already secured all the main British interests, did not return to Lausanne, but left Rumbold in charge. İsmet went back to face French insistence on special treatment for its economic and cultural interests. The capitulations were again the most troublesome problem. Adamant that they should be abolished, İsmet advanced to his objective step by step. In his reminiscences he gives this account of his discussions with the French legal expert, Henri Fromageot:

> His draft opened with the words 'To prepare the ground for the reform and abolition of the capitulations …'. 'No need,' I said, 'of preparing the ground … Why not say simply "the capitulations are abolished?"' 'You can't,' he replied, 'you must use legal language.' Well, I didn't master their legal language in nine months. Then one day Fromageot came to me with the same article. 'What do you want?' he asked. 'Write "the capitulations have been abolished, finished and done with"' I replied. 'All right,' he said. 'Have it your way.' 'What's happened to your legal language?' I asked. 'They have come to a decision to do away with the capitulations,' he replied. 'So they hadn't decided earlier? 'No they hadn't.'[23]

One by one the other difficulties were disposed of. The French agreed that their bondholders should be repaid in francs at the current rate of exchange, and not in gold, as they had insisted earlier. The Ottoman public debt was apportioned among all the successor states. Letters were exchanged on conditions governing foreign schools, concessions granted earlier to foreigners, and so on. Now and then, İsmet made some temporary concessions: he agreed that Turkey would not increase its customs duties for five years, and that, also for five years, it would employ a few foreign advisers in the administration of justice and public health. Only one difficulty remained. It was clear to İsmet that there was no point in pressing Greece for reparations. The Greeks could not pay anyway. He offered to waive Turkish claims in exchange for a frontier rectification by which Turkey would gain Karaağaç, a suburb of Edirne (Adrianople), and the site of the city's railway station, which lay on the western (Greek) bank of the Meriç (Maritza/Evros) River. But back in Ankara, Rauf would not hear of it. Exasperated, İsmet threatened to break off negotiations and return to Ankara if the concessions he had made were not endorsed.

Mustafa Kemal, to whom he copied the telegram, knew that this was a subject open to demagogic exploitation. Rauf could say 'We cannot give up our claim of reparations against the Greeks who have wrecked

---

23 Turan (ed), *İsmet İnönü*, p 305.

our country. Not after our great victory.' He proceeded carefully to save Rauf's face, while İsmet waited impatiently for permission to sign the peace Treaty. Finally, on 19 July, Mustafa Kemal cabled to İsmet: 'I congratulate you most warmly on your success and await confirmation that the treaty has been signed.'[24] Rauf did not associate himself with the congratulations. Nor did he meet İsmet when he returned to Ankara after the signing of the peace settlement. He resigned on 4 August. A week later, the newly elected Assembly held its first session and Mustafa Kemal's friend, Fethi (Okyar) became the new Prime Minister.

The Treaty of Lausanne was signed on 24 July 1923. It was an extraordinarily detailed document, running to 143 articles with 20 appendices and associated covenants. Agreement had not been easy, as Mustafa Kemal had realised from the start. 'The problems discussed round the peace table at Lausanne had not arisen during the last three or four years', he said. 'Centuries-old scores had to be settled.'[25] But in the end the work was done solidly. Of all the treaties concluded after the First World War, the Treaty of Lausanne alone has survived. The Turkish insistence that it should be a treaty freely negotiated by all the parties has paid off. Even Greece, whose defeat it sealed, accepted it as the permanent basis for its relations with its neighbour, Turkey.

However, there were two absent parties at Lausanne, and these continued to nurse grievances against the Middle Eastern peace settlement. The first was Armenia, a signatory to the unratified Treaty of Sèvres. The Treaty of Lausanne made no mention of Armenia, whose frontier with Turkey had been decided by the 1921 Treaty of Kars. However, it would be Kurdish nationalism that posed the more serious threat to the Lausanne settlement.

The Middle East after Lausanne

The conclusion of the Treaty of Lausanne drew a certain line in the affairs of the Middle East. For the Turks it brought to an end the period of continuous warfare which had begun with the Italian aggression in Cyrenaica and Tripolitania in 1911. Their achievement should not be underestimated. Their only friend, Imperial Germany, had been defeated, and their fate had seemed to lie in the hands of their seemingly

24 Kemal Atatürk, *Nutuk*, p 524.
25 Kemal Atatürk, *Nutuk*, p 466.

all-powerful enemies, all of which had ambitions at Turkey's expense. Out of these unpromising circumstances the Turks had through their own exertions and the clear-sighted leadership of Mustafa Kemal, successfully defended the integrity of their ancestral lands in Anatolia and eastern Thrace. As part of that transition they had acquiesced in the loss of their Arab subjects, but given the rising tempo of Arab nationalism they were none the worse for that, as the British were discovering. Able at last to pursue their own destiny, they were free to build a secular republic which would in time, Kemal believed, enable them to become the economic and social equals of the European states.

In May 1923, the British also recognised the Emirate of Transjordan as a national state being prepared for eventual independence, thus securing Abdullah's position.[26] The signing of this agreement caused King Hussein to fly into one of his by-now characteristic rages. Already estranged from Feisal by his acceptance of the crown of Iraq and a truce with Ibn Saud, he now furiously denounced Abdullah. He believed Abdullah's deal with the British acknowledged Jewish claims in Palestine and more importantly, in his now extraordinarily egocentric view of the world, denied his own claims to rule Transjordan. Abdullah, unlike Feisal, was still strongly under the influence of his father and when he met him in January 1924 was so bullied and dominated by him that the British feared that the Emir might give up his claims in Transjordan in favour of Hussein. By now that was the last thing they wanted to see.

Hussein made one final blunder. In spite of his financial and military weakness, he took the opportunity provided by the abolition of the Caliphate by the Turkish National Assembly in March 1924 to declare himself Caliph. The action attracted support in Syria and in Transjordan where Abdullah canvassed on behalf of his father. However, in Iraq and Saudi Arabia, there was rejection and outrage. Ibn Saud's *Ikhwan* warriors demanded that they be allowed to move against the Hejaz once and for all. In August 1924, Ibn Saud launched an offensive that rapidly took the towns of Taif and Mecca. Hussein abdicated in favour of his eldest son, Ali, though he continued to interfere from Akaba. Only Medina and Jeddah remained in Hashemite hands. Ibn Saud's forces blockaded Jeddah for more than a year. The foolishness of Hussein's decision to abandon his

---

26 Kamal S Salibi, *The Modern History of Jordan* (I B Tauris, London: 1993) p 88.

alliance with Britain was demonstrated when British military intervention routed an *Ikhwan* raid aimed at toppling Abdullah in 1924.[27] Ali might well have saved his regime, too. Instead, on 5 December 1925, Medina surrendered. This set off a mutiny amongst Ali's troops in Jeddah. Most of the Jeddah notables were by now willing to submit to Ibn Saud. Ali gave in to the inevitable and abdicated on 19 December 1925. The Kingdom of the Hejaz now ceased to exist. Ibn Saud and the *Ikhwan* remained a threat to both Transjordan and Iraq. It was not until 1928 that Ibn Saud accepted the borders with Abdullah and suspicion and mistrust would continue down the years between the two leading dynasties of the Middle East.

Iraq under the Hashemites[28]

The 1920s saw rapid political developments in Iraq after Feisal was finally confirmed on the throne. Britain was content to speed up the devolution of power, as it would reduce its financial commitment. The Anglo-Iraqi treaty of 1922 was followed by a supplementary agreement in 1924. The major external threat to the integrity of Iraq was Turkey's claim to the old Ottoman *vilayet* of Mosul. However, in 1925, a League of Nations commission declared in favour of continued Iraqi control over the area and Turkey accepted this. The League of Nation's commission also recommended that the Kurds be granted limited self-rule. In the same year, an oil concession was granted to a consortium of British, Dutch, French and American oil companies to exploit the large discoveries around Mosul. Iraq received royalties for the oil that was extracted though its demand for an actual share of the company was rebuffed.[29] This provided revenue to the government from the 1930s, reaching some £84.6 million a year by 1958.[30]

---

27 Avi Shlaim, *Lion of Jordan: The Life of King Hussein in War and Peace* (Allen Lane, London: 2007) p 17.

28 The history of Iraq since independence is well served by the Hanna Batatu's seminal *Old Social Classes and the Revolutionary Movements of Iraq: A Study of Iraq's Old Landed and Commercial Classes and of Its Communists, Ba'thists, and Free Officers* (Princeton University Press, Princeton, NJ: 1978). Two excellent general accounts are the aforementioned Marr, *The Modern History of Iraq* and Tripp, *A History of Iraq*.

29 Marr, *The Modern History of Iraq*, p 30.

30 William Roger Louis, *Ends of British Imperialism: the Scramble for Empire, Suez and Decolonization: Collected Essays* (I B Tauris, London: 2006) p 862.

Relations between the Iraqi leadership and Britain remained strained over the ending of the Mandate and over issues such as the introduction of conscription, especially between 1926 and 1929.[31] The election of a Labour government in Britain in 1929 saw an increased appetite on the part of Britain to advance Iraqi independence. In 1930, a new Anglo-Iraqi treaty was signed. In return for rights to military bases and guarantees for economic and oil interests, the British government agreed to recommend the termination of the Mandate and to support Iraqi entry into the League of Nations. This was achieved in 1932 and Iraq became the first of the Mandates to achieve independence. British advisers were now employees of the Iraqi government and no longer able to veto government policy. The Prime Minister at the time of formal independence was Nuri al-Said. He proved to be the strong man of Hashemite Iraq. Right from the start he silenced opposition from those opposed to any continued British influence.[32]

Feisal remained acutely aware of the underlying weakness of a regime that was dominated by Sunni Arabs in a land where they made up less than a quarter of the population. For this and for wider Arab nationalist reasons, Feisal continued to pursue wider pan-Arab ambitions. In short, he still wished to control Syria. If a union of the Fertile Crescent could be established with him at its head, the Shias and Kurds would be minorities in this wider entity. Furthermore, many of his key advisers and staff were Syrians who had come to Iraq. Perhaps the most important was the Yemenese-Syrian Sati al-Husri, who became Minister for Education. Part of the role of the embryonic school system of Iraq, which al-Husri developed, was to be 'a tool for nationalist indoctrination'.[33] However, Feisal, well aware of previous setbacks, was careful not to push pan-Arabism too far. For instance, he was reticent about supporting the 1925 Druze-led revolt in Syria. Nonetheless, Feisal complained about provisions of the 1930 Anglo-Iraqi treaty because they seemed to preclude the unification of the Arab-speaking states of the Middle East. Feisal, the British High Commissioner Francis Humphrys noted in 1930, 'still hopes and works for the close federation under the rule of his House of all the

---

31 See Peter Sluglett, *Britain in Iraq: Contriving King and Country* 2nd edition (I.B. Tauris, London: 2007) pp 108–20.
32 Marr, *The Modern History of Iraq*, p 34.
33 Tripp, *A History of Iraq*, pp 61–2.

Arab territories in Asia, and it seems that his intention is to endeavour to bring about first the union of Syria and Iraq'.[34] The Sunni elite at the pinnacle of Iraqi politics envisaged Iraq as the Piedmont or Prussia of the Arab world which would drive forward the cause of pan-Arabism. One of the biggest political issues was conscription, which the king and the Sunni elite also viewed as a means of nation-building in their ethnically divided country. For this reason, the Shias and Kurdish populations were strongly opposed, as were the British who saw it as both financially and ethnically destablising.[35]

There were other claimants for the mantle of 'leader of the Arab world'. Feisal's brother, Abdullah, who had consolidated his rule in Transjordan by the end of the 1920s, envisaged a role for himself in Syria. Indeed, as we have seen, he had stopped in Transjordan on his way to confront the French in Syria in 1920 and then hung on there in anticipation of being called to take the throne of Syria. He saw himself as the leader of any Hashemite restoration in Syria. His prospects were improved by the death of Feisal I of Iraq after a short illness in 1933. By then the Hashemite monarchy in Iraq was running into increasing difficulties, including sectarian problems with Shias, Kurds and the tiny Assyrian community. The last named were crushed with great brutality in a pogrom in 1933. The army was regularly called upon to put down tribal revolts in the Shia areas in the south of Iraq with the same heavy-handedness, especially after the introduction of conscription in 1933. This gave the army leadership increasing political influence.

In 1936, after Yasin al-Hashimi, the Prime Minister, began to demonstrate increasing authoritarian tendencies, General Bakr Sidqi, encouraged by al-Hashimi's enemies, staged a coup. King Ghazi, Feisal's young son and successor, did not especially object to the coup once the monarchy was not threatened. In any case, Ghazi tended to be in sympathy with the nationalist officer corps and lacked his father's political realism. Most importantly, the coup was a huge blow to constitutional rule in Iraq and signalled the beginning of violent faction-fighting among the Sunni elite.[36] Sidqi was assassinated in August 1937 and the older establishment

---

34 Cited in Khaldun S Husry, 'King Faysal I and Arab Unity, 1930–33', *Journal of Contemporary History*, Vol 10, No 2 (1975) p 324.

35 Sluglett, *Britain in Iraq*, p 94; Tripp, *A History of Iraq*, pp 61–2.

36 Marr, *The Modern History of Iraq*, pp 44–6.

figures such as Nuri al-Said and Rashid Ali returned to positions of power. However, from 1937 until 1941, despite the holding of elections, the arbiter of power in Iraq was a nationalist army clique known as the 'Golden Square'. Civilian governments fell if they incurred the displeasure of this group, whose pro-Nazi and anti-British views were greatly heightened by the Arab revolt in Palestine between 1936 and 1939.

Atatürk and the new Turkey

Turkey's major setback at Lausanne had been the failure to gain Mosul with its important oilfield, which was retained in the British-Mandated country of Iraq, where it was to remain. Would Turkey have been better off if it had regained Mosul in 1923? Its budget would have benefited from the revenue of the Kirkuk oilfields. But it would have had to administer many more Kurds, as well as more Arabs. The Ottoman Empire had practised multiculturalism, but this had hastened its demise. None of the successor states of the Ottoman, Austro-Hungarian and Russian Empires in eastern Europe and the Balkans followed the sort of multicultural policies which are recommended today. Mustafa Kemal recognised the problem, but he had other priorities. The modernisation of Turkey came first, and for its sake he opted for good relations with all the Great Powers.

The failure of the Treaty of Lausanne to award Mosul to Turkey was the main objection raised by the opposition when the newly elected Assembly debated ratification on 23 August. But the opposition had been reduced to a handful of deputies, and the Treaty was overwhelmingly approved. The immediate need was to end the Allied occupation of Istanbul, which was to follow ratification. On 2 October Allied occupation troops left Istanbul. Four days later Turkish troops entered the city, while the last Allied soldiers left Gallipoli. On 13 October, the Assembly voted to move the capital of the Turkish state from Istanbul to Ankara.

The old Ottoman capital was demoted to the status of a provincial city. Civil servants had to move to Ankara. Trade suffered, as the transit of goods to and from Russia was reduced to a trickle after the Bolshevik revolution. The city was impoverished by the departure of many foreigners and indigenous non-Muslims. The new regime was not popular in Istanbul. Sensing this, Mustafa Kemal kept away from the old capital, which he had last seen in May 1919. It was only in June 1927, after he had consolidated his personal power, that he went back to Istanbul on the first of what became his regular summer trips to the city. By then the first statue to Mustafa Kemal had been erected on Seraglio Point at the entrance to the harbour.[37]

The Treaty of Lausanne is the founding document of the Turkish national state. But the form, character and institutions of that state had yet to be decided when it was concluded. İsmet had signed it as the representative of the awkwardly named Government of the Grand National Assembly of Turkey. Soon the country was to acquire its new name. On 28 October 1923, Mustafa Kemal invited a group of supporters to dinner in his residence at Çankaya, on the outskirts of Ankara, and told them without further ado: 'Tomorrow we will proclaim the Republic.'[38] The following day a bill to this effect was tabled and approved by the Assembly after a brief discussion. Elected first President of the Republic, Mustafa Kemal appointed İsmet as his Prime Minister, while Fethi moved over to become Speaker of Parliament. The citizens of Istanbul, including the government's representative Re'fet, learnt of the decision only when a 101-gun salute greeted the birth of the Republic on 29 October.

The circle of Mustafa Kemal's companions in the War of Independence gradually fell apart. Rauf was the first to move away when he was overridden over the terms of the Treaty of Lausanne. The sudden proclamation of the Republic cost the friendship of all those nationalist commanders who had not been consulted beforehand. They believed that they were joint authors of the victory in 'Our War of Independence' – the title given to his memoirs by Kâzım Karabekir, the commander who first welcomed Mustafa Kemal in Anatolia and stood by him when he was dismissed by the Sultan. They wanted, therefore, a voice in the shaping and the government of the state, and they demanded this in the name of democracy. As an opposition journalist argued in Istanbul, the proclamation of a republic was not sufficient guarantee of the freedom of citizens. Republics could harbour dictators as in Latin America. Mustafa Kemal responded by hauling opposition journalists before a revolutionary court in Istanbul. They were acquitted, having been warned that criticism would not deflect Mustafa Kemal from the course he had chosen. In 1927 he offered this explanation for the defection of his original supporters: 'In the development of the nation's life which has led to today's

---

37 It was adjacent to the historic Topkapi Palace of the Ottomans.
38 Mango, *Atatürk*, p 394.

republic and its laws, some of the travellers who had started together on the road of national struggle began to resist and oppose me as we crossed the limits of what they could comprehend or sympathise with.'[39]

The radicalism of Mustafa Kemal's project was indeed hard for them to accept. The nationalist commanders who had sided with Mustafa Kemal had no particular love for the monarchy or for established religion. They were not reactionaries or backward-looking, as was claimed against them. They too admired the achievements of the West. But they were not prepared to sever all links with the past and alter their whole way of life. They were not democrats, but they wanted to have a voice in government. Mustafa Kemal was prepared to listen to other people's opinions. But he insisted that his decision should be final. Provided his will prevailed, he did not interfere with the administration. As a successful military commander, he knew how to choose subordinates capable of carrying out his orders, and how to delegate.

Mustafa Kemal's determination did not exclude prudence. Before proceeding with his cultural revolution in Turkey, he made sure that the army would remain loyal to him. The nation's will was sovereign, and the peasant, he declared, was the true master of the country. But power was in the barrel of a gun. Mustafa Kemal was lucky in that he found a respected professional soldier to whom he could entrust the command of the armed forces. Field Marshal Fevzi Çakmak was a German-trained battle-tried commander, who had started by opposing Mustafa Kemal, but having resolved to side with him, proved a totally loyal Chief of the General Staff during the War of Independence and then to the end of Kemal's life. The fact that he was a pious Muslim did not count against him. Fevzi Pasha was not an enthusiast; he professed the patriotic faith of regimental chaplains. When Mustafa Kemal died, opponents of İsmet's succession wanted to put him up as the candidate allegedly favoured by the first President. He declined, preferring to stay in command of the armed forces. But in the end Fevzi clashed with İsmet, objecting to being retired at the age of 68. He wanted to go on for ever.

On 15 February 1924, Mustafa Kemal and İsmet went to İzmir to watch army manoeuvres and meet military commanders. It was at this meeting that the decision was taken to abolish the Caliphate, just over a year after it had been set up as a separate institution. It had served its purpose of

---

39 Kemal Atatürk, *Nutuk*, p 11.

softening the blow of the abolition of the monarchy, and had no place in the new Republic, where it was bound to attract dissidents. A letter from the Aga Khan the previous November pleading for the preservation of the office was presented as an example of the foreign interference which it invited. But Mustafa Kemal had a wider purpose in mind. The presence of the Caliph in Istanbul was incompatible with the secularisation of the Turkish Republic which he was determined to introduce.

On 3 March 1924 a member of the Assembly who had received a clerical education was chosen to present a wide-ranging bill, going beyond the abolition of the Caliphate. Together with the Caliph Abdülmecid, all members of the Ottoman dynasty were to be exiled immediately. The bill was, of course, approved, and the same night the Caliph and his family were taken by car to a station outside Istanbul and put on a train to Europe. Any supporters he had in Istanbul were not given a chance to demonstrate. Abdülmecid was never to see the country again. He died in Paris in August 1944. Surviving members of the dynasty were allowed back after many years, princesses first in 1952, followed by male descendants in 1974. They enjoy social prestige, but do not attract political interest. The achievements of the Ottoman era, decried in the first years of the Republic, are now widely recognised. 'Ottomania' or Neo-Ottomanism is fashionable in the arts, architecture and cooking. But there never has been a movement favouring the restoration of the monarchy in Turkey.

The abolition of the Caliphate was accompanied by the removal of all religious influence on public policy and by the imposition of state control over religious practices. *Madrasahs* were banned. Religious education in lay schools was restricted and discouraged until it disappeared altogether. The Ministry of Islamic Canonical Affairs and Pious Foundations, which had replaced the office of the Sheikh-al Islam, was abolished and replaced by a Department of Religious Affairs attached to the Office of the Prime Minister. This department employed and supervised mosque personnel, and laid down the law on practice and worship. The religious institution had always been under the control of the Ottoman state, but it used to enjoy some autonomy and could at times influence public policy. Now it was totally nationalised.

The nationalist commanders who were excluded from power found a popular cause in public disquiet at the unfolding cultural revolution. Forced to choose between politics and a military career, some of Mustafa Kemal's original companions resigned their commissions and formed an opposition party. They named it the Progressive Republican Party to emphasise that they were not counter-revolutionaries, reactionaries or monarchists. But the promise in the party programme that they would respect religious feelings and beliefs made plain their opposition to the radical transformation of society. In response, Mustafa Kemal adopted a somewhat softer approach. İsmet, known as a hard-line supporter of Mustafa Kemal's radical project, was replaced by the more conciliatory Fethi.

The let-up was short-lived. In February 1925, a Kurdish sheikh raised the standard of rebellion in the east. As the revolt spread, Fethi was seen as hesitant and ineffective. He was replaced by İsmet, who this time stayed in power for over a decade. The suppression of the Kurdish rebellion was followed by the banning of the opposition Progressive Republican Party, and by an acceleration of Mustafa Kemal's reform programme. All Dervish orders were banned and their shrines closed. Over the next few years, modernisation became synonymous with Westernisation. European laws were introduced wholesale: the Swiss civil code, which put an end to polygamy, German commercial law, the Italian penal code. In November 1925, the fez, which had been for over a century the distinctive head-gear of Muslim gentlemen, was banned, and Muslims were ordered to wear European-style hats or peaked caps, both of which are inconvenient when Muslims press their heads against the ground during prayers. A month later the European calendar and European time-keeping replaced the Muslim calendar.

Wilder opponents now took to plotting. In June 1926 an attempt to assassinate Mustafa Kemal in İzmir was narrowly averted when one of the conspirators gave the game away. The discovery led to a wave of repression. There was a loose connection between the conspirators and figures of the old CUP who had not accepted Mustafa Kemal's leadership. One such was Cavid, the wartime Ottoman Finance Minister who had advised the Turkish delegation at Lausanne. Critical as he was of Mustafa Kemal, he was not involved in the attempt on his life. Nevertheless, he was hanged along with the conspirators. It was the high point of state terror.

With all his opponents silenced and the country pacified, Mustafa Kemal could now give his account of the events which had led to the proclamation of the Republic and the subsequent cultural revolution. He did so in October 1927 in a speech to the convention of his Republican

People's Party, by then the only party allowed in the country. The speech took six days to deliver. It started with the words, 'On the 19th day of May of the year 1919, I landed in Samsun.' Mustafa Kemal's life story had become the history of modern Turkey.

More radical changes followed. In April 1928, the reference to Islam as the official religion was dropped from the Constitution. In November that year the last important link with the Muslim Ottoman past was severed when the Latin alphabet replaced the Arabic one. The new alphabet was better suited to the phonetic structure of the Turkish language, and the change was made all the easier by the fact that the vast majority of the population was illiterate, so that most Turks learnt to read and write for the first time in the new script. Other changes were symbolic: Turkish women were given the vote, and some were elected or rather nominated town councillors and then Members of Parliament in uncontested elections. More importantly, the government encouraged career women. There had long been women teachers in girls' schools. Now there were women teaching in mixed schools and universities, practising medicine and law. The number of professional women grew gradually, although to this day the proportion of women employed outside the home in Turkey is low by European standards. Unlike the fez and clerical dress, the veiling of women was never banned. But it was discouraged and all but disappeared, the veil giving way to headscarves among older women in the cities and, more generally, in the countryside.

In 1934, after a law had been passed that all Turkish citizens should choose surnames in addition to the given Muslim names by which most of them were known, Mustafa Kemal was given the name of Atatürk, Father of the Turks, by the Assembly. The surname was restricted to him alone; it could not be used by his surviving sister or his adopted daughters. His marriage, which was dissolved in 1924, was childless.

Just as the reforms were being completed in Turkey, the settlement put in place after the First World War was beginning to break down in Europe. The first threat came from the Italian dictator Benito Mussolini. Then, in 1933, Hitler came to power in Germany. Proclaiming 'peace at home and peace in the world' as the principle of his foreign policy, Mustafa Kemal sided with the Western democracies in defence of the *status quo*. This allowed Turkey to win back two concessions it had made at Lausanne. In July 1936, a convention was signed at Montreux, abolishing the international commission of the Turkish Straits, allowing Turkish troops back into what had been the demilitarised zone of the Straits, and making Turkey responsible for applying rules for navigation through them. Then, on the eve of the Second World War, in exchange for a treaty of alliance with France and Britain, Turkish troops entered the district of İskenderun (Alexandretta), which had been administered as part of French-Mandated Syria. Renamed the province of Hatay (after Cathay, the area inhabited by Turkic tribes outside the Great Wall of China), the district became part of Turkey some six months after the death of Atatürk on 10 November 1938, at the age of 57. His work of laying the foundations of modern Turkey was complete. The country's subsequent history has shown that the foundations were solid.

The Palestine Mandate

With the formal confirmation of the League of Nations Mandate in 1922, the prospects for Zionism rested, above all, on how the National Home fared in Palestine. In 1922, the British estimated the population at 589,000 Muslims, 83,000 Jews and 71,000 Christians, who were mostly Arabs. By 1925, when Samuel's period as High Commissioner came to an end, the Jewish population had grown to 108,000, but this proved to be a boom year as far as immigration was concerned. That year some 33,801 Jews came into Palestine, while 2,151 left. Economic conditions in the country were far from easy, and in 1927 there were only 2,713 Jewish immigrants, whereas 5,071 left the country.[40] Even so, the National Home was beginning to make progress. By 1929, the population of Tel Aviv had grown to 46,000, and it was acquiring critical mass as a Jewish city.[41] Much of the organisation of the Jewish community turned on the powerful trade union movement, the Histadrut, or General Federation of Jewish Labour, which had been formed in 1920. Elected to its council in November 1921, Ben-Gurion became its driving force, rapidly emerging as the dominant personality in the *Yishuv*, as the Jewish community in Palestine was called. As his stature grew, it became evident that in time he would come to rival, and possibly eclipse, Weizmann.[42]

The highlight of this period for Weizmann undoubtedly came in April

---

40 *Palestine Royal Commission Report*, pp 43, 46, 62.
41 Howard M Sachar, *A History of Israel: From the Rise of Zionism to Our Time* (Basil Blackwell, Oxford: 1976) p 155.
42 Teveth, *Ben-Gurion*, pp 187–8.

1925 with the inauguration of the Hebrew University on Mount Scopus, the project he had lovingly nurtured for nearly a quarter of a century. The Weizmanns were accompanied to Palestine by Balfour, at the age of 77 and a poor sailor, paying his first visit to the country with which his name had come to be associated. The inauguration ceremony on 1 April was attended by many Jewish dignitaries, including Dr Judah Magnes, who was to be its first Chancellor and later President, but whose work on behalf of Arab-Jewish cooperation in the government of Palestine soon led to bitter recriminations by Weizmann, and alienated him from the mainstream of Zionism.[43] Samuel and Allenby were also present, but inevitably the spotlight fell on Balfour. As expected, the author of the Declaration was rapturously received by a crowd of some 10,000, as he was in Tel Aviv and the Jewish settlements he visited. The Arabs of Palestine, on the other hand, greeted his arrival with a one-day strike, but much worse was to follow when he attempted a somewhat ill-advised visit to Damascus. A crowd of about 6,000 advanced on his hotel and had to be dispersed by the French army, leaving three dead. Balfour's visit to Syria ended almost as soon as it began. He was no better loved by the Arabs than he had been by the Irish, it seemed.[44]

The comparative lull which settled on Palestine for much of the 1920s ended abruptly in 1928. Samuel's tenure as High Commissioner finished in 1925. He was succeeded by Field Marshal Lord Plumer of Messines, one of Britain's more successful commanders in the First World War. Between them, Samuel and Plumer managed to keep the political situation relatively calm, but political advance in Egypt, Iraq and Syria led to the Arabs of Palestine feeling left behind. Tension came to a head on 24 September 1928, Yom Kippur, the Jewish Day of Atonement, and it derived from the complex agreements and conventions which had come to surround the Western Wall. For centuries Jews had been allowed access to it, provided that nothing was erected on the pavement, and the British felt obliged to maintain this position. When the Jews put up a screen to separate men from women, the police forcibly took it down. In

43 Weizmann to Felix M Warburg, New York, 24 November 1929, in Camillo Dresner (ed), *LPCW*, Series A, Vol XIV, July 1929–October 1930 (Transaction Books, Rutgers University; Israel Universities Press, Jerusalem: 1978) 104, p 103.
44 Weizmann, *Trial and Error*, pp 390–400; Dugdale, *Arthur James Balfour*, Vol II, pp 267–72.

an atmosphere of increasing tension, each side protested to the League of Nations.[45]

This incident, disturbing as it was, was but the portent of a much more serious sequence of events the following year. The immediate prelude, perhaps, was the culmination of negotiations Weizmann had been pursuing for a number of years, that is, the creation of an enlarged Jewish Agency, which had been provided for in the terms of the Mandate. This was at last agreed at the Sixteenth Zionist Congress in Zurich in the summer of 1929. The Jewish Agency was to be representative of both Zionist and non-Zionist Jews, with Weizmann as its President. In any other circumstances, this would have marked a new high point in his career, but within days any sense of satisfaction he might have felt was shattered by events in Palestine. On 15 August 1929, there was a Jewish procession to the Western Wall; the next day the Arabs followed suit. Then, from 23 to 29 August, there were attacks on Jews across Palestine. In all, 133 Jews were killed and 339 wounded, while 116 Arabs were killed and 232 wounded, most of them by the security forces. Particularly disturbing was the fact that these attacks took place in the ancient Jewish holy cities of Hebron, where some 60 people were killed, and Safed. Jews had lived there for generations, untouched.

The Commission of Inquiry into these events, chaired by Sir Walter Shaw, reported its findings on 31 March 1930, just days after Weizmann had mourned the death of Balfour.[46] The subsequent report pointed to the fundamental differences in outlook between Arabs and Jews, but identified the basic reason behind the outbreak as being Arab fears over the level of Jewish immigration and the amount of land purchase. Shaw's recommendations were that the government should define what it meant by safeguarding the interests of the non-Jewish communities; revise the regulation of immigration, which he described as excessive; institute an inquiry into methods of cultivation and regulate land policy in the light of this; and emphasise once again that the Zionist Organisation could not take part in the government of Palestine.[47]

Weizmann had for some time sensed the hostility of Ramsay

---

45 *Palestine Royal Commission Report*, pp 65–7.
46 Weizmann to Gerald Balfour, Woking, 19 March 1930, *LPCW*, Vol XIV, 225, p 252.
47 *Palestine Royal Commission Report*, pp 67–71.

MacDonald's Colonial Secretary, Lord Passfield, better known as Sydney Webb, a veteran socialist perhaps best remembered for his work in founding the London School of Economics, and who, with his wife, subsequently wrote a highly sympathetic account of Stalin's Russia. The conclusions of the commission did not, therefore, come as a complete surprise to Weizmann, unpalatable though they were. Receiving the report in advance, Weizmann arranged a meeting with MacDonald and Passfield, at which he was joined by three prominent colleagues, Lord Reading, the former Viceroy of India, Lord Melchett, formerly Sir Alfred Mond, and the American banker Felix Warburg. MacDonald apparently confided his belief that Shaw had exceeded his brief, promising to make a statement to the House of Commons reaffirming British commitment to the National Home, which he did, being supported by Baldwin on behalf of the Conservatives and Lloyd George for the Liberals.[48] Weizmann was also in contact with Baldwin and Lloyd George, and, then, on 11 April the *Manchester Guardian* published Weizmann's lengthy riposte to Shaw, written in his capacity as President of the Jewish Agency. Reasserting that the Jews were in Palestine as of right, he responded that to restrict immigration and land purchase would set at nought the creation of the National Home.[49]

The government announced a further commission, under Sir John Hope Simpson, to carry forward the inquiry Shaw had recommended. Weizmann had hoped instead for the chairmanship of Smuts, whose sympathies he knew, and at a rather bitter meeting with MacDonald and Passfield he denounced the latter as a liar for reneging on a promise that he could meet Hope Simpson prior to his departure for Palestine.[50] News that immigration into Palestine had been suspended was a further unwelcome indication of the drift of events, followed, as it was, by amendments to land legislation, and restrictions on the work of the Jewish Agency.[51]

The best that Weizmann could do in the circumstances was try to

---

48 Weizmann to C P Scott, Manchester, 31 March 1930, *LPCW*, Vol XIV, 233, pp 256–7.

49 Weizmann to the Editor of the *Manchester Guardian*, 11 April 1930, *LPCW*, Vol XIV, 248, pp 266–8.

50 Weizmann to Vera Weizmann, Paris, 13 May 1930, *LPCW*, Vol XIV, 269, pp 281–3.

51 Weizmann to James Ramsay MacDonald, London, 16 May 1930, *LPCW*, Vol XIV, 275, pp 300–1.

anticipate through contacts with Passfield what the government's likely reaction might be. By the beginning of October he believed that there would be a five-year ban on land purchases, limits on Jewish immigration, and a loan to settle landless Arabs. His rather pessimistic conclusion was that Passfield, as he had recently done in Kenya with the Africans, would assert the rights of the Arabs as the indigenous population of the country.[52] On 13 October, he wrote to Passfield and MacDonald protesting that any prohibition on land purchases would undermine the National Home, and acknowledge that the Arabs had the greater claim to Palestine. He argued that such a policy would run counter to the Balfour Declaration and the provisions of the Mandate.[53]

Hope Simpson's report, published on 21 October and seen by Weizmann in advance, threatened to undermine one of the main planks of the Zionist platform; namely, that there was sufficient cultivable land to accommodate them without prejudice to the Arabs. Hope Simpson thought not, concluding that until there was further development of Jewish lands and better cultivation of Arabs lands, there was no room for any more settlers if the standard of living of the Arab cultivators were to be maintained. More optimistic from the Zionist perspective was his view that through development the countryside could not only sustain the present population, but accommodate at least an additional 20,000 families of settlers. The report was accompanied by a Statement of Policy which accepted Hope Simpson's figures and conclusions, but pointedly ignored his view that with development the land could absorb more Jewish immigrants.[54] The Passfield White Paper, as it soon became known, came as a devastating blow to the Zionists, and to Weizmann in particular, for whom cooperation with Britain had been the *sine qua non* of Zionist strategy. His response was that the White Paper dealt a serious blow to prospects for the National Home, and was contrary to the policy set out in the 1922 White Paper. Complaining to Passfield that by issuing a Statement of Policy the government had precluded negotiations, he announced his resignation as President of the Zionist Organisation and

---

52 Weizmann to Felix M Warburg, New York, 6 October 1930, *LPCW*, Vol XIV, 357, pp 376–81.

53 Weizmann to Lord Passfield, London, 13 October 1930, *LPCW*, Vol XIV, 359, pp 382–4.

54 *Palestine Royal Commission Report*, pp 71–3.

the Jewish Agency. To MacDonald, more in sorrow than in anger, he lamented the failure of his policy of working in harmony with the British government.[55]

Weizmann had long castigated the British administration in Palestine for being pro-Arab, but now he had to contend with the Colonial Office as well. As he began his lobbying campaign against the White Paper, he was probably correct in his suspicion that MacDonald was more sympathetic than Passfield. As well as mobilising support in Jewish circles, he enlisted his old friends Amery and Smuts, and the Conservatives Baldwin and Austen Chamberlain also joined in criticising the White Paper. MacDonald sought to defuse the issue by appointing a Cabinet Committee on Palestine, which would examine the question in consultation with the Jewish Agency. Despite his resignation as President, Weizmann co-operated fully throughout the winter of 1930/1, emphasising that the National Home could not be curtailed at its current level, and that the Jews had been the victims in 1929.[56] His reward came on 13 February 1931 in the form of a letter addressed to him from MacDonald, which, while it did not rescind the White Paper, substantially qualified it. In his letter, MacDonald challenged the view that the White Paper 'foreshadows a policy which is inconsistent with the obligations of the Mandatory to the Jewish people'. Emphasising that the Mandate put obligations on Britain towards both Arabs and Jews, he denied that there was any intention to end Jewish land purchases. On the even more vexed question of immigration, he reiterated the long-standing policy of absorptive capacity, confirming that the government did 'not contemplate any stoppage or prohibition of Jewish immigration in any of its categories'. To the Arabs the White Paper had been replaced by the 'Black Letter'.[57]

Once again, Weizmann had succeeded, but this time rather against the odds, and the whole episode had raised questions about his reliance on British good intentions. His critics, especially the Revisionists, the organisation Jabotinsky had formed after falling out with Weizmann in

55 Weizmann to Lord Passfield, London, 21 October 1930; Weizmann to James Ramsay MacDonald, London, 21 October 1930: *LPCW*, Vol XIV, 364, 368, pp 387–9, 391.

56 Weizmann, *Trial and Error*, pp 413–15.

57 J Ramsay MacDonald, House of Commons, 13 February 1931; *Palestine Royal Commission Report*, pp 74–7.

the 1920s, assailed him for accepting a letter rather than another White Paper. This accusation was as unjust as it was wrong-headed, since Mac-Donald's letter opened up the possibility of immigration into Palestine just as the Jews of Europe were to need it most. The sequel was that at the International Zionist Conference in Basle in July 1931, Weizmann's opponents managed to pass a motion of no confidence in him. It was the lowest point in his political career thus far.[58]

After such a bitter rebuff, it is hardly surprising that Weizmann turned for consolation to the other passion of his life, chemistry. Although he did not cut himself off entirely from Zionism, he built a small laboratory in London, and then another opportunity to revive his scientific career presented itself. This opening was the Daniel Sieff Research Institute at Rehovoth, funded by Weizmann's friend Israel Sieff in memory of his son, and inaugurated in April 1934. Here the Weizmanns built their home in Palestine, a classic piece of modernist architecture, designed by Erich (later Eric) Mendelsohn, one of Germany's leading architects, who had recently left the country.[59] After the tribulations he had just come through, this might have seemed an idyllic interlude in Weizmann's life when he could turn to domestic and scientific matters, except for the reason Mendelsohn had left Germany: the coming to power of Adolf Hitler on 30 January 1933.

The impact of Hitler and the Arab Revolt in Palestine

Adolf Hitler, an Austrian who had absorbed the anti-Semitic atmosphere of pre-1914 Vienna and who had harped on the so-called injustices of the Versailles settlement, was barely in power before he began the systematic exclusion of Jews, hitherto amongst the most patriotic of Germans, from national life. What followed hardly needs repetition: the Nuremberg Laws of 1935, the atrocities against the Viennese Jews which followed the Austrian *Anschluss* in 1938, the *Reichskristallnacht* of November 1938, culminating in Hitler's Reichstag speech of 30 January 1939 in which he foretold the fate of the Jews in the event of war, a conflict he was about to start. The result was an exodus of Jews from Germany and elsewhere in Europe. Since the United States was no longer an option for most of them as a result of the ethnic quotas imposed in the 1924 Immigration Act,

---

58 Weizmann, *Trial and Error*, pp 417–20; Rose, *Chaim Weizmann*, pp 289–93.
59 Rose, *Chaim Weizmann*, pp 294–300.

Palestine was the obvious choice, made possible by Weizmann's recent intervention with MacDonald. The figures speak for themselves. By 1938, Jews numbered some 401,600 out of a total population of 1,415,700..[60] Moreover, many of these immigrants were middle-class urban Jews who brought with them the cultural values of Central Europe. Tel Aviv was now a major urban centre of 150,000 people. Emblematic of the changing nature of the *Yishuv* was the arrival in 1936 of the legendary Italian conductor Arturo Toscanini to conduct the fledgling Palestine Orchestra, which had recently been founded largely from musicians dismissed in Germany, and, as the Israel Philharmonic, would later become one of the world's leading orchestras. The concert was attended by Weizmann.[61]

This transformation of the National Home provoked the Arabs into action. On 15 April 1936, a Jew was killed near Nablus and the Arab Revolt began. It lasted until 1939, tying down British forces just at the time when the ambitions of Germany, Italy and Japan were becoming increasingly ominous. The Arab Higher Committee was formed, led by Haj Amin al-Husayni, who was now clearly the leader of the Palestinians. The government's response was to send yet another commission of inquiry, chaired by Lord Peel, sadly ill with cancer, charged with making recommendations that might remove the grievances of both parties. Its most dynamic member was Reginald Coupland, Beit Professor of Colonial History at the University of Oxford, who had already analysed nationality problems in Ireland, Canada and South Africa. There then developed a fascinating dynamic between Coupland and Weizmann, who had returned to the presidency of the World Zionist Organisation in 1935. On 23 December 1936, when Weizmann was giving evidence on behalf of the Jewish Agency, Coupland threw out the suggestion of creating what he called two big areas in Palestine. Then, on 8 January 1937 he developed this concept by setting before Weizmann the idea of partition, which would lead in time to independent Arab and Jewish states. What underpinned Coupland's thinking was his conclusion that Arab civilisation was Asian, while that of the Jews was European, and, that, as a

---

60 *Palestine Partition Committee Report*, Cmd 5854 (Her Majesty's Stationery Office, London: 1938) p 23.
61 Sachar, *A History of Israel*, p 586; Michael Jackson, ed Janet Jackson, *A Scottish Life: Sir John Martin, Churchill and Empire* (The Radcliffe Press, London: 1999) p 89.

result, their national aspirations were incompatible. Weizmann grasped the significance of what Coupland was saying. What was being suggested was a state, not a National Home, albeit in part of Palestine. He was also aware that despite the growth in Jewish numbers, the Arab population was also expanding, and that the prospect of a Jewish majority was some way off. He also knew that partition would meet with resistance in Zionist ranks, especially since it was felt that the creation of Transjordan had already truncated the National Home.

At the end of January 1937, the two men consulted privately at the agricultural settlement of Nahalal, where Weizmann became convinced that partition offered the best way forward. When the Royal Commission reported on 7 July to the Colonial Secretary, none other than Weizmann's old friend Ormsby-Gore, it was in favour of partition. Rather like Caesar's Gaul, Palestine was to be in three parts: a Jewish state along much of the coast and Galilee; an Arab state in the interior; and Jerusalem retained as a British enclave with a corridor to the coast. This proposal was accepted by the Cabinet and in Parliament, though criticised in debate by the veteran pro-Zionist speakers Lloyd George, Churchill and Samuel, who saw partition as contrary to the Mandate. Their reservations were more than echoed in influential sections of the Zionist movement, as Weizmann had known from the start they would be.

The dispute within Zionism had unmistakable echoes of the 1903 'Uganda Offer' crisis, except that this time Weizmann was sitting in Herzl's seat, and it came to a head at the Zionist Congress in Zurich in August. Weizmann was supported by the bulk of European and Palestinian representatives, including Ben-Gurion, who had been initially opposed to partition. The opposition was spearheaded by Ussishkin, but the real threat came from the United States, whence Weizmann's old feud with Brandeis came back to bite him. Brandeis did not attend the Congress, but at a preparatory meeting with Felix Frankfurter, Rabbi Stephen Wise and the lawyer Robert Szold, partition was rejected. Wise, however, was not in Europe for long before the realities of the Jewish position in Palestine were impressed upon him, and his position changed. He was the prime architect of the compromise strategy that the Congress approved on 10 August 1937; namely, that the Zionists should reject the Peel Commission recommendations, but should negotiate with the British government for a more favourable scheme. While this formula left the door open for partition, it was a lukewarm endorsement, which was ultimately unhelpful to Weizmann, especially since on 11 September an Arab National Conference at Bludan in Syria totally rejected the scheme. It left the British government with the obvious question of whether they should press ahead with a partition plan neither side seemed really to want.

Buoyed up by an assurance from Ormsby-Gore that in a year's time he would be preparing for the establishment of a Jewish state, Weizmann left for Palestine, but the Colonial Office was a junior player compared with the Foreign Office. With war threatening in Europe and the Mediterranean, the last thing the Foreign Secretary, Anthony Eden, and his Prime Minister, Neville Chamberlain, wanted was a hostile Arab world. At a Cabinet meeting on 22 December 1937, it was decided to send a commission under Sir John Woodhead to explore the implementation of a partition scheme, but with a confidential letter to the effect that he was free to pronounce against it. His report duly did so on 9 November 1938, the day the *Reichskristallnacht* was unleashed upon the Jews of Germany. All Weizmann's attempts to influence the commission came to nothing, his view that its purpose had been to justify a course of action already determined being quite correct.[62]

If Weizmann felt that his relations with the British government had touched their nadir, much worse was to follow. In May 1938, Ormsby-Gore, whose pro-Zionism had become an inconvenience, was replaced at the Colonial Office by Malcolm MacDonald, son of the late Prime Minister. Even before Woodhead concluded his work, MacDonald had decided upon a conference to discuss the future of Palestine. The conference, held at St James's Palace, opened on 7 February 1939, and ended on 15 March, just as Hitler was taking over the rump of Czechoslovakia which Chamberlain thought he had saved at Munich the previous September. The conference was predictably inconclusive, but during its course, through, it seems, a clerical error, Weizmann became aware of what MacDonald was planning. There would be an independent Palestine, and limited Jewish immigration for the next five years, but after

---

62 For a fuller discussion see T G Fraser, *Partition in Ireland, India and Palestine: theory and practice* (Macmillan, London and Basingstoke: 1984) Chapter 6, 'Palestine: the Peel Commission'; and T G Fraser, 'A Crisis of Leadership: Weizmann and the Zionist Reactions to the Peel Commission's Proposals, 1937–8', *Journal of Contemporary History*, Vol 23, No 4 (October 1988) pp 657–80.

that immigrants would only be allowed with Arab consent. At the closing session, which Weizmann and Ben-Gurion did not attend, MacDonald outlined his proposal, which confirmed what Weizmann had already discovered, but in greater detail; namely, that Palestine would become independent in ten years, and that 75,000 Jews would be permitted to enter over the next five years, but after that only with Arab agreement. This meant, quite simply, that the Jews could only ever be a minority in the country.[63] These, in essence, were the policies which MacDonald went on to unveil in his White Paper of 17 May 1939. They were rejected by the Palestinian Arabs, despite the extent to which the White Paper favoured them, but they proved enough to help Britain's friends, Abdullah of Transjordan, Ibn Saud of Saudi Arabia and Nuri al-Said in Iraq, keep the Arab world largely quiescent in the Second World War.

The Zionist Congress that convened in Geneva on 16 August 1939 as Europe teetered on the edge of war could not have been other than a bleak affair. While there was no question but that the Jews would support Britain in war, the Congress denounced the White Paper in anguished terms. As it ended on 24 August came news of the Nazi-Soviet Pact, the cynical agreement between two hitherto bitter ideological foes, which opened the way for Hitler's imminent attack on Poland.[64] The German attack on 1 September triggered the Anglo-French declaration of war two days later, but this did nothing to save Poland or the millions of Polish Jews who were now at Hitler's mercy. Hitler's domination of the continent was extended with his successful campaign in western Europe the following year and then by his invasion of the Soviet Union on 22 June 1941. By the autumn of that year, Germany controlled what had been the Pale of Settlement, with the direst of consequences for its Jewish inhabitants.

The Middle East at war

Italy's entry into the war in June 1940 meant that the Middle East became an area of critical concern. It was, therefore, fortunate for the British that in August 1936 they had been able to conclude a treaty with Egypt which allowed them the use of key facilities in wartime, safeguarding strategic routes through the Suez Canal as well as access to oil supplies in

---

63 Weizmann, *Trial and Error*, pp 493–501; Rose, *Chaim Weizmann*, pp 344–6.
64 Esco, *Palestine*, Vol II, pp 928–31.

the Gulf. By June 1942, German and Italian forces were a mere 60 miles (97 kilometres) from Alexandria, and were only halted by General Sir Claude Auchinleck at the First Battle of El Alamein. At the same time, the German advance into the Caucasus was threatening the British position in the Middle East from the north. Once American resources were fully deployed, the Persia-Iraq Command became a major Allied supply centre for the Soviet war effort, offering an alternative to the hazardous Arctic convoys. Before then, however, certain events in Iraq had to be played out.

In 1939 Ghazi died in a car crash. His successor was his young son, Faisal II. Abdulilah, son of Ali ibn Hussein the last King of the Hejaz, became regent. He was by instinct pro-British. Consequently, tensions between the royal family and the nationalist officers in the army grew from the outbreak of the Second World War. These were exacerbated by British demands for full Iraqi compliance with their obligations under the 1930 treaty, including the breaking of diplomatic relations with the Axis Powers. In the spring of 1941 Abdulilah was forced to flee after months of political infighting culminated in the seizing of power by the nationalist Rashid Ali, who enjoyed the confidence of the 'Golden Square'. The British, convinced of a German-Italian plot to drive them from the Middle East, decided to secure their positions in the region. In a matter of a few weeks in late April and May 1941, British forces landed at Basra and toppled the Rashid Ali regime. In June, they moved against Syria and expelled the Vichy Governor. A second British occupation of Iraq followed and a pro-British ruling group around the regent was re-installed. Those who had opposed the British, such as Rashid Ali, found themselves exiled and excluded from power. His supporters who stayed behind were executed or imprisoned.[65] Nuri al-Said backed the British and became the dominant political figure in post-1941 Iraq. He viewed the British connection as an important support for the Hashemite monarchy in Iraq and its wider ambitions in the Middle East.

In sharp contrast to the hostilities being waged all around her, Turkey was at peace. On her borders were the British in Iraq, the Vichy French in Syria, Hitler's ally Bulgaria, the Soviet Union, and after the fall of Greece in 1941, the German army. Still emerging as a nation state, Turkey was in

---

65 For the 1941 coup and its aftermath see Marr, *The Modern History of Iraq*, pp 53–6, and Tripp, *A History of Iraq*, pp 99–106.

no military or economic position to match the combatant powers, especially after a devastating earthquake in December 1939. Even so, it was a major achievement of the President throughout the period, Atatürk's long-standing colleague İsmet İnönü (the surname he adopted to commemorate his victory over the Greeks near the village of that name), to steer the country's neutrality in the face of many pressures. His success was similar to that of Eamon de Valera in Ireland. In each case geographical realities meant pragmatic choices had to be made, and just as de Valera allowed British aircraft to fly over Irish territory, German military shipping passed through the Straits. Britain's desire to have Turkey's active participation in the war was signalled by Churchill's visit in January 1943, but İsmet İnönü played for time. The Turkish leader did not make de Valera's gesture of offering condolences on the death of Hitler. Instead, on 23 February 1945 Turkey declared war on Germany, thus ensuring its place at the forthcoming San Francisco conference which was to set up the United Nations Organization, and hence chart the diplomatic shape of the post-war world. Turkey thus emerged intact, unscathed, and on the winning side.[66]

The Holocaust[67]

The genocidal nature of Hitler's intentions towards the Jews became clear in the course of 1941, prior to which the Jews in occupied Poland, the General Government as it was called, had been confined to ghettos, principally in Warsaw, Cracow, Lodz and Lublin. On 31 July 1941 Hermann Goering, who had earlier been given responsibility for Jewish affairs, ordered Reinhard Heydrich of the SS to proceed to a 'final solution' of the Jewish question. That Hitler was behind the order, and certainly the actions which followed, need be in no doubt. Overall direction

---

66 Andrew Mango, *The Turks Today* (John Murray, London: 2004) Chapter 1.
67 Books on the Holocaust are too numerous to list, and the following can only be indicative: Lucy S Dawidowicz, *The War Against the Jews 1933–1945* (Holt, Rinehart and Winston, New York: 1975); Sybille Steinbacher, *Auschwitz: A History* (Penguin, London: 2005); Christopher R Browning, *The Origins of the Final Solution: The Evolution of Nazi Jewish Policy 1939–1942* (Arrow Books, University of Nebraska Press, Lincoln and Yad Vashem, Jerusalem: 2005); Richard J Evans, *The Third Reich at War: How the Nazis Led Germany from Conquest to Disaster* (Allen Lane, London: 2008; Penguin, London: 2009), especially pp 217–318, 'The Final Solution'.

was held by the head of the SS, Heinrich Himmler. *Einzatsgruppen* of his SS were already at work as the German army conquered much of the Soviet Union, and by the autumn of 1941 were engaging in the mass murder of Jews, some 34,000 in Kiev alone in September. Propaganda Minister Joseph Goebbels, who had been behind the 1938 *Kristallnacht* pogrom, was determined to remove the Jews from Berlin, where he was *Gauleiter*. November 1941 saw the killing at Riga and Kaunas of Jews from Germany, as well as the first gassing of Polish Jews at Chelmno and Belzec. From his headquarters in Lublin, the former *Gauleiter* of Vienna, SS police chief Odilo Globocnik, directed the extermination of the Jews in the General Government, killing around 1,700,000.

On 20 January 1942, Heydrich coordinated what was happening at a conference with other officials at Wannsee on the outskirts of Berlin. Jews from across Europe were to be divided into those fit or unfit for work, the latter to be killed, while the former were to be worked to death as forced labourers. Heydrich's subsequent assassination outside Prague made no difference to the course of events, which proceeded relentlessly under the supervision of the Austrian SS officer Adolf Eichmann. The camps at Chelmno, Belzec, Sobibor and Treblinka had no other function but extermination, while Maidanek outside Lublin and the vast Auschwitz-Birkenau complex near Cracow had a dual function, serving also as labour camps. It is estimated that over a million people were killed at the latter, most of them Jews. When the Allied victory brought the slaughter to an end, between 5,500,000 and 6,000,000 European Jews were dead.[68] The death, at their own hands, of Hitler, Himmler, Goering, Goebbels and Globocnik was no consolation. Eichmann escaped the immediate fate of his superiors, finding refuge in Argentina until being spirited to Israel in 1960, tried and executed two years later.

Palestine in the war

The fate of the European Jews more than justified the worst fears of the Zionist leaders who had met in Geneva in August 1939. There was no doubt what course of action they would take. On 29 August, Weizmann wrote to Neville Chamberlain that the Jews would fight on the British side. He was true to his word, tragically so, since his younger son Michael, a pilot in the Royal Air Force, went missing over the Bay of

---

68 Evans, *The Third Reich at War*, p 318.

Biscay in February 1942. By 1943, some 21,000 Palestinian Jews had reinforced the British in the Middle East, serving in such non-combat roles as transport and construction, although Jews were also allowed to enlist for fighting duties.[69] Frustration at being largely confined to an auxiliary role fuelled the demand for the formation of active Jewish fighting units, but the British, fearful of Arab reaction, were slow to move. Sanction for a Jewish brigade was only given in September 1944, and after training it went into action on the Italian front the following March, rather late in the day as the result of British procrastination.[70] Nevertheless, the scale of Jewish support for the Allied war effort contrasted with the position taken up by Haj Amin al-Husayni, who met Hitler and was photographed reviewing Bosnian Muslim recruits to the SS, actions which did nothing to help the Palestinian Arab position after the war.[71]

Britain's tepid reaction to the Jewish army proposal reflected its determination to hold to the White Paper policy. As news of what was happening in Europe started to reach the Jews of Palestine and the United States, resentment mounted over Britain's handling of the immigration issue. Two incidents brought this into sharp focus. On 25 November 1940, the *Patria*, which was about to transport illegal refugees to Mauritius, blew up in Haifa harbour, killing 257. Then, in February 1942, the *Struma*, which had arrived at Istanbul from Romania with 769 Jews on board, sank with the loss of almost all its passengers in the Black Sea after the British authorities had made it clear they would not be admitted to Palestine.[72]

By 1942, when news of Nazi extermination policies was reaching the western Allies, the focus of Zionist activity had steadily moved to the United States. The Biltmore Conference, held in New York in May of that year, pledged the movement to making Palestine a Jewish commonwealth, an important revision of the original Basle Programme. Under the banner of the American Zionist Emergency Council, American Jews began to mobilise their political influence, to considerable effect after

69 'Historicus, The Last Decade', in Paul Goodman, *The Jewish National Home: The Second November 1917–1942* (J M Dent & Sons Ltd, London: 1943), p 90.
70 Esco, *Palestine*, Vol II, pp 1020–35.
71 Mattar, *The Mufti of Jerusalem*, pp 102–7.
72 Esco, *Palestine*, Vol II, pp 945–8.

1945.[73] In Palestine itself right-wing sentiment, opposed to the policies of Weizmann and Ben-Gurion, saw the emergence of two underground organisations, the Irgun Zvai Leumi ('National Military Organisation') and the Leh'i ('Fighters for the Freedom of Israel'), often known as the Stern Gang after its founder, Avraham Stern. In 1942, Stern was killed by the police, but his mantle was taken up by Nathan Yellin-Mor. In November 1944, two of the organisation's members assassinated the British Minister in the Middle East, Lord Moyne. At their trial, they cited Britain's immigration policy as their reason.[74] In February 1944, led by the young Polish Jew Menahem Begin, the Irgun set off bombs at the Department of Migration in Tel Aviv and Jerusalem.[75] These activities were an ominous sign of what might develop after the war should the British still adhere to their White Paper immigration strategy.

73 T G Fraser, *The Arab-Israeli Conflict*, 3rd edition (Palgrave Macmillan, Basingstoke: 2007) pp 20–1.
74 Esco, *Palestine*, Vol II, pp 1042–9.
75 Esco, *Palestine*, Vol II, pp 1040–1.

7

Conclusion: The Legacy

Unlike its predecessor, the Second World War was not followed by a peace conference. Germany had surrendered unconditionally, its immediate future lying with the military authorities of the United States, United Kingdom, France and the Soviet Union, each of which had its zone of occupation. The future shape of international relations found its focus in San Francisco in the spring of 1945 when the victorious powers came together to create the new United Nations Organization which was to ensure that the world would not have to endure another conflict, or so its founders hoped. President Franklin D Roosevelt had entertained the perhaps utopian, but certainly admirable, vision of a world in which peace would be guaranteed by the victorious powers cooperating through the United Nations. This was not to be. Instead, by 1949 East and West were locked into the Cold War, which lasted until the fall of Communism and collapse of the Soviet Union some four decades later. Although the peoples of the Middle East had their own concerns throughout this period, no part of the world could entirely escape the consequences of this seemingly intractable ideological conflict.

The war had finally set the clock ticking for European imperialism. Recovering as it was from four years of occupation, France was in no fit state to reassert its position in Lebanon and Syria. Whilst the Americans had always been clear that they were not fighting the war in order to restore the European empires, they were prepared to acknowledge the Middle East as a British sphere of influence. They did not, however, realise at first that Britain had been ruined financially and economically by the war. Their acknowledgement of the growing importance of the Middle East came in February 1945 when, on his return from the Yalta Conference, Roosevelt took the time to meet Ibn Saud in Egypt, assuring the Saudi king that 'he would do nothing to assist the Jews against the Arabs and would make no move hostile to the Arab people'.[1] The meeting illustrated the importance that the future of Palestine was assuming. By the time the two men met, the Red Army's liberation of Auschwitz at the end of January had amply confirmed the appalling reality of the Holocaust. Jews were now resolved that statehood was the only means by which such a tragedy could never recur, and were determined to achieve it.

Turkey and the Western Alliance

A neighbour of the Soviet Union, Turkey controlled Moscow's access to the Mediterranean through the Straits. The Montreux Convention, signed in 1936, made Turkey responsible for implementing its provisions on navigation through the Straits. Enlisting Turkey's sympathy was, therefore, of vital importance for both East and West. This became clear as early as the Potsdam Conference in the summer of 1945 when Josef Stalin signalled the Soviet Union's interests in the Straits, including the possibility of a base. The basis of the Soviet case was that Axis ships had been allowed through during the war. The British and Americans were not initially unsympathetic to the Soviet Union's needs as a Black Sea power, but clearly the establishment of a base was a step too far. In addition, the Armenian and Georgian issues made a reappearance with a Soviet claim to the districts of Kars and Ardahan in north-eastern Anatolia. At all events, the Potsdam Conference had more urgent issues to hand, and the future of the Straits was postponed until another day.

Turkish-Soviet relations deteriorated in the winter of 1945/6 at a time when the Americans were annoyed by Moscow's failure to withdraw its troops from parts of Iranian territory where they had been stationed during the war. American fears were signalled by the decision in March 1946 to return the body of the deceased Turkish Ambassador to Washington on board the USS *Missouri*, the battleship on which the Japanese surrender had been signed the previous year. The presence of this

---

1 T G Fraser, *The USA and the Middle East since World War 2* (Macmillan, Basingstoke: 1989) p xi.

powerful vessel with her nine 16-inch guns reflected the deterioration of relations between Washington and Moscow, and symbolised American power in an area which had hitherto been a British preserve. By the summer of 1946, relations between Ankara and Moscow were so bad, with reports of major Soviet troop build-ups along the Caucasus and in Bulgaria, that Turkey began a general mobilisation. On 15 August, President Harry S Truman convened a meeting of senior advisers, including the chiefs-of-staff, to review American policy on the Straits. The Department of State's advice was that Soviet pressure on Greece and Turkey was designed to dominate the eastern Mediterranean. Such pressure should be resisted, even at the risk of hostilities. Considering also the civil war between Nationalists and Communists in China, Truman agreed that it was time for America to test Soviet intentions. It was decided to reinforce the *Missouri*, which was still in Istanbul, with the navy's newest and most powerful aircraft carrier, the uss *Franklin D. Roosevelt*, and to make clear both support for Turkish sovereignty, and that responsibility for the defence of the Straits rested exclusively with the Turks.[2]

Since 1945, Britain had provided the main economic support to Turkey, and to Greece, but this proved to be too much of a financial burden on its depleted resources. On 21 February 1947, Washington was informed that Britain could no longer continue its aid to the two countries. This decision, coming at a time when East-West relations were already coming under severe strain, led to a major statement by Truman, which set American foreign policy on a new course. Addressing Congress on 12 March 1947, while asking for $400 million in aid for Greece and Turkey, Truman also announced that America would support free peoples, a speech which became known as the 'Truman Doctrine'. Turkey's strategic importance in the fast-deteriorating relationship between Washington and Moscow was clear.[3]

From then on, the country moved steadily, but decisively, into the American and Western orbit. An American military mission arrived in May 1947 to advise on the modernisation of Turkish armed forces. In

2 Walter Millis (ed), *The Forrestal Diaries* (Viking Press, New York: 1951) p 192; Dean Acheson, *Present at the Creation: My Years in the State Department* (W W Norton & Company, Inc, New York: 1969) pp 195–6.
3 T G Fraser and Donette Murray, *America and the World since 1945* (Palgrave Macmillan, Basingstoke: 2002) pp 23–4.

July 1948, the economic assistance provided under the European Recovery Program, commonly known as the Marshall Plan, was extended to Turkey. By 1950, the United States had provided $108 million in direct and $75 million in indirect aid, as well as military assistance amounting to some $200 million.[4] The next logical step for Turkey was to be admitted to the North Atlantic Treaty Organization (NATO), formed in April 1949. Turkey was hardly on the North Atlantic, but then neither was Italy, one of the original signatories. The geography was ignored. Two things paved the way for Turkey's entry. On 14 May 1950, free elections, based upon a secret ballot, were held, bringing to power a new government under Adnan Menderes. Then, in the Korean War which broke out a few weeks later, Menderes committed a Turkish brigade to the United Nations forces, under American command. In February 1952, Turkey became a full member of NATO, the cornerstone of American defence and foreign policy. It was now a fully-fledged member of the Western defence community, bringing to an end the non-alignment which had marked its foreign policy since Lausanne, but which had been increasingly difficult to sustain since 1945.[5]

The Arabs in the post-war world

During the war, the Free French under General Charles de Gaulle promised independence to Syria and Lebanon subject to the conclusion of an acceptable treaty, but France's power in the region was in tatters. Britain and the United States now wielded increasing and decisive influence and they saw little gain for the West in the continuation of French rule. In 1943, the nationalists in Syria won elections called by the Free French administration under huge pressure from the British and the United States. Shukri al-Quwwatli, a radical pan-Arab, became President. France still controlled the *les Troupes Spéciales*, the locally recruited paramilitary force which they had used to try to prevent independence until French interests were guaranteed. Its refusal to withdraw culminated in May 1945 in the outbreak of anti-French riots. Subsequent attempts to restore order and control were strongly criticised by the British, who demanded France withdraw its forces. Bowing to

---

4 George Kirk, *The Middle East 1945–1950* (Oxford University Press, London: 1954) p 42.
5 Mango, *The Turks Today*, pp 44–7.

international pressure, France finally conceded defeat and withdrew its forces in April 1946.[6]

Lebanon's path to independence was no less troubled. The French arrested much of the Lebanese government after elections in 1943 brought anti-French groups to power. As in Syria, this was a forlorn attempt to maintain control and the British forced the French to retreat. In 1946, France withdrew its forces and Lebanon became independent under President Bishara al-Khouri. However, gaining independence was only part of Lebanon's political problems. The country's population was divided virtually 50/50 between various Christians sects (the most significant being Maronite Christians) and Muslims. Muslims were again split between Sunnis and Shias, with a substantial Druze minority. Muslims were generally sympathetic to union with Syria. An unwritten grand political compromise, called the National Pact, was agreed between the Christian leaders and Muslims in 1943. This provided for a permanent division of political spoils between Christians, who received the Presidency in perpetuity, and Muslims who were guaranteed the office of Prime Minister. A ratio of six Christians to five Muslim members of parliament was also enshrined. The Christians compromised by accepting that Lebanon would be an Arab state.

A strong supporter of the British reconquest of the Middle East during the Second World War was Emir Abdullah of Transjordan, who provided military backing with his British-trained Arab Legion. Abdullah, by default, was now *de facto* leader of the Hashemite family. However, he ruled the weakest of the Arab states and the one most dependent on British support. Transjordan remained desperately poor and underdeveloped. With a tiny population, lacking oil or other natural resources, Abdullah, even more so than his relatives in Iraq, considered it necessary to further his ambitions by merging Transjordan in a wider Arab entity. For one thing, it would allow him to throw off the shackles of the British. He was anxious that he should have a leading role in the post-war settlement of the Middle East when it was assumed that the Mandate system would come to an end. Abdullah, and virtually all pan-Arabists, believed that this would presage the union of all of the Arab countries in the Fertile Crescent (Iraq, Syria, Transjordan and Palestine).

6 Malcolm E Yapp, *The Near East Since the First World War: A History to 1995* (Longman, Harlow: 2007) pp 96–7.

Anxious that talks on Arab unity should take place before Trans-jordan, Syria, Palestine and Lebanon became independent, and fearful that he would be too weak to achieve union on his own, Abdullah had decided that his best chance of success was to co-operate with the British in the hope that they would use their enhanced influence in Syria after 1941 to get him the throne there. His big plan was to create a Greater Syria, essentially a Syrian-Jordanian federation. However, he was mis-trusted by much nationalist opinion in the Arab world as a British stooge.[7] Syrian nationalist leaders such as Faris al-Khouri were reluc-tant to commit themselves while vestiges of French influence remained. Shukri al-Quwwatli, the President of Syria, rejected Abdullah's over-tures decisively in 1946 and the creation of the Arab League, formed by Egypt, Syria, Lebanon Jordan, Iraq and Saudi Arabia, in March 1945 gave Egypt an increasingly important role in Arab unity discussions. Neither did the British themselves have much interest in backing Abdul-lah in Syria. While they had come to the view that Abdullah was one of Britain's most useful Middle Eastern allies, they were sceptical about his wider regional ambitions. Reward for his loyalty came in 1946 when Transjordan was granted formal independence and renamed the Hash-emite Kingdom of Jordan; Emir Abdullah became King Abdullah. By then, however, it was clear that the future of Palestine was the most burning issue in the Middle East.

Palestine: the Jewish Revolt

When the war ended, Weizmann's long-standing dominance of Zionist affairs began to ebb. British policy under the Labour government, which came into office in the summer of 1945, adhered stubbornly to the terms of the 1939 White Paper, the Foreign Secretary, Ernest Bevin, and his principal adviser on Palestine, Harold Beeley, incurring Jewish oppro-brium as a result. With Hitler's atrocities now fully revealed, Jews were determined to secure their state, and were in no mood to indulge the British. In the circumstances, Weizmann's reliance on Britain seemed to belong to another age. On 1 October 1945 three Jewish groups in Pales-tine, the Haganah, the Irgun and Leh'i, began the Jewish Revolt against the Mandate. On the political front, Weizmann seemed a spent force. His relations with Ben-Gurion had become increasingly uneasy since

---

7 See Wilson, *King Abdullah, Britain, and the Making of Jordan*, pp 129–68.

1942, and he now had a new adversary in Rabbi Abba Hillel Silver, a rising star in American Zionism. His support for partition was not dead, however. At a Zionist Executive in Basle in July 1946, it was agreed that partition could be the basis of a solution.[8] Frustrated by the continuing crisis in Palestine, the British announced plans for a conference in London.

The simmering crisis within Zionism came to a head at the Twenty-Second Zionist Congress, held at Basle from 9–24 December 1946. It was the first since 1939, and in his presidential address Weizmann mourned the 6 million fellow Jews who had been murdered. Castigating the 1939 White Paper, he expressed understanding for the temper of the young Palestinian Jews, but still condemned violence as something alien to Zionism, and pleaded for restraint. The only way forward, he argued, was the establishment of a Jewish state. But the times were not with him. Now dominated by the representatives of Palestinian and American Zionism, the Congress voted to boycott the London conference, which had already got under way in September without them, or, indeed, the Arabs. Weizmann, who had advocated taking part, took this as a vote of no confidence and resigned the presidency. He never again attended a Zionist Congress.[9]

Despite spurning him, Zionism had not finished with Weizmann. When the London conference reconvened in January 1947, the Palestinian Arabs attended, and the Jewish Agency, despite the December vote, came for what, with some sophistry, it called informal talks. Partition was now top of the agenda, but the Arabs were adamantly opposed, as always, and the Jewish Agency was too Delphic in its attitude for the British to proceed along this path. Unable to see a way forward, in February, the British government agreed to hand over the future of Palestine to the United Nations. On 15 May, the United Nations Special Committee on Palestine (UNSCOP) was established. Consisting of representatives of Guatemala, Uruguay, Peru, Australia, Canada, Sweden, the Netherlands,

---

8 Fraser, *Partition in Ireland, India and Palestine*, p 156.
9 *Presidential Address by Dr Chaim Weizmann, Twenty-Second Zionist Congress, Basle, 9th December 1946* (The Jewish Agency for Palestine, London: nd); Weizmann, *Trial and Error*, pp 543–4; Vera Weizmann, *The Impossible Takes Longer*, pp 211–13; Getzel Kressel, 'Zionist Congresses', in *Zionism*, Israel Pocket Library (Keter Publishing House, Jerusalem: 1973) p 253.

Czechoslovakia, Yugoslavia, India and Iran, it was charged with making recommendations for the future of Palestine by 1 September. The Arabs decided to boycott its proceedings, but the Jews made no such mistake. The first task confronting the Zionist leaders was to convince UNSCOP that the British Mandate should end. This was brilliantly accomplished when the refugee ship *Exodus 1947* was intercepted by the Royal Navy on 17 July. Two days later, two members of UNSCOP watched its passengers disembarking at Haifa prior to their return to Germany.

On the more crucial question of the future of Palestine, the Zionist movement was still committed to the 1942 Biltmore Program, but privately Ben-Gurion had concluded that partition was the more realistic option. Weizmann, of course, had been its advocate since 1937. When Ben-Gurion presented the Jewish Agency's case before UNSCOP in Jerusalem, he did not mention partition. This task was left to Weizmann, who testified on 8 July 1947. Arguing that partition would mean a sacrifice for the Zionists, he conceded that they knew they could not have the whole of Palestine. He appealed for a more generous line than the one offered in the Peel Commission report by including the Negev Desert in a Jewish state. It was a clear signal to UNSCOP of what the Zionists would accept. Recalled before the committee, Ben-Gurion confirmed that they would consider a Jewish state in an area less than the whole of Palestine; privately, he assured them that he would support partition provided he got the Negev.[10]

When UNSCOP reported on 1 September, its members recommended termination of the Mandate. On the future of Palestine, there was less agreement. The Indian, Iranian and Yugoslav members supported a bi-national federal state, the Australian could not support any scheme, while the majority ruled in favour of partition. There was to be an Arab state, a Jewish state, a *corpus separatum* for Jerusalem, and economic unity. The Jewish state was to include the Negev, as Weizmann had argued. The Arabs, backed by the British, rejected partition, while the Jews, strongly supported by the Americans, worked assiduously to achieve it. The Americans, however, were concerned that the projected Jewish state contained too many Arabs, and the obvious way to reduce this was to exclude the Negev with its Bedouin population. Faced with this prospect, the Zionists turned again to their old warhorse.

On 19 November, Weizmann met President Truman at the White

---

10 Fraser, *Partition in Ireland, India and Palestine*, pp 162–3.

House. Persuaded by Weizmann that the Negev was vital to the Jewish state, Truman issued immediate instructions to his delegation at the United Nations that it should not be assigned to the Arab state. Not only was this an important intervention, but the impression Weizmann had made on Truman was to prove even more invaluable the following year. When the Ad Hoc Committee on the Palestinian Question took the vote on partition on 25 November 1947, it was supported by 25 votes to 13, with 17 abstentions and 2 absentees. This vote was some way short of the two-thirds majority needed to make it a formal recommendation of the General Assembly, where the vote was due to be taken on the 29th. Once again, Weizmann was brought into action, successfully telegraphing his friend Leon Blum to get France's vote changed to one of support for partition. In fact, it took direct action from the White House to secure a change in intention by enough states, so that when the vote was held, partition passed by the necessary majority of 33 votes to 13, with 10 abstentions. Exactly 50 years after the First Zionist Congress, sanction had been given for a Jewish state, and Weizmann was given a rapturous reception at a rally in New York.[11]

His services were not yet at an end, however. With the Arabs resolutely opposed to partition, and the British determined not to implement it, the situation in Palestine deteriorated dramatically. While partition had been strongly supported by Truman and his advisers, this was far from the case amongst key officials in the Department of State, and events in Palestine in early 1948 enabled them to mount a campaign against it. What they recommended was that if the United Nations resolution could not be implemented, then the question of Palestine should be referred back to the General Assembly. Truman agreed to this in principle, though with the caveat that he should see the final draft of any speech. Irritated as he was by the amount of lobbying he had been subjected to on the issue of Palestine, he gave instructions that no more Zionist leaders were to see him, and that included Weizmann.

Knowing nothing of the State Department's campaign against partition, but sensing the coldness coming from the White House, the Zionist leaders searched for a way through the embargo. The key proved to be Eddie Jacobson, Truman's old army comrade and business partner from

11 Fraser, *Partition in Ireland, India and Palestine*, pp 179–82; Fraser, *The USA and the Middle East since World War 2*, pp 31–4.

Kansas City. On 13 March 1948, Jacobson saw Truman at the White House. He persuaded an initially reluctant President to meet Weizmann, whom he compared with Truman's political hero, Andrew Jackson. The subsequent meeting on 19 March, at which no minutes were kept, proved crucial, with Truman reassuring Weizmann that he still supported partition. The following day, unaware of this development, Warren Austin made a speech to the Security Council in which the United States repudiated partition, casting doubt on the prospects for a Jewish state. Jewish opinion, equally ignorant of the White House meeting, was outraged, but as the controversy swirled around the White House, Weizmann kept silent, trusting in Truman's good faith, and earning the President's goodwill in the process. It was not the least of Weizmann's services to Zionism.[12]

The State of Israel: Weizmann as President

When the British Mandate for Palestine ended on 14 May 1948, Ben-Gurion proclaimed the establishment of the State of Israel in the Tel Aviv museum; 11 minutes later it was accorded *de facto* recognition by Truman. Still in New York, Weizmann was not present at these historic events. On 17 May, he received the news that the Provisional Council of State led by Ben-Gurion had elected him President, and this was subsequently confirmed in Israel's first election in January 1949. To become the first President of the State of Israel should have been the triumphant finale to Weizmann's career, but it proved instead to be a coda played out in a minor key. Before returning to Israel, he performed one last service. At an official meeting with Truman on 23 May, Weizmann learned that the United States was willing to make a loan of $100 million to the new state. But he was not long home when the picture darkened.

Now in his mid-70s and in declining health, Weizmann still hoped to play an active part in affairs as President, along the lines of certain continental European countries. Ben-Gurion, for his part, was determined that the role of the President should, like that of the British monarch, be purely symbolic, precisely the word Foreign Minister Moshe Sharett used, with rather insulting honesty, when describing its functions to Weizmann. He was not consulted by Ben-Gurion's government on affairs of state, nor was his request to receive Cabinet minutes granted. Of particular chagrin was the omission of his signature from the Declaration of the

---

12 Fraser, *The USA and the Middle East since World War 2*, pp 38–43.

Establishment of the State of Israel. He had, of course, not been present in Tel Aviv at the time, but it galled him that there were 34 signatories to the historic document, and that space had been left for three others who had been absent, but not for him. At best, it seemed a curious omission of the man who had guided Zionism through its pivotal phase, and who was the first President of the State.[13] He was honoured, of course, but that was not what he had wanted. He made one final visit to the United States in 1949 on behalf of his beloved research institute, now named after him, but it was as 'The Prisoner of Rehovoth' that he now saw himself. For the final year of his life, Weizmann was almost entirely confined to his bed. On 9 November 1952, he died.[14]

The First Arab-Israeli War and the Palestinian *al-Nakba*[15]

The day after Ben-Gurion proclaimed the State of Israel, it was attacked by armies from the Arab League, Egypt, Syria, Lebanon, Jordan, Iraq and Saudi Arabia, beginning a war which was to end in February 1949 with Israel's victory. The Israelis were fighting on interior lines against forces from six Arab countries, but which lacked modern weapons and were far from united in their purpose. The armistice agreements of 1949, which brought hostilities to an end, left Israel with borders more extensive and rather more secure than those which had been set out in the UNSCOP plan. Israel now compromised some 78 per cent of pre-1948 Palestine. Even so, the coastal plain was narrow, and the towns and cities still potentially vulnerable to attack, since the armistice agreements did not end the state of war. Rather the contrary, since defeat generated radicalism in the Arab world. In 1952, the Free Officers movement overthrew the monarchy in Egypt. The leading revolutionary, Colonel Gamal Abdul Nasser, became President in 1954, and was to become the charismatic voice of a new Arab nationalism at odds with the West and with Israel. Security, or rather the lack of it, would be an abiding Israeli

---

13 Rose, *Chaim Weizmann*, p 446
14 Weizmann, *Trial and Error*, pp 585–9; Vera Weizmann, *The Impossible Takes Longer*, pp 237–52; R H S Crossman, 'The Prisoner of Rehovoth', in Meyer W Weisgal and Joel Carmichael (eds), *Chaim Weizmann: A Biography by Several Hands* (Weidenfeld and Nicolson, London: 1962) pp 325–6; Rose, *Chaim Weizmann*, pp 445–59.
15 The discussion of the Arab-Israeli conflict in the following paragraphs is drawn from Fraser, *The Arab-Israeli Conflict*, *passim*.

concern. Israel also secured west Jerusalem, but not the Old City which held the Western Wall, a source of bitter regret.

With Weizmann's old colleague and sometime rival Ben-Gurion as Prime Minister, Israel could now proceed with the business of nation building. By the mid- 1960s, aided by reparations from West Germany, its economy had reached a level comparable with that of southern Europe. The new state had absorbed large numbers of Jews, mainly from the Middle East and north Africa. The arrival of immigrants from these areas altered the nature of Israel's population, hitherto almost entirely European in origin. Because of Hitler's genocide, substantial immigration from Europe was no longer possible, although the country was able to take in survivors from the Holocaust. Relations between the Ashkenazim, Jews of European origin, and the Sephardim from the Middle East and north Africa, were not always easy. The country also experienced tensions between secular and religious Jews, but whatever their differences the overwhelming bulk of Israelis were united behind the ideal of a Jewish state, and took pride in its achievements.

The Palestinians were the principal losers in all of these events. Although they had vehemently rejected partition in 1947, no Palestinian political entity came into being. Instead, the remaining 22 per cent of Mandated Palestine fell into two parts. The area which became known as the West Bank, including east Jerusalem, was held by Abdullah's Arab Legion, and was formally annexed by him in 1950. Abdullah viewed the creation of Israel more phlegmatically than did the other Arab states, and Jordanian and Israeli negotiators maintained discreet contact after the war. These negotiations included proposals for a final partition of Palestine that would include a Jordanian corridor to the Mediterranean and a non-aggression pact. However, there was strong opposition within Abdullah's government and in the wider Arab world. Israel was also unwilling to make the necessary territorial concessions to make an agreement work. These talks came to an abrupt conclusion with the assassination of Abdullah by an extremist Muslim outside the al-Agsa Mosque in Jerusalem on 20 July 1951. After a brief interval, he was succeeded by his 17-year-old grandson Hussein, who proved to be one of the most durable leaders in the region, dying of cancer in 1999, by which time he had steered the Hashemite dynasty through many challenges.[16]

16 Avi Shlaim, *The Iron Wall: Israel and the Arab World* (Penguin, London: 2001) pp 62–8.

The Gaza coastal strip, which had been bitterly contested by the Israeli and Egyptian forces in 1948–9, remained occupied and administered, but not annexed, by Egypt. Its fate was lamentable, and prospects dim. Much of it comprised sand dunes, it had no resources worth the name, and its farmlands and groves were divided by the armistice lines. A pre-1948 population of 70,000 was swollen by 200,000 refugees. The total number of Palestinian refugees by 1949 was around 750,000. Some had fled, others been expelled in the course of the fighting. Without homes, businesses or land, consigned to refugee camps in Jordan, Gaza, Lebanon, Syria, Iraq and Israel itself, they had to rely for support in the decades to come on the United Relief and Works Agency for Palestine Refugees (UNWRA), established in December 1949. The events of 1948–9 were for the Palestinians *al-Nakba*, 'the catastrophe'. The future of the Palestinian refugees became one of the great unanswered questions of the Middle East, their numbers growing appreciably over the years.[17]

The Arab-Israeli Wars

The war of 1948–9 was the first of many. In February 1955, Palestinian raids into Israel resulted in a major incursion into Gaza. On 29 October 1956, Israel attacked Egypt in the Sinai Desert as part of a plan secretly agreed with Britain and France, which had been building up their forces in response to Nasser's nationalisation of the Suez Canal Company. The ill-conceived Anglo-French military landing at Port Said on 5–6 November was brought to a swift stop by an irate President Dwight D Eisenhower. The United Nations Emergency Force (UNEF) was put in place.

The 'Suez Crisis', as it was known, signalled the end of Britain's role in the Middle East, and confirmed America's predominance, which was to grow in the decades ahead. In June 1967, Egypt and Syria began to mass their forces in response to an ill-founded Soviet message that Israel was planning to attack the latter. When Nasser demanded the withdrawal of UNEF and then announced a blockade of the Straits of Tiran, something which Israel had said would constitute a *casus belli*, the crisis assumed critical proportions. Israel reacted with a lightning campaign, which in

---

17 Fraser, *The Arab-Israeli Conflict*, pp 46–7, 54–8, 201; Benny Morris, *The Birth of the Palestinian Refugee Problem, 1947–1949* (Cambridge University Press, Cambridge: 1987) pp 203–12. A recent study is Ilan Pappe, *The Ethnic Cleansing of Palestine* (Oneworld, Oxford: 2006)

a matter of days saw her forces advance to the Suez Canal and capture the strategic Golan Heights from Syria. King Hussein rallied to the Arab cause, losing east Jerusalem and the West Bank as a result. After one of the most dramatic military victories of the post-war world, Israel now occupied all of pre-1948 Palestine, as well as extensive Egyptian and Syrian territory.

On 6 October 1973, Egypt's President Anwar al-Sadat and Syria's President Hafez al-Asad, seemingly frustrated by the lack of diplomatic progress, launched a surprise attack on Israeli positions along the Suez Canal and on the Golan Heights. After initial Egyptian and Syrian successes along the Suez Canal and on Mount Hermon, the Israelis counter-attacked, aided by a massive American resupply operation. When hostilities ended, largely as the result of American Secretary of State Henry Kissinger's diplomacy, the Israeli army was deployed on the western bank of the southern part of the Suez Canal, surrounding the Egyptian Third Army, and also threatening Damascus after successful operations on the Golan front. The result of the war was far from clear-cut. The Israeli forces had recovered well after their initial reverses. Critically, however, Egyptian and Syrian military pride and confidence had been restored, opening the way for diplomatic moves, as Sadat had certainly hoped. With his success in negotiating a ceasefire behind him, Kissinger was well placed to begin the process.

Iraq: the end of the Hashemite monarchy

In contrast with Abdullah's willingness to seek peace with Israel, Iraq, despite its pro-Western orientation, was militantly opposed to any compromise with the new state. The year 1948 was a very unsettled year for the country. Severe riots erupted over the Palestine conflict and over the new Anglo-Iraqi agreement, the Treaty of Portsmouth. The former were aimed at the large Jewish population in Baghdad, who soon concluded they had no future in Iraq and the vast majority of them left, abandoning most of their property, in the early 1950s.[18] Nuri, now the dominant figure in Iraqi ruling circles, took the opportunity offered by the death of Abdullah I of Jordan to reclaim Iraqi leadership of schemes for unity in the Fertile Crescent. However, with the coming to power in 1952 of the new military regime in Egypt, he now faced a rival for

---

18 Tripp, *A History of Iraq*, pp 125–6.

regional leadership. Nasser's earliest achievement was to sign an agreement that ended British base rights in peacetime in Egypt. This contrasted with Nuri and the Iraqi royal family's continued advocacy of the British connection and the maintenance of British bases. Britain would retain air bases and military facilities and rights in Iraq until after the 1958 revolution.

Moreover, Nuri, influenced by a deep distrust of the Russians dating back to his days in the Ottoman army, was deeply committed to bringing Iraq firmly into the Western Alliance. To this end, in early 1955 he orchestrated the creation of a regional defence organisation, the Baghdad Pact, which included Britain, Iran, Turkey and Pakistan. Nuri eventually hoped to bring other Arab states, including Jordan and Syria, into the alliance. The Baghdad Pact provoked fierce opposition from Nasser, who saw it as a challenge to his own preference for Arab states to be neutral in the Cold War and a block to his own ambitions for regional leadership.[19] The Egyptian leader directed the full weight of an increasingly powerful propaganda machine against the Iraqi leadership. Jordan decided not to join after Egyptian-inspired riots, and Syria became increasingly entranced by Nasser's brand of Arab nationalism. The Hashemites faced increasing isolation – a situation only exacerbated by the Anglo-French-Israeli invasion of Suez.[20] An international crisis over Syria in the summer and autumn of 1957, in which, with British encouragement, Nuri floated a number of schemes for Iraqi intervention, only strengthened Egyptian influence. This culminated in a union of Egypt and Syria, called the United Arab Republic, under Nasser's leadership in February 1958. Nuri, in desperation, floated a counter-proposal – the Arab Union – made up of Iraq and Jordan, but it had little popular support.

Domestically the regime remained unstable. Iraq had huge social divisions between the peasant masses that saw little benefit from increased oil revenues and the landlord classes that grew ever more prosperous. The landed classes also excluded a growing middle class from the levers of power. A Development Board tasked with spending the oil revenues was the subject of criticism for moving too slowly. Nasserite propaganda over the Baghdad Pact tapped into widespread political disquiet about Iraq's

19 See Robert McNamara, *Britain, Nasser and the Balance of Power in the Middle East* (Cass, Portland: 2003) pp 42–6.
20 Louis, *Ends of British Imperialism*, p 860.

pro-Western foreign policy.[21] The government treated even mild political opposition as subversion, leaving little opportunity for legitimate political opposition.[22]

Within the army the wider political discontent was reflected in the growth of groups in the officer class modelled on the Egyptian Free Officers. They became increasingly determined to end the regime. The opportunity arose in July 1958, when Iraqi troops were ordered to Jordan to bolster the regime there. Instead they marched on Baghdad and seized power. In appalling scenes, the royal family, including the youthful king and the former regent Abdulilah, were slain. Nuri was captured attempting to reach a friendly foreign embassy, allegedly disguised in women's clothes, and murdered. Iraq was proclaimed a republic under Brigadier General Abd al-Karim Qasim.

Fatah and the PLO

It took the Palestinians fully a decade to rally politically after the events of 1948–9. When they did so, the key figure was an engineer from Gaza who had fought in the war, Yasser Arafat. In 1959, with a small group of friends, he formed Fatah, 'The Movement for the Liberation of Palestine'. Its moment came after the 1967 war when its fighters challenged the Israeli army at Karameh in Jordan, and established networks in the West Bank. In 1968–9, the Palestine Liberation Organization (PLO), a hitherto largely ineffectual body which had been created in 1964, was restructured under Fatah's leadership with Arafat as chairman, a position he was to hold until his death in November 2004.

Armed Palestinian resistance to the Israeli occupation took several forms. While Fatah mounted conventional raids inside the West Bank, the Popular Front for the Liberation of Palestine (PFLP) targeted airliners, ensuring that the Palestinian issue was never far from the world's headlines. This phase reached a climax in September 1970 when the hijacking of three airliners to Jordan led King Hussein, in an operation which became known as 'Black September', to strike at the Palestinian bases in his country. The term 'Black September' reappeared at the 1972 Munich Olympics when an organisation of that name killed eleven Israeli athletes.

---

21 Stephen Longrigg and Frank Stoakes, *Iraq* (Praeger, New York: 1959) p 225.
22 See George Lawrence Harris, *Iraq: Its People, Its Society, Its Culture* (HRAF Press, New Haven: 1958) p 83 and Longrigg and Stoakes, *Iraq*, p 242.

In the period after the 1973 war, the PLO increasingly followed a political path, never likely to be easy since the Israelis understandably regarded it with deep hostility and Fatah was only one of a number of groups within it. Its high point came when Arafat addressed the General Assembly of the United Nations in New York in November 1974, but this momentum could not be sustained, not least since the Palestinians became caught up in the crisis which developed in Lebanon the following year, leading to a prolonged civil war in the country.

Until the 1970s, Lebanon was the financial centre of the Middle East and appeared to be the most successful of the Arab states. However, beneath the surface of calm and prosperity lay substantial communal tensions. The country also found itself drawn into the inter-Arab disputes of the 1950s, the Israel-Palestine conflict owing to the presence on its soil of a sizeable population of Palestinian refugees, as well as the wider world struggle between the United States and the Soviet Union. Lebanon's National Pact held until the late 1950s when the tensions caused by the intra-Arab struggle and the growing internal troubles of a divided communal society led to a brief civil war. From the late 1960s Lebanon-based Palestinian guerrilla attacks on Israel provoked ever greater Israeli reprisals that destabilised relations between the Christian and Muslim communities. In 1975, full-scale fighting broke out between Christians and Palestinians. This widened into a Muslim-Christian civil war, which lasted until 1989, eventually involving, in various capacities, Syria, Israel, the United States, France, Italy and the United Kingdom.

Attempts at an Arab-Israeli peace settlement

Attempts at a diplomatic settlement began almost as soon as the 1967 war ended, the key document being United Nations Security Council Resolution 242 of 22 November, which served as the basis of negotiations thereafter. At its heart was the provision that Israel armed forces should withdraw from territories occupied in the recent conflict, a condition that could be, and was, interpreted in different ways. It did, nevertheless, acknowledge the sovereignty of every state in the area. Accepted by Egypt and Jordan, this carried their implicit recognition of Israel. The resolution also called for a just settlement of the refugee problem, but this was not a description the Palestinians accepted. Two years later, American Secretary of State William Rogers announced an ill-fated peace plan, but it took the 1973 war for any progress to be made. In 1974-5, Henry

Kissinger negotiated important disengagement agreements between Israel and its two major antagonists, Egypt and Syria, which defused much of the immediate danger. A ceasefire line along the Golan Heights was agreed, and both banks of the Suez Canal were restored to Egypt. In return, Sadat announced that Israeli cargoes would be allowed through the Suez Canal.

The next major move was made by President Sadat, who, to universal surprise, addressed the Knesset in Jerusalem in November 1977 with a plea for a peace settlement, which would include not just a peace agreement between Egypt and Israel but a settlement for the Palestinians. In the meantime, the Labour Party, which had dominated Israeli politics since the foundation of the state, had lost power to the right-wing Likud led by former Irgun leader Menaham Begin and General Ariel Sharon, who had commanded the Israeli crossing of the Suez Canal in 1973. Their victory reflected in part the growing power of Jews of Middle Eastern origin.

Despite Sadat's dramatic intervention, it took the determined intervention of US President Jimmy Carter for progress to be made. Two Frameworks were agreed between Egypt and Israel at the Camp David summit which he convened in September 1978. The first provided for a peace treaty between the two countries, which was signed on 26 March the following year, and survived Sadat's assassination in October 1981. In return for giving back the Sinai Desert, Israel had removed the threat from its most powerful Arab adversary. The second Framework, which sought to address the future of the West Bank and Gaza, failed in its purpose. This was to provide 'full autonomy' for the inhabitants of the West Bank and Gaza, but it proved impossible to agree what this meant.

The war in Lebanon and the Intifada

On 6 June 1982, 'Operation Peace for Galilee' began when Israeli troops invaded Lebanon and within days were on the outskirts of Beirut, close to Muslim areas of the city and Palestinian refugee camps. It was a controversial war, even within Israel itself, and sustained bombardment of parts of the city bought intense pressure from President Ronald Reagan for a resolution. As a result, a joint American, French and Italian Multinational Force oversaw the evacuation of Yasser Arafat and his PLO forces from the city. President Reagan followed this with a new peace plan, which within days was overtaken by events when the Maronite leader, Bashir Gemayel, on whom Israel had placed considerable hopes, was assassinated. Lebanese supporters of the slain leader massacred hundreds of Palestinians in the Sabra and Shatila refugee camps, in an area of west Beirut which the Israelis had occupied in the aftermath of Gemayel's murder. A new Multinational Force of American, French, Italian and British soldiers was sent to Beirut, but its mission became inseparable from the passions of the Lebanese conflict. The crisis came on 23 October 1983 when suicide bombers killed 241 American marines and 78 French soldiers. By the following spring, the Multinational Force had been withdrawn.

The focus of events then moved to the West Bank and Gaza where there had been mounting frustration at the lack of diplomatic progress, and anger over Israeli settlement activities, which had steadily built up in the course of the 1980s. The Intifada, or Uprising, which began in Gaza in December 1987 and then spread to the West Bank, was an unprecedented and widespread challenge to the Israeli occupation. Out of the Intifada came a new movement which in time was to challenge not just Israel but Fatah. This was Hamas, the Islamic Resistance Movement, founded by Sheikh Ahmed Yassin. The movement combined social work and an intense Islamic commitment with a military wing, the Izz al-Din al-Qassam Brigade. Hamas was destined to grow in opposition to the secular Fatah.[23]

Iraq after the Hashemites

The Iraqi Republic which emerged from the ruins of the Hashemite monarchy was prey to conflicting political ambitions and ideologies, Qasim himself being overthrown and shot in 1963. In July 1979, Saddam Hussein, a leading member of the Ba'th Party which had built up a strong power base in the security services, became President, inaugurating his rule with a ruthless purge of party rivals.[24] He soon had his country in a firm grip, his power based in the Sunni heartland, the Ba'th Party and the armed forces, and began an adventurous foreign policy. While Saddam Hussein's regime was secular, Sunni Arabs had been the dominant element in the country since its creation. Shia Iran, where the Shah was overthrown in 1979 and which was in the process of establishing an

---

23 See Beverley Milton-Edwards and Stephen Farrell, *Hamas* (Polity Press, Cambridge: 2010).
24 Tripp, *A History of Iraq*, pp 213–14.

Islamic republic, was Saddam Hussein's first target. The Shatt al-Arab waterway, Iraq's sole maritime outlet, had long been an issue between the two countries, and the upheaval caused by the revolution in Iran seemed to present a unique opportunity for action. In September 1980, Iraq began a series of attacks on Iranian territory. Revolutionary Iran proved to be a stern opponent, however. The war dragged on until 1988, leaving Iraq with massive debts, and no gains.[25]

The war with Iran was not Saddam Hussein's last misreading of the international situation. His next target was Kuwait. Here, too, there were long-standing border disputes, as well as a debt of $30 billion result-ing from the war with Iran. On 2 August 1990, the Iraqi army invaded. Kuwait was in no position to resist, but Saddam Hussein seriously mis-judged the effect his conquest would have in the rest of the Middle East, and in Washington. On 5 August, President George Bush announced that the aggression would not stand unopposed. Saudi Arabia gave its permission for American troops to enter its territory, while Britain and France announced their support. They were joined by troops from a number of countries, most notably Egypt and Syria, an indication of how the Iraqi leader's ambitions were seen elsewhere in the Middle East. Turkish opinion was divided. Turkish troops did not take part, but per-mission was given for operations from the NATO air base at Incirlik in southern Turkey. On 29 November 1990, the United Nations Security Council passed a resolution demanding Iraqi withdrawal from Kuwait by 15 January. When this deadline expired, air attacks on Iraq began. The coalition's ground assault was launched on 24 February 1991, liberating Kuwait in three days. The Security Council had not sanctioned further action, and certainly not an advance on Baghdad. Hopes that defeat would lead to Saddam Hussein's overthrow were confounded, since he had carefully husbanded his Republican Guard, an essential prop of his government. Risings in the Shia south and Kurdish north were ruthlessly suppressed, and although Iraq was subject to United Nations sanctions, his power remained intact.[26]

After the 9/11 attacks of 2001 on New York and Washington by al-Qaeda, the United States decided to remove Saddam Hussein. While his

25 Tripp, *A History of Iraq*, pp 224–39.
26 Fraser and Murray, *America and the World since 1945*, pp 248–54; Tripp, *A History of Iraq*, pp 244–50; Mango, *The Turks Today*, pp 90–1.

regime was swiftly removed in the spring of 2003, the ensuing years saw a violent insurgency and widespread destruction. Tens of thousands of Iraqis died in the conflict. American forces captured Saddam Hussein in December 2003. Put on trial in 2005 for the murder of 148 Shia villagers, he was found guilty, and was executed on 30 December 2006. In the meantime, a new government under Nuri al-Maliki, leader of the Da'wa Party, had been formed in May, following elections in December 2005. Elections for the 325-member Council of Representatives on 7 March 2010 were less decisive, however, leaving Maliki's State of Law Coalition with 89 seats and the opposing Iraqi National Movement led by former premier Iyad al-Allawi with 91. The political future of Iraq was beginning to emerge, however tentatively, and in the face of many challenges.[27]

An uncertain peace process

In the course of 1993, a highly secret dialogue between key Israeli and PLO representatives had been maturing in Norway, culminating in an historic exchange of letters, the Declaration of Principles, on 9 September. In this dramatic development, the PLO recognised Israel's right to exist and renounced terrorism, while Israel promised to withdraw from Gaza and the city of Jericho on the West Bank. There were to be elections for a Palestinian Council, which was to administer the West Bank and Gaza for five years, while a final settlement was being negotiated. In a ceremony at the White House on 13 September, presided over by President Bill Clinton, Arafat and Israeli premier Yitzhak Rabin shook hands and signed the agreement. A meeting in Cairo in May 1994 paved the way for the creation of a Palestinian Authority with Arafat as President. It was followed by a peace treaty between Israel and Jordan in October. Even so, the Oslo peace process had its opponents on both sides. Hamas waged a campaign against it, while Rabin was assassinated at a rally in Tel Aviv on 4 November 1994 by a young Israeli. Suicide bombers undermined Israeli support.

Despite the iconic handshake in the Rose Garden of the White House, the peace process did not flourish, defying the best efforts of the Clinton

---

27 Tripp, *A History of Iraq*, pp 303–8; 313–14; see also Kenneth Katzmann, *Iraq: Politics, Elections and Benchmarks* (Congressional Research Service, The Library of Congress, Washington, DC: 24 August 2010) <http://fpc.state.gov/documents/organization/147288.pdf>.

administration. Suicide bomb attacks in Israel and continuing Israeli settlement activity in the West Bank did not encourage goodwill, quite the reverse. Elections for the Palestinian Council took place in January 1996. The Council was addressed by Clinton after the Nye Valley conference in 1998 arranged for 40 per cent of the West Bank to be placed under its control and provided that the Palestinians would implement security measures. In July 2000, Clinton made a valiant and imaginative attempt to bring Arafat and Israeli premier Ehud Barak to a settlement at a summit at Camp David. At issue was the prospect of a Palestinian state within the 1967 borders, but with territorial adjustments that would transfer most of the Jewish settlements to Israel, while compensating the Palestinians with some Israeli territory. The Palestinians would have full sovereignty in parts of east Jerusalem and custodial rights on the Haram al-Sharif shrine in the city. It seems that Barak was prepared to concede to the Palestinians 91 per cent of the West Bank, as well as custodianship over the Haram al-Sharif/Temple Mount, sovereignty in part of Jerusalem, and a solution for the refugees. Arafat could not agree.[28]

The collapse of the summit was quickly followed by a return to violence. The occasion, if not the actual cause, of the outbreak was the visit to the Haram al-Sharif Temple Mount on 28 September 2000 by Israeli opposition Likud leader Ariel Sharon, an object of particular dislike to Palestinians. When Palestinian protesters were fired on by police the following day, killing four people, what came to be called the al-Aqsa Intifada began. It was more violent than the first Intifada, with suicide bomb attacks provoking Israeli retaliation with tanks and helicopter gunships.[29] In January 2001, at the very end of his presidency, Clinton made a final attempt to reach a settlement, but again Arafat could not be persuaded, his sticking points being the Old City of Jerusalem and the right of return of the Palestinian refugees. The Israeli election which immediately followed was won by Sharon.

By 2002, Israeli-Palestinian relations had deteriorated into a depressing

---

28 Clinton's efforts can be studied in Bill Clinton, *My Life* (Hutchinson, London: 2004) pp 911–16 and Dennis Ross, *The Missing Peace: The Inside Story of the Fight for Middle East Peace* (Farrar, Straus and Giroux, New York: 2004) pp 650–711.
29 George Mitchell, *Sharm El-Sheikh Fact-Finding Committee Report* (Washington, DC: 30 April 2001) <http://www.state.gov/p/nea/rls/ppt/3060.htm>.

and bloody spiral of suicide bombings and Israeli retaliation. On 27 March, a suicide bomb at a Passover celebration in Netanya killed 28 and injured 140. In response, Sharon launched 'Operation Defensive Shield' across the West Bank, effectively isolating Arafat in his Ramallah head-quarters. Casualties as the result of operations in the Jenin refugee camp were particularly controversial. On 30 April 2003, following the fall of Baghdad, President George W Bush announced a 'Performance-Based Roadmap to a Permanent Two-State Solution to the Israeli-Palestinian Conflict', which was to see a final settlement by 2005. This proved no more successful than its predecessors, although the American commit-ment to the pursuit of a two-state solution was in itself significant.

There were critical developments affecting the West Bank and Gaza. In the former the Israelis began the construction of a security fence intended as a barrier against suicide attacks. It was a formidable affair which in Jerusalem took the form of a concrete wall. Palestinians viewed it as a wall of annexation, since it took in settlement blocks beyond the 1967 border and impacted adversely on a number of communities, notably Bethlehem whose economy depended on the tourist trade. In Gaza, con-tinuing suicide attacks led the Israelis to target the Hamas leadership. On 22 March 2004, the movement's founder, Sheikh Ahmed Yassin, was killed by a missile, to be followed a month later by his successor in the leadership. These strikes did not inhibit the movement's growth. In Ramallah, Arafat's health had been declining. Flown to France for treat-ment, he died on 11 November, his burial at his Ramallah headquarters being the occasion for widespread mourning amongst Palestinians for whom he had long embodied their cause.

Sharon had the capacity to surprise. Despite strong opposition in his party, he forged ahead with a disengagement plan for Gaza. By Septem-ber 2005, all settlements and military units had been withdrawn. This disengagement was followed by a dramatic political move. In November, Sharon resigned from Likud, forming a new centrist party, Kadima, or 'Forward'. While committed to Israel's security, the party promised to pursue the peace process based upon two states. How Kadima would have developed under Sharon's leadership was never put to the test, since the following January he was struck down by a cerebral attack. In the Israeli election of March 2006, now led by former Jerusalem mayor Ehud Olmert, Kadima emerged as the largest party, and was able to form a coalition government with Labour. Olmert's government had to confront new realities, since in the Palestinian elections in January, Fatah was eclipsed by Hamas. In March, Hamas's Ismail Haniya became Prime Minister of the Palestinian Authority.

As tensions between the two new governments rose, in July 2006 serious fighting broke out on Israel's border with Lebanon, where the Islamic militia Hezbollah mounted a raid killing eight Israelis. In the subsequent large-scale fighting northern Israel was hit by some 4,000 rockets, while 144 Israelis and over 1,000 Lebanese are believed to have been killed.[30] Israel was also being attacked by rockets from Gaza, where tensions between Hamas and Fatah were coming to a head. In June 2007, bitter fighting between them left Hamas in firm control of Gaza and Fatah holding on to the West Bank.

This *de facto* fragmentation of the Palestinian Authority did not bode well for the success of a major conference presided over by President Bush at Annapolis on 27 November, at which the parties committed themselves to strive for an agreement based on two states by the end of 2008. This did not happen. Instead, Israel's increasingly bitter relations with Gaza held the stage. Continuing rocket attacks led to an Israeli closure of the border crossings in January 2008. As the situation in Gaza deteriorated, gaps were blown in the border fence with Egypt, leading thousands of Palestinians to cross into Egyptian territory. In June a ceasefire was arranged by the Egyptians, but this collapsed in December as a result of Israeli operations against the tunnels connecting Gaza with Egypt. When rocket attacks on Israel resumed, on 27 December 2008 the Israelis launched air attacks. 'Operation Cast Lead' soon involved major ground operations, lasting until 18 January. As it drew to a close and the scale of the conflict and of the casualties began to emerge, it was believed that over 1,000 Palestinians, including many civilians, had been killed, while Israel had lost thirteen.[31] Southern Israel continued to be vulnerable to rocket attacks, while Gaza remained subject to border restrictions which impeded attempts at reconstruction.

---

30 Fraser, *The Arab-Israeli Conflict*, p 191.

31 See Jim Zanotti, Jeremy M Sharp, Carol Migdalovtz, Casey L Addis and Christopher M Blanchard, *Israel and Hamas: Conflict in Gaza (2008–2009)* (Congressional Research Service, Library of Congress, Washington, DC: 15 January 2009) p12, <http://fpc.state.gov/documents/organization/116003.pdf>.

Modern Turkey

Post-war Turkey continued to present a paradox. It was firmly linked to the West through NATO membership, but its relations with its neighbour and fellow alliance member, Greece, were frequently acrimonious. There were disputes over Aegean islands, but the principal source of friction was Cyprus, which Britain had acquired from the Ottomans in 1878, but where Turks were only some 20 per cent of the population. The Greek Cypriot campaign in the 1950s for *Enosis*, union with Greece, raised fears in the predominantly Turkish north of the island. The island became independent in 1960 with Archbishop Makarios as President. In 1974, the National Guard mounted a coup against him with a view to securing union with Greece, but this provoked a Turkish military landing, leading to the creation of the Turkish Republic of North Cyprus, effectively partitioning the island. The unresolved future of Cyprus was to complicate Turkey's foreign relations, not least its bid to join the European Union, especially since the (Greek) Republic of Cyprus became a full member in 2004.

Membership of NATO meant that relations with Washington were central to Turkey's foreign policy for much of the period, its security powerfully guaranteed by the American Sixth Fleet in the Mediterranean. In 1954, the United States acquired a major military asset with the construction of the Incirlik air base in south-eastern Turkey. This substantial facility enabled NATO to threaten the Soviet Union on its southern flank. In 1980, the Defense and Economic Cooperation Agreement between the two countries set the terms for the base's use. With the ending of the Cold War, its function changed, placing American aircraft significantly closer to the Middle East than did the Rhein-Main air base in Germany.[32] In 1962, loyal NATO membership also allowed the United States to base 17 Jupiter missiles targeted on the Soviet Union on Turkish territory.[33] This deployment presented a significant threat to the Soviets, but in October President Kennedy agreed to withdraw the Jupiters as part of the resolution of the Cuban Missile Crisis. Agreement with Moscow was

---

32 Carol Migdalovitz, *Turkey: Selected Foreign Policy Issues and U.S. Views* (Congressional Research Service, Library of Congress, Washington, DC: 29 August 2008) pp 16–17, <http://fpc.state.gov/documents/organization/110398.pdf>.
33 Robert Dallek, *John F. Kennedy: An Unfinished Life 1917–1963* (Allen Lane, London: 2003) p 536.

negotiated, it seems, over the head of the Turkish government. Such was the *realpolitik* of the time.

The Iranian revolution of 1979 reinforced Turkey's importance for the United States, which had seen its most powerful ally in the Middle East suddenly turn bitterly hostile.[34] During the first Gulf crisis of 1991, Turkey permitted the use of the Incirlik air base, but the Second Gulf War of 2003 provoked a major crisis in its relations with the American administration. In its planning, the Pentagon had hoped to mount a two-pronged invasion of Iraq, with a northern attack mounted from Turkey. On 1 March, however, the Turkish parliament voted against the American troop deployment.[35]

The military remained a powerful force in national life and politics, seeing itself as the heir to, and principal buttress of, the secular republic Atatürk had created. Under the banner of the National Unity Committee, in May 1960 a group of officers overthrew the Menderes government. The following year, the ousted premier and two of his ministers were executed. He has since been rehabilitated to the extent that the thousands of holidaymakers who visit the flourishing resorts of the Aegean coast, and those who come to appreciate the glories of the region's classical heritage at Ephesus and Bergama, pass through Izmir's Adnan Menderes airport, possibly unaware of how it came to be named.

The tension long inherent in the maintenance of a secular state in a country which remained 99.8 per cent Muslim began to surface in November 2002 with the coming to power of the Justice and Development Party (AKP), which had only been founded the previous year, led by Recep Tayyip Erdogan, a former mayor of Istanbul. The party, while pledging loyalty to the secular state, had a broadly conservative ethos. In 2007, its Foreign Minister, Abdullah Gul, a trained economist, was elected President, reinforcing the party's position. The fears of secularist supporters surfaced the following year when the government introduced constitutional amendments to remove the long-standing ban on the

---

34 Feroz Ahmad, *Turkey: The Quest for Identity* (Oneworld Publications, Oxford: 2005) pp 145–6.

35 Jim Muir, 'The Northern Front and the Kurds' Endgame', in Sara Beck and Malcolm Dowling (eds), *The Battle for Iraq: BBC News Correspondents on the War against Saddam and a New World Agenda* (BBC Worldwide Ltd, London: 2003) p 158–69.

318 THE MAKERS OF THE MODERN MIDDLE EAST

wearing of headscarves by women in the universities. The amendment was invalidated by the Constitutional Court, which, however, rejected a petition to have the AKP banned.[36]

A more immediate threat to the stability of the Turkish state was Kurdish nationalism. The Treaty of Sèvres had provided for an independent Kurdistan, to be carved out of Turkey, should the Kurds want it and prove capable of sustaining it. Turkish Kurdistan could then link up with the Kurdish areas of the Iraqi province of Mosul. The Treaty of Lausanne did not mention the Kurds. But their cultural rights were covered obliquely by Article 39. This provided that:

> ... no restrictions shall be imposed on the free use by any Turkish national of any language in private intercourse, in commerce, religion, in the press, or in publications of any kind or at public meetings. Notwithstanding the existence of the official language, adequate facilities shall be given to Turkish nationals of non-Turkish speech for the oral use of their own language before the Courts.[37]

This provision awaits implementation to this day. Restrictions placed on the use of the Kurdish language (or rather languages) in Turkey were resented by all Turkish citizens of Kurdish origin. Nationalists among them wanted more, their demands ranging from autonomy to full independence. In 1984, the Kurdistan Workers' Party (PKK) launched a guerrilla campaign, which increased in intensity after the 1991 Gulf War, as the movement had established bases in northern Iraq, from which Saddam Hussein's forces were excluded after the first Gulf War. By 1999, the insurrection had been largely suppressed, following the arrest of its leader Abdullah Öcalan, but the demand for some from of Kurdish autonomy remained.[38]

---

36 Ahmad, *Turkey*, pp 181–2; Carol Migdalovitz, *Turkey: Update on Crisis of Identity and Power* (Congressional Research Service, Library of Congress, Washington, DC: 2 September 2008) <http://fpc.state.gov/documents/organization/110367.pdf>.

37 <http://www.hri.org/docs/lausanne/part1.html>.

38 Carol Migdalovitz, *Iraq: The Turkish Factor* (Congressional Research Service, Library of Congress, Washington, DC: 31 October 2002) pp 2–3, <http://fpc.state.gov/documents/organization/14957.pdf>; Carol Migdalovitz, *Turkey: Selected Foreign Policy Issues and U.S. Views*, pp 4–5; Mango, *The Turks Today*, pp 214–25.

In foreign affairs, Turkey engaged on a process of active engagement with its neighbours in the region. This included a dialogue with Iran, which lay under a blanket of international disapproval as a result of its nuclear enrichment programme. Fears over Iran's possible intentions were of particular concern to the United States and Israel, but Turkey maintained that the country was entitled to have a peaceful nuclear energy programme.

At the same time that Ankara was pursuing this policy, Turkish relations with Israel went into sharp decline. The two countries had long enjoyed a positive relationship, not least in military cooperation, but a series of events associated with Israeli policies towards Gaza changed this. This was dramatically symbolised in January 2009 by Prime Minister Erdogan leaving the stage when Israeli President Shimon Peres defended 'Operation Cast Lead' at the World Economic Forum. The blockade of Gaza led to a number of attempts to send supply ships, which Israel diverted to Ashdod, where the cargoes were first inspected before being sent on. In May 2010, six ships, including the Turkish vessel MV *Mavi Marmara* sailed for Gaza, refusing to make for Ashdod. On 31 May, they were intercepted by Israeli commandos. Fighting on the *Mavi Marmara* resulted in the death of eight Turks and one Turkish-American. Turkish opinion was outraged, and the Ambassador to Israel was recalled.[39]

Active engagement with Turkey's Middle Eastern neighbours went alongside the country's long-standing ambition to join the European Union. Membership of the Union was neither straightforward nor pre-ordained, as the British had learned to their cost. Applicants were required to meet the complex requirements of the 35 chapters of the acquis communautaire, and a final accession treaty had then to be ratified by all 27 member countries as well as the applicant. Turkey's path to membership was prolonged. An Association Agreement was signed as early as 1963. The country's first application to join was in 1987, but was put on hold since new applicants were not then being considered. Subsequently, however, the Union dramatically expanded to include most of the states of Central and Eastern Europe, as well as Malta and Cyprus, which left Turkey's position looking anomalous.

---

39 See Carol Migdalovitz, *Israel's Blockade of Gaza, the Mavi Marmara Incident, and its Aftermath* (Congressional Research Service, Washington, DC: 23 June 2010), http://fpc.state.gov/documents/organization/145581.pdf.

In October 2005, the European Union agreed to begin the negotiating process with Ankara. Opinion inside the Union was divided on the
issue. The unresolved position of Cyprus was an obvious difficulty. With
a population of nearly 78 million, almost all of them Muslims, Turkey
would be the largest member state close behind Germany with just over
82 million, 2.4 per cent of whom were of Turkish origin. Supporters
of the Turkish application pointed to the country's key strategic position. Turkish membership would give the Union an extensive frontier
with states in the Middle East and the Caucasus, the merits of which
could be argued either way. The Union would almost certainly become
more closely involved with contentious areas and issues hitherto at some
remove. Conversely, however, Turkey's powerful armed forces would add
considerably to the Union's military potential. Membership of the Union
would certainly send an important signal for the 21st century that Islam
and Christianity could work in harmony.[40]

On 12 September 2010, Turkish voters overwhelmingly endorsed a
government-backed list of 26 amendments to the country's 1982 Con-
stitution, which were designed to reinforce its bid to join the European
Union, but which were strongly opposed by secularist parties. Areas of
Europe across the Balkans and in Andalucia had an Islamic as well as
Christian heritage, and Istanbul was declared European City of Culture
for 2010. Perhaps the case for Turkey's admission into the European
Union was put most eloquently by President Barack Obama before the
Turkish Parliament on 6 April 2009 when he when he reminded his listeners that Turkey and Europe were united by more than the bridges across
the Bosporus. Europe, he said, gained by diversity and this would be
enhanced by Turkish membership.[41]

No longer imperial, nor as cosmopolitan as it had been in Ottoman
times, Istanbul remained one of the world's great cities, still uniquely

---

40 Commission of the European Communities, *Commission Staff Working
Document. Issues Arising from Turkey's Membership Perspective* (COM: 2004, 656
Final, Brussels: 6 October 2004) <http://ec.europe.eu/enlargement/archives/pdf/
key_documents/2004/issues_paper_en.pdf>; CIA, *The World Factbook: Turkey*,
<https://www.cia.gov/library/publications/the-world-factbook/geos/tu.html>;
CIA, *The World Factbook: Germany*, <https://www.cia.gov/library/publications/
the-world-factbook/geos/gm.html>.
41 'Remarks by President Obama to the Turkish Parliament', 6 April 2009,
<http://www.whitehouse.gov/the-press-office/remarks-president-obama-turkish-parliament>

embracing Europe and Asia across the narrow waters of the Bosphorus, a symbol for the future many hoped.

Envoi

The Middle East in 2010 was a region of promise and paradox. Long gone were the empires of the Ottomans, British and French, the last two never having been other than birds of passage. The major outside power was the United States, but the problems of Iraq after 2003 showed that even it had limitations, and 31 August 2010 was to see the end of an active American combat role in the country. Despite the problems of reconstruction, and the divisions between Shia and Sunni, Arab and Kurd, which had festered since its very creation, Iraq possessed one of the world's most important oil reserves, offering possibilities for the future. If the Hashemites were long gone from Baghdad, the family still ruled Jordan under King Abdullah II. Israel was a fully-fledged democracy with a sophisticated economy, but the security problems apparent since its victory in 1949 remained. American diplomacy had closely engaged with the Israeli-Palestinian conflict for decades, but had failed to resolve it. The Palestinians lacked statehood, and the two components of the fledgling Palestinian Authority were divided by a secular Fatah in the West Bank and an Islamic Hamas in Gaza. Turkey moved in international affairs as an increasingly confident regional power. In contrast with an ageing European Union, which it aspired to join, Turkey had a young population, as, indeed, had the Middle East in general.

The end of the Cold War did not diminish the Middle East's importance in world affairs, as two wars involving Iraq demonstrated. Failure to resolve the Israeli-Palestinian impasse had ramifications well beyond the region, as well as tragedies for those directly involved. It was significant that President Obama's first overseas trip after his inauguration included Turkey. Then, on 4 June 2009, he made a major speech at Cairo University in which he declared that he had come to look for a new beginning in the relationship between his country and the world's Muslims. In a wide-ranging review, in which he explored issues of extremism, nuclear weapons, democracy, religious freedom, women's rights and economic development, he stressed the need for an Israeli-Palestinian settlement.

Obama's choice of Cairo reflected Egypt's key position. In the decades since it had thrown off British tutelage the country had grown in population to over 80 million and enjoyed considerable natural wealth, as well as its invaluable tourist revenue.[42] The Suez Canal retained its critical importance. Hosni Mubarak, Vice-President and veteran air force officer, had replaced the assassinated Sadat as President in 1981, ruling the country for the next three decades through his National Democratic Party, maintaining the peace treaty with Israel, and receiving substantial aid from Washington. On 25 January 2011, this apparent stability was shattered when thousands of protesters assembled in Cairo's central Tahrir Square, and then in other cities, demanding democratic reforms and an end to the existing regime. Clashes with the police and government supporters failed to quell or deter them. Faced with the scale of the protests, Mubarak announced that he would not seek re-election in the presidential election scheduled for September, and the government began negotiations with opposition groups. Even so, the protests maintained their intensity. On 10 February, the President made a television address. Confounding the hopes and expectations of the protesters, he made it clear that he would continue in office for the rest of his term. The following afternoon, as crowds massed across the country, Vice-President Omar Suleiman came on state television, and in a brief statement announced that Mubarak was stepping down from the office of President, putting the country's affairs in the hands of the high council of the armed forces. As normality started to return, the army confirmed its commitment to the country's international treaties and to the transfer of power to an elected civilian government. The potential for a new era was there.[43]

This book has analysed the ways in which these societies, Arab, Jewish and Turkish, emerged out of the complex series of events which affected the Middle East between 1914 and 1923. The war and the peace agreements which followed set new agendas for this historic and complex region. If the war of 1914–18 was the product of European rivalries and ambitions, not the least of its consequences was a transformed Middle East in which leaders of courage and imagination, notably Feisal, Weizmann and Mustafa Kemal Atatürk, were inspired to seize the moment, often against difficult odds. Their successes and failures have been traced in this book. Nine decades later, their legacy remains.

---

42 Useful statistics may be found at: CIA, The World Factbook, Egypt, https://www.cia.gov/library/publications/the-world-factbook/geos/eg.html
43 'Egypt protests: Key moments in unrest', http://www.bbc.co.uk/news/world-middle-east-12425375 "Source – BBC News/bbc.co.uk – © 2011 BBC". "BBC Credit".

Further Reading

The First World War, the Peace settlements and their legacy

The subject of the First World War, the Peace settlement and its after-math in the Middle East has generated a vast bibliography of popular and academic studies. This note only refers to those the authors have found most useful in preparing this book. The most recent concise history of the First World War is Norman Stone's *World War I: A Short History* (Allen Lane, London: 2007). The context of the Peace Conference for the region is set in H W V Temperley (ed), *A History of the Peace Conference of Paris*, Volume VI (Oxford University Press, Oxford: 1924; reprinted 1969). Essential modern accounts of the Peace Conference are Alan Sharp, *The Versailles Settlement: Peacemaking after the First World War, 1919–1923* (Palgrave Macmillan, Basingstoke: Second Edition, 2008) and Margaret MacMillan, *Peacemakers: The Paris Peace Conference of 1919 and its attempt to End War* (John Murray, London: 2003).

In 2008, Haus Publishing (with some volumes published by Harvard University Press in the United States) embarked on a 32-title series, 'Makers of the Modern World' covering the participants in the Peace Conferences following the First World War, including those of the Middle East, and and the consequences of the peace settlements.

The Middle East

The best general account of the Middle East in the period from the French Revolution to the First World War is Malcolm Yapp's excellent

The Making of the Modern Near East, 1792–1923 (Longman, Harlow: 1987). Two useful books that cover the period from 1914 to 1922 in great detail are Howard Morley Sachar, *The Emergence of the Middle East, 1914–1924* (Allen Lane, Penguin Press, London: 1970), and the more recent and bestselling David Fromkin, *A Peace to End All Peace: Creating the Modern Middle East, 1914–1922* (Deutsch, London: 1989). Both view the Middle East very much from a Eurocentric point of view and are primarily based on the excellent collections of British documents produced under the *Documents on British Foreign Policy 1919–1939* series. Fromkin's volume has the advantage of building on the vast documentation in the relevant companion volumes of Martin Gilbert's official biography of Winston Churchill.

A wealth of articles can be found in the following journals: *The Historical Journal, International Journal of Middle East Studies, Journal of Palestine Studies* and *Middle Eastern Studies.* The middle two tend to reflect a line sympathetic to the Arab cause, while *Middle Eastern Studies* was founded and edited for many years by Elie Kedourie and reflects his sceptical line.

The Hashemite Kingdom

Broad overviews of Middle Eastern history include the late Albert Hourani's justly acclaimed *A History of the Arab Peoples* (The Belknap Press of Harvard University Press, Cambridge, MA: 1991) and Ira M Lapidus's massive study *A History of Islamic Societies* (Cambridge University Press, Cambridge: 2002 edition). Both are focused more on developments within the region and its societies than the influence of external powers. Lapidus' work, as its title indicates, has a broader compass that ranges beyond the Middle East. Both are highly sophisticated works of history and broadly sympathetic to the region and its inhabitants. Peter Mansfield and Nicholas Pelham, *A History of the Middle East* (Penguin Books, New York: 2004) is much more focused on the international history of the region and the impact of foreign powers.

The fall of Feisal's kingdom in Syria is the subject of Zeine N Zeine, *The Struggle for Arab Independence: Western Diplomacy & the Rise and Fall of Faisal's Kingdom in Syria* (Khayats, Beirut: 1960); Malcolm Russell, *The First Modern Arab State: Syria Under Faysal, 1918–1920* (Bibliotheca Islamica, Minneapolis: 1985); and James Gelvin, *Divided Loyalties: Nationalism and Mass Politics in Syria at the Close of Empire*

(University of California Press, Berkeley: 1998). The fate of the successor states, Syria, Iraq and Jordan, can be traced in Charles Tripp, *A History of Iraq* (Cambridge University Press, Cambridge: Third Printing: 2010); Phoebe Marr, *The Modern History of Iraq* (Westview Press, Boulder, CO: 2004 edition); Kamal S Salibi, *The Modern History of Jordan* (I B Tauris, London: 1993); and Philip S Khoury, *Syria and the French Mandate: The Politics of Arab Nationalism, 1920–1945*, Princeton Studies on the Near East (Princeton University Press, Princeton: 1987). The post-First World War history of the entire Middle East is skilfully drawn in Malcolm Yapp, *The Near East Since the First World War: A History to 1995* (Longman, Harlow: 1996).

Arab Nationalism and Palestine

Arab nationalism is central to this story. For an Arab perspective on these events, George Antonius, *The Arab Awakening* (Hamish Hamilton, London: 1938) remains indispensable. Antonius viewed Arab nationalism as an organic vibrant force even before the First World War. C Ernest Dawn, whose work beginning more than 40 years ago is perhaps best encapsulated in *From Ottomanism to Arabism: Essays on the Origins of Arab Nationalism* (University of Illinois Press, Urbana: 1973) frames much of the current debate. There are important syntheses in the essays in Rashid Khalidi *et al* (eds), *The Origins of Arab Nationalism* (Columbia University Press, New York: 1991) and in A Dawisha, *Arab Nationalism in the Twentieth Century: From Triumph to Despair* (Princeton University Press, Princeton: 2003). Eliezer Tauber, *The Emergence of the Arab Movements* (Frank Cass, London: 1993) and *The Formation of Modern Syria and Iraq* (Frank Cass, London: 1995) are recent detailed reconstructions of Arab national movements before, during and after the war based on huge research. A useful counterpoint is the critical essay on Arab nationalism by Efraim and Inari Karsh, 'Myth in the desert, or not the Great Arab Revolt' in the journal *Middle Eastern Studies* (1997). There is useful information in Philip Mattar, *The Mufti of Jerusalem: Al-Hajj Amin al-Husayni and the Palestinian National Movement* (Columbia University Press, New York: 1988).

British Relations and the Middle East

The late Elie Kedourie wrote two of the key texts on Britain's relations with the Hashemites in *England and the Middle East* (Bowes & Bowes,

London: 1956) and *In the Anglo-Arab Labyrinth: The McMahon-Husayn Correspondence and Its Interpretations, 1914–1939* (Cambridge University Press, Cambridge: 1976). Kedourie was a tireless interpreter of the vast documentation on the First World War Middle East in the British National Archives. He tends to be a harsh critic of the Hashemites and those British politicians and administrators who accepted their version of British betrayal as articulated in George Antonius' *The Arab Awakening*. Isaiah Friedman's *The Question of Palestine, 1914–1918: British-Jewish-Arab Relations* (Routledge and Kegan Paul, London: 1973) is another book sceptical of the Hashemite viewpoint. Both Kedourie and Friedman are challenged by Charles D Smith in his article 'The Invention of a Tradition: The Question of Arab Acceptance of the Zionist Right to Palestine during World War I' in the *Journal of Palestine Studies* (Winter 1993). More recently Efraim and Inari Karsh have followed on from the Kedourie position and extended it into an even harsher critique of the Hashemites, Arab nationalism and Islamic assertiveness in a series of books and articles, most notably *Empires of the Sand: The Struggle for Mastery in the Middle East, 1789–1923* (Harvard University Press, Cambridge, MA: 1999). The Karshs' work is characterised by wide-ranging research, judgemental conclusions and a very hostile tone towards the Hashemites.

British policy during the war and its aftermath is well covered in Jukka Nevakivi, *Britain, France and the Arab Middle East 1914–1920* (Athlone Press, London: 1969) and Timothy J Paris, *Britain, the Hashemites, and Arab Rule, 1920–1925: The Sherifian Solution* (Frank Cass, London: 2003), as well as Fromkin and Sachar. The best overview contextualising half a century of British Middle Eastern policy remains Elizabeth Monroe's acclaimed classic *Britain's Moment in the Middle East 1914–1956* (Methuen, London: 1963). D K Fieldhouse, *Western Imperialism in the Middle East 1914–1958* (Oxford University Press, Oxford: 2006), is an excellent modern assessment. French policy can be traced in Jan Karl Tanenbaum's lengthy essay 'France and the Arab Middle East, 1914–1920' in *Transactions of the American Philosophical Society* (1978) and C M Andrew and A S Kanya-Forstner, *France Overseas: The Great War and the Climax of French Imperial Expansion* (Thames and Hudson, London: 1981). German policy is described by Sean McMeekin in his recently published magisterial *The Berlin–Baghdad Express: the Ottoman Empire and Germany's Bid for World Power 1898–1918* (Allen Lane, London: 2010).

Zionism and the history of Israel

The standard account of Zionism remains Walter Laqueur, *A History of Zionism* (Schocken Books, New York: 1972; 1989 edition), and for the period under review it can be supplemented by David Vital, *Zionism: The Crucial Phase* (Oxford University Press, Oxford: 1987). Nahum Sokolow's two-volume *History of Zionism 1600–1918* (Longman, Green and Co., London: 1919) remains invaluable. Herzl's career is best studied in Alex Bein, *Theodore Herzl: A Biography*, translated by Maurice Samuel (The Jewish Publication Society of America, Philadelphia: 1940), and his thinking in *The Jewish State: An Attempt at a Modern Solution of the Jewish Question*, translated by Sylvie d'Avigdor (H Pordes, London: 1972). Leonard Stein's *The Balfour Declaration* (Valentine, Mitchell, London: 1961) is a classic piece of historical writing, but since he did not then have access to the British records, it should be used together with Isaiah Friedman, *The Question of Palestine, 1914–1918: British-Jewish-Arab Relations* (Routledge & Kegan Paul, London: 1973), who did. A recent study is Jonathan Schneer, *The Balfour Declaration: The Origins of the Arab-Israeli Conflict* (Bloomsbury, London: 2010).

There are also worthwhile perspectives in the works of two British Zionist sympathisers: Herbert Sidebotham, *Great Britain and Palestine* (Macmillan, London: 1937); and Trevor Wilson (ed), *The Political Diaries of C. P. Scott 1911–1928* (Collins, London: 1970). There is a mine of information in *Palestine: A Study of Jewish, Arab, and British Policies*, two volumes (Yale University Press, New Haven: 1947). No student of the period can afford to ignore the *Palestine Royal Commission Report* (Cmd 5479, London: 1937), especially since Weizmann adopted its views on partition; these are analysed in T G Fraser, 'A Crisis of Leadership: Weizmann and the Zionist Reactions to the Peel Commission's Proposals, 1937–8', *Journal of Contemporary History*, Volume 23, No. 4 (October 1988).

From the Ottoman Empire to modern Turkey

There are two recent short histories of modern Turkey: Erik Zurcher's *Turkey: A Modern History* (revised edition, paperback, I B Tauris, London: 2004) and Sina Akşin's *Turkey: From Empire To Revolutionary Republic* (Hurst, London: 2007). Andrew Mango, *Atatürk* (John Murray, London: 1999) and its sequel *The Turks Today* (John Murray, London: 2004) relate the birth and development of the Turkish Republic.

For more detailed treatment consult Reşat Kasaba (ed), *The Cambridge History of Turkey, Volume.4: Turkey in the Modern World* (CUP: 2008) and Caroline Finkel, *Osman's Dream: The Story of the Ottoman Empire 1300–1923* (John Murray, London: 2005). Alan Palmer's *The Decline and Fall of the Ottoman Empire* (John Murray, London: 1992) provides a readable non-academic treatment of the subject.

More specialised books on Turkey's participation in the First World War include Ulrich Trumpener's *Germany and the Ottoman Empire 1914–1918* (Princeton University Press: 1968), which remains a classic. Consult also Edward Erickson, *Ordered to Die: A History of the Ottoman Army in the First World War* (Greenwood Press, Westport, Conn.: 2001) and Hikmet Özdemir, *The Ottoman Army 1914–1918: Disease and Death on the Battlefield* (University of Utah, Salt Lake City: 2008). There are several studies of the Gallipoli campaign, the best known being Alan Moorehead's *Gallipoli* (latest reprint of paperback, Aurum Press, London: 2007). The British campaign in Mesopotamia is described in A J Barker's *The Neglected War* (Faber and Faber, London: 1967). For the 1922 Chanak Crisis, consult David Walder, *The Chanak Affair* (Hutchinson, London: 1969). The highly controversial subject of the Armenian deportations is ably covered in Guenter Lewy's *The Armenian Massacres in Ottoman Turkey: A Disputed Genocide* (University of Utah, Salt Lake City: 2005). Michael Llewellyn Smith's *Ionian Vision: Greece and Asia Minor 1919–1922* (Allen Lane, London: 1973) is impartial and readable.

Biographies and Memoirs

The Hashemites have been the subject of a number of studies. The dearth of primary source material means they tend to be based on British, and to a lesser extent, French documents. The only memoir is Abdullah's *Memoirs of King Abdullah of Transjordan* (Cape, London: 1950). J Nevo assesses its value in his essay 'Abdullah's memoirs as historical source material' in Asher Susser and Aryeh Shmuelevitz (eds), *The Hashemites in the Modern Arab World: Essays in Honour of the Late Professor Uriel Dann* (Frank Cass, London: 1995). Mary C Wilson, *King Abdullah, Britain, and the Making of Jordan*, Cambridge Middle East Library (Cambridge University Press. Cambridge: 1987) is a study of his relations with Britain but contains a wealth of biographical material. Feisal, perhaps the most interesting Hashemite, is given voice in Beatrice Erskine, *King Faisal of Iraq: An Authorised and Authentic Study*

(Hutchinson, London: 1933), which was based partly on interviews with him before his premature death. A popular and highly readable biographical study of the family is James Morris, *The Hashemite Kings* (Faber and Faber, London: 1959). Hussein has received coverage ranging from the hagiographic in Randall Baker, *King Husain and the Kingdom of Hejaz* (Oleander Press, Cambridge: 1979) to the insightful and critical work of Joshua Teitelbaum in a number of books and articles, most notably *The Rise and Fall of the Hashimite Kingdom of Arabia* (Hurst, London: 2001).

For Turkey, Andrew Mango's *Atatürk* (John Murray, London: 1999), and its sequel *The Turks Today* (John Murray, London: 2004) relate the birth and development the Turkish Republic and Mustafa Kemal's role in it. There are two English-language academic studies of İsmet İnönü: Faruk Loğoğlu, *İsmet İnönü and the Making of Modern Turkey* (İnönü Vakfı, Ankara: 1997) and Metin Heper, *İsmet İnönü, Turkish Diplomat and Statesman* (Brill, Leiden: 1998). Enver Pasha awaits his English-language biographer.

The student of Weizmann is fortunate in many respects. The essential starting point for any study of his life and career is his autobiography, *Trial and Error*, which he published in 1949 (Hamish Hamilton, London: 1949). Book One, which covers the period down to the Balfour Declaration, was finished in 1941; Book Two, which takes his story down to November 1947, was completed that year; and in 1948 he wrote an Epilogue. The autobiography is full of fascinating insights, not least into his early life in Tsarist Russia and the formative years of the Zionist movement, but it sometimes strays over dates and the sequence of events. Shortly before her death in September 1966, Vera Weizmann recounted her memoirs to David Tutaev, and these were published the following year as *The Impossible takes Longer* (Hamish Hamilton, London: 1967). It is full of sharp observations, as well as valuable extracts from her diary.

The Letters and Papers of Chaim Weizmann are the rock on which any study of his career must be based. Of fundamental importance are: Leonard Stein (ed), Series A, Volume VII, August 1914–November 1917 (Oxford University Press, Israel Universities Press, London and New York: 1975); Dvorah Barzilay and Barnet Livinoff (eds), Series A, Volume VIII, November 1917–October 1918 (Transaction Books, Rutgers University, Israel Universities Press, Jerusalem: 1977); Jehuda Reinharz (ed), Series A, Volume IX, October 1918–July 1920 (Transaction Books,

Rutgers University, Israel Universities Press, Jerusalem: 1977). Weiz-mann's appearance before the Paris Peace Conference may be studied in M Dockrill (ed), *British Documents on Foreign Affairs: Reports and Papers from the Foreign Office Confidential Print, Part II: From the First to the Second World War, Series I, The Paris Peace Conference of 1919*, General Editors Kenneth Bourne and D Cameron Watt, *Volume 2: Supreme Council Minutes, January–March 1919*, (University Publications of America, Frederick, Maryland: 1989).

Weizmann has been well served by his biographers. *Chaim Weizmann: A Tribute on his Seventieth Birthday*, edited by Paul Goodman (Victor Gollancz, London: 1945), contains reminiscences, appropriately rever-ential, from a number of colleagues, and a particularly valuable section on his scientific work. An even more useful collaborative work is *Chaim Weizmann: A biography by several hands*, edited by Meyer W Weisgal and Joel Carmichael (Weidenfeld and Nicolson, London: 1962). In 1976, Barnet Litvinoff published a well-written overview, *Weizmann: Last of the Patriarchs* (Hodder and Stoughton, London: 1976). Norman Rose wrote a masterly account in *Chaim Weizmann: A Biography* (Weidenfeld and Nicolson, London: 1987). It is replete with insights. Finally, there are the two magisterial volumes by Jehuda Reinharz: *Chaim Weizmann: The Making of a Zionist Leader* (Oxford University Press, Oxford: 1985), covering his life down to 1914, which was followed by *Chaim Weizmann: The Making of a Statesman* (Oxford University Press, Oxford: 1993), which continued the story down to 1922.

Four published lectures on Weizmann by his friends and contemporar-ies also give valuable insights. In 1955, the British international historian and veteran of the Paris Peace Conference Sir Charles Webster deliv-ered 'The Chaim Weizmann Memorial Lecture' on *The Founder of the National Home*, subsequently published by the Yad Chaim Weizmann. The next year, Weizmann's American colleague, Louis Lipsky, continued with 'The Chaim Weizmann Memorial Lecture' on *Herzl, Weizmann and the Jewish State* (Yad Chaim Weizmann, n.d.: c. 1957). The 1958 Herbert Samuel Lecture at Hebrew University was given by the eminent scholar Isaiah Berlin, and published as *Chaim Weizmann* (Herzl Institute, New York: 1958). Finally, in 1960 a lecture given at Rehovoth entitled 'Chaim Weizmann' by the British politician R H S Crossman appeared in the journal *Encounter*. All four repay study.

The British military administration of Palestine is covered, somewhat opaquely, in the memoirs of Ronald Storrs, *Orientations* (Ivor Nicholson and Watson, London: 1939). The *Memoirs of Viscount Samuel* (The Cresset Press, London: 1945) provide his important testimony. Balfour's role is traced in *Arthur James Balfour: First Earl of Balfour*, by his niece Blanche E C Dugdale, two volumes (Hutchinson, London: 1939), especially useful since she became a close friend of Weizmann. For biographies of the major British participants in the Near Eastern peace settlement, consult Alan Sharp, *David Lloyd George* (Haus Publishing, London: 2008), David Gilmour, *Curzon* (John Murray, London: 1994) and Martin Gilbert, *Sir Horace Rumbold: Portrait of a Diplomat 1869–1941* (Heinemann, London: 1973). Crown Copyright materials are published with the permission of the Controller of Her Majesty's Stationery Office.

Index